THE RASHTRAKUTAS AND THEIR TIMES

THE RASHTRAKUTAS AND THEIR TIMES

A. S. ALTEKAR

GYAN

Published by

Gyan Publishing House
5, Ansari Road
Daryaganj, New Delhi-110002
Phone: 011-47034999, 9811692060
E-mail: books@gyanbooks.com

Distribution Network
gyanbooks.com
India, USA, Canada, UK, Australia

ISBN: 978-93-6920-342-0 (HB)

First Published, 1934

2nd Impression 2025

Printed at: Gyan Press, Delhi.

THE RASHTRAKUTAS AND THEIR TIMES
Author : A. S. ALTEKAR

THE RĀSHTRAKŪTAS
AND THEIR TIMES

being

a political, administrative, religious, social, economic and literary history of the Deccan (*i. e.* Southern Gujarat, Maharashtra, Karnatak, Nizam's Dominions, and Northern Mysore,) during C. 750 A.D. to C. 1000 A.D.

BY

Anant Sadashiv Altekar, M.A., LL.B., D. Litt.

Manindrachandra Nandi Professor of Ancient Indian History and Culture, Benares Hindu University. Author of 'A History of Important Towns and Cities in Gujarat and Kathiawar,' 'A History of the Village Communities in Western India', 'Education in Ancient India,' 'A New Gupta King' etc.

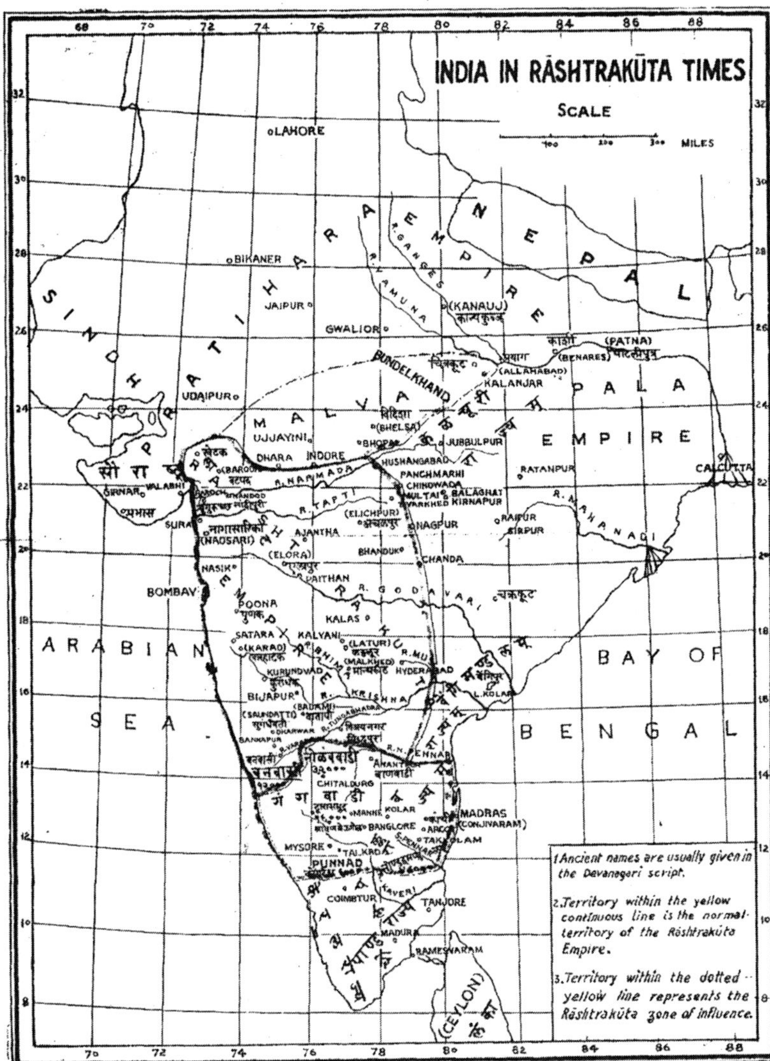

Balodyan Press, 689 Sadashiv peth, Poona 2

TRANSLITERATION

In the transliteration scheme followed in this book the following deserve to be noted :—

Long vowels : by a line above the short ones.

ऋ ṛ, ङ् ṅ, च् ch, छ् chh, ञ् ñ

ट् ṭ, ठ् ṭh, ड् ḍ, ढ् ḍh, ण् ṇ

श् ś, ष् sh, स् s, ळ् ḷ, विसर्ग ḥ

Sanskrit, Prakrit and Pali words and ancient names are spelt according to the above system ; modern current names and terms are spelt without any diacritical marks.

BOOKS BY THE SAME AUTHOR

1. **A History of Important Ancient Towns and Cities in Gujarat and Kathiawar;** reprinted from the *Indian Antiquary*, 1924–25. *Out of print.*

2. **A History of the Village Communities in Western India.** Oxford University Press, Bombay, 1927, Pp. xvi + 144. Price Rs. 3

3. **Education in Ancient India.** The Indian Book Shop, Benares City, 1934. Pp. vi + 386. Price Rs. 3

PREFACE

The reconstruction of Ancient Indian History has passed through several stages. In the beginning, almost everything appeared to be of the nature of a dim legend; hardly any historical data were available. When the key to the ancient Indian inscriptions was discovered, abundant historical material became available, and the energies of scholars were for some time directed towards the task of assorting it. The first generation of scholars was naturally engaged in determining the chronology and giving the frame-work of the political history. These problems became more or less settled in course of time. Owing to the commendable zeal of the Indian Government and of the various research societies, both in India and abroad, immense historical material became available in course of time. The discovery of the *Arthas'āstra*, which coincided with the political awakening in the country, gave a powerful impetus to the study of the political institutions of Ancient India. The material now available is, however, so ample that the historian need not longer be exclusively or mainly occupied with the court, but can give equal attention to the cottage.

In this book, which substantially represents a thesis accepted for the D. Litt. degree of the Benares Hindu University, an attempt has been made to give a comprehensive history of the Deccan under the Rāshṭrakūṭas (c. 750–1000 A.D.).

The first Part (Chapters I–VI) deals with the political history of the Rāshṭrakūṭa dynasty. More than 40 years have elapsed since the late Drs. R. G. Bhandarkar and Fleet wrote upon this subject. During this time, several new inscriptions of the Rāshṭrakūṭas and their contemporaries have been published, necessitating the rewriting of the history of the dynasty. Some idea of the new material, that has become subsequently available in this period, may perhaps be gained, when it is pointed out that in the present work, it was found necessary to devote about four times the space that was found more than sufficient by Bhandarkar and Fleet for narrating the political history of the house. Like a novel, political history cannot be all new or original. It is, however, hoped that scholars will find the history of the Rāshṭrakūṭas expounded here much more fully than in any book so far published. Several new suggestions, view-points, and conclusions will be met with, and Chapter I, dealing with the predecessors of Dantidurga, will be found to be substantially new and original. The political relations of the Rāshṭrakūṭas with their contemporaries and feudatories have been fully discussed. The history of the feudatories, however, has not been dealt with in detail as it was outside the scope of the present work.

Part II (Chapters VII–XII,) contains a comparative study of the Rāshṭrakūṭa administration. The books on the subject of Ancient Indian Politics are now so numerous, that the students of the subject may be inclined to feel some apprehension at the prospect of a new one being added to their number. It is, however, confidently hoped that a perusal of this part will show that epigraphical documents have a rich store of material bearing on the subject, which has been practically untouched to the present day. The information from the Rāshṭrakūṭa inscriptions has been in several places compared to, contrasted with, and in some cases, where it seemed justifiable to do so, supplemented by the data supplied by the earlier, contemporary, and later inscriptions and works on the *Nītis'āstra*, *Dharmas'āstra*, and *Arthas'āstra*.

Part III (Chapters XIII-XVII) attempts to delineate the religious, social, literary, educational and economic conditions of the times. Here the back-ground had to be necessarily wider. The method in this part is also comparative. I have not only tried to show what the things were in the Deccan under the Rāshṭrakūṭas, but also introduced comparisons with a view to illustrate the state of affairs in the earlier and later times. In this part the treatment has been mainly confined to the Deccan under the Rāshṭrakūṭas; in a few cases evidence from Northern India is also considered with a view to emphasise the points of similarity and contrast. While considering the economic conditions, the data supplied by some Chola records had to be utilised, as it was necessary to do so in order to interpret properly the numerous Rāshṭrakūṭa inscriptions, hailing from the northern districts of Tamil country. Epigraphical sources have been primarily relied upon, but at every step an effort has been made to show how far the realities of the situation, as disclosed by the inscriptions, confirm, modify or contradict the picture based upon the Smṛtis and Purāṇas. As social and religious customs and institutions do not change suddenly, the information in this part is in some cases supplemented by the data supplied by the 7th and the 11th century inscriptions also.

The reader will thus find in this work not only the political history of the times, but also the religious, social, economic, literary and administrative history of the age. Unlike most of the books on the subject of Ancient Indian History, he will find here equal attention given to the cultural as well as to the political history. A perusal of the book will show that there hardly exists any work at present, which offers so complete and comprehensive a study of any period in Ancient Indian History.

The main sources of the book are the inscriptions of the Rāshṭrakūṭas, their contemporaries, and their immediate predecessors and successors. These are supplemented by the accounts of the Arabic travellers and the valuable book of Alberuni. Contemporary works like Somadeva's *Yas'astilaka* and *Nitivākyāmṛta*, Pampa's *Vikramārjunavijaya* and later Smṛtis and Purāṇas have also been utilised. Later travellers like Marco Polo, Ibn Batuta, Bernier and Tavernier have also been consulted with a view to see whether they could throw any light on our period.

For the purpose of Parts II and III, I have thoroughly studied the whole of the *Dharmas'āstra*, *Nitis'āstra*, and *Arthas'āstra* literature, and the relevant portions from the Purāṇas and the later Nibandhas. My principal aim is to find out how far the epigraphical data confirm, modify or contradict the conclusions based upon the theoretical works on the subject.

In Part III the aim is merely to describe the social, religious and economic conditions of our period. No attempt is made to account for the changes that we witness taking place at this time. To a student of the Dharmas'āstra literature, the temptation to initiate this enquiry is almost irresistible, but that would have been beyond the scope of the present work and would have unnecessarily increased its size. I hope to write in course of time a few monographs on the origin, development and history of the various socio-religious institutions of the Hindus. The first of these, dealing with the history and development of Education in Ancient India, has been just published.

In conclusion I would like to offer my hearty thanks to the Oriental Book Agency and its enterprising manager Dr. N. G. Sardesai for undertaking the publication of this work, and to Mr. S. R. Sardesai, the manager of the Samarth Bharat Press, for printing it neatly.

Benares Hindu University,
February 20, 1934.

A. S. Altekar

CONTENTS

ABBREVIATIONS

Amg.	Ardhamāgadhī
A. S. R.	Archæological Survey of India, Annual Reports, New Series.
A. S. S. I.	Archæological Survey of South India Annual Reports.
A. S. W. I.	Archæological Survey of Western India, Annual Reports.
B. G.	Bombay Gazetteer.
B. I. S. M. J.	Journal of the Bhārata Itihāsa Samshodhaka Maṇḍala, Poona (Marathi).
C. I. I.	Corpus Inscriptionum Indicarum.
Dynasties.	Dynasties of the Canarese Districts of the Bombay Presidency.
E. C.	Epigraphia Carnatika.
E. I.	Epigraphia Indica.
Elliot	Elliot, History of India, 7 vols.
I. A.	Indian Antiquary.
J. A. S. B.	Journal of the Asiatic Society of Bengal.
J. B. B. R. A. S.	Journal of the Bombay Branch of the Royal Asiatic Society, Bombay.
J. B. O. R. S.	Journal of the Bihar and Orissa Research Society, Patna.
J. M.	Jain-Mahārāshṭrī.
J. R. A. S.	Journal of the Royal Asiatic Society, London.
M.	Mahārāshṭrī.
S. I. I.	South Indian Inscriptions.
Sachau	Alberuni's India, edited by Sachau.
Skt.	Skt.

PART I—POLITICAL HISTORY

CHAPTER I

Early Rāshṭrakūṭa Rulers, Their Stock, Home, and Relations with the Predecessors of Dantidurga.

Before proceeding to narrate the history of the Imperial Rāshṭrakūṭa dynasty, the historian has to consider a few preliminary but important questions. Who were the Rāshṭrahūṭas? What was their home? When and how did they first rise into political prominence? Were there any ruling Rāshṭrakūṭa families before the time of Dantidurga? These questions have to be first considered to clarify the later history. We shall first discuss the question of the early Rāshṭrakūṭa families as it will naturally throw considerable light over the remaining problems mentioned above.

Earlier Rāshṭrakūṭa Ruling Families.

Ancestors of Dantidurga excepted, Abhimanyu of Mānapura, Nannarāja of the Multai grant and Karkkarāja of the Antroli-Chharoli record are the only Rāshṭrakūṭa rulers, whose houses are known to have flourished earlier than the house of Dantidurga. A number of other rulers, however, have been considered as belonging to the Rāshṭrakūta stock by some earlier writers; it will be first shown why these views are untenable.

(1) While editing the Kadaba plates[1], Hultzsch had suggested that Akālavarsha Śubhatuṅga, mentioned in Merkara plates[2] as having flourished in the 5th century A.D., might be a Rāshṭrakūṭa prince, possibly the father of Indra who, according to the Kauthem plates, was defeated by the early

1. I. A., XII, pp. 13 ff.
2. I. A., I, p. 363.

Chālukya prince Jayasinha. Akālavarsha Subhatunga no doubt looks like a Rāshṭrakūṭa name, but we have to omit this king altogether from our consideration, as the Merkara plates have been shown to be a forgery.

It is no doubt true that a few records of the later Chālukya dynasty, *viz*., the Kauthem plates of Vikramāditya V[3], Yewoor[4] and Nilgunda[5] plates of Vikramāditya VI, and Sonavade[6] and Miraj[7] plates of Jayasinha refer to a Rāshṭrakūṭa dynasty said to have flourished earlier than that of the Chālukyas of Badāmi. We are told in these records that after ruling for 59 generations at Ayodhyā, the Chālukyas migrated to the south and ruled there for 16 generations. Then their glory was eclipsed for a time owing to the ascendancy of the Rāshṭrakūṭas. But soon there arose the valiant Jayasinha, who conquered the Rāshṭrakūṭa king Indra, the son of Kṛshṇa, and reestablished the fortunes of his family. If this version of history be true, no doubt we have evidence for the existence of a Rāshṭrakūṭa dynasty, ruling prior to c. 500 A.D., somewhere in central Mahārāshṭra or northern Karnātak. But there is ample evidence to show that the defeat of the Rāshṭrakūṭas, attributed in these records to Jayasinha, is not based upon any reliable tradition. In the first place, the records in question are full of mythological details; a Chālukya dynasty ruling for 59 generations at Ayodhyā is not known to sober history. The most conclusive reason, however, for ignoring the theory, that Jayasinha had really defeated a Rāshṭrakūṭa king Indra in c. 500 A.D., is the fact that not a single record of the early Chālukyas of Badāmī refers to this incident. This silence will appear the more significant when we remember that the Chālukya records mention a number of petty rulers like the Kadambas, the Mauryas, the Naḷas etc., who were supplanted by the early rulers of the dynasty. It is inexplicable why

3. I. A., XVI, pp. 151 ff. 4. I. A., VIII, pp. 11 ff.
5. E. I., XIII, pp. 12 ff. 6. B. I. S. M. J., X, pp. 87 ff.
7. E. I., XII, pp. 142 ff.

the Chālukya rulers of Badāmi should have conspired to condemn to oblivion the most significant achievement of Jayasinha, whom they were claiming as the founder of their dynasty. Fleet's theory in this respect appears as the most plausible one; the defeat of Rāshṭrakūṭa Indra, son of Kṛshṇa, attributed to Jayasinha in c. 500 A.D., is probably due to the fact that the historians of the later Chālukyas, like some of their present-day successors, believed that history repeats itself. They knew that Taila II, the founder of the later Chālukya empire, had defeated Rāshṭrakūṭa king, Indra IV, the (grand-) son of Kṛshṇa III; they attributed an exactly similar feat to the founder of the early Chālukya dynasty as well. Coins of a king Kṛshṇa have been discovered in the Central Provinces which seem to belong to a fairly early date. But there is nothing to connect the king Kṛshṇa of the coins with Kṛshṇa, the father of Indra, said to have been defeated by Jayasinha. The Kṛshṇa of the coins may be perhaps the Kalachuri ruler Kṛshṇarāja, whose grandson Budharāja was defeated by Mangaliśa.(8)

(2) Fleet had suggested that king Attivarman, mentioned in a grant hailing from Guntur district (9), may probably have been a Rāshṭrakūṭa prince (10). This suggestion also is to be ruled out of order, because there is hardly anything to support it. The provenance and the characters of the grant show that it is very probably a Pallava record. The mythological descent from Hiraṇyagarbha, which Attivarman claims, would also suggest that he was a Pallava, rather than a Rāshṭrakūṭa ruler. Rāshṭrakūṭa rulers of no branch whatever make any mention of Ānandamaharshi with whom Attivarman claims to be connected. The only ground for suggesting that Attivarman may have been a Rāshṭrakūṭa is the expression '*Kandharanṛpatikulodbhūtena*', used with reference to Attivarman. But this expression is hardly sufficient to prove

8. E. I., V, p. 295. 9. I. A., IX, p. 102.
10. *Dynasties of the Canarese Districts*, p. 334.

ı is lion, whereas that of the Rāshṭrakūṭas of that Attiv"is either S'iva or Eagle. Nor is there any similarity Kr.ne names of the members of the two families. The territory over which Abhimanyu was ruling was, however, immediately to the north of the kingdom of the Rāshṭrakūṭa king Nannarāja who was, as will be presently shown, very probably either a direct or a collateral ancestor of Dantidurga. Since on palaeographical grounds, the grant of Abhimanyu can be placed in the middle of the 7th century, Mānāṅka, Devarāja, Bhavishya and Abhimanyu become the contemporaries, as will be shown below, of Durgarāja, Govindarāja, Svāmikarāja and Nannāraja respectively of the Tivarkhed and Multai plates. The kingdoms of these Rāshṭrakūṭa families were also contiguous to each other. It is not unlikely that the two houses may have been connected with each other by blood relationship; but definite evidence to establish such connection is still wanting.

The next definite mention of Rāshṭrakūṭa kings is to be seen in the Tivarkhed and Multai plates. The name of the grantor of the Multai plates has been read by Fleet as Nandarāja[17] but an examination of the facsimile published by him makes it absolutely certain that the name of the king is *Nannarāja* and not *Nandarāja*. Fleet has mistaken the partially faint lower *na* for *da*; a comparison of this letter with *nda* in ll. 2 and 6 will show clearly that the letter in question is *nna* and not *nda*.

If we compare the genealogies in the Tivarkhed and Multai plates, we shall find that they are absolutely identical. In both the plates the grantor is Nannarāja and his father, grand-father and great-grand-father are Svāmikarāja, Govindarāja and Durgarāja respectively. But the Tivarkhed plates were issued by Nannarāja in Śaka 553 or in 631–2 A.D. [18], whereas the Multai plates purport to be issued by the same ruler in S'aka 631 or 709–710 A.D. If Fleet's reading in the

17. I. A., XVIII, pp. 230 ff. 18. E. I., XI, pp. 276 ff.

the locality of the territory over which Abhimanyu was ruling, we can get some idea from the statement in the plates that he was gracing Mānapura by his presence, when he made the grant of village Uṇḍivāṭikā to the Śiva temple at Peṭhapāṅgārikā, which is recorded in the charter. Dr. Bhagwanlal's view that Mānapura is the same as Mānyakheṭa or modern Malkhed[14] has to be rejected; for, if the later Rāshṭrakūta capital was really known as Mānapura in the 7th century, it is difficult to understand why the epithet *pura* of Mānapura should have been changed into *kheṭa*, especially since this change was calculated to belittle the importance of the place. For, *pura* denotes a city or a capital, while *kheṭa* is used only in connection with small towns. Further, it must be remembered that Abhimanyu and his ancestors were petty rulers, and if we identify their Mānapura with Malkhed, their dominions, we shall have to suppose, were very extensive. For, Pāṅgārikā, the Śiva temple of which received the grant, has been identified by Hultzsch[15] and Fleet[16] with Pagārā, 4 miles north of Panchmarhi in Houshangabad district, C. P., and Uṇḍivāṭikā, the village given, with one of the two villages called Oontia in the same locality. Abhimanyu would thus be ruling over a kingdom at least 400 miles in length, which would hardly have been the case, since such a kingdom in the 7th century would have cut across the dominions of the early Chālukyas. Fleet's suggestion that Mānapura, which was probably founded by Mānāṅka, may be Mānapura in Malva, the chief town of Mānapura sub-division, 12 miles southwest of Mhow, seems more probable, for it is only about 100 miles west of the village granted.

The Rāshṭrakūṭa house of Abhimanyu was thus ruling over the Mhow-Houshangabad tract in Central India. The question whether it can be connected with the house of Dantidurga cannot be settled at present. The seal of the grant of

14. J. B. B. R. A. S., XVI, p. 89. 15. E. I., VIII, p. 163.
16. I. A., XXX, p. 503.

Abhimanyu is lion, whereas that of the Rāshṭrakūṭas of Malkhed is either S'iva or Eagle. Nor is there any similarity in the names of the members of the two families. The territory over which Abhimanyu was ruling was, however, immediately to the north of the kingdom of the Rāshṭrakūṭa king Nannarāja who was, as will be presently shown, very probably either a direct or a collateral ancestor of Dantidurga. Since on palaeographical grounds, the grant of Abhimanyu can be placed in the middle of the 7th century, Mānāṅka, Devarāja, Bhavishya and Abhimanyu become the contemporaries, as will be shown below, of Durgarāja, Govindarāja, Svāmikarāja and Nannāraja respectively of the Tivarkhed and Multai plates. The kingdoms of these Rāshṭrakūṭa families were also contiguous to each other. It is not unlikely that the two houses may have been connected with each other by blood relationship; but definite evidence to establish such connection is still wanting.

The next definite mention of Rāshṭrakūṭa kings is to be seen in the Tivarkhed and Multai plates. The name of the grantor of the Multai plates has been read by Fleet as Nandarāja(17) but an examination of the facsimile published by him makes it absolutely certain that the name of the king is *Nannarāja* and not *Nandarāja*. Fleet has mistaken the partially faint lower *na* for *da*; a comparison of this letter with *nda* in ll. 2 and 6 will show clearly that the letter in question is *nna* and not *nda*.

If we compare the genealogies in the Tivarkhed and Multai plates, we shall find that they are absolutely identical. In both the plates the grantor is Nannarāja and his father, grand-father and great-grand-father are Svāmikarāja, Govindarāja and Durgarāja respectively. But the Tivarkhed plates were issued by Nannarāja in Śaka 553 or in 631–2 A.D. (18), whereas the Multai plates purport to be issued by the same ruler in S'aka 631 or 709–710 A.D. If Fleet's reading in the

17. I. A., XVIII, pp. 230 ff. 18. E. I., XI, pp. 276 ff.

Multai plates were correct, it was possible to argue that Nandarāja was a younger brother of Nannarāja and, therefore, may have been on the throne even 78 years later than the elder brother. But it is shown above that the grantor of the plates in question is Nannarāja, and not Nandarāja, and therefore identical with the ruler who had issued the Tivarkhed plates. In his grant issued in 631–2 A.D., Nannāraja claims that unlike his ancestors he was a ruler entitled to the dignity of the *pañchamahās'abda*, which he had personally won. He must be at least 25 at this time; could he be then still on the throne 78 years later? We have got the case of Nizam-ul-Mulk, who died when he was 104; so this is not impossible. But we must confess that such a long reign, as distinguished from life, is very rare, and it is therefore almost certain that the date of one of the two records is wrong.

There are good grounds to hold that the date 709–10 A.D. supplied by the Multai plates may not be genuine. The genealogy of the Multai plates starts in verse, but after the first verse there is a sudden break. A sentence in prose follows but the concluding portion of it, *tasyātmavānātmajo*, is again the fragment of a verse. The record, therefore, does not seem to be genuine, at least it is not carefully drafted or copied; and the date it supplies to us may not be genuine.

The genealogy of this Rāshṭrakūṭa house, as we gather it from these two records, is as follows:—

(1) Durgarāja.
|
(2) Govindarāja, son of No. 1.
|
(3) Svāmikarāja, son of No. 2.
|
(4) Nannarāja Yudhāsura, son of No. 3.
Known dates, 631–2 A.D. and 709–10 A.D. (?)

Since the reign of Nannarāja commenced earlier than 631 A.D., we may assign his predecessors to the following periods, assuming an average reign of 20 years.

Durgarāja 570–590 A.D.
Govindarāja 590–610 A.D.
Svāmikarāja 610–630 A.D.
Nannarāja, known dates, 631 A.D. and 710 A.D. (?)

Can we establish any connection between the Rāshṭrakūṭas of the Tivarkhed and Multāi records with the predecessors of Dantidurga? It may be at once admitted that direct evidence to connect the two houses is not yet forthcoming: but the available data make it extremely probable that Dantidurga was either a direct or a collateral descendant of Nannarāja of the Tivarkhed and Multai records. The seal of the two plates issued by him is Garuḍa or Eagle, which was also the seal of Dantidurga and his descendants. The names of Nannarāja and his ancestors are either similar to, or identical with, the names of many of the predecessors and successors of Dantidurga. One of the latter's uncles, who was probably a younger brother of Kṛshṇa I, and was governing the territory round Daulatabad in 793 A.D. [19] was Nannarāja. The formation of the name Svāmikarāja is similar to the *biruda* Pṛchhakarāja which was borne by Indra[20]. Govindarāja, the name of Nannarāja's grand-father, is repeated four times in the main Rāshṭrakūṭa line ruling at Malkhed, and once in the Gujrat branch. The great-grand-father of Nannarāja was Durgarāja and his name may have paved the way of the formation of the name Dantidurga. This close similarity in the names of the members of the two houses can hardly be explained, except on the assumption that the two families were connected with each other. Indra, Karka, Govinda, Dhruva, Akālavarsha Subhatuṅga, Akālavarsha Kṛshṇa and Dantivarman were the names of the different rulers in the Gujrat Rāshṭrakūṭa branch, whose blood relationship with the house of Malkhed cannot be doubted; and all these names are repetitions of the names of the earlier rulers of the main line. The names of four out of five rulers of the Gujrat branch of the Chālukyas, *viz.* the two

19. E. I., IX, pp. 195 ff. 20. E. I., XVIII, p. 235.

Jayasinhavarmans, Vinayāditya, Mangalarasa and Avanijanāś-raya Pulakeśin are borrowed from those of the main Chālukya line. If the names of Nannarāja and his ancestors are identical with or similar to those of the predecessors and successors of Dantidurga, the presumption is possible that there was a close family connection between the two houses.

It will be presently shown that the early exploits of Dantidurga and his father, Indra, *e. g.* the latter's feat of carrying away by force (*rākshasa vivāha*) a Chālukya princess from Kaira, Dantidurga's occupation, at the beginning of his career, of Gujrāt and northern Mahārāshtra and the defeat of the kings of Sindh, Mālvā and Kos'ala, would indicate that the family must have been ruling in the feudatory capacity somewhere in the central or western portion of Central India, prior to the rise of Dantidurga in c. 745 A.D. We learn from the Tivarkhed and the Multāi grants, that Nannarāja was also ruling in a portion of the territory above indicated. The Tivarkhed plates were issued from Achalapura, which is the same as Elichpur in Berar; Tivarkhed itself was granted away by the charter, and it is only 55 miles from Elichpur. The villages referred to in the Multāi plates have not yet been identified, but Multāi, where the plates were discovered, is only about 20 miles from Tivarkhed. Nannarāja and his ancestors were ruling in Berar and their capital was probably at Elichpur. The exploits of Dantidurga also can best be explained if we assume that his patrimony was somewhere in Berar. This province occupies a central position with reference to Kaira, Ujjain, Sirpur and Satara, where we know that his forces were operating at the beginning of his career.*

And finally, the known chronology of the two houses does not only not go against the proposed connection between them but does support it. Assuming an average reign of 20 years (except where the succession was not from father to son), and

* See the adjoining map.

working back from the known dates of Kṛshṇa I, we get the following genealogical and chronological table:—

(1) Durgarāja, c. 570-590 A.D.
(2) Govindarāja, son of No. 1, c. 590-610 A.D.
(3) Svāmikarāja, son of No. 2, c. 510-630 A.D.
(4) Nannarāja Yudhāsura, son of No. 3, c. 630-650 A.D.
Known dates, 631 A.D. and (?) 709 A.D.
(5) Dantivarman, probably son of No. 4, 650-670 A.D.
(6) Indra Pṛchhakarāja, son of No. 5, c. 670-690 A.D.
(7) Govindarāja, son of No. 6, c. 690-710 A.D.
(8) Karka I, son of No. 7, c. 710-730 A.D.
(9) Indra I, son of No. 8, c. 730-745 A.D.
(10) Dantidurga, son of No. 9, c. 745-756 A.D.
Known date, 754 A.D.
(11) Kṛshṇa I, uncle of No. 10, c. 756-775 A.D.
Known dates, 758, 768 and 772 A.D.

N. B.—In the case of Indra I and his son Dantidurga, a reign of 15 years only has been assumed, as Nanna Guṇāvaloka, a younger brother of Indra I, was still alive in 792 A.D., as the Daulatabad plates show [21].

If we reject the date 709 A.D., supplied by the Multai plates, as not genuine, it will appear very probable that Nannarāja was the predecessor, and very likely the father, of Dantivarman, the earliest known ancestor of Dantidurga. If, on the other hand, that date has to be accepted as genuine, the probability would be that Dantivarman was a younger brother of Nannarāja Yudhāsura, ruling somewhere in Khāndesh, over part of the dominions of his elder brother. Nannarāja may have had no sons, or they and their descendants may have been eclipsed altogether by the successors of Dantivarman.

To sum up, the similarity and identity of the names of the members of the two families, the close contiguity of the places where they were ruling, the identity of the seal design, and the striking manner in which the known dates of the members

21. E. I., III, pp. 195 ff.

of the two families can be worked up into a mutually adjusting chronological and genealogical table,—all these make it extremely probable, if not almost certain, that the ancestors of Dantidurga were ruling somewhere in Berar, and were either the direct or collateral descendants of the Rāshṭrakūṭa king Nannarāja Yudhāsura, who was ruling at Elichpur in Berar in the middle of the 7th century A.D.

There remains to be considered the Rāshṭrakūṭa family disclosed by the Antroli-Chharoli plates of Karkarāja II, dated 757 A.D.[22] The following genealogy is supplied by the record:—

(1) Karkarāja I, c. 690–710 A.D.
(2) Dhruva, son of No. 1, c. 710–730 A.D.
(3) Govinda, son of No. 2, c. 730–750 A.D.
(4) Karka II, son of No. 3, c. 750–770 A.D.
Known date 757 A.D.

From this record we learn that the village of Sthāvarapallikā, *i. e.* modern Antroli-Chharoli, was granted away by Karka II in 757 A.D. Since Antroli-Chharoli is 10 miles to the north-east of Surat, and since the donee hailed from Jambusāra in the Bharoch District, it is clear that Karka II was ruling over Surat and Bharoch districts. It is, however, almost certain that the immediate ancestors of Karka II were not living in this locality, or if they were doing so they were wielding no ruling powers. For, in the early decades of the 8th century A.D. the districts in question were being governed partly by the Gujrat Chālukyas, and partly by the Bharoch house of the Gurjaras. The rule of Karka II in southern Gujrat, therefore, must have been of recent origin.

The seal of Karka II of the Antroli-Chharoli record is the same as that of the main Rāshṭrakūṭa branch, *viz.* eagle; the names of the ancestors of the donor are those, which frequently figure in the main Rāshṭrakūṭa line. Karka II was a contemporary of Dantidurga and was ruling over a portion of

22. J. B. B. R. A. S., XVI, pp. 106 ff.

Lāṭa, which the latter claims to have conquered. It is therefore quite clear that the house of Karka must have been closely cȯnnected with that of Dantidurga, but what precisely that relationship was we do not know. Bhagwānlāl Indraji has suggested[23] that Dhruva of the Antroli-Chharoli record may be assumed to be another brother of Indra I, the father of Dantidurga. On this hypothesis the genealogy of the main line with known dates will be as under:-

Karka I

Dhruva	Indra I	Kṛshṇa I	Nannarāja
Govinda	Dantidurga 754 A.D.	758, 768 and 772 A.D.	793 A.D.
Karka II 757 A.D.			

There is nothing impossible in the above genealogy and chronology. Nanna, the youngest brother of Karka I, we may assume, was born in c. 715 A.D. and Dhruva, his eldest brother, may have been his senior by about 20 years. Dhruva's son Govinda may have been born in c. 715 A.D. and his grandson Karka II, in c. 735 A.D. Indra may have been two years younger than Dhruva, and his son Dantidurga may have been born in c 720 A.D. Indra seems to have been the most ambitious of the four brothers and his son Dantidurga may have begun his military career in c. 745 A.D. when he was only about 25. Shivaji and Babar are known to have begun their careers at even an earlier age. Dantidurga's nephew may have actively assisted him in his conquests when he was only a youth of 20; the uncle may have rewarded the services of the nephew by appointing him the governor over the newly conquered province of Lāṭa. After the death of Dantidurga in c. 760 A.D. Kṛshṇa, his eldest surviving uncle, may have succeeded him, being the most senior member of

23. J. B. B. R. A. S., XVI, pp. 106 ff.

the house. The drawback in this theory is the necessity of assuming that Dhruva, Govinda and Karka II were, all of them, the eldest sons of their parents, and even after making this assumption we find that Karka II has to be assumed to have joined his uncle, when he was only just a boy of 18 or 20. It is also difficult to understand why a youth of about 20 should have been preferred by Dantidurga for the Gujrat viceroyalty to his two mature uncles.

Recently Dr D. R. Bhandarkar has tentatively advanced the view[24] that Karka II and his father Govinda of the Antroli-Chharoli record may be identified with Karka and Govinda, father and grand-father respectively of the Indra I of the main Rāshṭrakūṭa house. He points out that the genuineness of the Samangad plates of Dantidurga is not above suspicion and therefore we may ignore the date 754 A.D., supplied by this record for Dantidurga.

This view also is not free from difficulties. If Karka and his father Govinda of the Antroli-Chharoli record are to be identified with the father and grand-father of Kṛshṇa I of the main line, Dhruva and Karka I of the former record will have to be identified with Indra I and Dantivarman of the main house. We shall have to assume that either Dhruva and Karka were the *birudas* of Indra I and Dantivarman or *vice versa*. Rāshṭrakūṭa kings have used several *birudas*, but there is not a single instance of any of the names Dhruva, Karka, Indra or Dantivarman being used as a *biruda*. So far these names have been known only as personal names.

In the second place the known dates of Dantidurga and Kṛshṇa I militate against this view. Even supposing it to be proved that the Samangad record is a later forgery, the chronological difficulties involved in this theory are not solved. The new plates [25] published by the Bhārata Itihāsa Samshodhaka Mandala now supply 758 A.D. as the earliest date for Kṛshṇa I, and if we accept 757 A.D. as the date of Dantidurga's

24. E. I., XVIII, p. 238. 25. B. I. S. M. J., VIII, pp. 165-8.

grandfather Karka, the reigns of Dantidurga and his father Indra will have to be crammed in the incredibly short space of about a year! The reigns of both these rulers were eventful; Indra I had come into hostile contact with the Gujrat Chālukyas, and Dantidurga had in the course of a brilliant career defeated the kings of Mālvā, Sindh, Kośala, Lāṭa and Sris'aila, besides annexing the northern dominions of the early Chālukyas. How could all this be achieved in the course of a single year? Even if we assume that Indra had predeceased his father, the difficulty would not be got over, for one year is too short a period for the achievements of Dantidurga.

A third possible view in this connection is to regard Karka I of the Antroli-Chharoli record as a younger brother of Indra Pṛchhakarāja of the main line, and to make his descendants Dhruva, Govinda and Karka II contemporary cousins of Govinda, Karka and Indra of the main line. This view presents no chronological difficulties like those in the first two theories; Karka II, according to this theory, becomes an elder contemporary of Dantidurga and he may quite possibly have rendered him valuable assistance in his military plans, in return for which Dantidurga may have appointed him his deputy in southern Gujrat. It must, however, be admitted that the assumption that Karka I was a younger brother of Indra I is based upon mere conjecture. It has to be confessed that the precise relation of the main line with the Rāshṭrakūṭas of the Antroli-Chharoli record still remains to be discovered. That the two houses were related in some way is fairly certain; the ill-behaved relative, whom Kṛshṇa I ousted soon after his accession, was very probably either Karka II or his successor.

The Naravana plates of Vikramāditya II, dated Saka 664, (January 743 A.D.)[26] state that the village Naravana in Chiplun taluka of Ratnāgiri district was given to certain Brahmanas by that Chālukya king at the request of Rāshṭrakūṭa Govindarāja, son of Śivarāja. The charter was issued when the

26. B. I. S. M. J., X, pp. 9 ff.

king was encamped at Ādityavāṭika or modern Aitavade in Satara district. It is not possible to connect this Rāshṭrakūṭa Govindarāja either with the main line or with the ancestors of Karka II of the Antroli-Chharoli record. He cannot be Govinda of the main line, for the latter was great-grand-father of Dantidurga and he could not have been possibly alive in 743 A.D., when the Naravana plates were issued. Nor can we identify him with Govinda, the father of Karka II of the Antroli-Chharoli record. It is true that no chronological difficulty arises in connection with this identification; for the known date of Karka II, *viz.* 757 A.D., fits in well with the known date of Govinda of the Naravana plates, *viz.* 743 A.D. The father of Govindarāja may have been an officer under Vikramāditya II in northern Konkan and his son may have carved out a principality in southern Gujrat at the downfall of the Chālukyas. There is, however, an almost fatal objection to this view; the father of Govindarāja of the Naravana plates is Sivarāja, whereas that of Govindarāja of the Antroli-Chharoli record is Dhruvarāja. There is no evidence so far forthcoming to indicate that either Dhruvarāja or Śivarāja was ever used as a *biruda* by the Rāshṭrakūṭas. It may be also pointed out that Govindarāja of the Antroli-Chharoli record was using feudatory titles, whereas Govindarāja of the Naravana plates has not even the title of a *Sāmanta*. The latter was probably a mere district officer ruling over some portions, either of Satara or of Ratnagiri district. It is, therefore, very likely that he was in no way connected with the Rāshṭrakūṭa family that later ousted the Chālukyas.

Having indicated the probable relationship of the main Rāshṭrakūṭa line with earlier and contemporary Rāshṭrakūṭa ruling families, let us now consider the question of the stock and nationality of the house of Dantidurga. We may refer only very briefly to mythological or semi-mythological views in this connection. Later Rāshṭrakūṭa records claim that the dynasty was descended from the race of Yadu. Bhagwānlāl

Indraji had conjectured that this theory was started in c. 930 A.D., to explain the change in the emblem of the Rāshṭrakūṭa seal from lion to eagle, which is the *vāhana* of Vishṇu. This suggestion, however, is not happy; lion was the emblem of the Rāshṭrakūṭas of Mānapura and not of Malkhed. The seal-emblems on the early Rāshṭrakūṭa records, *e. g.* the Alas plates of Yuvarāja Govinda, the Paiṭhan plates of Govinda III, are of Garuḍa or eagle. On some of the later records the emblem is that of seated Śiva but the lion emblem figures nowhere.

The earliest date, now known, when the Rāshṭrakūṭas are seen claiming descent from Yadu is 871 A.D., when the Sanjan plates were issued. 63 years earlier, however, the Rāshṭrakūṭas had not even dreamt of claiming this descent. The Wani-Dindori plates of Govinda III, dated 808 A.D., while referring to the birth of that monarch, observe that when he came on the horizon the Rāshṭrakūṭa race became invincible like the race of the Yadus when Murāri was born in it.[27] It is fairly certain that the birth of Govinda III in the Rāshṭrakūṭa family would not have been compared to that of Kṛshṇa in the Yadu race, if the Rāshṭrakūṭas had at that time thought of claiming connection with it by descent. It is probably the simile in this verse,[28] which suggested to the later kings and poets the idea of claiming a descent from the Yadus, especially since it seems fairly probable, from the seal emblem of the eagle, that the earlier rulers were, like the Imperial Guptas, Vaishṇavas.

R. G. Bhandarkar had suggested that the Rāshṭrakūṭas had probably sprung from a family that was known by the name of Tuṅga[29], since in the Karhad [30] and Deoli plates[31] of Kṛshṇa III it is stated that the family had its origin from

27. I. A., XI, pp. 157 ff.

28. Cf. Yasmin sarvaguṇās'raye kshitipatau S'ri-Rāshtrakūtānvaye|
Jāte Yādavavans'avanmadhuripāu āsīdalanghyaḥ paraiḥ ||

29. E. I. IV, pp. 278 ff. 30. E. I., V, pp. 192 ff.

31. B.G., III, p. 384.

a king named Tuṅga. The above plates, however, mention in the immediately next line Raṭṭa as a descendant or perhaps a son of Tuṅga, and observe that the Rāshṭrakūṭa family was known after him. Both Tuṅga and Raṭṭa are imaginary rather than real rulers, and even if we suppose that the family was descended from them, we find ourselves in no better position about the solution of the question of the stock and the original home of the Rāshṭrakūṭas.

Fleet has suggested [32] that since the names Rāṭhor and Rāṭhod are to be derived from the term Rāshṭrakūṭa, we may connect the Rāshṭrakūṭas with the Rājputānā–Kanauj country, which seems to be the original habitat of the Rāṭhor clans of the Rajputs. But the Rāṭhors come to our notice much later than the southern Rāshṭrakūṭa families, and it is quite possible that the Rajput Rāṭhors may be the descendants of some members of the Deccan Rāshṭrakūṭa families, left behind in northern India during the northern campaigns of Dhruva I, Govinda III, Indra III and Kṛshṇa III.

Burnell was inclined to hold that the Malkhed Rāshṭrakūṭas were Telgus and were of the same stock as the Reddies of the Andhra land.[33] This view, however, does not bear close scrutiny. The Reddies are at present scattered even over Tamil country and north-eastern portions of Mysore State; but their original home and present stronghold is the Andhra country. The Reddies of Mysore are undoubtedly of Telgu origin,[34] and those in Tamil districts still speak a broken Telgu dialect, which clearly proves their northern origin. If we suppose that the Rāshṭrakūṭas were the ancestors of the modern Reddies, their original home will have to be located somewhere in the Krishna-Godavari *doab*. In that case it is reasonable to expect that they would have first come into prominence in that locality. As it is, not only did the Rāshṭrakūṭa expansion not

32. B. G. I. ii, p. 384.
33. *South Indian Palaeography*, p. 10.
34. *Imperial Gazetteer*, XVIII, p. 191.

begin from the Telgu-speaking area, but most of it was never included in the Rāshṭrakūṭa dominions. The Chālukya rulers overthrown by them were those of the main and the Gujrat lines. The Vengi kings continued to defy them down to their fall. The mother-tongue of the Rāshṭrakūṭas was Canarese and not Telgu, as will be presently shown. The Reddies were a class of traders and cultivators and they are not known to have distinguished themselves by military exploits in any period of ancient Indian history. It is but once that they are known to have founded a kingdom, and that was after the fall of the Gaṇapatis of Warangal, when for about a century, c. 1350-1450 A.D., they were holding portions of Krishṇā and Rajmahendri districts.(35) The change of Rāshṭra into Raḍḍa or Reḍḍies is also not possible in the Telgu dialect, though it can take place in the Tamil one.(35) Under these circumstances it is not possible to identify the Rāshṭrakūṭas with the ancestors of modern Reddies.

Mr. C. V. Vaidya holds that the Rāshṭrakūṭas of Malkhed were a Marathi-speaking family, and were the ancestors of the modern Marathas.(36) This view also seems to be untenable, for it can be shown that the family belonged to the Canarese stock and its mother-tongue was Canarese.

A survey of earlier history is necessary in order to decide whether the Rāshṭrakūṭas of Malkhed hailed from Mahārāshṭra or Karnāṭak. It is as early as the time of Aśoka that we first hear of the Raṭhikas, a term to which we have to trace the Raṭṭas and Rāshṭrakūṭas of later centuries. There is no philological difficulty in postulating this derivation; the name is spelt as Risṭika at Girnar, Rasṭika at Shahabazgarhi, and Raṭraka at Mansera, showing that all these terms are to be derived from the Sanskrit term Rāshṭrika. It is true that there is no trace of the sibilant of the original word in the terms Raṭṭika or Raṭṭa, but the Mansera form Raṭraka shows

35. *Ibid*, VII, p. 158.

36. *History of Medieval Hindu India*, II p. 249 (Marathi Edition).

that the term Rāshṭrika assumed a form altogether devoid of any sibilant in some dialects. As a matter of fact the form Raṭraka of Mansera supplies us the link between Rāshṭrika and Raṭṭika or Raṭṭa. Pischel besides quotes several cases of a Sanskrit *shṭa* becoming a simple *ṭṭa* in Prakrits. Cf.

Skt. Ishṭa;	M., J. M. and Amg. Iṭṭa.
Skt. Aushṭrika;	J. M. Uṭṭiya.
Skt. Sandashṭa;	M. Sandaṭṭa.[37]

It will be seen that this tendency to change the original *shṭa* into *ṭṭa* is to be mainly seen in the Mahārāshṭri and Jaina-Mahārāshṭrī, and it is precisely in the south, where these dialects were spoken, that we find the change of original Rāshṭrika into Raṭṭa.

In my opinion the various Raṭṭa or Rāshṭrakūṭa families of our period were the descendants of some of the Raṭhika families, that were ruling over small tracts in the feudatory capacity since the time of Aśoka. Aśoka inscriptions describe Raṭhikas as westerners, but they also associate them with the Bhojakas, which will show that they were occupying portions of Mahārāshṭra and Berar as well. The next reference to them is in the Nānāghaṭ inscription of Queen Nayanikā, where we learn that she was the daughter of Mahāraṭhi Tranakayira, whose statue was erected by the side of his daughter at Nānāghaṭ. There existed at this time numerous feudatory rulers known as *raṭhikas.* In connection with the western expedition of king Khāravela his Khandagiri inscription tells us that he carried away the wealth and crowns of all the *raṭhikas* and *bhojakas.* There are two records at Kārli[38] belonging to a little later period, recording the benefactions of Mahāraṭhi Gotiputa Agimitanaka and Mahāraṭhi Vasithiputa Somadeva. The latter grants a village which shows that he was a ruling chief. A Bhājā record[39] discloses the existence of a Mahāraṭhi Viṇhudatta, and a Kaṇheri one that of a

37. *Grammatik der Prakrit-Sprachen*, Section 304.

38. J. B. B. R. A. S., V, pp. 152-3. 39. *Ibid*, p. 62.

Mahāraṭhinī Nāgamūlanikā, who was the daughter of a mahārāja and sister of a mahābhoja. This record again shows, like that of king Khāravela, that *raṭhis* and *mahāraṭhis* were feudal chiefs, and not mere generals or local district officers.

It is usually supposed that the Raṭhis and Mahāraṭhis were in power in Mahārāshṭra only, but there is definite evidence to show that some of them were occupying portions of Karnāṭak as well. Lead coins bearing the legend 'Sādakani-Kaḷalāya-Mahāraṭhi' have been found near Chitaldurga.[40] These coins belong to the middle of the 3rd century A.D. The Hirahadagalli grant of Dharmamahārājādhirāja S'ivaskandavarman[41] is addressed, among others, to Raṭhikas. We further find that some of the Mahāraṭhis were closely connected with Canarese families. The cumulative evidence of two Kaṇheri records shows that Nāgamūlanikā, who was married to a Mahāraṭhi, was the daughter of Hāritiputra Vishṇu-kada Chūtu-Sātakarṇi, who was a Canarese prince ruling at Banavasi.[42] Some of the Mahāraṭhis were Nāga-worshippers; the name of the queen of Sātakarṇi I, Nayanikā or Nāganikā, suggests that her Mahāraṭhi father was a Nāga-worshipper. One of the lion-pillars at Karli was the gift of a Mahāraṭhi, Agimita-naka or Agnimitra-nāga, whose name also shows that he was a Nāga-worshipper. The donor of one of the Kaṇheri inscriptions, who was the wife of a Mahāraṭhi, is Nāgamūlanikā or Nāgamūlanikā and her son's name was Skandanāga.[43] One of the inscriptions of her father Viṇhu-kaḍa-chutu, discovered at Banavasi, is upon a stone slab bearing the representation of a five-headed cobra. Nāga-worship was extensively practised by the early inhabitants of Mysore,[44] and since some of the Mahāraṭhis were Nāga-worshippers and connected

40. Rapson, *Catalogue*, p. 57, Plate VIII, No. 233.
41. E. I., I, P. 2.
42. Rapson, *Catalogue*, p. LIII, Luders, *List*, No. 1021.
43. A. S. W.I., V, p. 86.
44. Rice, *Mysore and Coorg from Inscriptions*, p. 202.

by marriage with Canarese families, we are justified in concluding that Rathis and Mahārathis were in power also in parts of Karnatak, especially since coins of Sadakana Kalalāya Mahārathi are discovered in the heart of Karnātak near Chitaldurga. In the face of these facts it can no longer be maintained that the Rathi and Mahārathi families were confined only to Mahārāshtra.

We can now take up the question as to whether the Rāshtrakūtas of Malkhed originally belonged to Mahārāshtra or Karnātak. We have shown already how the main line, that was later established at Malkhed, has to be connected with the Rāshtrakūta family ruling at Elichpur. But Dantidurga and his ancestors were not natives of Berar. Canarese was their mother-tongue. It was Canarese and not Mahārāshtrī literature that flourished at their court.[45] Amoghavarsha I of the line was either himself the author, or at least the inspirer, of the oldest Canarese work on poetics. The sign-manuals of Karka and Dhruva of the Gujrat branch of the house in the Naosāri plates of 816 A.D.[46] and the Baroda grants of 812[47] and 835[48] A.D. are in the south-Indian proto-Canarese characters, whereas the records themselves are to be seen inscribed in the usual script of the locality of the period in question. If the home of the Malkhed Rāshtrakūtas were in Mahārāshtra, it is difficult to explain how they could be using the script of Karnātak as their mother script. It is true that much earlier than 812 A.D. the Rāshtrakūta empire had embraced the whole of Karnātak, but if the family had originally belonged to Mahārāshtra, its members deputed to rule over southern Gujrat could not be seen using for their sign-manual a script that was current neither in southern Gujrat, nor in Mahārāshtra but in Karnātak. The fact that the recently published Jura inscription of Kṛshṇa III, found in Bundelkhand, should be using the Canarese language

45. See Supra, chapter. XV. 46. J. B. B. R. A. S., XX, p. 135.
47. I. A., XII, p. 157. Plate III a. 48. *Ibid*, XIV, p. 197.

to describe his achievements can also be explained only on the assumption that Canarese was the mother tongue of the Rāshṭrakūṭas of Malkhed.

The use of the Canarese script and language by the members of the family of Dantidurga is not, however, inconsistent with the theory, here advanced for the first time, that Dantidurga's ancestors were direct or collateral descendants of Nannarāja of Elichpur. It is shown already how a number of Raṭhi families were long domiciled in Karnāṭak even before the 3rd century A.D. Under the Chālukyas of Badāmi, a Canarese-speaking dynasty was founded in southern Gujrat, and another in the Telgu-speaking Andhra country. The predecessors of Dantidurga may similarly have carved a domain in Berar away from their home in Karnāṭak.

There is also evidence available to show that the home of the house of Dantidurga was in a Canarese-speaking locality. A number of Rāshṭrakūṭa records describe the rulers by the epithet *Laṭṭalūrapuravarādhīs'a* 'lord of Laṭṭalūra, the best of towns.'[49] This epithet is changed into *Laṭṭalūrapura-vinirgata* 'emigrants from Laṭṭalūra, the best of towns' in some of the records of the Raṭṭas of Saundatti.[50] Laṭṭalūra, to which the Rāshṭrakūṭas belonged, need not have been necessarily included within the jurisdiction of Nannarāja and his ancestors. Maṇalera, a general of Kṛshṇa III, has been

49. Sirur and Nilgund inscriptions of Amoghavarsha I, I.A., XII, p. 218; and E. I., VI, p. 102.

50. J. B. B. R. A. S., X pp. 167 ff. In two of the Saundatti Raṭṭa records Kṛshṇa the founder of the house is described as *Khandara-puravaradhis'a*. This, however, cannot show that Kandharapura was the home of the Rāshṭrakūṭas, since the vast majority of records describe them as *Laṭṭalūrapuravarādhis'a*. It is likely that Kandharapura was only an imaginary city since we do not hear of it anywhere else. If at all it was a real city, Kṛshṇa III alone may have been associated with it: it was not the home of the family.

described as *Valabhipuravarādhīs'a*, 'lord of Valabhi, the best of towns' at a time when it is clear that he had no control over that city.[51] The Kalachurya kings of Kalyāni, the Gutta princes of Guttavolal, and the Yādava rulers of Devagiri called themselves lords of Kālañjara, Ujjayinī, and Dvārakā respectively,—places which were never included in their dominions. The identification of Laṭṭalūra is not yet definitely certain. Fleet had once suggested that Laṭṭalūra may be Ratanpur in Vilaspur District of the Central Provinces, pointing out how most of the Rāshṭrakūta families belonged to Central India. But later on he himself abandoned this theory, when it was found from a 12th century inscription from Ratanpur itself, that the name of the place was originally Ratnapura and not Laṭṭanūrapura. His later view that Laṭṭalūra may be Lāṭūr in Bedar District of Hydrabad State seems to be hitting the truth.[52] Phonetically the change of Laṭṭalūra into Lāṭūr is quite natural. The second *la* in Laṭṭalūra, being dropped by haplology, the original form will assume the garb of Laṭṭaūra in Prakrit ; this form will later change into Lāṭūra, the loss of the double consonant *ṭṭa* being compensated by the doubling of the preceding vowel.

Since there is no phonetic difficulty, there is nothing to stand against the identification of Laṭṭalūra with Lāṭūr. As a matter of fact all the known facts of history can be explained only on this hypothesis. It has been shown already that the Raṭhis and the Mahāraṭhis were spread over portions of Karnāṭak as well, in the early centuries of the Christian era. So there may, quite possibly, have been a Raṭhi family holding local sway at Lāṭūr, which is almost due east of Poona and south of Berar. This family may have later migrated to Elichpur or some other place nearby in Berar, where Nannarāja was ruling in 631-2 A.D. Elichpur is only about 150 miles north of Lāṭūr, and the emigration is quite possible. And by assuming that Dantidurga's ancestors in Berar were

51. E. I., VI, pp. 56 ff. 52. E. I., VII, pp. 186 ff.

immigrants from Lāṭūr, we can well understand how they were using Canarese language and proto-Canarese script. Lāṭūr is now a Canarese-speaking town and such was also the case during our period; for we learn from the *Kavirājamārga*, which was composed in the 9th century A.D., that Canarese was then spoken between the Godāvari and the Kāveri.[53] The immigrant rulers naturally stuck to their language and script during their stay in Berar. When we remember how the Maratha families ruling in Baroda, Indore, and Gwallior still use their mother tongue and script in personal matters, there is nothing impossible in the supposition that the Canarese Rāshṭrakūṭa family, ruling in Berar, which was and is just contiguous to Canarese-speaking area, preserved its mother tongue and script.

If we assume with Fleet and Vaidya that the home of the Malkhed Rāshṭrakūṭas was either in Mahārāshṭra or somewhere in Central India, we cannot explain how they were using the Canarese language and the southern script. If we assume that they were local chiefs somewhere in central or southern Karnatak, we cannot understand how Dantidurga's exploits were most of them performed in Gujrat, Malva, Central India, and northern Mahārāshṭra, and how the Chalukyas of Badāmi continued to hold the southern portions of their dominions down to the reign of Krishṇa I. If on the other hand, we assume that they were immigrants in Berar from Lāṭūr, we can understand why they call themselves Laṭṭalūrapuravarādhīśa, why they were using the proto-Canarese script and the Canarese language, why their early exploits were performed in Central India, Gujrat and northern Mahārāshṭra and why the early Chalukyas continued to hold their own so long in the southern portion of their kingdom.

It will have become already clear from what has been said so far, that the terms *raṭhi*, *mahāraṭhi*, *raṭhika*, *rāshṭriya*, *rāshṭrapati* and *rāshṭrakūṭa* possessed merely political and

53. *Kavirājamārga*, I, 46.

administrative significance; none of them was used to denote any tribal or ethnical stock. R. G. Bhandarkar has argued that the name Mahārāshṭra is due to the province being occupied in the early days by the *raṭhis* and the *mahāraṭhis*,[54] but with due deference to the views of that learned scholar, it must be confessed that there is no evidence to show that the *raṭhis* and the *mahāraṭhis* were the names of any tribes, Aryan, non-Aryan or mixed. Mr. C. V. Vaidya holds that the Rāshṭrakūṭas represent the captains of the Aryan army, who parcelled out the districts in Mahārāshṭra among themselves. This view again ignores the presence of the Rāshṭrakūṭas in Andhra country, and of the *raṭhis* and the *mahāraṭhis* in Karnatak right upto Chitaldurga. The Nāga worship, which prevailed extensively among the *raṭhi* and the *mahāraṭhi* families, is surely no argument to prove their Aryan origin. We must, therefore, conclude that the facts so far known do not support the view that the Rāshṭrakūṭas belonged to any particular stock, either Aryan or non-Aryan.

A point of minor importance remains to be considered, *viz.* what was the real and original name of the Rāshṭrakūṭa family. After an elaborate analysis of the epigraphical evidence upon the point,[55] Fleet has come to the conclusion that 'while Rāshṭrakūṭa was the formal appellation which it was customary to apply to the kings of Malkhed in ornate language, the real practical form of the family name was Raṭṭa.' He then points out that the form Raṭṭa was not derived from the form Rāshṭra or Rāshṭrakūṭa, but that the reverse was the case.

This controversy as to the original form of the word Rāshṭrakūṭa is partly due to a misunderstanding as to what we mean by the term 'original.' Fleet, while maintaining that Raṭṭa was not derived from Rāshṭra, does not assert that Raṭṭa is a *des'ī* or Dravidian word of non-Aryan parentage. We have already pointed out a number of cases, where original *shṭa* in Sanskrit becomes simple *ṭṭa* in Mahārāshṭrī and Jain-

54. B. G., I. ii. p. 143. 55. E. I., VII, pp. 220 *ff*.

Mahārāshṭrī.[56] There is, therefore, no phonetic difficulty in deriving the term Raṭṭa from the Sanskrit term Rāshṭra or Rāshṭrakūṭa. As to the question which of these was the original form, the answer will entirely depend upon what we mean by 'original'. From the 3rd century B.C. to about the 4th century A.D., Prakrits were usually used for epigraphical purposes, and perhaps for daily intercourse as well. The form *raṭhī* was therefore the original or earlier form in vogue, when the terms *Rāshṭrakūṭas* and *Rāshṭrapatis* began to be generally used on the use of Sanskrit becoming common for epigraphical purposes. In this sense *Raṭhi* or *Raṭṭa* is no doubt the earlier form, but philologically and historically the term *Raṭṭa* has to be admitted as a derivation from and contraction of the term Rāshṭrakūṭa.

The Raṭhis and the Mahāraṭhis were, as we have seen above, small local rulers. The Hindu imperial theory and practice were generally against the policy of annexation, as will be shown in Chapter XII, Section B; the local chiefs were often converted into district officers and *vice versa*, according to the changes in the political situation. The terms *Raṭhika*, *Rāshṭriya*, *Rāshṭrapati* and *Rāshṭrakūṭa* were used to denote local chiefs, district officers, and big landlords. From the Girnar inscription of Rudradāman we learn that the Mauryan governor in Kathiawār was styled *Rāshṭriya*. From the Hirahadagalli grant of S'ivaskandavarman we find that district officers were known as *Raṭhikas*.[57] Numerous Vengi records show that the term Rāshṭrakūṭa denoted important landlords in Andhra country during our period.[58] A number of Gurjara and Valabhi plates show that Rāshṭrapati was the title of the district governor.[59] In the recently published Naravana plates of Vikramāditya II,[60] Govindarāja,

56. *Ante*, p. 19. 57. E. I., I, pp. 2 ff.
58. E. I., V, p. 122, 133; I. A., VII, pp. 186 ff. etc.
59. I. A., X, p. 284; XIII, p. 15; p. 77 etc.
60. B. I. S. M. J., X, pp. 9 ff.

who is called Rāshṭrakūṭa in the record, may have been either a district officer or a big landlord, who wielded a fair amount of influence with the Chālukya emperor.

Whether the Rāshṭrakūṭas of Malkhed were originally local rulers or district officers or mere landlords is difficult to judge. Many of the Raṭhis of the 3rd century B.C. must have been reduced to the position of district governors at the rise of the Andhra empire. Some of them must have again become petty local rulers with the fall of that empire. Their status in many cases must have been again reduced by the early Chālukyas, when they rose to power. With reference to the ancestors of Dantidurga we notice that Yudhāsura Nannarāja was the first to claim the *Pañchamahās'bdas*. His predecessors, therefore, may have been either local officers or mere landlords. They rose to power first under Nannarāja, and it is possible that his descendants may have continued to enjoy the feudatory status, won for the family by Nannarāja.

We shall conclude this chapter with a survey of the careers of the predecessors of Dantidurga. The earliest of them known from the records of the Malkhed house is Dantivarman who, according to the theory here proposed, was either a son or a brother of Nannarāja. He is known to us only from the Daśāvatāra cave inscription,[61] which gives us only a conventional account of his bravery and career. It is doubtful, however, whether he was in any way greater than his predecessor, who was proud to announce the fact of his having won the *Pañchamahās'abdas.* One of the scions of the Gujrat Rāshṭrakūṭa branch, the younger brother of Dhruvarāja, was named after him.[62] The probable time when Dantivarman ruled is 650-670 A.D., whether we make the calculation from the known date of Dantidurga or of Nannarāja, allowing an average of about 20 years per reign.

The next two members of the family, Indra alias Pṛchhakarāja and Govinda I, are equally shadowy. They pro-

61. A. S. W. I., V. p. 87. 62. E. I., VI. p. 285.

bably ruled from c. 670–690 A.D. and 690–710 A.D. respectively. The Baroda plates of Karkarāja Suvarṇavarsha of the Gujrat branch, dated 812 A.D., inform us that even among gods, with the exception of S'ankara, none was saluted by Govinda I.[63] This may show that he was a zealous Saivite. Fleet[64] and R. G. Bhandarkar[65] have suggested that this Govinda may be identified with the king Govinda, who along with Āppāyika, invaded the Chālukya dominions from the north of the Bhima, taking advantage of the confusion of the war of succession between Mangalīśa and Pulakes'in.[66] This theory looks plausible when it is remembered that Govinda I was ruling in Berar, and could therefore have invaded the Chālukya dominions only from the north of the Bhima. The proposed identification is, however, impossible; Govinda I must have been at least 25 when he attacked Pulakes'in in c. 610. A.D., and we know that his grandson Kṛshṇa I was alive and ruling in 772 A.D. *i. e.* 162 years later than the time of his grand-father. This chronological difficulty is fatal to the theory of Fleet and Bhandarkar, that Govinda, first an opponent and then an ally of Pulakes'in, is the same as the grand-father of Kṛshṇa I.

The next ruler was Karka I, who unlike his father was a Vaishnavite.[67] Very little that is historical is known about him. He had at least three sons,[68] of whom Indra I, the father of Dantidurga, seems to have been the eldest. He may have been born very probably in c. 700 A.D. Kṛshṇa I, who succeeded his nephew, seems to have been a younger brother of Indra I. He may have been junior to Indra I by about ten years; his age at the time of his death in c. 775 A.D., may have been about 65. Nanna Guṇāvaloka seems to have been the youngest child of Karka I, since he is known

63. I. A., XII, pp. 158 ff. 64. *Dynasties*, pp. 386-7.

65. *Early History of the Deccan*, p. 194.

66. Aihole inscription, E. I., VI. pp. 5 ff.

67. Baroda plates of Karka, I. A., XII, pp. 158 ff.

68. If we accept the view of Bhagwanlal Indraji, (see *ante*, pp 12-13) the number of the known sons of Karka becomes four.

to have been alive in 793 A.D., when the Daulatābad plates were issued by his son Śaṅkaragaṇa.[69] His birth may be placed in c. 715 or 720 A.D.

Of the three brothers Indra seems to have been the most ambitious. That he had married a Chālukya princess was known since the publication of the Samangad plates, the name of the princess Bhavanāgā came to light with the Bhandak plates[70] of her brother-in-law Kṛshṇa I. The recently published Sanjan plates inform us that Bhavanāgā was carried away by force from her marriage pandal at Kaira by Indra I.[71] Since Datidurga, the issue of this union, began his career earlier than c. 750 A.D., the marriage must have taken place some time in c. 725 A.D.. A few more facts about the career of Indra will be narrated in the next chapter, where the career of his illustrious son Dantidurga will be described.

CHAPTER II

The Rise of the Rāshṭrakūṭas
Indra I, Dantidurga, and Kṛshṇa I

A bird's-eye-view of the political condition of India in general, and the Deccan in particular, in the first half of the 8th century would be necessary to understand properly the rise of the Rāshṭrakūṭa house. The history of Kashmir need not be considered, for after the death of Lalitāditya Muktāpīḍa that kingdom did not come into contact with the kingdoms in the rest of India for a long time. We do not know who was occupying the imperial throne of Kanauj after Yaśovarman. It would appear from the *Chachnāmā*[1] that Rai Hari Chander

69. E. I., IX, pp. 195 ff. 70. E. I., XIV, pp. 121 ff.

71. Cf.—Indrarājastatogrihṇādyas'Chālukyanṛpātmajām
Rākshaseṇa vivāhena raṇe Khetakamaṇḍape.

1. Elliot, I, pp. 207-208.

was ruling there in c. 715 A.D., but this king is yet a mere name to us. The same is the case of Vajrāyudha, who is supposed to have been the predecessor of Chakrāyudha by some writers. Bengal was just recovering from anarchy under the leadership of Gopāla I. In the Deccan itself the Chālukya empire was powerful, but its strength was being wasted in hereditary wars with Pallavas. The precise extent of the Chālukya kingdom at the time of its overthrow is not easy to determine. Its southern boundary line must have been a changing one, as the wars with the Pallavas were being continuously fought with varying success. A subordinate branch, related by blood-relationship to the main line, was no doubt ruling at Vengi; but it had become practically independent of the main line at this time, though the imperial title *Mahārājādhirāja Parames'vara Parama-bhaṭṭāraka* was not assumed by its rulers before the time of Vijayāditya II. The northern boundary of the Chālukya kingdom was probably the Kim in southern Gujrat; beyond that river stretched the kingdom of the Gurjaras of Bharoch (or rather of Nāndīpurī, to be precise) which embraced the territory between the Kim and the Mahi. How much further east of the Kim valley the sway of the Chālukyas extended is difficult to determine, for the history of the Central Province of this period is still shrouded in mystery. Portions of this province must have passed under the Chālukya sway with the overthrow of the Kaḷachuri prince S'aṅkaragaṇa by Maṅgalis'a towards the end of the 6th century A.D., but whether they continued to be ruled by the Chālukyas by the beginning of the 8th century is not known. Portions of Berar were being ruled by the ancestors of Dantidurga; the Multai and Tivarkhed records[2] do not mention the name of the suzerain ruler, but it is almost certain that he must have been the Chālukya king upon the throne. From the Udayendiram plates of doubtful authenticity[3] it would

2. I. A., XX, p. 100.
3. I. A., VII, pp. 275 ff.

appear that there was a fairly powerful king in the Vindhya regions at this time named Pṛthvīvyāghra, who is claimed to have been defeated by the Pallava ruler Nandivarman. Who this Pṛthvīvyāghra was, and how far he had encroached upon the Chālukyan kingdom, we do not know. It is, however, possible that Pṛthvīvyāghra may have been another name of Jayavardhana of S'ailodbhava dynasty who, in his Ragholi plates, which on palæographical grounds have been assigned to the middle of the 8th century by Rai Bahadur Hiralal,[4] styles himself *Paramamāhes'vara Sakalavindhyādhipati Mahārājādhirāja Parames'vara*. Whether this identification is true or not, it is clear that the Chālukyas must have lost a portion of their dominions in the north by the rise of Jayavardhana. In the eastern Kos'ala, there was kingdom at Sirpur near Raipur, where king Udayana was ruling by the middle of the 8th century. In Rajputānā and Mālvā there ruled two Gurjara houses, one at Bhinmal and another at Ujjain. Both these, along with the kingdoms of Valabhi and Nandīpurī, were being considerably harassed by the raids of the Arabs of Sindh in the second quarter of the 8th century A.D.

Such then was the political condition in India, when Indra I began his political career. The Sanjan plates inform us that he had married the Chālukya princess Bhavanāgā by *rākshasa* form of marriage at Kaira.[5] This event must have taken place some time after 722 A.D. Kaira was then still under the rule of the Valabhi house, as the Gondal plates of Silāditya V show.[6] Very soon thereafter Kaira and Panchmahal districts were lost by the Valabhi kingdom; no record belonging to that dynasty comes from this area during the next 29 years. This negative evidence is confirmed by the Kavi plates of Jayabhaṭṭa III of Bharoch,[7] where that ruler claims to have defeated the king of Valabhi by the skill of his sword.

4. Hiralal, *List of Inscriptions in C. P. and Berar*, p. 18.
5. E. I., XVIII, pp. 235 ff.
6. J. B. B. R. A. S., XI, p. 112. 7. I. A., V, p. 112.

It would seem that Jayabhaṭṭa III had made an alliance with the Gujrat Chālukya ruler Maṅgalarasa, and that the allied forces had wrested away the continental districts from the Valabhi king in c. 725 A.D. Indra I seems to have, very probably, served in this campaign as one of the feudatories of the Chālukya king; it was in that capacity that he may have been present in Kaira, when he carried away the Chālukya princess by force from the marriage pandal there. Bhavanāgā may have been a daughter of Maṅgalarasa or Pulakeśin. Hindu marriage is indissoluble and, therefore, the estrangement caused by this *rākshasa* marriage could not have lasted long. The Chālukya ruler may have soon reconciled himself with the accomplished fact; the marriage may have also added to the prestige and patrimony of Indra in Berar.

The Kairā and Panchmahāl districts were not held for a long time by the Gurjara-Chālukya forces. From Al Biladuri we learn that Junaid, the Arab governor of Sindha, had sent expeditions to the kingdoms of Marwar, Bharoch, Ujjain, Mālvā and Bhinmal.[8] The account of the Muslim chronicler is confirmed by the Naosari plates of Pulakeśiraja, dated 739 A.D.,[9] which state that the Muslim army, which had defeated the kings of Sindh, Kachchha, Kathiawar and the Chavda, Maurya, and Gurjara rulers, was repulsed by Pulakeśin. Since the grant is dated 739 A.D., and since Pulakeśin's accession took place in 731 A.D., the Muslim raid must have taken place between these two dates. The havoc of the Muslim raid and the effort to repulse it must have weakened the states in Gujarat and Malva, and Dantidurga must have decided to fully exploit this situation when he began his career in c. 745 A.D. at the age of about 22 or 23. His imagination must have been fired to some extent by his descent from the Chālukyas on his mother's side.

8. Elliot, I, p. 109.
9. B. G., I. i, p. 109.

Our sources of information about Dantidurga are two contemporary records, the Samangad plates[11] dated 754 A.D.

11. I. A. XI, pp. 111 ff. The genuineness of this record has been recently called into quetion by Drs. Sukhtankar and Bhandarkar (E. I. XIV, pp. 121–2; *Ibid*, XVIII, p. 236). Dr. Sukhtankar's conclusion, which is mainly based on palæographical grounds, is that the plates are a few decades later than the alleged time of their issue. The palæographical test is, however, a hardly convincing one when the difference is only of a few decades. If we compare the Talegaon plates of Krishṇa I with the Samangad plates, we no doubt find that the duct of the former is much more archaic than that of the latter; but the *s'a* in the latter record is more archaic than the s'a in the former. The sign-manual of Dadda Pras'āntarāga in his Kaira Plates of 659 A.D. is in characters at least two centuries later than that date. (J. R. A. S., 1864, p. 205). The same is the case of the Mathura Jain inscriptions of the Kushana period, whose characters are much in advance of their age. It is clear from the last two cases that the current hand was considerably in advance of the monumental writing, and it is not impossible that the characters of the Samangad plates appear a few decades later than the date of the record, not because it is not genuine but because it is written in the current, rather than in the monumental script of the period. The names of the villages have been tampered with in this record, and if we have to suppose that the record is not genuine, it will be a case of double forgery. Palæographical evidence being inconclusive in this matter, attention may be drawn to a few points which would show that the record is a genuine one.

i. The verse :—

महीमहानदीरेवारोधोभित्तिविदारणम् ।
लोका विलोकयन्त्युच्चैः कृतं यज्जयकुञ्जरैः ॥

does not occur in any other Rāshtrakūta record; and it will be soon shown that the armies of Dantidurga had operated in the vallies of these rivers. If the record were not genuine, or based upon a genuine record, and if it were forged by the *kramavid* Brahmanas of Karad, the donees of the grant, the rivers mentioned in connection with the exploits of Dantidurga would have been big rivers like the Ganges, the Jumna etc. and not insignificant ones like the Mahī, the Mahānadī and the Revā. The fact that these comparatively unimportant rivers are mentioned would show that the grant is either genuine or based on an original document issued by Dantidurga.

[*P. T. O*

and the fragmentary Ellora Daśāvatāra cave inscription.[12]

(*Continued from last page*)

ii. The writer of the Talegaon plates of Kṛshṇa I is the same individual as the writer of the Samangad plates issued 15 years earlier. It is very likely that Indra, who composed the grant, was serving both under Dantidurga and Kṛshṇa. When it is remembered that the Talegaon grant is not based or modelled on the Samangad one or vice versa, the identity of the composers can be explained only on the assumption that the record is a genuine one. Forged records are not likely to be correct on such minute points.

iii. The date of the Antroli-Chharoli record, 757 A.D., is not the date of Karka, the grandfather of Dantidurga, as shown in the last chapter. So there is nothing impossible in Dantidurga being a ruling prince in 753-4 A.D. when the Samangad grant was issued.

It may be pointed out that even if we accept the view of Dr. Sukhatankar, the plates will have to be pronounced to be a few decades later than the alleged date of their issue. If such is the case, we will have to assume that the present plates are a later copy of an originally genuine grant, and therefore their value as a record describing contemporary incidents cannot be much diminished. The Samangad plates in that case will stand on the same level as the Konnur Inscription of Amoghavarsha. The latter record was no doubt not written in S'aka 782, but it has been shown recently by Dr. D. R. Bhandarkar (E. I., XVIII, p. 235 ff.) that the record is a genuine copy of an earlier grant.

12. Kielhorn seems to assign this record to the reign of Amoghavarsha I. (E. I. VII, Appendix, p. 13) but this view is not correct. The record does not refer to any king later than Dantidurga but merely supplies S'arva as an epithet of that king. This becomes quite clear from an analysis of the record. V. 23 describes Dantidurga's victory over the rulers of Lāta, Mālva, Badāmi, etc., V. 24 compares him to a number of gods according to the usual notions on that subject, and V. 25 after describing his bravery concludes with the line:—

बीभत्सुर्दुष्टनागो जयिनमिव परं श्रीमहाराजशर्वः ॥ 'S'rī Maharaja S'arva was terrible like a mad elephant to the enemy who was ambitious of conquest.'

Then immediately follows the line:—

दत्तं येनोज्जयिन्यामपि नृपतिमहादानमाश्चर्यभूतम् । 'Who had made in Ujjayini in a wonderful way the great gift prescribed for kings.'

P. T. O.

and the notices about him in the records of his successors. From these we learn that the rulers of Kānchī, Kalinga, Śrīśaila, Kośala, Mālava, Lāṭa, Ṭaṅka, and Sindh were defeated by Dantidurga.(13) Our records, however, do not supply any clue as to whether the overthrow of the Chālukyas preceded or followed the defeat of other kings mentioned in them.

But before we proceed to determine the probable chronology of these wars, we have to consider a serious discrepancy

(Continued from last page)

This line obviously refers to हिरण्यगर्भ महादान which Dantidurga had given at Ujjayini, as we know from the recently published Sanjan plates of Amoghavarsha I. It is, therefore, clear that Maharaja S'arva who is mentioned in V. 25 of the Das'āvatāra record must be obviously Dantidurga, whose exploits are the topic of eulogy from V. 23. If we assume that it is Amoghavarsha I and not Dantidurga who is referred to in the last line of V. 25, which refers to king S'arva, we shall have to suppose that the record passes over, entirely unnoticed, as many as four rulers, *viz.* Krishna I, Govinda II, Dhruva and Govinda III. This is extremely improbable, since the author of the Das'āvatāra inscription has devoted several verses to describe the imaginary careers of the predecessors of Dantiduaga. He would have waxed ten times eloquent in describing the *all-India* exploits of Dhruva and Govinda III! Buhler, who had edited the record, had realised that king S'arva could not be identified with Amoghavarsha I; he had proposed to regard him as a brother or a minister of Dantidurga. (A. S. W. I., V, pp. 186 ff.) This view, however, overlooks the fact the V. 25 describes the महादान ceremony of S'arva as something which other *kings* could not have thought of emulating, even in dream. This statement would have been altogether inappropriate and wide of the mark, if S'arva were a younger brother or a minister of Dantidurga. To conclude, the last ruler mentioned in this record is Dantidurga S'arva and therefore the record may well be a contemporary document. But as it is incomplete, one cannot be positive on the point.

13. Cf. Ellora Inscription V. 23, Samangad grant lines, 21-22, Begumra plates of Indra III, E. I. IX, pp. 24 ff. The Das'āvatāra record gives the name of the last mentioned king as *Sandhubhūpa* but this is obviously a mistake for *Sindhubhūpa*.

in the Rāshṭrakūṭa records about the overthrow of the Chālukyas. Some of the records ascribe the defeat of Kīrtivarman II to Dantidurga and others to Kṛshṇa I. There can, however, be no doubt that Kṛshṇa I only completed the work of his nephew. It is no doubt true that the Wani-Dindori[14] and Radhanpur[15] plates of Govinda III, dated 808–9 A.D., Baroda plates of Karka,[16] dated 812 A.D., and the Kāpadwanj plates of Krishṇa II,[17] dated 910 A.D., give the credit of the overthrow of the Chālukyas to Kṛshṇa I, but this is obviously due to the fact that these records altogether pass over Dantidurga, because he was only a collateral ancestor. The Sanjan plates of Amoghavarsha I,[18] dated 871 A.D., and the Cambay[19] and Sangli[20] plates of Govinda IV, dated 930 and 933 A.D. respectively, no doubt mention Dantidurga, but give the credit of the Chālukya overthrow to Kṛshṇa I. But these are late records and their testimony will have to be rejected in favour of the undoubtedly earliest and almost contemporary records, *viz.* the Bhārata Itihāsa Samshodhaka Mandala[21], Talegaon[22] and Bhanduk[23] plates of Kṛshṇa I dated 758, 770 and 774 A.D. respectively. These records were issued by Kṛshṇa I himself, and they not only do not claim the credit of the Chālukya defeat for him, but actually give it to Dantidurga. There can, therefore, be no doubt that it was Dantidurga, and not Kṛshṇa I who gave the first decisive blow to the Chālukya house. The later records ascribe that feat in some cases to Kṛshṇa I, partly because they pass over Dantidurga altogether, and partly because Kṛshṇa I completed the work of his nephew and humbled the Chālukyas of Vengi as well.

Dantidurga seems to have begun his career by attacking

14. I. A., XI, pp. 157 ff.
15. E. I., VI, pp. 242 ff.
16. I. A., XII, pp. 158 ff.
17. E. I., I, pp. 52 ff.
18. E. I., XVIII, pp. 235 ff.
19. E. I., VII, pp. 36 ff.
20. I. A., XII, pp. 249 ff.
21. B. I. S. M. J., VIII, 165–8.
22. E. I., XIII, pp. 275 ff.
23. E. I., XIV, pp. 101–02.

his eastern neighbours in Kos'ala,[24] Udayana of Sirpur near Raipur and Jayavardhāna of Srīvardhana near Ramtek, who was probably also known as Pṛthvīvyāghra.[25] If the Udayendiram plates,[26] issued by Nandivarman II in his 21st year, are geniune or based, like the Konnur inscription of Amoghavarsha I, on a genuine record, it would appear that Dantidurga and Nandivarman II were co-operating with each other in this expedition: for the Udayendiram plates claim that Nandivarman II had captured Udayana, the king of the Sabaras, and defeated Pṛthvīvyāghra, another S'abara chief, who was presumptuous enough to perform an Aśvamedha sacrifice. Since several records of Dantidurga claim for him also the credit of defeating the Kośala ruler or rulers, it seems very likely that he had made an alliance[27] with the Pallava ruler Nandivarman, the natural enemy of his prospective

24. Udayana's great-grand-son Chandragupta was defeated by Govinda III in c. 810 A.D. It is, therefore, very likely that Udayana himself was on the throne at this time. See E. I., XVIII, pp. 240 and XI, pp. 185 ff.

25. Jayavardhana is called परमेश्वरमहाराजाधिराजसकलविन्ध्याधिपतिः। in the Ragholi plates; he may, therefore, well have been the same as the S'abara chief, Prithvīvyāghra, who attempted to perform an As'vamedha according to the Udayendiram plates. With reference to Nandivarman he was a northerner.

26. S. I. I. II., pp. 365 ff.

27. Dubreuil has suggested that Dantivarman cemented this alliance by giving his daughter S'ankhā in marriage to Nandivarman (*Pallavas*, p. 75) There are several difficulties in accepting this theory. In the first place it may be pointed out that the Bahur plates simply mention that S'ankhā was a Rāshṭrakūṭa princess; the name of her father is not given. (S. I. I., II, p. 515). We have seen already how there were several Rathi or Rāshṭrakūṭa families in Andhra and Karnatak; it is not impossible that S'ankhā may have belonged to one of these and may have been altogether unconnected with the house of Dantidurga. In the second place it may be pointed out that Nandivarman, who had married S'ankhā, was the son of Tantivarman (See V. 12 of the Bahur plates; S. I. I., II, p. 515), while Nandivarman, who was the ally and [*P. T. O.*

opponent Kīrtivarman II. It is no doubt true that a number of records, like the Daśāvatāra one, state that Dantidurga had defeated the king of Kanchi as well; but this statement is not against the theory of alliance. For Nandivarman I was not the son of his predecessor Parameśvaravarman, as the Udayendiram plates were supposed to prove. He was born in a collateral branch and seems to have supplanted by force either Parameśvaravarman or his successor.[28] Dantidurga may probably have helped Nandivarman in this war against his predecessor. Hence his records may well claim that he had defeated the Pallava king. It was probably when Dantidurga was cooperating with the forces of Nandivarman that he may have defeated or come into hostile contact with the ruler of Śrīśaila in Karnul district.

After strengthening his position by the defeat of his eastern neighbours and by his alliance with Nandivarman, Dantidurga seems to have attacked the Gurjaras of Bharoch and the Chālukyas of the Gujrat branch, and annexed their dominions. These kingdoms were already exhausted by the Muslim raid and its repulsion, and Dantidurga's task may not have been very difficult.

Dantidurga's successes must have made a collision with Kīrtivarman II inevitable, and it seems to have taken place before January 754 A.D. when the Samangad plates were issued. We are told that the Chālukya emperor was easily defeated merely by the frown without even any weapons

(*Continued from last page*)

contemporary of Dantidurga, was the son, either of Parames'varavarman, according to the earlier view based upon the Udayendiram plates, or of Hiraṇya, according to the present view based upon the Kasakudi and Velurapalaiyam plates. No record, however, designates his father as Tantivarman. It must, therefore, be admitted that there is no conclusive evidence to prove that S'ankhā, the Rāshṭrakūṭa princess, was a daughter of Dantidurga married to Nandivarman II.

28. See Kasakudī plates of Nandivarman, S. I. I., II, No. 78, and Velurapalaiyam plates of Vijayanandivarman III, S. I. I., II, No. 98.

being raised ;[29] this statement, if not an exaggeration, would show that the overthrow of the Chālukya emperor was brought by strategem or treachery. Dantidurga was enabled by this victory to occupy Khandesh, Nasik, Poona, Satara and Kolhapur districts, as the findspot and the villages mentioned in the Samangad plates would show. Kīrtivarman, however, continued to hold sway in Karnatak right up to Sholapur even after this defeat. In 757 A.D. we find him encamped with his army at Bhadara–Gaviṭṭage,[30] a village on the northern bank of the Bhima in Sholapur district. Either Dantidurga or his successor Kṛshṇa I soon completed the Chālukya overthrow. The second defeat, the whereabouts of which are still unknown, was decisive ; for not only do we not find any record of Kīrtivarman subsequent to 757 A.D. but the records of the later Chālukyas themselves state expressly that the glory of the Chālukyas set with Kīrtivarman II.[31]

Dantidurga's attacks on the rulers of Tank, Sindha and Malva now remain to be considered. Tanka has not been so far identified. Arabs of Sindh were now and then attacking their western neighbours and Dantidurga seems to have defeated some of these raids. Some time after the first defeat of Kīrtivarman, Dantidurga seems to have led an expedition to Ujjain either to help the Gurjara–Pratihāra ruler Devarāja, or to take advantage of the defeat that was inflicted on him by the rival Gurjara-Pratihara king, Siluka, ruling at

29. Cf. सभ्रूविभङ्गमगृहीतनिशातशस्त्रम् ।
अश्रान्तमप्रतिहताज्ञमपेतयत्नम् ॥
यो वल्लभं सपदि दण्डबलेन जित्वा ।
भृत्यैः कियद्भिरपियः सहसा जिगाय ॥ I. A., XI, pp. 111.

30. Vakkeri plates of Kīrtivarman II, E. I., V, pp. 202 ff.

31. तद्भवो विक्रमादित्यः कीर्तिवर्मा तदात्मजः ।
येन चालुक्यराज्यश्रीरन्तरायिन्यभूद्भुवि ॥
Yewoor Inscription, I. A., VIII, pp. 11 ff.

Bhinmal.[32] This becomes quite clear from the Das'āvatāra record which states that Dantidurga was occupying a palace of the Gurjara ruler[33] and from the Sanjan plates where we are informed that when Dantidurga performed the *Hiraṇya-garbhadāna* ceremony at Ujjain, the Gurjara ruler acted as his door-keeper.

After the conquest of Gujrat, Dantidurga appointed Karka II of the Antroli-Chharoli record as his governor of the province. Karka II was a relative of his as shown already. The Antroli–Chharoli record does not claim that either Karka or any of his ancestor had conquered southern Gujrat. Since a number of records ascribe that conquest to Dantidurga, it is clear that Karka owed his position in Gujrat to that king. It may be pointed out that Karka's titles do not show that he was an independent ruler,

A review of Dantidurga's career will show that he was a leader gifted with political insight and possessed of great organising capacity. He could see how the Chālukya empire had become weakened by its incessant wars with the Pallavas and how the petty states of Gujrat, exhausted by the Muslim forays, could no longer hold their own against a resolute conqueror. Forming wise alliances, proceeding cautiously step by step, utilising the services of his youthful nephews and mature uncles, he gradually enlarged his kingdom until it included southern Gujrat, Khandesh, Berar, and northern

32. The line: 'पूर्वां श्रीमदवन्तिभूभृति नृपे वत्साधिराजे' in the colophon of *Harivans'a* of Jinasena has to be construed to mean that Vatsarāja was ruling at Avanti; the lines in the Sanjan plates.

हिरण्यगर्भ राजन्यैरुज्जयिन्यां यदासितम् ।
प्रतिहारीकृतं येन गुर्जरेशादिराजकम् ॥

make this construction most plausible.

For the defeat of Devarāja, see Jodhapur Inscription of Pratihara Bauka and Dr. Majumdar's remarks thereon; E. I., XVIII, pp. 87 ff.

33. यस्याखण्डितविक्रमस्य कटकेनाक्रम्य क्षीरक्षितिम् ।
सौधेऽस्मिन्कृतगुर्जरेन्द्ररुचिरे.,, ॥

Mahārāshṭra. The theory that he oppressed his subjects and was overthrown by his uncle Kṛshṇa I is, as will be shown in the next section, no longer tenable. Like most other founders of new dynasties he seems to have been a wise and able ruler. In religion he shared orthodox Hindu beliefs. When he was at the sacred *tīrtha* Ujjain, he performed there the *Hiraṇyagarbhamahādāna*; he must have obviously believed that the ritual would endow him with a divine body. On the *rathasaptamī* day of 754 A.D he weighed himself against gold and distributed the money among the Brahmanas. He showed his devotion to his mother by bestowing, at her request, lands in several villages on worthy Brahmanas.[34] The precise date of his death is not known but since his successor was on the throne in 758 A.D., it is clear that he must have died not long after 754 A.D., when he could hardly have been much above 30. When we remember how young he died, his achievements will have to be pronounced as unique.

Krishṇa I

Dantidurga was succeeded by his uncle Kṛshṇa I probably because he left no male issue. This reason is no doubt given by the Kadba plates which were issued in the reign of Karka II, but a record from Chitaldurg confirms it. This record[35] informs us that when Dantidurga died without a son, Kannara, his junior uncle, succeeded him.

The view that Dantidurga was deposed by his uncle Kṛshṇa for oppressing the subjects was based upon a misunderstanding of the verse:—

34. Samangad plates, I. A., XI, pp. 111 ff.

35. E.C., XI, Chitaldurga No. 49, Alas plates of *Yuvarāja* Govinda refer to मानावलोकरत्नवर्षश्रीविजयादित्य, son of Dantivarman, as the person at whose request the grant was made. But since Dantivarman of this record is not the son of Indra, it will not be possible to identify him with Dantidurga.

तस्मिन्दिवं प्रयाते वल्लभराजेऽकृतप्रजाबाधे ।
श्रीकर्कराजसूनुर्महीपतिः कृष्णराजोऽभूत् ॥

occurring in the Begumra plates of Kṛshṇa II. The reading of the last part of the first line is 'Kshataprajābādhaḥ' in the Talegaon plates of Kṛshṇa I himself, and the Paithan plates of Govinda III, 'Kṛtaprajāpālaḥ' in the Daulatabad plates of S'aṅkaragaṇa, and 'kshitau prajāpālaḥ' in the Alas plates of Kṛshṇa's son Govinda II. It is, therefore, clear that this line either praises Kṛshṇa I for removing the miseries of the subjects or observes that Dantidurga was also a ruler of the same category; the correct reading of the last word of the first line in the Begumra plates is clearly, 'akṛtaprajābādhe' and not kṛtaprajābādhe.[36] A verse in the Baroda plates of Karka of the Gujrat branch no doubt says that Kṛshṇa I had ousted a relative, who had gone astray, but the Bharata Itihasa Samshodhaka Mandala,[37] Talegaon[38] and Bhanduk[39] plates of Kṛshṇa I himself make it abundantly clear that this relative could not have been Dantidurga. As Dr. D. R. Bhandarkar observes,[40] Kṛshṇa I would not have tolerated a eulogy of his murdered nephew in his own grant, and added at the end that when the victim of his machinations had departed from this world, he ascended the throne. The relative ousted by Kṛshṇa was very probably Karka II of the Antroli-Chharoli record who, we have seen, was a distant cousin of his. The Antroli-Chharoli record itself shows that Karka II was even then entertaining imperial ambition. Karka there styles himself '*Samadhigatapañchamahās'abda-parama-bhaṭṭāraka-mahārājādhirāja-parames'vara*: It will be seen that here Karka is trying to smuggle cleverly for himself the imperial title after first using the feudatory one to which alone he was entitled. After the death of Dantidurga he may have openly declared himself emperor. It is, therefore, very

36. I. A., XIII, pp. 66 ff.
37. B. I. S. M. J., VIII, p. 165.
38. E. I., XIII, pp. 275 ff.
39. E. I., XIV, pp. 121 ff.
40. E. I., XIII, pp. 275 ff.

probable that the relative ousted by Kṛshṇa was Karka II, he was certainly not Dantidurga.

A verse occurring in four records of the Gujrat branch[41] states that Kṛshṇa obtained the title of *Rājādhirājaparames'vara* after defeating Rāhappa who had become inflated with pride about his strength. This Rāhappa must have been different from the relative, whom Kṛshṇa had ousted, for he is nowhere described as a relative of Kṛshṇa. He cannot be, therefore, Karka of the Antroli-Chharoli record. The present state of our knowledge, however, does not enable us to identify this potentate with certainty. A ruler of Mewar, bearing that name, is known to have flourished in c. 1200 A.D.; an inscription from the same province, dated 725 A.D., refers itself to the rule of *Mahārājādhirāja Parames'vara* S'rī–Dhavalappadeva.[42] It may thus appear that in some of the ruling families of Mewar, names ending in *ppa* were current, and it is not impossible that Rāhappa, the opponent of Kṛshṇa I, may have been a ruler in Mewar, possibly a hitherto unknown son or successor of king Dhavalappa just referred to. It has also to be remembered that the last part of the name Rāhappa bears a Canarese appearance, and since Kṛshṇa I is said to have obtained the imperial position after defeating Rāhappa, it is not impossible that Rāhappa may have been either another name of Kīrtivarman, or a *biruda* of the contemporary Vengi ruler Vishṇuvardhana defeated by his heir-apparent. It must, however, be confessed that in the present state of our knowledge no identification, that can be unreservedly accepted, can be proposed.

41. Kavi Plates of Govinda, 827–8 A. D., I. A., V, pp. 145 ff.
Bogumra plates of Dhruvarāja II, 867–8 A. D., I. A., XII, pp. 181 ff.
" " " Kṛshṇa, 888–9 A. D., I. A., XIII, pp. 46 ff.
Surat plates of Karka, 821 A. D. (being edited by the writer in E. I.)

42. E. I., XII, pp. 11 ff.

Kṛshṇa was a mature man of about 45 when he succeeded his nephew in c. 756. He had very probably participated in many of the campaigns of his nephew, and it is very probable that the final defeat of Kīrtivarman was his achievement. For Kīrtivarman was holding his own in Karnatak as late as 757 A.D., *i. e.* three years after the last known date of Dantidurga and one year before the first known date of Kṛshṇa I. The Bharata Itihasa Samshodhak Mandala plates of Kṛshṇa, issued in September 758, do not refer to his defeat of the Chālukyas; it is probable that the event was yet to take place then. But not much later than that date he must have completed the Chālukya overthrow, and annexed the southern part of that kingdom.

He must have spent some time in consolidating his position; but that was not much. Soon he undertook an offensive expedition against Gangavadi; for his Talegaon plates[43] show him encamped in 768 A.D. at Maṇṇe in Mysore state during the course of that expedition. An echo of this invasion of Gangavadi is heard in a lithic record from Tumkur district,[44] immortalising the memory of a hero, who had fallen in the war caused by the rising of the Raṭṭas against Gangavadi. Since this record refers itself to the reign of Srīpurusha, it is clear that this aged ruler was on the throne of Gangavadi when Kṛshṇa invaded it after annexing the Chālukya dominions. The issue of Talegaon plates from Maṇṇe, the Ganga capital, shows that Kṛshṇa was successful in his expedition. Kṛshṇa's expedition against the Gangas was not known before the publication of his Talegaon plates.

The Chālukyas of Vengi were next attacked, and this expedition was under the charge of *Yuvarāja* Govinda whom we find encamped on the confluence of the Musī and the Kṛishna—hardly 100 miles from Vengi itself—in 770 A.D. while

43. E. I., XIII, pp. 275 ff. 44. E. C., XII, Maddagiri, No. 99.

conducting that expedition[45]. Vishṇuvardhana IV, who was then upon the Vengi throne, was defeated by Govinda. As a result of this victory a major part of the modern state of Hyderabad must have passed under the Rāshṭrakūṭa sway. The recently published Bhanduk plates[46] of Kṛshṇa show that in 772 A.D. practically the whole of Marathi C. P. was then under his rule.

Kṛshṇa I had also brought under his sway southern Konkan. From the Kharepatan plates of Raṭṭarāja, we learn that Saṇaphulla, the founder of the line, had obtained the territories between the Sahya and the sea through the favour of Kṛshṇarāja.[47] S'ilāhāras were for a long time very loyal feudatories of the Rāshṭrakūṭas; allowing about 25 years per generation for the ancestors of Raṭṭarāja, we find that Saṇaphulla has to be placed in the latter half of the 8th century It is therefore evident that Kṛshṇarāja, who had placed Saṇaphulla in charge of Konkan, must be Kṛshṇa I.

The date of the death of Kṛshṇa I is not known, but it must have taken place some time between the 23rd of June 772 A.D., when the Talegaon plates were issued and October 775 A.D., when the Pimperi plates[48] were issued by his son Dhruva, which do not refer to Kṛshṇa I as living or ruling.

Kṛshṇa was undoubtedly an able ruler and a skilful general. During his short reign of about 18 years he enlarged the kingdom he had inherited to three times its original size by annexing Konkan, Karnatak and the major portion of Hyderabad state to his empire. He had humbled down the Ganga and Vengi rulers and the expression '*Kāñchīguṇālaṅkṛtā vis'vambharā nijavaniteva sā tena bhuktā*' occurring in his Talegaon plates, may perhaps be referring to the defeat of the Pallava ruler of Kanchi as well, though we have no other evidence on the point. It is clear that by his conquests

45. Alas plates of Yuvarāja Govinda, E. I., VI, pp. 208 ff.
46. E. I., XIV, pp. 121 ff.
47. E. I., III, pp. 292 ff.
48. E. I., X, pp. 81 ff.

Kṛshṇa I had secured for his house a dominating position in the Deccan paving thereby the way of his successors to participate in the politics of the north. He was also a great builder and caused to be excavated the Ellora Kailasa temple which is one of the architectural wonders of the world, since the whole structure is hewn out of solid rock.

The overthrow of the Chālukyas was complete and decisive, and it is only rarely that we come across even Chālukya feudatories in the first century of the Rāshṭrakūṭa rule. Only three such feudatories come to our notice. (i) Kaṭṭiyira of Diḍgur inscription[49] was possibly a Chālukya chief but he was a very petty ruler. Kaṭṭiyiradeva, who is mentioned as an ancestor of later Chālukyas in Managoli inscription,[50] may possibly be this Kaṭṭiyira. (ii) Kadba plates of Govinda III[51] disclose another Chālukya feudatory named Yaśovarman, but since he had to requisition the services of the Ganga chief to secure the permission of Govinda III for certain grants it is doubtful whether he was a ruler of even a mediocre feudatory status. (iii) Mahāsāmanta Budhavarsha of the Torkhede plates of Govinda III[52] was possibly of Chālukya extraction, but his feudal sway extended over only 12 villages. Arikesarin was a powerful Chālukya feudatory, but he belongs to the eve of the rise of the later Chālukyas. It seems clear that Kṛshṇa had not permitted any member of the dethroned dynasty to occupy a position of any political importance in his empire.

It was only for the sake of convenience that the house of Dantidurga was designated as the Malkhed Rāshṭrakūṭa house in the present and the preceding chapter. Malkhed became the capital in the time of Amoghavarsha I, and the pre-Malkhed capital of the house cannot yet be determined with certainty. On the strength of a verse in the *Kathākosha*, it was once suggested that Malkhed was the capital of the

49. E. I., VI, pp. 251 ff.
50. E. I., V, pp. 16 ff.
51. I. A., XII, pp. 13 ff.
52. E. I., III, pp. 54 ff.

Rāshṭrakūṭas from the beginning, since the verse in question mentions Śubhatuṅga, which was one of the *birudas* of Kṛshṇa I, as ruling at Malkheḍ. This view, however, does not seem to be correct, since Śubhatuṅga is known to have been a *biruda* of Kṛshṇa II as well. Besides a verse in the Karda plates of Karka II distinctly states that Amoghavarsha I built Mānyakheṭa, which could put to shame even the capital of gods.[53] It would, therefore, seem that before the time of Amoghavarsha I some other city than Malkhed was the capital of the empire, especially as no record earlier than his time refers to Malkhed as capital. It has been suggested that Mayūrakhiṇḍi or Morkhind, a fort in the district of Nasik, may have been the pre-Malkhed capital, since Wani-Dindori, Radhanpur and Kadba plates of Govinda III were issued from that place. But the expression used in these records is *Mayūrakhiṇḍīsamāvāsitena mayā* and not *Mayūrakhiṇḍīvāstavyena mayā*. It is, therefore, quite possible that at the time of the issue of these records Govinda III may have temporarily encamped in this fort. In the Wani-Dindori plates the village granted is described as included in Vaṭanagara *vishaya* of Nāsika *des'a*. If Morkhinda of Nasik district were really the capital at this period, it is strange that the *vishaya* or *des'a* in which it was situated should not have been designated after it. It would, therefore, appear that Mayūrakhiṇḍī was only a military station and not a capital. This same circumstance would go against the view that Nasik was the capital. The Dhulia[54] and Pimperi[55] plates besides show that Nasik was the seat of a viceroy, and not of the central Government, in the 8th century. Lāṭūra was the original home of the family, from which it had migrated in Berar a few centuries earlier; and it was also included in the Rāshṭrakūṭa kingdom in the reign of Kṛshṇa I. But there is no evidence to show that the earlier rulers of the family had made their ancestral home

53. I. A., XII, pp. 263 ff. 54. E. I., VIII, pp. 182 ff.
55. E. I., X, pp. 81 ff.

once more their capital. Paithan also was not the capital as the Paithan plates of Govinda III would show. As it is, we have to confess that the early capital of the house cannot be determined with certainty. It is, however, not improbable that Elichpur in Berar, where the ancestors of Dantidurga were ruling before the rise of the house, may have continued to be the capital, till it was changed to Malkhed. Cousens has recently suggested[56] that the Rāshṭrakūṭa capital may have been located somewhere in the vicinity of the Elora caves in the time of Dantidurga. He thinks that the place called as 'Sooloobunjun' in the Indian atlas sheets, which is just above the plateau near the Elora caves, may have been the actual locality of the capital, since what look like the remains of a town and a very large tank are still to be seen in the place. This view is a probable one, but the identification of the pre-Malkhed capital with Sooloobunjun can be accepted as proved only when more substantial evidence can be adduced. As it is, we have to admit that we have no definite knowledge as to the precise site of the capital before it was shifted to Malkhed.

CHAPTER III

The Empire at its Zenith
Govinda II

Kṛshṇa I was succeeded by his eldest son Govinda Prabhūtavarsha Vikramāvaloka soon after 772[1] A.D. He had been

56. Cousens, *The Chalukyan Architecture*, p. 1.

1. Fleet's a view that Govinda II did not succeeed at all to the throne cannot be maintained any longer. The expression 'ज्येष्ठोल्लंघन' can support the theories both of dethronement and supercession; for the root 'उल्लंघ्' means to jump over as well as to set aside or transgress. Baroda plates of Karka Suvarṇavarsha dated 881-2 A.D., Kapadwanj grant of Krishna II, dated 910-11 A.D., and Begumra plates of Indra III, dated 914-5 A.D., no doubt omit the name of Govinda II from the genealogy; but this was because [*P. T. O.*

selected by his father as his successor and was annointed as *yuvarāja* some time between 770 and 772[2] A.D. He had already distinguished himself on the battlefield by defeating Vishṇuvardhana IV of Vengi.[3] He appears to have been a great cavalry leader, for the Kadba plates issued by Govinda III, a son of Dhruva I who had deposed him, mention how Govinda II used to win victory by the sole help of his favourite horse.

Daulatabad plates describe how Govinda II relieved Govardhana and despoiled a king named Pārijāta[4]. But at present we neither know who this king Pārijāta was, nor why it was necessary to relieve Govardhana. Since Govardhana is

Continued from last page

he was a collateral member. It may be pointed that the first two of the above-mentioned records omit the name of Dantidurga as well. Deoli and Karhad plates of Kṛshṇa III mention the name of Jagattunga as a prince who did not ascend the throne; but they make no such statement about Govinda II. Govinda III was the son of Dhruva I who had deposed Govinda II, and still his earliest record—the Paithan plates of 794 A.D.—describe how Govinda II appeared under the white imperial umbrella. Another record of his, the Kadba plates of 814 A.D., actually describes the coronation of Govinda II. Daulatabad plates of 793–4 A.D., issued in the reign of Dhruva himself, describe how Govinda had to be deposed by Dhruva in the interest of the dynasty, as he had entrusted the administration to some strangers and was being deserted by the feudatories. There can, therefore, be no doubt that Govinda II did actually rule, although it may be only for a short time. This conclusion is supported by the Chalkeri record No. 34 (E. C. XI) which uses the expression '*Prithvirajyam-geyye*' 'ruling over the earth' with reference to जगत्तुंग-प्रभूतवर्षप्रतापावलोक, son of Akālavarsha. Cf. अकाल ..पृथिवीवल्लभ...सवरस्य पुत्रेण. Prabhūtavarsha was a *biruda* of Govinda III as well, but he cannot be the king here referred to, for he was not the son of Akālavarsha but of Dhārāvarsha. The title 'प्रतापावलोक' is also a variation of the title 'त्रिकभावलोक' which we find him using in his Alas plates. (E. I., VI, pp. 208 ff.)

2. The Talegaon plates of 770 refer to him as simple Govindarāja, while the Alas plates of 772 describe him as *Yuvarāja*.

3. Alas plates, E. I., VI, pp. 208 ff. 4. E. I., IX, pp. 185 ff.

situated in Nasik district, it is probable that its relief may refer to a temporary victory of Govinda over Dhruva, his rebellious brother, who, we know from the Dhulia[5] and Pimperi[6] plates, was ruling over Nasik and Khandesh as the governor under his elder brother.

Soon after his accession Govinda abandoned himself to a life of pleasure and vice[7]. This must have made his administration unpopular and inefficient. Karhad plates of Kṛshṇa III[8] state that Govinda practically entrusted the whole administration to Dhruva, as his mind was engrossed with the enjoyment of pleasures. This must have given Dhruva a golden opportunity to usurp the throne for himself. He proceeded cautiously; we find him sometimes issuing grants under his own authority, sometimes we notice him recognising Govinda as the *de jure* sovereign, but nevertheless issuing the land grant on his sole responsibility[9]. It seems that Govinda soon realised what his brother was aiming at; he immediately removed him from the administration and entrusted it to some stranger. Feudatories, realising the internal dissensions, became lukewarm in their loyalty. This supplied Dhruva with a sufficient excuse to revolt openly against his brother; declaring that there was the danger of the Rāshṭrakūṭa family itself being ousted from the throne, he proceeded to fight with his brother, not so much to gain the throne for himself, as to

5. E. I., VIII, pp. 182 ff. 6. E. I., X, pp. 81 ff.

7. See Karhad plates of Kṛshṇa III, E. I., IV, pp. 278 ff. and the Kharda plates of Karka, I. A., XII, pp. 263 ff.

8. E. I., IV, pp. 278 ff.

9. In the Pimperi grant issued in 775 A.D., Dhruva altogether ignores his elder brother Govinda, who was the reigning sovereign; in the Dhulia plates of 779 A.D. (E. I., VIII, pp. 81 ff.), we find that Govinda II is mentioned as the ruling emperor, but the grantor Karka makes the grant with the sanction, not of Govinda, the emperor, but of his own father Dhruva.

retain it for the Rāshṭrakūṭas[10]. He first tried to induce Govinda to abdicate, which he naturally refused to do. Govinda tried his best to put down the rising of his brother; he sought and obtained help from the rulers of Kanchi, Gangawadi, Vengi,[11] and Malva. Dhruva, however, succeeded in defeating the confederacy and winning the throne for himself. This event probably took place in c. 780 A.D.[12]

10. Cf. तस्यानुजा निरुपमस्तमुदीर्णमीक्ष्य ।
त्यक्तं नृपैरपि नयने विलुप्यमानम् ॥
राज्यं बभार गुरुभक्तिवतोऽन्यसंस्थम् ।
मा भूत् किलान्वयपरिच्युतिरत्र लक्ष्म्याः ॥

Daulatabad plates; E. I. IX, pp. 193 ff.

11. Pampa in his *Vikramārjunavijaya* states that Arikesarin I, the sixth ancestor of his patron Arikesarin II, (c. 925–950 A.D.) had penetrated into the kingdom of a king named Nirupamadeva, with the ministers of Bengerivishaya. (J. B. B. R. A. S. XIV. p. 19). Allowing 25 years for each generation, the time of Arikesarin I works out to be 775-800 A.D. It would, therefore, appear that this Chālukya feudatory had joined the party of Govinda against Dhruva. Can king Bengerivishaya possibly stand for the Vengi ruler ?

12. The above account of the reign of Govinda is based on the assumption that his Dhulia plates are genuine. It must be admitted that this record, though issued in 779 A.D., appears to be some decades later than the Pimperi plates of 779 A.D. But it has been shown already [*ante* pp. 33–4] that the palaeographical test cannot be regarded as the most decisive one, when the difference is only of a few decades. The important factor in connection with the genuineness of the Dhulia plates is the genuineness of their date. The plates were issued on the 10th day of the bright half of Pausha of S'aka 701. Prof. Kielhorn, after making the necessary calculations, wrote: 'The date of this inscription for S'aka Samvat 701 expired regularly corresponds to the 22nd of December 779 A D. On this day Makara or Uttarāyaṇa Sankrānti took place at 4 h. 30 m., and the 10th *tithi* of the bright half of Pausha commenced 6 h. 44 m. after the mean sunrise.' (E. I., VIII, p. 183, n. 2.). Astronomical calculations thus show that the Dhulia plates are genuine, or at least based on a genuine original document. The Pimperi record is also genuine, but we cannot suppose that Govinda was expelled as early as

[*P. T. O.*

Nothing is known about the scene of this war of succession, but since most of the allies of Govinda hailed from the south, it is not improbable that the decisive battles may have been fought in that direction. It is not known as to what fate overtook Govinda after his defeat; nothing is further heard of him. He may have died in battle or may have been imprisoned or killed by his brother Dhruva. It is not known whether Dhruva treated his elder brother with the same consideration with which Govinda III treated his own elder brother, Stambha, when the latter had risen in rebellion.

Dhruva Dhārāvarsha

After the overthrow of his elder brother above described, Dhruva ascended the throne. From the Dhulia plates of Govinda II, we find that Dhruva was still professing himself to be a subordinate of his elder brother in 779 A.D. In what year precisely he overthrew his brother and ascended the throne is not definitely known at present. From Jinasena's *Harivans'a*, we learn that in 783 A.D. king Śrīvallabha, son of Kṛshṇa, was ruling the south. This statement, however, does not enable us to determine the date of the accession of Dhruva, for the description 'Śrīvallabha, son of Kṛshṇa,' can suit Govinda II as well as Dhruva. It is true that the Paithan plates of Govinda III issued soon after his accession, mention

(*Continued from last page*)

October 775 A D. Kṛshṇa I was still on the throne in June 772 A.D. It would be difficult to imagine that in the short space of about 3 years all the following events took place :—accession of Govinda II, his misrule, his entrusting the administration, first to Dhruva, and then to some strangers when the former showed disloyalty, Dhruva's effort to induce Govinda to abdicate, the latter's successful attempt in securing for himself the help of the hereditary enemies of his house, and the defeat of this big confederacy by Dhruva. As both the Pimperi and the Dhulia plates are genuine, the above reconstruction of history, here proposed for the first time, seems to be the only way out of the difficulty, created by the overlapping dates of these documents.

Srīvallabha as an epithet of Govinda II and Kalivallabha as that of Dhruva. But Srāvanbelgola Inscription No. 24, which is an almost contemporary document, describes the father of Stambha, *i. e.* Dhruva, as Srīvallabha.[13] Another contemporary record from Matakeri in Mysore district[14] refers to Dhārāvarsha Śrīvallabha as the overlord of Kambarasa, proving thereby that Dhruva was known both by the epithets of Srīvallabha and Kalivallabha. Since Srīvallabha was thus the epithet of both Govinda II and his immediate successor Dhruva, Śrīvallabha mentioned by Jinasena as ruling in 783 A.D. can be either Govinda or Dhruva. But since the latest known date of Govinda II is 779 A.D. which is supplied by the Dhulia plates discussed above, it may be reasonably assumed that Srīvallabha, who is mentioned by Jinasena as ruling over the south in 783 A.D. may have been Dhruva rather than Govinda II. For, if we place the usurpation subsequent even to 783 A.D., say in 784 or 785 A.D., Dhruva will have a short reign of about 8 years. His extensive conquests in the south and north, which will be soon described, will make it abundantly clear that they presupposed a somewhat longer reign.

At the time of his accession in c. 780 A.D. Dhruva was a mature man of about 50; for, when the Dhulia plates were issued in 779 A.D., his son was a grown-up man invested with the *Pañchamahās'abdas*, and taking an active part in the administration. Dhruva's age, however, had not quenched his military ambition as his *biruda* '*Kalivallabha*', 'one who loves strife or war,' will show. After his accession Dhruva must have spent some time in consolidating his position by compelling the refractory feudatories, who were about to overthrow his brother's yoke,[15] to recognise his sovereignty. Then he proceeded to punish those of his neighbours who had

13. E. C., I. 14. E. C., IV, p. 93.

15. See *ante*, p. 51 foot-note No. 10.

sided with his brother in the war of succession. We have seen already how the rulers of Talwad, Kanchi, Vengi, and Malva had championed the cause of his brother. It is precisely against these kings that we find the armies of Dhruva operating during the greater part of his reign.

Dhruva first proceeded to punish his southern neighbours. The first blow was directed against the Ganga principality. The aged Ganga ruler Śrī-purusha Mutta-rasa who was defeated by his father Kṛshṇa I, was now dead, and was succeeded by his son Sivamāra II. The Manne plates,[16] alleged to have been issued in 797 A.D., are no doubt spurious, but the statement made therein, that Sivamāra was interested in logic, dramaturgy and *Pātañjala-Mahābhāshya* may well have been founded on good tradition ; it would show that he was more a scholar than an administrator. His authorship of a book on war-elephants did not prove to him of much avail against the elephant-phalanx of Dhruva, who managed to defeat and imprison him. The statement in the Rāshṭrakūṭa records that the Ganga ruler was imprisoned[17] is confirmed by some Ganga documents as well. The Manne grant, above referred to, states that Śivamāra was entangled on all sides in difficulties. The Gattiyadpur plates inform us[18] that Sivamāra put his younger brother Vijayāditya upon the throne who, like Bharata, knowing the earth to be his elder brother's wife, refrained from enjoying her. The simile makes it quite clear that Śivamāra was absent from the kingdom in the Rāshṭrakūṭa prison, and that his younger brother was trying to carry on the struggle against the invading forces in the absence of the *de jure* ruler. Dhruva, however, was completely successful in his expedition; he appointed his eldest son Stambha to govern the newly conquered province.

16. E. C., XI, p. 41.

17. See Wani-Dindori plates, 11, 9—10; I.A., XI, p. 157.

18. E. C., XII, Nanjangad No. 129.

After the annexation of the Ganga principality, Dhruva attacked the Pallava ruler and besieged his capital Kanchi. A verse in the Radhanpur plates informs us that the Pallava ruler was defeated and compelled to surrender a large number of war-elephants to the victor.

After punishing his southern neighbours for siding with his elder brother, Dhruva turned his attention to Northern India. As Dharmapāla of Bengal is known to have married a Rāshṭrakūṭa princess, Raṇṇādevī, daughter of king Parabala,[19] it was once believed that Dhruva had undertaken the northern expedition as an ally of Dharmapāla against their common enemy Vatsarāja, the Gurjara-Pratihāra ruler. This view is, however, no longer tenable as the *v.* 14[20] of the Sanjan plates of Amoghavarsha I, recently published, distinctly says that Dhruva fought also against the Gauda ruler in his northern expedition. The real motive of the northern campaign of Dhruva seems to have been to teach a lesson to Vatsarāja,[21] who had tried to espouse the cause of Govinda II.

19. The identity of this Rāshṭrakūṭa prince is still uncertain. He cannot be Parabala of the Pathari pillar inscription, for the latter's date is 861 A.D. (E. I., IX, p. 248). The reign of Dharmapāla had ended about 50 years at least before that year, and therefore he could not have been Parabala's son-in-law. Fleet had proposed to identify him with Govinda III (*Dynasties*, p. 198), but this ruler is not known to have had this *biruda*.

20. Cf. गङ्गायमुनयोर्मध्ये राज्ञो गौडस्य नश्यतः ।
लक्ष्मीलीलारविन्दानि श्वेतच्छत्राणि योऽहरत् ॥

21. The statement of Jinasena

पूर्वाम् श्रीमदवन्तिभूभृतिनृपे वत्सादिराजे......।

has to be understood to mean that Vatsarāja was ruling at Avanti', especially since we know from the Sanjan plates that there was a Gurjara-Pratihāra ruler at Avanti in the time of Dantidurga also. The Malava ruler, who helped Govinda II, must, therefore, have been this Vatsarāja or perhaps a local governor of his, and one of the reasons that induced Dhruva to undertake this expedition in the north must have been to punish the Gurjara-Pratihāra ruler for his partisanship with Govinda II.

Later on Dhruva may have attacked Dharmapāla as well, as the latter may have tried to thwart his plans, regarding him as a possible rival in the overlordship of the north towards which he himself was aiming.

It is not necessary for us to enter into a detailed discussion of the very complicated history of northern India of this period. Only facts, relevant for our enquiry, need be referred to. The Gwalior inscription of Bhoja I[22] of the Gurjara-Pratihāra dynasty informs us that his great-grand-father Vatsarāja had wrested away the empire from the Bhaṇḍi family. Kanauj in our period was occupying the position of Pataliputra in an earlier age, and we know from the *Harshacharita* that Bhaṇḍi was a maternal-uncle of Harsha. Indrāyudha, who was at this time ruling over Kanauj, may probably have been a descendant of this maternal-uncle of Harsha, and it is possible that his family in that case may have been known as Bhaṇḍikula. The statement in the Gwalior inscription that Vatsarāja forcibly wrested the empire from Bhaṇḍikula may support the view that soon after 783 A.D., Vatsarāja attacked Kanauj and defeated its ruler Indrāyudha. Indrāyudha does not seem to have been immediately deposed; for some time he continued to occupy the imperial throne at Kanauj as a mere puppet in the hands of the conqueror. This must have roused the jealousy of Dharmapāla, who was also an aspirant for the overlordship of northern India. Dharmapāla decided to champion the cause of Chakrāyudha, who was probably a relative of Indrāyudha. The Bengal ruler, however, suffered a reverse in the beginning; for a verse[23] in the Waṇi-Diṇḍori plates states that Vatsarāja was elated by the easy victory that he had scored over the lord of the Gaudas. The Bengal ruler defeated by him could not have been Gopāla, for the latter is not known to have sent any expedition outside the

22. A. S. R., 1903–4 p. 280.

23. *Cf.* हेलास्वीकृतगौडराजकमलामत्तम्......वत्सराजम् ।

province of Bengal. The Sanjan plates, on the other hand, show that the armies of Dharmapāla were operating in the Ganges-Jumna Doab in the course of his wars with the Gurjara-Pratīhāras.

At the time of Dhruva's intervention in the northern Indian politics, Dharmapāla had again rallied up his forces and advanced into the Doab with a view to capture Kanauj. Dhruva must have first attacked Vatsarāja, his immediate neighbour, in c. 789 A.D. The latter was probably engaged in meeting the second invasion of Dharmapāla, and so Dhruva could get a decisive victory, capturing the two white umbrellas of the Bengal ruler which Vatsarāja had snatched away from him in a former battle. This defeat of Vatsarāja brought Dhruva into contact and conflict with Dharmapāla, who was already in the Doab. Each must have regarded the other as standing in the way of the realization of his imperial ambition and a conflict was inevitable. We have no details of the military operations, but the Sanjan plates of Amoghavarsha I, distinctly assert[24] that the defeat of the Gauda king took place in the Ganges-Jumna Doab. The statement in the Sanjan plates is confirmed by verse 22 of the Surat plates of Karka Suvarṇavarsha, which I am at present editing for the Epigraphia Indica, where Dhruva and God Śiva are both described as 'Gāṅgaughasantatinirodhavivṛddhakīrtiḥ.'[24a] There is a pun on the expression, and with reference to Dhruva, it can refer both to his imprisonment of the Ganga ruler, as well as to his campaign in Ganges valley. The term *ogha* is not very happy if taken in connection with the imprisonment of the Ganga ruler. It can be more appropriate with reference to the campaign in the Ganges valley, when the huge southern army, consisting of elephants, horses and soldiers

24. गङ्गायमुनयोर्मध्ये राज्ञो गौडस्य नश्यतः ।
लक्ष्मीलीलारविन्दानि श्वेतच्छत्राणि योऽहरत् ॥

24*a*. Likely to be published in E. I., vol. XX or XXI.

may have, while encamped on the banks of the Ganges, appeared to be obstructing the flow of that river either while bathing in it or crossing it across.

And finally the verse:—

> यो गङ्गायमुने तरङ्गसुभगे गृण्हन्परेभ्यः समम् ।
> साक्षाच्चिह्ननिभेन चोत्तमपदं तत्प्राप्तवानीश्वरम् ॥

in the Baroda plates [25] of Karka Suvarṇavarsha has now to be interpreted as referring to Dhruva's occupation of the Ganges-Jumna Doab; the poet imagines that the acquisition of heaven by Dhruva, which is mentioned in the latter half of this verse, was due to his being in possession of the holy Jumna and the Ganges. Prinsep's view that this verse refers to Dhruva's drowning himself in the confluence of the Ganges and the Jumna [26] can no longer be accepted.

Dhruva's expedition in northern India was merely of the nature of a *digvijaya*. It probably brought him no substantial gain, apart from fame and booty, that might have been obtained. Boundaries of the Rāshṭrakūṭa empire did not alter as a result of his successes against Vatsarāja and Dharmapāla. It does not seem that he was in a position to follow up his victories in the Doab by marching upon the capital of either of his opponents. He was far away from his base; and perhaps he was too old to press his armies on to Kanauj. It is also possible that he was anticipating some trouble about the succession after his death, and was, therefore, anxious to return to the south in order to abdicate in favour of his favourite son Govinda. Whatever the real causes, the Rāshṭrakūṭa armies soon retired to the south, enhancing no doubt the military prestige of the empire, but adding very little to its area.

Dhruva died some time between April 793 and May

25. I. A., XII, pp. 157 ff. 26. J. A. S. B., 1839, pp. 304 ff.

794 A.D.[27] He was one of the ablest of the Rāshṭrakūṭa rulers. During a short reign of about 13 years he not only reestablished the Rāshṭrakūṭa ascendency in the south, which was seriously endangered by his predecessor's loose and vicious government, but made the Rāshṭrakūṭas an *all-India* power. For the first time after the Andhra occupation of portions of Northern India, after a lapse of nearly nine centuries, a Deccanese force crossed the Vindhyas and entered into the very heart of *Madhyades'a*, defeating each of the two rival claimants for the imperial position in the North. His deposition of his elder brother is an unfortunate circumstance casting reflections upon his moral character; but if Govinda was really a weak and vicious ruler, which certainly seems to have been the case, there was more than ample political justification for the step taken by Dhruva. His northern campaigns no doubt did not result in the enlargement of the Empire in that direction, but in the south, after the imprisonment of the Ganga ruler, his dominions were annexed[28] and the boundary of the Empire was pushed to the Kāverī.

Govinda III

Dhruva had a number of sons. The names of four of them are known,—Stambha Raṇāvaloka, (Kambarasa in Canarese), Karka Suvarṇavarsha, Govinda and Indra, and it is not unlikely that he may have had more. Stambha was a viceroy over the newly annexed province of Gangawadi,[29] Karka Suvarnavarsha was carrying on the administration of Khandesh,[30] even before his father's accession; Govinda,

27. Dhruva was living when the Daulatabad plates were issued in April 793 and dead when the Paithan plates were issued by his son in May, 794 A.D.

28. From an inscription at Matakeri in Mysore district, we learn that Stambha was the governor of Gangawadi when Dhārāvarsha S'rīvallabha was ruling the earth. E. C., IV, p. 93.

29. E. C., IV, p. 93.

30. Dhulia plates of Govinda II, E. I., VIII, pp. 182 ff.

who was selected by the father for succession and Indra, who was later put in the charge of southern Gujrat by Govinda, were probably co-operating with their father in the military expeditions. All these sons were grown up, able, and ambitious, and the old emperor must have realised that if a war of succession was to be avoided, some one among them must be selected for the throne and formally anointed as the heir-apparent. His choice fell upon Govinda, because he was the ablest and the worthiest among them,[31] well competent to protect the wide empire that he was to inherit. The selection was followed by a formal coronation, and Govinda was invested with a *kaṇṭhikā* or necklace which was the insignia of the heir-apparent.

But the old emperor apprehended trouble in spite of the Yuvarāja coronation of his son Govinda, and proposed to abdicate in favour of the heir-apparent, as the verse quoted in the last footnote would show. Govinda, however, opposed this proposal. It is difficult at present to determine whether the proposed abdication did actually take place. The Paithan plates definitely state that Govinda obtained the kingdom from his father at a formal coronation[32] and their testimony is supported by v. 30 of the Surat plates of Karka, which states that Govinda obtained not Yuvarājaship but emperorship from his father. Cf.

राज्याभिषेककलशैरभिषिच्य दत्ताम् ।
राजाधिराजपरमेश्वरतां स्वपित्रा ॥

It is possible that the expressions 'Rājyābhishekasamaya' and 'Rājyābhishekakalaśa' may have been used rather loosely in these records with reference to Yuvarāja coronation.

31. यस्याकारममानुषं त्रिभुवनव्यापत्तिरक्षोचितम्: ॥
कृष्णस्येत्र निरीक्ष्य यच्छति पितर्येकाधिपत्यं भुवः ।
आस्तां तात...इति पितरं युक्तं वचो योऽभ्यधात् ॥

Radhanpur plates, E. I., IV, pp. 242 ff.

यश्च प्रभु ...पितुस्सकाशात् मूर्धाभिषिक्तनृपसंमतमाशुराज्यम् आसेदिवान्...॥

But it is equally probable that realising that installation as a Yuvaraja was no guarantee against a war of succession, as was shown by his own overthrow of his elder brother, Dhruva may have actually abdicated in favour of Govinda in spite of the filial protests of the latter. Govinda's actual installation as an emperor, he may have thought, may minimise the prospects of his succession being opposed after his death. In the present state of knowledge, therefore, it is difficult to decide whether Dhruva had actually abdicated towards the end of his career : it may, however, be safely assumed that Govinda was the *de facto* ruler in full charge of the administration when his father died.

The accession of Govinda III took place peacefully, for the Paithan plates, issued within less than a year of the death of Dhruva, do not refer to any war of succession. But Stambha, who was an elder brother of Govinda, was smarting under the humiliation of his supercession, and soon formed a formidable confederacy of twelve kings to gain the throne to which he was legally entitled. The names of the allies of Stambha are not known, but we cannot be far wrong in assuming that they must have been some of the neighbouring and feudatory rulers[33] who must have been smarting under the treatment they had received from the dead emperor. The Sanjan plates inform us that a number of high officers of the state also joined the cause of Stambha.

33. Such was the case with the Ganga ruler whom Govinda had released, probably with the intention of creating a rival against his brother, who was governing Gangawadi, the patrimony of the released king. S'ivamāra Muttarasa, the Ganga ruler, however, joined Stambha who, anticipating the imperial crown, may have promised Gangawadi to its legitimate ruler in order to get his assistance in the fight with Govinda. Fleet's suggestion that the glorious Kaṭṭiyira who is mentioned as reigning over the earth, while Dosirāja was governing Vanavasi 12000, may have been an ally of Stambha, would be plausible only if we assume that this Dosirāja was different from the Dosirāja who was governing portions of Karnatak under Kīrtivarman in 757 A.D. (E. I., VI, pp. 253 ff.)

Govinda had anticipated the storm and was well prepared to meet it. By following a policy of conciliation he had endeared himself to a number of his feudatories,[34] who now stood by his side. His brother, Indra, helped him zealously, and it was probably in recognition of his services on this occasion, that he was appointed to the Gujrat viceroyalty. Besides, Govinda was himself a great soldier and skilful general. He, therefore, soon defeated Stambha and his twelve allies and made his position secure. A verse in the Sanjan plates claims[35] that Govinda treated his enemies leniently after the revolt was put down. Such really was the case, for the ring-leader of the confederacy, Stambha, was reinstated by Govinda in his Ganga governorship where he continued to govern at least till 802 A.D.[36]

Stambha was governing Gangawadi during his father's life-time, and it is therefore very likely that the centre of campaign against him must have been south Karnatak. Govinda's expedition against the Ganga ruler must have been undertaken immediately thereafter. Seeing a war of succession impending, Muttarasa, the Ganga ruler, (c. 765 – c. 805 A.D.) assumed imperial titles soon after his release from the Rāshṭrakūṭa captivity;[37] he may have very probably joined the side of Stambha, who may have promised to restore his kingdom to him when he would become the Emperor. We can, therefore, well understand why the Radhanpur plates call him haughty,[37] and the Sanjan plates ungrateful.[38] Govinda defeated him easily, for the Radhanpur plates observe that

34. Sanjan plates of Amoghavarsha, v. 17, E. I., XVIII, p. 244.

35. *Ibid*, v. 18. 36. See note No. 39 below.

37. In his earlier inscriptions, as Fleet has pointed out, his title is simple Maharaja whereas, in his Holawadi record he assumes the imperial title Konguṇi Rājādhirāja Parames'vara S'rīpurusha E. I., V., pp. 156-158 ff.

37. Cf. दर्पविसराय: प्रातिकूल्ये स्थित: । E.I., VI. p. 242.

38. Cf. उपगताविकृति: कृतघ्नगङ्ग : ।। v. 18. E.I. XVIII p. 244..

a mere frown was sufficient for the purpose. The defeated ruler was again imprisoned in c. 798 A.D., and Gangawadi was again annexed to the Rāshṭrakūṭa empire. Stambha was reappointed to the Ganga viceroyalty which he continued to rule down to 802 A.D. at least.[39] Later on he was succeeded by Chākirāja, sometime before the issue of the Kadba plates in 814 A.D. Grown wiser by the fate of Ganga ruler, Charuponnera of Nolambawadi recognised the suzerainty of Govinda.[40]

Govinda next turned his arms to Kanchi. That kingdom had been already once attacked by his father, but Govinda found it necessary to invade it once more, probably because its ruler had sided with Stambha. The Kanchi ruler was defeated sometime before 803 A.D.; for we learn from the British Museum plates of Govinda III,[41] that at the time when they were issued in 804 A.D., Govinda was encamped at Rameśvara Tīrtha, while returning from his victorious expedition against the Pallava king. Govinda's victory was not decisive, for towards the end of his reign, he had to attack the Pallavas once more.

Freed from the worries in the south, Govinda turned his attention to the east. Vishṇuvardhana IV and Vijayāditya Narendrarāja were his contemporaries, but since we have to

39. A copper-plate grant from Manne, dated 802 A.D., mentions Raṇāvaloka S'aucha Kambhadeva as the elder brother of Prithīvivallabha Prābhūtarasa Govindarājadeva who meditated on the feet of Dhāravarshadeva. This grant was made by Stambha with the permission of Govinda, a fact which clearly shows that Stambha had been pardoned by Govinda and reinstated in the Ganga viceroyalty after the imprisonment of the Ganga ruler. E. C. IX, Nelamangal No. 61.

40. Some records from Chitaldurga district show that Charuponnera of Noḷawbaḷge was a feudatory of जगत्तुंग-प्रभूतवर्ष-गोविन्द्. This Govinda is obviously Govinda III. E. C., XI, Nos. 33-34.

41. I. A., XI, p. 126.

place the expedition against Vengi later than 804 A.D.,[42] his Chālukya opponent was very probably Vijayāditya, who is known to have ruled from c. 799 to 843 A.D. Govinda attacked him probably because of the old feud between the two houses. He was a new ruler and therefore a good target for an aggressive conqueror. The Vengi ruler was defeated; a verse in the Radhanpur plates states that he was compelled to prepare a compound for the conqueror's stables, and another in the Sanjan plates of Amoghavarsha I describes the humiliation to which he was subjected, when compelled to cleanse the floor of Govinda's camp. The war which broke out at this time between the two states, lingered for twelve years in which as many as 108 battles are said to have been fought;[43] during the lifetime of Govinda the victory seems to have been with the Rāshṭrakūṭa forces, but things changed with the accession of the boy emperor Amoghavarsha.

After reducing to subjection almost all the important kings to the south of the Narmada, Govinda organised an expedition into northern India. Many new developments had taken place there since his father's retirement to the south. Taking advantage of the crushing defeat inflicted upon Vatsarāja by Dhruva, and of the preoccupation of Govinda III in the south, Dharmapāla had captured Kanauj and put his own nominee Chakrāyudha on its throne with the assent, genuine or forced, of most of the kings of Madhyadeśa and the Punjab.[44] But Dharmapāla did not enjoy his

42. Govinda's armies were fighting against the southern powers down to 804 A.D.; and the defeat of the Vengi ruler is first mentioned in the Radhanpur grant of 809 A.D.

43. See Idara grant of Ammaraja I, I. A., XIII, pp. 56 ff.

44. जित्वेन्द्रराजप्रभृतीनरातीन् ।
उपार्जिता येन महोदयश्रीः ॥
दत्ता पुनस्सा................
चक्रायुधायानतिवामनाय ॥ Bhagalpur grant.
भोजैर्मत्स्यैस्समद्रैः कुरुयदुयवनावन्तिगान्धारकीरैः ।
............:साधु संगीर्यमाणः ॥
Khalimpur grant of Dharmapala, E. I., VI, pp. 248 ff.

imperial supremacy in northern India for a long time. Nāgabhaṭa II, who had succeeded Vatsarāja on the Pratihāra throne, soon recovered his position. He formed an alliance, as Dr. R. C. Majumdar has pointed out, with the Mahomedans of Sindh, the Chalukyas of Vengi, and the local rulers in eastern and western C. P., and attacked Dharmapāla and Chakrāyudha.[45] His attack was successful and both Dharmapāla and Chakrāyudha were defeated.[46] He then subjugated the territory round Dholpur and led an expedition to the west defeating the chiefs in Malva and northern Gujrat.[47] Nāgabhaṭa II was thus at the height of his glory and power, when Govinda III decided to attack him sometime in 806 or 807 A.D.

The northern expedition of Govinda was boldly planned and skilfully executed. He entrusted a number of his generals with the work of subduing or keeping in check the rulers of Vengi, Orissa, Kosala and Malva, his brother Indra was sent to attack the Gurjara-Pratihāras in their home province, and then he himself proceeded in the direction of the Doab and Kanauj to attack Nāgabhaṭa himself[48] sometime in 806 or 807 A.D.[49]

45. E. I., XVIII, pp. 87 ff.

46. जित्वा पराश्रयकृतस्फुटनीचभावम् ।
चक्रायुधं विनयनम्रवपुर्व्यराजत् ॥
निर्जित्य वङ्गपतिमाविरभूद्विवस्वान् ।
- Gwalior inscription of Bhoja, A. S. R., 1903–4.

47. *Ibid.* v. 8.

48. The Sanjan plates actually mention the name of the Gurjara-Pratihāra ruler as Nagābhaṭa (v. 22). Before the publication of this record the name of the Gurjara opponent had to be inferred, since it was given in no Rāshṭrakūṭa record. Buhler had proposed to identify him with some member of the Chāvoṭaka house. (I. A., XII. p. 158.)

49. Since the Gurjara defeat is mentioned in the Radhanpur plates issued in August 809 A.D., and since Govinda was just completing his expedition against the Kanchi ruler in 804 A.D. the above conclusion about the date of this expedition will appear as very probable, when it is also remembered that the Vengi expedition was undertaken prior to the advance to the north.

Apart from a few local reverses,[50] success seems to have attended Govinda's arms everywhere. The army under the Gujrat viceroy Indra was ultimately victorious; the Baroda plates of his son Karka, issued in 811-2 A.D., state that Indra was able to rout out single-handed the lord of the Gurjars. The expeditions against the central Indian rulers were equally successful.[51] After defeating the ruler of Chitrakūṭa Govinda himself marched into the Doab. He defeated Nāgabhaṭa II and apparently pressed right up to the Himalayan ranges.[52] Nāgabhaṭa's defeat was fairly decisive; he had to retire to the deserts of Rajputana. Chakrāyudha was a mere puppet and offered voluntary submission. Dharmapāla also is said to have done the same,[53] probably because he was shrewd enough to realise that it was politically wise to humour Govinda III, who had indirectly obliged him by overthrowing his greatest enemy, Nāgabhaṭa II. Govinda, he knew, would soon retire to the south, leaving him free to exploit the situation created by the defeat of the Gurjara-Pratīhāra ruler.

50. Bāhukādhavala, a contemporary and feudatory of Nāgabhaṭa II in Kathiawar, is said to have defeated a Karnataka army in a grant of his grandson Balavarman (E. I., IX, pp. 1 ff). This victory may have been a local success against the army of Indra, the Gujrat viceroy.

51. The defeat of Kosala king, Chandragupta, is specifically mentioned in the v. 22 of the Sanjan record; v. 24 makes the general statement that all the central Indian kings were reduced to submission by the generals of Govinda. E. I., XVIII p. 245.

52. V. 23 of the Sanjan record refers to the resounding of the Himalayan caves by the noise made at the time of the bath of the army of Govinda in the Ganges. It is possible, however, that this resounding of the Himalayan caves may be merely poetic, and the armies of Govinda may not have marched much beyond the Ganges-Jumna Doab. The Rāshṭrakūṭa records do not claim the conquest of Kanauj at this time; and since Kanauj was not conquered, it is not likely that Govinda could have gone in the close vicinity of the Himalayas.

53. स्वयमेवोपनतौ च यस्य महतस्तौ धर्मचक्रायुधौ । Sanjan plates, *ibid.*

Govinda's expedition in northern India was merely of the nature of a *digvijaya.* He compelled both Nāgabhaṭa II and Dharmapāla, each of whom was seeking to make the titular king Chakrāyudha a puppet in his own hands, to recognize his suzerainty. He did not annex any portions of their normal kingdoms, though he must have exacted heavy tributes from them. The same was the case with the central Indian rulers, perhaps with the exception of Malva. We do not know who the Malva ruler was, who in the Wani-Dindori[54] plates is described as submitting to Govinda. He may possibly have been a feudatory governor of Nāgabhaṭa II, appointed to govern Malva when his master was preoccupied with the conquest of Kanauj. The statement in Baroda plates of Karka, issued in 812 A.D., that Karka was made a door-bolt to protect Malva against the Gurjara attack, suggests that Malva was almost assimilated to the Rāshṭrakūṭa dominions as a result of this expedition.

Govinda then marched westward and was welcomed by king Śarva at his capital Sribhavana or modern Sarbhon in Bharoch[55] district with the presents of the choicest heir-looms.

54. I. A., XII, p. 157.

55. An inscription hailing from Gudigeri in Dharwar district (E. I., VI, p. 257) which, on paleographical grounds can be assigned to c. 800 A.D., refers to a glorious mahārāja, Mārassaḷba by name, as ruling over that district. Fleet had opined (*Ibid*) that this ruler may be the same as king Mārās'arva, who, in the Rādhanpur plates, is described as submitting to Govinda at the mere news of his approach to the Vindhya regions. This view is, however, untenable. Mārās'arva was a petty ruler ruling at Sarbhon in Bharoch district as will become evident from the following reasons :—

(i) The statement in the Wani-Dindori plates, that Mārās'arva hastened to present his heir-looms to Govinda, as soon as his spies reported to him the arrival of the conqueror in the vicinity of the Vindhyan ranges, makes it abundantly clear that his dominion must have been in the vicinity of that mountain; if he were really ruling in Dharwar district, the advent of Govinda in the Vindhyan regions would not have frightened him. (*Continued on the next page*)

Govinda spent the major part of the rainy season of 808 A.D. at his capital, maturing the plans of the campaigns against the kings of the south, who had shown signs of insubordination during his absence in northern India and formed a confederacy against him.[56] It was during his stay at Sarbhon that Amoghavarsha was born in the monsoon of 808 A.D.[57]

Continued from last page

(ii) The reference to the presentation of the choicest heir-looms by Mārās'arva would show that before that time, he was an independent ruler. But Dharwar was in the very heart of the Rāshṭrakūṭa empire under the direct imperial administration; no independent king could have survived there down to c. 808 A.D. Mārassaḷba of the Gudigeri record must have been a third-rate feudatory,—supposing that he belonged to this period—; for an inscription from the district of Shimoga shows that Rājdāityarasa was Govinda's governor over Banavāsī 12000, and that Chitravāhana was ruling over Alurakhed 6000 under him at this time. [See E. C., VIII, Sorab Nos. 10 and 22].

(iii) At the beginning of the monsoon of 808 A.D. Govinda's army had just returned after prolonged operations in Northern and Central India, and it is therefore very unlikely that he would have subjected it to a long march to the Tungabhadrā. The fact that the Rādhanpur plates were issued from Mayūrakhindī in Nasik district in July 808 A.D. would also show that Govinda did not proceed to the south, immediately after his northern campaign but spent the rainy season in the north. S'rībhavana ought to be, therefore, identified with Sarbhon in Bharoch district, and not with Shiggaon, the headquarters of Bankāpur Taluka in Dharwar district, about 30 miles north of the Tungabhadrā, as Fleet has suggested. There is also some phonetic difficulty in identifying Shiggaon with S'rībhavan. The same difficulty is encountered in considering the view of Wathen that S'rībhavana, where Govinda was encamped, is modern Cowldurg in Mysore.

(iv) The Sanjān plates of Amoghavarsha I, recently published, show conclusively that S'rībhavana is Sarbhon in Bharoch district. They describe the capital of Mārās'arva, as situated in the Narmadā valley at the foot of the Vindhyas (v. 25). This description applies very accurately to Sarbhon in Bharoch district, and not to Shiggaon in Dharwar district. It need not be added that king S'arva of the Sanjān record is the same as king Mārās'arva of the Rādhanpur plates.

56. Sanjān plates of Amoghavarsha, v. 30 E. I., XVIII, p. 246.

57. *Ibid*, vv. 26–27.

From Srībhavana or Sarbhon he proceeded to the south to teach a lesson to the Dravidian kings who had formed an alliance against him. The members of this confederacy were the rulers of Gangawādi, Kerala, Pāṇḍya, Chola and Kānchī kingdoms. These were all of them defeated.[58] Several battalions of the Ganga army, or perhaps some members of the royal family,[59] were put to the sword, Kānchī was once more occupied, and the Chola and Pāṇḍya kingdoms were overrun. The fate of these states frightened the king of Ceylon who hurried to offer submission, sending his own statue and that of his minister to Govinda, while the latter was encamped at Kānchī.[60] Govinda sent them on to Mālkhed to be put in front of a Śiva temple as columns of victory.

The southern campaign, which was undertaken subsequent to the monsoons of 808 A.D., must have required at least two years and may have terminated sometime in 810 or 811 A.D. Govinda probably undertook no more expeditions; he was getting old, his end was approaching, and towards the close of his reign he must have been occupied in making some arrangements to ensure the succession of his only son, Amoghavarsha, who was born as late as in 808 A.D. Govinda was alive on the 4th of December 813 A.D. when the Torkhede plates[61] were issued by him. His death took place soon thereafter, for there is evidence to show that Amoghavarsha ascended the throne sometime in the next year.

58. *Ibid*. v. 30 59. *Ibid*, v. 33

60. *Ibid*, v. 34, Cf :—

लंकातः किल तत्प्रभुप्रतिकृती काञ्चीमुपेतौ ततः ।
कीर्तिस्तंमनिभौ शिवायतनके येनेह संस्थापितौ ॥

It is clear from this verse that the statues were transported from Kanchi to 'here' i e. Mālkhed from where the plates were issued. It is, besides, very unlikely that Govinda would have ever thought of erecting these *Kīrtistambhas* at Kānchī which he had only temporarily occupied.

61. E. I., III, p. 54.

Govinda was, perhaps, the ablest of the Rāshṭrakūṭa emperors. He not only put down the confederacy that was formed to oppose his accession but also enhanced the prestige of his kingdom and added to its area. Mālva in the north and Gangawadi in the south were annexed to the empire. Both Nāgabhaṭa and Dharmapāla, who were aspiring to the imperial position in the north, were overthrown by him. The victorious march of his armies had literally embraced all the territory between the Himālayas and Cape Camorin. Even the king of Ceylon was terrified into submission. Never again did the prestige of the Rāshṭrakūṭas reach this high level. Indra III, no doubt, conquered Kanauj but he could not proceed beyond the North Pennar in the south. Kṛshṇa III had indeed conquered all the states defeated by Govinda III in the south but could not enter the Madhyadeśa and defeat the principal kings in north India. The statement of the Wani-Dindori plates that with the advent of Govinda III the Rāshṭrakūṭa dynasty became invincible to its enemies is no boast of a court panegyrist but a plain statement of fact.

The success of Govinda was due to his bravery, statesmanship and power of organisation. He is compared to Pārtha in the Baroda plates of his nephew Karka,[62] and the Naosari plates[63] issued by the same ruler describe how Govinda was accustomed to plunge straightway into the thick of battle without caring to consider the odds against him. His fondness for sport[64] also attests to active habits and personal bravery. His successful campaigns in the north and the south attest to his generalship and power of organisation. His victory over Stambha at the beginning of his reign speaks volumes for his diplomacy. His creation of the Gujrat viceroyalty[65] under his

62. I. A., XII, pp. 158 ff. 63. J. B. B. R. A. S., XX, pp. 135 ff.

64. I. A., XI, pp. 126 ff.

65. It is usually supposed that Gujrat was reconquered by Govinda and handed over to his brother Indra. But no record, contemporary

P. T. O.

brother Indra not only secured the northern boundaries of the empire, but enabled his child successor to regain the throne. For, both Indra, who predeceased him, and his son Karka, were loyal to the imperial throne[66] and defended it against internal and external enemies.

CHAPTER IV

Amoghavarsha I and the Gujrat Branch

As shown already Govinda III was alive in December 813. He died early in the first half of the next year[1] and was succeeded by his only son Amoghavarsha. He was a boy

Continued from last page

or later, attributes the conquest of that province to him. The word 'Ī's'vara' in the expression 'तद्दत्तलाटेश्वरमंडलस्य' which occurs in the Baroda plates (I. A., XII, p. 160) may well be due to metrical exigencies. It may be pointed out that the Baroda plates of Dhruva II use the expression 'लाटीयं मंडलं यस्तनय इव निजस्वामिदत्त ररक्ष.' The fact that the donee in the Pimpri plates of Dhruva is a resident of Jambusara would also suggest that southern Gujrat was included in the Rāshṭrakūṭa kingdom before the accession of Govinda III.

66. Bhagwanlal Indraji's view that Indra aided certain Rāshṭrakūṭa feudatories, who had risen against Amoghavarsha, (B. G., I. i., p. 124) was based upon a wrong interpretation of a verse in the Baroda plates. Indra was dead before the accession of Amoghavarsha and, therefore, could not have helped any feudatories against him.

1. Sirur inscription of Amoghavarsha I (E. I., VII, p. 203) is dated in the 52nd year of his reign, the day being the new moon day of Jyeshṭha, S'aka 788. The new moon day of Jyeshṭha, S'aka 737, which must have fallen sometime in May or June of 815 A.D., must have therefore fallen in the first year of Amoghavarsha's reign which, therefore, must have commenced sometime between May-June of 814 and May-June of 815. The death of Govinda may probably have then taken place in the first half of 814 A.D.

of six at his accession[2] and Govinda, foreseeing his approaching end, may have arranged for a regency during his son's minority. Karka Suvarṇavarsha, a son of his brother Indra of the Gujrat branch, who had loyally stood by his side during the revolt of Stambha and others, was selected as the head of the regency,[3] and for some time the administration continued

(2) The statement of v. 35 of the Sanjān plates of Amoghavarsha I that Govinda III went to heaven because, inter alia, the one son, he had, was able to bear the yoke of the three worlds, would no doubt suggest that Amoghavarsha was a grown up youth at the time of his father's death. But this statement is more poetic than real and is contradicted by the earlier statement in vv. 25-6 of the same plates, that he was born at the close of the northern campaign of his father.

(3) This inference is based upon the fact that all the records of the Gujrat Rāshṭrakūṭa branch, which mention the restoration of Amoghavarsha give its credit to Karka. The recently published Sanjān plates of Amoghavarsha I, however, tell us that it was with the help of Pātālamalla that the boy emperor could regain the throne. But the Surat plates of Karka, which I am editing, give the credit of the restoration to Karka himself. These plates were issued in May 821 A.D. and are thus almost a contemporary document; and their testimony can hardly be brushed aside. The discrepancy between these two records can be explained in two ways: (1) Pātālamalla may have been another relative or feudatory of Amoghavarsha, who may have co-operated with Karka in overthrowing the confederacy against the boy-emperor. The Gujrat branch records would naturally ignore him and give the entire credit to Karka who belonged to it. (2) Or, Pātālamalla may be the same as Karka, the former being an epithet of the latter. Pātālamalla is obviously a *biruda* rather than a proper name; Bhagwānlal Indraji avers that it was a *biruda* of Karka, but cites no authority for the statement (B. G., I. i., p. 124). It is not improbable that he made that statement on the authority of some unpublished Rāshṭrakūṭa record, like the Baroda grant of Dhruva II to which he refers, but which is yet to see the light of the day. But so far, no published records including the Surat plates of Karka himself, which I am editing for the Epigraphia Indica, assigns this *biruda* to him. I believe that it may eventually be found out that Pātālamalla was a *biruda* of Karka, as Bhagwānlal had asserted. Were he really a different relative or feudatory of Amoghavarsha, it is difficult to imagine why the

P. T. O.

to be carried on without any hitch; for the Naosari plates of Karka Suvarṇavarsha,[4] which were issued in 816 A.D., mention Amoghavarsha as the ruling emperor and are altogether silent about the revolt and the part which their donor had played in quelling it.

But clouds were gathering fast. Almost at each previous succession there were troubles, and the presence of the boy emperor on the throne must have aroused imperial ambitions in several hearts. There arose factions in the imperial family ; ministers became disloyal ; the Ganga ruler, who had been set at liberty, declared independence and sheltered rebels against his feudal lord ; feudatories began to kill imperial officers and assert their own independence ;[5] and the hereditary enemies of the empire began to invade it. No records have handed down the names or the localities of the rebels. They were completely successful for a time. Amoghavarsha was deposed [6] and there followed confusion and anarchy, probably because the rebels must have begun to fight among themselves for the imperial crown. The records, published so far, enable us to determine the time of this rebellion only very roughly ; it is not mentioned in the Naosari plates issued

Continued from the last page

Sanjān plates of Amoghavarsha should ignore him altogether and give the whole credit of the restoration to Pātālamalla. It is possible to argue that the omission of Karka in the Sanjān record is deliberate ; his descendants having rebelled against Amoghavarsha, the latter may have naturally ignored the services that he had rendered to him, in a document that he had issued when the memory of that rebellion was still fresh in his memory. This explanation is, however, not quite convincing, and I will prefer to assume that Pātālamalla was a *biruda* of Karka.

4. J. B. B. R. A. S., XX, pp. 135.

5. Sanjan plates of Amoghavarsha, vv. 38-39.

6. V. 40 of the Sanjan plates describes the setting of the Rāshṭrakūṭa sun Amoghavarsha and v. 41 his subsequent rise. A later record also says that Amoghavarsha regained the throne which he had lost. See Kapadwanj grant of Kṛshṇa II, 910 A.D., E. I., I., pp. 54 ff.

in 816 A.D. whereas its quelling is described in the Baroda plates of Karka's son, Dhruva, issued in 835 A.D. The Surat plates of Karka, which I am editing, enable us, however, to determine the time of the rebellion almost accurately. They were issued on the 13th of May 821 A.D., and describe the restoration of Amoghavarsha to the throne, brought about by the exertions of Karka. It is, therefore, clear that the rebellion took place sometime between 816 and 821 A.D. It may have very probably lasted for about 3 or 4 years, since the description given thereof by the Sanjan record makes it clear that it was a very serious and prolonged affair.

Karka, alias Pātālamalla, soon retrieved the situation. We do not know what steps he took to restore the boy emperor to the throne, but the Surat plates issued by him in 821 A.D. make it clear that he was completely successful before May of that year. At his restoration, Amoghavarsha was still a boy of 12 or 13 and the entire credit for his reinstatement must, therefore, go to persons other than himself.

Idar grant of Amma I of the eastern Chālukya dynasty refers to a 12 years' war waged by Vijayāditya II with the forces of the Raṭṭas and the Gaṅgas[7] sometime between c. 799 and c. 843 A.D. This war took place in the beginning of his career and we have seen how Govinda III, who commenced it, was successful in his own time.[8] The later period of this war coincided with the early years of the reign of Amoghavarsha, when there was complete anarchy in the Rāshṭrakūṭa empire. At this time, Vijayāditya must have carried everything before him. V. 13 of the Begumra plates of Indra III states that Amoghavarsha I raised the glory of his house that had sunken deep in the Chālukyan ocean;[9] this statement no doubt occurs in a late record, but there is nothing improbable in Vijayāditya having fully exploited his successes by helping the rebels to oust the boy-emperor, whose father

7. I. A., XIV, pp. 197 ff. 8. See *ante*, p. 64.
9. E. I., IX, p. 24.

had put him to the humiliation of being compelled to cleanse his court-yard. Nay, the rebellion itself may have arisen as a result of Vijayāditya's successes.

In the Sirur grant of Amoghavarsha I, dated 866 A.D.,[10] he is being represented as being worshipped by the ruler of Vengi. Three later records supply more information in this connection. The Sangli plates of Govinda IV[11] issued in 933 A.D. state that a right royal feast was offered by Amoghavarsha I to Yama on the battlefield of Vingavalli, where he met the Chālukyas and the Abhyūshakas. The Karhad plates of Kṛshṇa III, issued in 958 A.D.,[12] observe that the wrath of Amoghavarsha I was not extinguished even when the Chālukya house was burnt to ashes. The Karda plates of Karka II[13] describe him as the fire of destruction to the Chālukyas. It is, therefore, clear that Amoghavarsha had signally defeated the Vengi ruler sometime before 866 A.D. This defeat cannot be placed in the first half of the 9th century; for Vijayāditya was upon the throne till c. 843 A.D. and the wording of the Idar plates of Amma makes it clear that he was ultimately successful against the Rāshṭrakūṭas. Amoghavarsha was not in a position to inflict such a defeat for a pretty long time after his attaining the majority, as he was soon thereafter involved in a war with his Gujrāt cousins and had besides to face a number of minor risings.

The success of Amoghavarsha against the Vengi forces has to be placed sometime about 860 A.D., when he had emerged successful from the preoccupations above referred to. The king of Vengi defeated by him was then Guṇaga Vijayāditya (c. 844–c. 888 A.D.). It is no doubt true that the Idar grant, above referred to, states that after defeating the Gangas and killing Mangi, this ruler had frightened Kṛshṇa and burnt his city, the name of which is given as Kiraṇapura

10. I. A., XII, p. 218.
11. I. A., XII, pp. 249 ff.
12. E. I., IV, pp. 281 ff.
13. I. A., XII, pp. 264 ff.

in the Maliapundi grant;[14] this incident, however, refers to the reign of Kṛshṇa II and not to that of his father Amoghavarsha I. The statement in the Rāshṭrakūṭa records, that Amoghavarsha finally inflicted a crushing defeat upon the Vengi opponent is supported by some of the Chālukya records themselves. The Idar grant, above mentioned, observes that after the time of Guṇaga Vijayāditya, the Vengi kingdom was occupied by Rāshṭrakūṭa forces[15] and that Bhīma had to reconquer it from Kṛshṇa II, sometime after his own accession in c. 888 A.D. The claim of the Rāshṭrakūṭa records to a crushing victory over Vengi is then correct, and we may place it sometime about c. 860 A.D.

Dr. D. R. Bhandarkar has recently shown[16] that there are no real genealogical discrepancies in the Konnur inscription of Amoghavarsha I ; we would, therefore, be justified in assuming that though the record was put on stone about a couple of centuries later than the time of the events it narrates, it must have been based upon a genuine document. From this record it appears that the reign of Amoghavarsha was a period of internal revolts and that before 860 A.D. at least three serious rebellions had broken, challenging the imperial authority. The first of these was the one that had broken out when he was a child, the second when he was engaged in his wars with his Gujrat cousins, and the third sometime later. Details about these revolts are not given, but it seems that the third was a very serious one[17] when the situation was saved only by the timely arrival of his Banavāsi viceroy, Bankeya. It would seem that Kṛshṇa, the heir-apparent, had joined the rebels, and Bankeya defeated and destroyed the enemy forces

14. E. I., IX, p. 48.

15. विजयादित्यश्चतुश्चत्वारिंशद्वर्षाणि । तदनु सवितर्यस्तंगते, तिमिरपटलेनेव रट्टदायादबलेनाभिव्याप्तम् वेंगिमण्डलम्।

16. E. I., XVIII, pp. 236-7.

17. See Konnur Inscription, vv. 28-9, E. I., VI, pp. 30 ff.

when Kṛshṇa had left them.[18] In return for his loyalty and signal services, Baṅkeya was made the governor of Banavsi 12,000, Belgol 300, Kundarge 70, Kundur 500 and Purigeri 300.

What with these internal revolts and what with his naturally spiritual temperament, Amoghavarsha had neither the time nor the inclination to take energetic part in the politics of northern India. The revolt of his Gujrat cousins, which will be soon described, had also seriously handicapped him. His Gurjara-Pratihāra contemporary, Mihiṛa Bhoja, was extending his dominions right upto Kathiawar, but Amoghavarsha did not lift even a finger to arrest his progress. Had he the ability or the temper of his father, he would surely have opposed tooth and nail the Gurjara-Pratihāra expansion just beyond his own borders. Nor does he seem to have interfered much with the affairs of Bengal. A passage in his Sirur inscription no doubt states that the ruler or rulers of Anga, Vanga and Magadha also paid homage to him. But some of the Pāla records also claim that Nārāyaṇapāla had defeated a Dravida king, who must in all probability have been Amoghavarsha I himself. The conflict with Gauda kingdom must have taken place towards the end of his career, sometime after the defeat of the Vengi ruler. It would seem that after occupying Vengi *maṇḍala* the generals of Amoghavarsha advanced through Orissa[19] further eastwards, when they may have come into hostile contact with Vanga forces. Only a

18. Cf. इत्युक्त्वा क्रमविक्रमोच्छिखशिखाज्वालावलीढे व्रजे ।
धूमश्यामलिते तिरोहिततनौ प्रायः परप्रेषिते ॥
याते मत्तनये स्थितान्यनृपतीन्निर्जित्य यो जित्वरः ।
बंधीकृत्य रिपून्निहत्य च तदा तीर्णप्रतिज्ञोऽभवत् ॥

19. A march through Baghelkhand and Bihar was impossible owing to the rise of the Gurjara-Pratihāras. Amoghavarsha's conflict with the Gauda ruler could not have taken place before the rise of Mihira Bhoja, for he had not attained majority before 830 A.D. His own position was for a long time very insecure.

few minor skirmishes may have happened and they too of an indecisive nature; as a result each side was free to claim the defeat of the other.

The Sirur record of Amoghavarsha I states that the lord of Malva was also a feudatory of that emperor. It is not possible to identify this feudatory; he could not have been the ruler of the whole of eastern and western Malva, for the larger part of that territory was under the influence of the Gurjara-Pratihāras. Parmāras rose to power under Upendra sometime after 900 A.D.; so Amoghavarsha's feudatory could not have been that ruler. He may probably have been some petty local magnate, now professing allegiance to Bhoja and then to Amoghavarsha I, according to the exigencies of the political situation.

S'ilāhāras were put in charge of Konkan by Kṛshṇa I. In the time of Amoghavarsha Pullaśakti was ruling that province as a Rāshṭrakūṭa feudatory[20] from his capital at Puri or modern Elephanta. Gujrat and Konkan, however, continued to be governed by Gujrat Rāshṭrakūṭa feudatories down to 888 A.D., as the Bharoch plates of Kṛshṇa II show.

Amoghavarsha's policy towards his southern neighbours was also a defensive one. From his Konnur inscription, we learn that his Banvāsī viceroy Bankeya had defeated a Ganga chief who may have been Pṛthvīpati II, who claims to have saved king Dindi's son from Amoghavarsha I.[21] On another occasion he had crossed the Kāveri and invaded the territories beyond, but was compelled to retire by a sudden and urgent call of his master to quell a rebellion. These southern expeditions seem to have been rather defensive than offensive; even Gangawadi, which had recovered its independence towards the beginning of his reign, could be annexed no more. Amoghavarsha had to follow a policy of conciliation, and an

20. I. A., XIII, pp. 134 ff.
21. Udayendiram plates of Pṛthvīpati II, S. I. I., II, p. 384.

alliance was brought about with the Gangas, which was cemented by the marriage of his daughter Chandrobelabbā with the Ganga crown prince Bhūtuga.

Gujrat Rāshṭrakūṭa Branch

Gujrat Rāshṭrakūṭa branch founded by Indra was, roughly speaking, contemporary with the life of Amoghavarsha I. It would be convenient to discuss its history from the beginning to the end at this place, as it is essential to do so to understand the career of Amoghavarsha properly.

Sometime after his accession Govinda III put his younger brother Indra in charge of southern Gujrat, probably in c. 800 A.D. He was thoroughly loyal to his elder brother,[22] protected the province assiduously and cooperated with his feudal lord in defeating Nāgabhaṭa II. Soon thereafter he died, for we find that his eldest son Karka Suvarṇavarsha was ruling the Gujrat kingdom in 812 A.D.[23] From the Torkhede plates issued in December of the next year, we find that Karka's younger brother was then occupying some important administrative post, having the power of creating sub-feudatories.[24]

Karka's valuable services to the imperial house, when he managed to restore Amoghavarsha to the throne, have been already described. Karka was probably acting as regent for the boy-emperor in his minority throughout, and may therefore have spent most of his time at Malkhed. It is usually supposed that his younger brother Govinda, who had issued the Kavi plates[25] in 827 A.D., was a usurper,

22. The lines भीतासंहतदाक्षिणापथमहासामन्तचक्रं यतः।
रक्षामाप विलुण्ठ्यमानविभवं श्रीवल्लभेनाद्दरात् ॥
in the Baroda plates of Karka refer to Indra's successful intervention with Govinda III in favour of southern feudatories, who had joined Stambha, and not to any hostile action against his imperial overlord.

23. Baroda plates, I. A., XII, pp. 157 ff.

24. E. I., III, pp. 53 ff.

25. I. A., V, p. 146.

but this view ignores the most significant fact that Govinda in these plates devotes as many as full four verses to the praise of the administration of his brother Karka, and two of these, which contain a very genuine and heart-felt tribute, do not occur in any grant either of Karka himself or of any of his descendants. Is it likely that a usurper or rebel would go out of his way to describe in glowing terms the administration of the victim of his usurpation ?[26] It appears to me that all the known facts can be explained by the assumption that Govinda of the Kavi plates was simply Karka's deputy, acting on his behalf during his stay at Mālkhed, while engaged in acting as Amoghavarsha's regent. Kavi plates do not refer to Govinda's accession at all. It is true that they refer to Karka as "Sūnurbabhūva Khalu tasya mahānubhāvaḥ," but the verb *babhūva* need not denote that Karka was dead; for the Torkhede grant of Govinda III[27] uses precisely the same line for Karka, although there can be no doubt that Karka was living when that grant was issued in 813 A.D. Dhruva, who succeeded Karka in c. 830, was not his eldest son;[28] he was probably an inexperienced youth during his father's absence in the south, whereas Govinda was already a responsible officer in 830 A.D. Karka, therefore, may have naturally selected him to act on his behalf during his absence. At the time of the Kavi plates, he was still merely the regent, since he does not refer there to his accession. The later records of Gujrat Rāshṭrakūṭas omit

26. Cf. :— सौराज्यजल्पे चलिते प्रसंगान्निदर्शनम् विश्वजनीनसंपत् ।
प्राज्यं बले: पूर्वमहो बभूव क्षिताविदानीं तु नृपस्य यस्य ॥
I. A., V, p. 145 ff.

27. E. I., III, p. 53.

28. Baroda grant of Karka refers to another son, Dantivarman, who was the *Dūtaka* of that grant. He must have been then a grown up youth. Since Dhruva succeeded his father, Dantivarman may have probably predeceased him.

him from the genealogy, not because he was a usurper, but because he was never a *de jure* ruler. The supposition that he was a rebel against Amoghavarsha received some support from the fact that his Kavi plates take the genealogy of the main line down to Govinda III, and omit Amoghavarsha altogether. But this omission was accidental ; for if Govinda was a rebel against Amoghavarsha he must have been an enemy of Karka as well; for the latter was championing the cause of the former. In that case Govinda would not have praised his brother against whom he was fighting. Nor would a favourite of his have been selected by Karka's son, Dhurva I, as the recipient of a land grant.[29]

Karka Suvarṇavarsha was succeeded by his son Dhruva I alias Dhārāvarsha in c. 830 A.D.; we have a land grant of his, issued in 835 A.D., wherein he recognises Amoghavarsha as his feudal lord.[30] But very soon thereafter, the Gujrat branch was entangled in a long war with a king called Vallabha, which lasted for three generations. Dhruva I lost his life on the battle-field while repelling the forces of his enemy, his followers joined the enemy and his son Akāla-varsha S'ubhatuṅga too had to regain his ancestral dominions from the enemy, *viz.* king Vallabha. His victory over his enemy, however, was not a decisive one, for his son Dhruva II had to continue the fight. He had to face a powerful Gurjara army on one side and the forces of Vallabha on the other And his relatives had grown disloyal and an unnamed younger brother of his was conspiring against him.[31] He was able to tide over this situation with the assistance of his brother Govinda. We find him firm upon the throne in 867 A.D., when he had emerged victorious from the crisis.

The identity of king Vallabha, the enemy of the Gujrat line, presents some difficulty. The Gurjara–Pratihāra ruler,

29. See Baroda grant of Dhruva II, I. A., XIV, p. 197.
30. See Baroda grant of Dhruva II, I. A., XIV, p. 197.
31. Begumra plates of Dhruva II, I. A., XII, p. 179.

Bhoja I, was at this time engaged in subduing Central India, Northern Gujrat, and Kathiawar; and one is tempted to conclude that the long-drawn war of the Gujrat house may have been with him. But the name of the enemy-king is stated to be Vallabha, and Bhoja is not known to have been known by that title. This title, Vallabha, makes it clear, that the opponent of the Gujrat branch was a Rāshṭrakūṭa ruler. There were several Rāshṭrakūṭa feudatories under the Malkhed house who had to be subdued by Amoghavarsha before he could regain the throne. Was this king Vallabha who was fighting with the Gujrat house for about twenty-five years (c. 838–c. 863) a Rāshṭrakūṭa feudatory of Amoghavarsha, or was he Amoghavarsha himself?

Pathari pillar inscription of king Parabala[32] discloses the existence of a Rāshṭrakūṭa family in Malva during the first half of the nineth century. This inscription, which is dated 861 A.D., informs us that an unnamed elder brother of Jejja, the grand-father of Parabala, had conquered Lāṭa country, after defeating the Karnāṭaka army, and that his father Karkarāja had inflicted a crushing defeat upon a king called Nāgāvaloka. It cannot, however, be maintained that Dhruva I, his son and grandson were engaged in fighting with a king or kings of this Rāshṭrakūṭa branch. It is no doubt true that Jejja's elder brother is represented as the conqueror of Lāṭa, when Dhruva and his successors were ruling; but Akālavarsha Śubhatuṅga had lost his thrown in his war with Vallabha in c. 840 A.D., while Jejja's elder brother must have flourished much earlier, as his grandson was ruling in 861 A.D. It is possible to argue that Jejja's elder brother conquered Lāṭa in c. 840 A.D. from Akālavarsha Śubhatuṅga and was succeeded not by Jejja but by his son Karkarāja, and that the king Nāgāvaloka defeated by the latter may have been Akālavarsha or his son Dhruva of the Gujrat line with an *avaloka*-ending epithet. This argument, besides

32. E. I., IX, p. 248.

being based upon an unproved assumption that Nāgāvaloka was an epithet of Akālavarsha or Dhruva II, ignores the fact that the Pathari pillar record nowhere states that Nāgāvaloka was a ruler of Lāṭa or Gujrat. The fact, that even the name of Jejja's elder brother, who had conquered Lāṭa, is not mentioned in Parabala's record, suggests that Parabala and his father Karka had nothing to do with Lāṭa, and, therefore, could not have been the enemies of the Gujrat Rāshṭrakūṭas.[33]

33. The identity of the elder brother of Jejja, who had conquered Lāṭa, and of king Nāgāvaloka who was defeated by his nephew, Karka, is still a matter of uncertainty. The *avaloka*-ending epithets were peculiarly associated with the Rāshṭrakūṭas; Dantidurga was Khadgāvaloka, Govinda II was Vikramāvaloka, a relative of his, Vijayāditya, at whose request he had issued the Alas plates, was Mānavaloka, Stambha was Raṇāvaloka, Nanna and his grandson Tuṅgā of the Bodhagaya record were Guṇavaloka and Dharmāvaloka respectively. It is possible to argue, especially since we know from the Konnur record that Amoghavarsha had to face several rebellions of his feudatories, that Nāgāvaloka, the opponent of Karka, was Amoghavarsha himself. But Nāgāvaloka as an epithet of Amoghavarsha is not known from any record, and the Pathari inscription does not give the least hint that the war with Nāgāvaloka was a war with the Mālkhed Rāshṭrakūṭas. Under the present circumstances, Dr. D. R. Bhandarkar's theory that Jejja was a younger brother of Govinda III and Indra and his son Karka had cooperated with him in defeating Nāgāvaloka or Nāgabhaṭa II of the Gurjara-Pratīhāra dynasty seems to be the most probable one (I. A., XL, pp. 239-40). Karka's reign may be placed between c. 810 and c. 840 A.D. and that of Parabala between c. 840 and c. 865 A.D. Nāgāvaloka's identity with Nagabhaṭa II is rendered all but certain by a statement in *Prabhāvakacharit*, according to which, Nagāvaloka, the grand-father of Bhoja I, died in c. 834 A.D. The date of the death of Bhoja's grand-father seems to be wrong since Bhoja himself is now known to have ascended the throne earlier than 836 A.D. (Ahar plates of Bhoja, E. I., XIX, pp. 18 ff.). But *Prabhāvakacharit* may be right in stating that Nāgabhaṭa was also known as Nāgāvaloka. It is very likely that Karka may have been appointed by his uncle Govinda III to rule over Mālva after its conquest and annexation.

The Vallabha opponent of the Gujrat branch was an obviously powerful ruler and he could not have been a mere feudatory. We have, therefore, to identify him with Amoghavarsha I himself[34]. Pṛthvīvallabha[35] and Lakshmīvallabha[36] are known to have been his epithets, and these may have contracted into simple vallabha. The Begumra record of Dhurva II[37] and Gujrat plates[38] of Dantivarman further make it quite clear that Dhruva I, Akālavarsha, and Dhruva II were fighting against one and the same enemy, a fact which supports the identity of Vallabha with Amoghavarsha, since he was a contemporary of all these kings. From the Konnur record[39] we further know that Amoghavarsha was twice deserted by his feudatories in the latter half of his reign and could not retain his hold upon the throne without the help of his zealous general Bankeya. It would, therefore, appear that the friendly relations between Amoghavarsha and his Gujrat cousins came to an end soon after 835 A.D.; either Amoghavarsha was ungrateful or Dhruva I became too overbearing, puffed up by the consciousness that it was his father who had restored Amoghavarsha to the throne.[40]

34. Bhagwanlal Indraji had seen in the following verse of the Kapadwanj grant of Kṛshṇa II (E. I., I, page 54) an evidence of Amoghavarsha's invasion and devastation of the coastal tract between Bombay and Cambay in his war with the Gujrat Rāshṭrakūṭas (B.G., I, i., p. 126):—

सूनुस्तस्यातिवीरः ... ... ।
भूपालात्कण्ठिकाभि (?) सपदि विघाटितान् वेष्टयित्वा ददाह ॥
राज्यं यश्चाभिमानी निजमपचालितं बाहुवीर्याद्वाप ।

But the third line shows that 1, 2 refers to the trouble at the beginning of the reign and therefore "Kaṇthikābhi" must be regarded as a mistake for "Kaṇṭakābhān."

35. Kanheri inscription, I. A., XIII, p 133.

36. Nilgund inscription, E. I., VI, p. 99. 37. I. A., XII, p. 179.

38. E. I., VI, p. 287. 39. E. I., VI, p. 29.

40. It is not likely that the rebellion of the Gujrat house was instigated by the Gurajara Pratīhāras, for in one place, we are definitely informed that the Gujrat house had to face King Vallabha on the one hand and the Gurjara ruler on the other. (Begumra grant, I.A., XII, p.179)

A war broke out in which Amoghavarsha was first successful. Akālavarsha, however, managed to regain the throne after defeating the imperial forces. Amoghavarsha then recalled Bankeya, who had been sent to reconquer Gangawadi, and with his assistance he was once more able to harass Akālavarsha and Dhruva II. It would seem that ultimately sometime is c. 860 A.D., a peace was concluded. probably because Bhoja I had threatend an invasion. Dhruva II may have consented to recognise Amoghavarsha's sovereignty and Amoghavarsha may have helped him in frustrating Bhoja's plans. Bhoja's invasion was not apparently a serious one, and Dhruva claims to have repulsed it single-handed sometime before 867 A.D.[41] This seems to be the only occasion when Bhoja I and the Rāshṭrakūṭas came into conflict with each other. Neither side seems to have been anxious to renew the old historic wars between the two houses.

It would be convenient to discuss the remaining history of the Gujrat branch at this stage though it continued to rule down to the reign of Amoghavarsha's successor. Dhruva II had three brothers, one of whom had joined his enemy. Of the remaining two, Govinda had rendered him valuable assistance in his wars with Amoghavarsha, and Dantivarman was ruling under him as a local governor in 867 A.D. This latter succeeded him some time after 867 A.D., and in 888 A.D. we find Dantivarman's son Kṛshṇarāja Akālavarsha upon the throne. This Kṛshṇarāja participated in his feudal lord's wars with the Gurjara Pratīhāras and claims to have defeated the enemy at Ujjain.[42]

Soon after 888 A.D., the Gujrat branch came to an end. The reasons for its disappearance are not yet known. On the

41. Cf: गूर्जरबलमतिबलवत् समुपतं बृंहितं च कुल्येन ।
एकाकिनैव विहितं पराङ्मुखं लीलया येन ॥
Begumra plates, I. A., XII, p. 154.

42. I. A., XIII, p. 67.

one hand, we do not know of any successor of Kṛshṇarāja and on the other, we find that Kṛshṇa II and Indra III were directly administering Southern Gujrat.

The territories over which the Gujrat branch ruled were bounded on the north by the Mahi. The Baroda grant of Karka grants Baroda itself, his Naosari plates were issued from Kaira; Baroda plates of his successor Dhruva I were issued from Sarvamangala near Kaira; all these show that the Mahi was the northern boundary.[43] The territory beyond was being governed by the feudatories of the Gurjara-Pratihāra empire. The southern boundary seems to have varied: according to an unpublished Baroda grant of Dhruva II, dated 867 A.D., his dominion stretched from the Mahi to the Narmada only.[44] But a copper plate of this very monarch issued four years earlier grants a village near Naosari,[45] showing that his jurisdiction had then extended upto the Tapi. The strip of the territory between the Narmada and the Tapi seems to have been transferred between these two dates to the Śilāhāras of Konkan by Amoghavarsha I. The Surat plates of Karka, which I am editing at present, grant a piece of land in Ambāpāṭaka, a village near Naosari, showing that in his time the Tapi was the southern boundary. It is very likely that Amoghavarsha may have granted the territory between the Narmada and the Tapi as a reward for the loyal

43. Fleet suggests the possibility of the Rāshṭrakūṭa rule having extended for some time right upto Sindh after the fall of Valabhi, since two Arab writers, Ibn Haukal and Al Istakhri state that the Rāshṭrakūṭa kingdom extended from Kambaya to Saimur. This view, however, is untenable, for Kambaya and Saimur are not on the confines of Sindh. The first is Cambay at the mouth of the Mahi and the second is Chaul, 30 miles to the south of Bombay. It is not improbable that some portion of the territory near the mouth of the Mahi may have been lost to Balavarman or his feudal lord Bhoja I soon after 867 A.D. See Una inscription of Balavarman, E. I., IX, p. 1.

44. Referred to by Bhagwanlal Indraji in B. G., I., i. p. 127.

45. Begumra plates, I. A., XII, p. 179.

services of Karka, which the Gujrat Rāshṭrakūṭas continued to hold till c. 862 A.D. It was probably taken away from them at the end of the long feud with Amoghavarsha I. Eastwards their authority could not have extended beyond the longitude 75, for the Ujjain kingdom was not permanently included in the Rāshṭrakūṭa empire.

Let us now revert to the career of Amoghavarsha. His latest known date is Phālguna Śuddha 10, Saka 799 (*i. e.* March, 878 A.D.) when the *Jayadhavala-ṭikā* of Vīrasena was finished. He had at this time completed the usual allotted span of human life and ruled for about 64 years.(46) His death, therefore, may well be presumed to have taken place not long after this date. We may place that event in c. 880 A.D.

Kṛshṇa II, who succeeded him, is the only known son of Amoghavarsha. Chandrobelabbā, who was married to the Ganga Crown Prince Bhūtuga, is the only daughter of the emperor.(47)

Amoghavarsha's reign was long, but it was not brilliant from the military point of view. During his rule Gangavadī and Malva were lost to the empire. The defeat of the Vengi ruler Guṇaga Vijayādityā was the only substantial military achievement. Amoghavarsha did not, like his father and grand-father, intervene in the politics of northern India, although there were provocations enough for such an intervention. The frequent internal revolts that broke during his reign left him no time to undertake an expedition in the north. He does not, besides, seem to have been a military leader or a lover of war, like his father and grand-father. It was rather peace,

46. R. G. Bhandarkar had suspected that there might be something wrong about the dates of Amoghavarsha on the ground that it was very improbable that a king should have ruled for so long a period (*Early History of the Deccan*. supplement p. 2). But the Sanjan plates hav now shown that Amoghavarsha was a child of six at his accession; he could, therefore, have ruled for 64 years.

47. E. C., XII, Nanjangud No. 129.

literature and religion that attracted him. He was either the author or the inspirer of *Kavirājamārga*, the earliest work in Canarese on poetics. He was a patron of literature: Nāgavarman II (c. 1150 A.D.), Keśirāja (c. 1225 A.D.) and Bhaṭṭakalaṅka (c. 1600 A.D.) all agree in stating that Amoghavarsha was very liberal to men of letters.[48] His Sanjan plates also aver that he was more liberal than the famous Vikramāditya himself.[49] In religion Amoghavarsha had great leaning towards Jainism. Jinasena, the author of *Ādipurāṇa*, claims that he was the chief preceptor of Amoghavarsha.[50] *Gaṇitasārasaṁgraha*, a Jain mathematical work by Mahāvīrāchārya, written in the reign of Amoghavarsha, describes him as a follower of *Syādyāda*. Though there can be thus no doubt that Amoghavarsha was immensely impressed by the gospel of Mahāvīra, he had not altogether ceased to believe in the tenets and beliefs of Hinduism. He was a devotee of Mahālakshmī and the Sanjan record states that he had on one occasion cut off and offered one of the fingers of his left hand to that Goddess, in order to ward off a public calamity. That this is not a cock-and-bull story is proved by the unexpected confirmation of the Sanjan record by the *Karnāṭakas'aabdānus'āsanam* of Bhaṭṭakalaṅaka, where we are told that Nṛpatuṅga excelled Bali twice, Dadhīchi three times, and Jīmūtavāhana a hundred times and Śibi certainly a thousand times.[51] These comparisons remind us of the wording of v. 47 of the Sanjan plates, where also the sacrifice of his finger by Amoghavarsha is compared to the sacrifice of Jīmūtavāhana, S'ibi and Dadhīchi, and shown to be immensely superior to theirs.

Amoghavarsha thus not only listened to the precepts of religion, but also practised them. The concluding verse of

48. I. A. 1904, pp. 197 ff. 49. Sanjan plates vv. 47-48.

50. B. G. I., ii. p. 200. Amoghavarsha referred to by these writers could not have been Amoghavarsha II or III since Ādipurāṇa was completed in the reign of Krishṇa II. 51. I. A., 1904, pp. 197 ff.

Pras'nottaramālikā was first to inform us that its author, Amoghavarsha, had abdicated, convinced of the futility of life. This statement was not believed by all, for the authorship of this poem was ascribed in some quarters to Saṅkarāchārya and in others to Vimala. The Sanjan record affords conclusive evidence that Amoghavarsha had abdicated. v. 47 informs us that he had given up the kingdom more than once. It would seem that he was often putting his Yuvarāja or the ministry in charge of the administration, in order to pass some days in retirement and contemplation in the company of his Jain gurus. This again shows the pious monarch trying to put into practice the teachings both of Hinduism and Jainism, which require a pious person to retire from life at the advent of old age in order to realise the highest ideals of human life.

We can now understand the discrepancy between the Saundatti record of Pṛthvīrāma[52] according to which Kṛshṇa II was ruling in 875 A.D., and the Kanheri record[53], according to which Amoghavarsha I was on the throne in 877 A.D. Even before 861 A.D., when the Sanjan plates were issued, Amoghavarsha had abdicated more than once; during the concluding years of his reign, his retirements from the administrative duties must have been more frequent and prolonged. He may have been at that time only a theoretical sovereign, his son Kṛshṇa being the *de facto* ruler for all practical purposes. It was, therefore, natural that in the documents issued in this period, there should be some confusion as to the name of the ruling king; some would mention the name of the *de jure* ruler, and some of the *de facto* one.

52. J. B. B. R. A. S., X, p. 200. It may also be added that the date of this record is not quite above suspicion. Pṛthvīrāma's grandson was ruling in December 980 A.D. (*Ibid*, pp. 211 ff.) ; it is, therefore, not very likely that his grandfather could have been upon the throne in 875 A.D. To get over this difficulty Fleet has suggested (B. G., I., ii, p. 211, note 1) that Pṛthvīrāma's overlord may be taken to be Kṛshṇa III and not Kṛshṇa II. The date of the record goes, however, against this view.

53. I. A., XIII, p. 135.

CHAPTER V

From Krishna II to Govinda IV

Krishna II

Unlike most of his predecessors, Kṛshṇa II could ascend and retain the throne without a war of succession. The exact date of his accession is still not possible to determine, but it cannot be much later than March 878 A.D., which is the last known date of his father, since the latter was by that time more than 70. We may, therefore, tentatively place his accession in c. 880 A.D.[1]

Kṛshṇa II had to engage in wars with most of his neighbours. On the south, he had to fight with the Gangas and the Nolambas, on the east with the Vengi Chālukyas, and on the north with the Gujrat Rāshṭrakūṭas and Gurjara-Pratīhāras. He was the son-in-law of Kokkala, the Chedi ruler,[2] and his son Jagattuṅga was married to Lakshmī, a daughter of his wife's brother Saṅkargaṇa *alias* Raṇavigraha. He derived considerable help from these Chedi relatives in times of need. The statement in the Bilahari inscription[3] of Yuvarāja II that Kokkala had conquered the whole earth planting Bhojarāja and Kṛshṇarāja as his columns of fame in the north and south respectively, is not to be interpreted and understood too literally to mean that

1. The earliest known date of Kṛshṇa II is 888 A.D. supplied by the Bettigiri inscription. (E. I., XIII, p. 189) An inscription from Kunimellihalli in Dharwar district, dated 896 A.D., refers itself to the reign of Mahāsāmantādhipati Kannaravallabha. It is quite certain that Kṛshṇa was not a Yuvarāja at this time. The feudatory title applied to him in this record must be either an accidental mistake, or Kannaradeva of the record was different from Kṛshṇa II. The later alternative is improbable, as Dharwar was at this time under direct imperial administration, the local governor being Lokāditya, the son of Bankeya, the famous general of Amoghavarsha.

2. Sangli plates of Govinda IV, I. A., XII, pp. 247 ff.

3. E. I., I, p. 156.

Kokkala had defeated his son-in-law Kṛshṇa II. It simply means that he had rendered assistance to him, an interpretation, which is supported by the Benares plates of Karṇadeva,[4] which simply say that Kokkala had extended protection to Kṛshṇa and Bhoja. Kokkala's conquests are nowhere described, and it is not unlikely that he may have derived his importance from his family connections with the Rāshṭrakūṭas and possibly with the Gurjara-Pratihāras.

The political relations between the Chālukyas of Vengi and Kṛshṇa II are very difficult to determine at present. A synthesis of the known facts in this connection presents almost insuperable difficulties. Vijayāditya III (c. 844–c. 888 A.D.) and Bhīma I (c. 888–c. 918 A.D.). were the Chālukya contemporaries of Kṛshṇa II. We have seen how Amoghavarsha claims to have defeated the Vengi ruler and how the Idar record admits that towards the end of the reign of Vijayāditya III, Vengi Maṇḍala was overrun by the Raṭṭas. The Kaluchamburu grant, however, states how Bhīma I defeated a great army sent by Kṛshṇavallabha along with some relatives of his own and then protected the earth.[5] It is, thus, clear that Bhīma I succeeded in regaining independence for his house sometime in the reign of Kṛshṇa II.

But the relations of Vijayāditya III with the Rāshṭrakūṭas after his defeat by the latter are still a great mystery. The Idar plates inform us that Vijayāditya III attacked the Gangas at the instigation of the lord of the Raṭṭas, cut off the head of Maṅgi in battle, frightened Kṛshṇa and his ally Sankila, and burnt their capital whose name, however, is not stated.[6] The

4. E. I., II, p. 396.
5. Cf. जित्वा संयति कृष्णवल्लभमहादण्डं सदायादिकम् ।
भीमो भूपातिरन्वभुंक्त भुवनम् ... ... ॥
6. Cf. गंगानां गजवारिशाकिरसमान् रट्टेशसंचोदित: ।
जित्वा मंगिशिरोऽहरद् युधि महावाहासर्वायार्यमा ।

P. T. O.

killing of Maṅgi was an undoubted historic fact; it is referred to in several eastern Chalukyan records[7] and the Musulipattan plates of Vijayāditya III himself record a grant to a Brahmana, Vinayāḍiśarman by name, who had suggested to the grantor the way to kill Maṅgi[8] while the battle was raging. From the Maliyapundi grant we learn that Maṅgi was a Nolamba chief, and that Sankila, who had joined with fierce Vallabha was a ruler of Dahāla country.[9] The same grant tells us that the city burnt was Kiraṇapura and that Kṛshṇa was statying there at that time.[10] The Pithapuram inscription[11] of Mallapadeva, however, states that Vijayāditya burnt Chakrakota, frightened Sankila (who was residing at Kiraṇa-

Continued from last page

कृष्णं संकिलमंकिताखिलबल (?) प्रासोरुसद्विक्रमः।
भीतार्तं च विधाय तत्पुरवरम् यो निर्ददाह प्रभुः ॥

The expression 'रट्टेशसंचोदितः' in this verse is translated by Fleet as 'Challenged by the lord of the Raṭṭas,' but the root संचुद् does not possess the sense of challenging.

7. The Pithapuram inscription describes the incident with a grim humour; Cf. :—

मंगिराजोत्तमांगेन यो वीरस्समरांगणे
चकार कन्दुकक्रीडां नाम्ना त्रिभुवनांकुशः ॥ E. I., IV, p. 233 v. 9.

8. हत्वा मंगिं विजितसकलाराति भूपालवर्गम् ।
रागोद्रेकाध्यसितनृपतित्यागशौर्यप्रतापम् ।
नाना हेत्या हतहयभटोन्मत्तहस्तिप्रकीर्णे ॥
युद्धे यस्य द्विजगणवरस्याद्भुतादेशतुष्टः ॥
तस्मै विनयाडिशर्मणे चंद्रग्रहणनिमित्तम् ग्रामं दत्तवान् । E. I., V, p. 125.

9. हत्वा भूरि नोदम्बराष्ट्रपतिं मंगिं महासंगरे
गंगानाश्रितगंगकूटशिखरान्निर्जित्य सद्दाहलाधीशम्
संकिलमुग्रवल्लभयुतम् यो माययित्वा विजयादित्यो ररक्ष क्षितिम् । *Ibid.*

10. किरणपुरमधाक्षीत् कृष्णराजस्थितम् यः । E. I., IX, p. 51.

11. योधाक्षीच्चक्रकूटं किरणपुरगतं संकिलं कृष्णयुक्तम् ।
योऽभैषीत्, वल्लभेन्द्रं निजमहिमयुतं योऽव्यथात्, अग्रहीच्च ॥
कालिंगप्राहृतेमान्,...। E. I., IV, p. 239.

pura and was helped by Kṛshṇa), acquainted[12] (lit. united) Vallabhendra with his bravery (*i. e.* by defeating him), and accepted elephants from the Kalinga ruler. And finally we learn from the Kalachumbaru grant that Vijayāditya III was worshipped by king Vallabha who could be obviously none other than Kṛshṇa II.

The above-mentioned exploits of Vijayāditya divide themselves into two parts : those performed in the south and those in the north. We have already seen how Vijayāditya was signally defeated by Amoghavarsha I. It seems that after this defeat either Amoghavarsha or Kṛshṇa II suggested to the defeated ruler the idea of attacking the Gangas and their feudatories, the Nolambas, offering free passage to the Vengi army and probably some help also in men and money.[13]

12. 'निजमाहिमयुतं योऽव्यथात्' can mean 'who restored (Kṛshṇa) to his dignity' as well. It will be shown below that the known situation requires a sense similar to the one suggested in the text. The root 'yu' means to unite as well as to separate ; the translation, 'who separated Krishna from his glory' would be better still.

13. Cf. the expression '"रट्टेशसंचोदित:' in the passage quoted in the foot-note No. 6 above. This lord of the Raṭṭas who incited the Vengi ruler could not have been Prithvirāma, the Raṭṭa feudatory of Kṛshṇa II; besides being a petty ruler, he was not an immediate neighbour either of Vijayāditya or of the Gangas to make his incitement to the former to attack the latter probable. I freely admit that the theory advanced in the text above that Vijayāditya attacked the Gangas at the instigation of his enemy Amoghavarsha or Krishna II looks a little unconvincing. In politics, however, the enemies of today become friends of tomorrow ; the conduct of Greece and Italy in the last world war is a pertinent example. It is possible to argue that the Raṭṭa chief, who incited Vijayāditya, may have been a hitherto unknown feudatory Rāshṭrakūṭa ruler, whose advice the Vengi ruler may have followed without any suspicion. The term Raṭṭes'a, however, can hardly be appropriate with reference to a mere feudatory and can properly denote only the Rāshṭrakūṭa emperor ruling at the time. Fleet's view that Vijayāditya was challenged by the Rattas to attack the Gangas is also unconvincing, for 'sanchodita' cannot mean 'challenged by.' The theory propounded above in the text is therefore the only one that explains the facts known so far.

The suggestion was a diplomatic one, for whosoever may succeed in the campaign, the Rāshṭrakūṭas were bound to be benefitted as both the Gangas and the Vengis were their enemies; and the defeat or stalemate would weaken either or both of them. At this time (c. 870–880 A.D.), Satyavākya Koṅguṇivarma Būtuga I had just come to the throne or his father Rāchamalla's reign was drawing to a close. It was, therefore, a nice opportunity to attack. The Nolambas of Nolambawadi who were the feudatories of the Gangas, had to bear the brunt of the attack as Nolambawadi lay between Vengi-maṇḍala and the Ganga territory. Vijayāditya defeated Nolamba army killing, probably by some trick,(14) its general Maṅgi, who seems to have been a relative of the ruler of Nolambawadi. He then advanced into Gangawadi and besieged and apparently captured a fort.(15)

Emboldened by these successes Vijayāditya and his nephew, Yuvaraja Bhima, must have tried to throw off the Rāshṭrakūṭa yoke, especially since Kṛshṇa II had just ascended the throne. With this end in view Vijayāditya led some daring raids in the north-eastern portions of the Rāshṭrakūṭa empire. The passages quoted in foot-notes Nos. 6, 9, 10 and 11 make it clear that Kṛshṇa and Sankila, who were the opponents of Vijayāditya, could only have been Kṛshṇa II of Malkhed and his brother-in-law Sankula or Sankaragaṇa of the Chedi house. The passage in the foot-note No. 9

14. In the passage quoted in foot-note No. 9 above we find Vijayāditya making a grant to a learned Brahmana on the occasion of an eclipse as a reward for the advice that he had given in the thick of battle which enabled him to kill Mangi. Since Vijayāditya could bring about the death of Mangi by following the advice of a Brahmana who, to judge from his name and from the fact that he is the donee of a grant made on the occasion of an eclipse, was a non-fighter, it is probable that some trick may have been played to bring about his death.

15. It may be pointed out that about half a century later the Chālukya ruler of the time, Amma I, was also engaged in fighting with a combination of the Gangas and Nolambas, E. I., VI, p. 47.

distinctly says that Sankila was a ruler of Ḍahāla and the Sangli plates[16] of Govinda IV inform us that the wife of Kṛshṇa II was a younger sister of Sankula, a son of Kokkala. Sankila of the passages quoted in foot-notes Nos. 6, 9 & 11, is obviously the same as Sankula of the Sangli plates. This conclusion is further supported by the localities mentioned in connection with this raid. The passage in the foot-note No. 11 refers to the burning of Chakrakūṭa and this is the same as the fort of Chakrakoṭya in the centre of Bastar state.[17] Kiraṇapura[18] which was subsequently besieged or burnt has not yet been identified, but I think that it is the same as Kiranpur, a small town in Baleghat district of C. P. about 150 miles to the north of Chakrakūṭa or Chakrakoṭṭya. By construing together the verses in foot-notes Nos. 6, 10 and 11, it becomes clear that Kiraṇapura was not a capital of Sankila or Kṛshṇa, but that these rulers were for the time being staying in that city. Kṛshṇa, the ally of Sankila, can be none other than his brother-in-law Kṛshṇa II. Jouveau Dubreuil's theory that he may be the Ganga-Pallava Prithvī-Kṛshṇa cannot be accepted, since both Chakrakūṭa and Kiraṇapura lay far away from the Ganga-Pallava principality. He cannot be Kṛshṇa of the Gujrat Rāshṭrakūṭa branch. The epithet "Ugravallabha" given to Sankila's ally,[19] shows that he was a great ruler and not a petty feudatory. Besides, Sankila

16. I. A., XII, p. 247.

17. Chakrakotya occupied a strategic position and was, in later times, captured by Rājendra Chola. See S. I. I., I, No. 67.

18. Fleet had conjectured that Kiraṇapura may be a mistake for Kṛshṇpura *i. e.* Malkhed, the capital of Kṛshṇa. (I. A, XX, p. 102 n. 26). This view has to be abandoned since the reading in the Pithapuram inscription (foot-note No. 11) is now confirmed by the Maliyapundi record (foot-note No. 10). Foot note No. 11 further shows that Kiraṇapura was a city of Sankila and not of Kṛshṇa. The latter may have been simply staying there for the time being. In view of my identification of this place there is now no scope for conjectures.

19. See foot-note No. 11.

may have, when in difficulty, invoked the aid of his mighty brother-in-law, whose territories were contiguous to his own, rather than that of a petty feudatory, living hundreds of miles from the battle-field. Nor can Sankila's ally be Kṛshṇarāja, the founder of the Paramāra dynasty, firstly because he was not a ruling prince in c. 880 A.D., and secondly because he did not bear the epithet of Vallabha. The only Kṛshṇarāja, then, who flourished in c. 880 A.D., and who could have participated in Sankila's battles near Chakrakūṭa and Kiraṇapura, is the Rāshṭrakūṭa emperor Kṛshṇa II, who was Sankila's brother-in-law. The verse in the foot-note No. 11 does not go against this identification; for Vallabhendra in clause (*c*) of that verse need not be taken as different from Kṛshṇa in clause (*b*); the verse is to be translated as follows :—" Who (Vijayāditya III) burnt Chakrakūṭa, frightened Sankila staying in Kiraṇapura and joined by Kṛshṇa, acquainted (lit. united) Vallabhendra (*i. e.* Kṛshṇa II) with his (*i. e.* Vajayāditya's) own prowess (by defeating him), and took away the elephants from the Kalinga ruler."

Kṛshṇa was not able to retrieve the situation after Vijayāditya's death. His successor Bhima I claims to have defeated Kṛshṇa and his Lāṭa and Karṇātaka allies in the battles of Niravadyapura and Peruvanguragrāma.[20] Bhīma had to pay rather heavily for his successes; for his eldest son, a lad of 16, was killed while fighting in this war. It may, however, be observed that Kṛshṇa's authority remained supreme right up to Chitaldurg during the dark days of his Vengi and Gujrat wars; an inscription from Kadajji in Chitaldurg District, dated 889 A.D., refers to Kannaradeva's kingdom as extending on all sides.[21]

Soon after his accession and some time before 888 A.D., Kṛshṇa II came into hostile contact with Bhoja I. The scene

20. *Inscriptions from Madras Presidency*, Kistna Dt. No. 9.

21. E. C., XI, Davanagare No. 17.

of war was Malva; a fragmentary Pratihāra inscription from Bhavanagar Museum, recently published,[22] refers to the Narmada in connection with Bhoja's attack on a king called Kṛshṇarāja, who must be obviously Kṛshṇa II; and the Begumra plates of Kṛshṇa of the Gujrat branch, dated 888 A.D.,[23] tell us how the grantor feudatory defeated the enemy at Ujjayinī, while king Vallabha was watching the army movements. Begumra plates of Indra III[24] inform us that old men vividly remembered in 914 A.D. (when the plates were issued) the brave feats of the late Rāshṭrakūṭa emperor in the sanguinary wars with the Gurjaras. The crown prince Jagat-tuṅga also participated in these wars as also the Chedi ruler.[25] These wars seem to have profited neither party; they may have been of the nature of the frontier affrays. From Al Masudi, we learn that the Gurjara-Pratihāras used to maintain a strong force in the south to keep the Rāshṭrakūṭas in check;[26] frontier clashes were therefore inevitable, and victory must have remained some time on one side and some time on the other. Kṛshṇa was too weak to think of emulating the example of Dhruva I or Govinda III, and Bhoja was too old to undertake a serious expedition against his southern neighbour.[27]

22. E. I., XIX., pp. 174-7.
23. I. A., XIII, p. 66.
24. E. I., IX, p. 24.
25. I. A., XII, p. 265.
26. Elliot: *History of India*, Vol. I, p. 22.
27. In his historical appendix to *Uttarapurāṇa*, which was completed in S'aka 820 *i.e.* 908-9 A.D., the elephants of Kṛshṇa are represented by Guṇachandra to have drunk the waters of the Ganges and enjoyed the cool shade in the forests at Cape Kamorin. cf:—

यस्योत्तुंगमतंगजा निजमदस्रोतस्विनीसंगमात् ।
गांगं वारि कलंकितं पट्ठ मुहुः पीत्वाप्यगच्छत्तृषाम् ॥
कौमारं घनचंदनं...अस्तभारकरच्छायं...समाशिश्रियन् ॥

Bhandarkar Oriental Research Institute Ms. No. 1191 of 1886-91, folio 360.

This is conventional praise; we know that Kṛshṇa's rule did not extend beyond Banavāsi 12,000 and so his army could not have reached Cape Kamorin. Similarly his soldiers could not have entered the waters of the Ganges as the Gurjara Pratihara rule was firmly established in the Ganges vally.

It was some time in the last decade of the 9th century, that the career of the Gujrat Rāshṭrakūṭa branch came to an end. 888 A.D. is the latest date, so far known, for its last ruler Kṛshṇa, when he was fighting at Ujjayinī under his feudal lord Kṛshṇa II. But soon thereafter the two rulers became enemies and a war ensued. Sangli[28] and Cambay[29] plates of Govinda IV refer to the evacuation of Kheṭaka by the enemies of Kṛshṇa II; this must refer to the expulsion of the Gujrat ruler Kṛshṇa or his successor from Kaira.[30] We come across no inscriptions of the Gujrat branch after 888 A.D.; the Kapadwanj grant of Kṛshṇa II, dated 910 A.D.,[31] reveals the existence of a new feudatory Prachaṇḍa of Brahmāvaloka house. To judge from the names of its members, this seems to have been a Canarese family, ruling under direct imperial supervision over the Kapadwanj Kaira area, which was formerly being governed by the Gujrat Rāshṭrakūṭas. In the time also of the next ruler Indra III we find Gujrat being directly controlled from Malkhed. In his Begumra plates of 914 A.D. Indra regrants a village named Trennā, which had been formerly bestowed upon the donee's ancestors both by Dhruva I and Dhruva II of the Gujrat branch. The donee's descendant was anxious for a regrant of the village, obviously because the grantor's family was no longer in power in southern Gujrat. We may, therefore, conclude that the Gujrat branch came to an end in c. 900 A.D.

Kṛshṇa II was not an able and gifted ruler like his grand-father. His only military achievement was the defeat and destruction of the Gujrat branch, which certainly was not a very great exploit, considering how petty that kingdom

28. I. A., Vol. XII, pp. 247, 29. E. I., VII, p. 29.

30. The view that Kheṭaka in this passage is the same as Malkhed is hardly tenable. Mānyakheṭa is nowhere known to have been referred to as Kheṭaka; whereas the ancient name of Kaira was Kheṭaka. Besides Mānyakheṭa is not known to have been occupied by any enemies at this time. 31. E. I., I, p. 52.

was. He could just maintain his own against Bhoja I and Mahendrapāla, and he was worsted by Chālukya Bhīma of Vengi. Gangavadi, which had seceded from the Rāshṭrakūṭa empire during the weak rule of his father, could not be reconquered by him.[32] He was just able to maintain a *status quo* and that too with the assistance of his father-in-law and brother-in-law. Like his father he was a Jain; Guṇabhadra, the famous Jain author of the last five chapters of *Ādipurāṇa* was his preceptor.[33] There is no sufficient evidence to investigate into the question as to how far the adhesion to Jainism of Amoghavarsha I and his son Kṛshṇa II was responsible for the military and political decline of the Rāshṭrakūṭa empire during their rule. It may, however, be pointed out that a number of fervent followers of Jainism like Baṅkeya, Chālukya Nārasimha, Srīvijaya, and Noḷambāntaka Nārasimha were very able and fiery military leaders. [See also, *supra*, Chapter XIII, section C, in this connection.]

Indra III

Kṛshṇa II was succeeded by his grandson Indra III. His son Jagattuṅga had predeceased him; both the Karhad[34] and Deoli[35] plates of Kṛshṇa III inform us that Jagattuṅga was taken to heaven by the Creator before his accession to the throne, as if at the pressing request of the heavenly damsels. Nausari plates[36] of Indra III describe him as meditating on the feet of Akālavarsha, showing that Indra III was the successor of Kṛshṇa II, and not of his own father Jagattuṅga. The latest known date of Kṛshṇa II is 912 A.D.;[37] but the aged emperor lived for two years more. He died towards the close of 914 A.D.; for we know from the Nausari plates of

32. *Mysore Inscriptions*, No. 113, p. 29.
33. J. B. B. R. A. S., XXII, p. 85.
34. E. I., IV, p. 278.
35. E. I. V, p. 190.
36. J. B. B. R. A. S., XVIII, pp. 253 ff.
37. E. C., VIII, Sorab No. 88.

Indra III that he had gone to Kurundhaka[38] from his capital Mānyakheṭa on the 7th day of the bright half of Phālguna, S'aka 836 (24–2–915 A.D.) for the purpose of Paṭṭabandhotsava or coronation ceromony. Since on this occasion Indra granted afresh four hundred villages resumed by previous rulers, it must obviously have been the time of his formal coronation. His accession, which was a peaceful one, could not therefore have taken place much earlier.

Indra was probably a man of 35 at the time of his accession and he ruled for about five years only. His career, if short, was a brilliant one. Before his formal coronation in February 915, he had sacked Meru and conquered a king named Upendra who had annexed or relieved Govardhana.[39] The historical information conveyed by the second quarter of this verse is still a mystery. Kielhorn thinks that Meru may be Kanauj.[40] Dr. D. R. Bhandarkar suggests that Upendra may have been another name of Mahīpāla, the Gurjara-Pratīhāra emperor;[41] both these suggestions, besides being based upon pure assumption, ignore the significant fact that the feats, referred to in the verse in question, were performed by Indra before his coronation. It is almost inconceivable that Indra would have carried out his expedition against Kanauj during the short interval between his father's death and his own formal coronation. Upendra, conquered by him, seems to be the Paramāra chief Kṛshṇarāja, who, according to the Udaipur Praśasti, was also known as Upendrarāja. Vākpati *alias* Muñja, who was a contemporary of Tailapa, (c. 980 A.D.) was Upendra's great grandson. The

38. R. G. Bhandarkar identifies Kurundhaka with Kandoḍa on the Tapti. B. G., I, ii, p. 203. It is equally possible that the place may be Kurundwad in Kolhapur state.

39. कृतगोवर्धनोद्धारं हेलोन्मूलितमेरुणा ।
उपेन्द्रमिन्द्रराजेन जित्वा येन न विस्मितम् । J. B. B. R. A. S., XVIII, p. 253.

40. E. I., VII, Appendix p. 16 n. 2.

41. *Ibid*, pp. 38 ff.

known dates of Sīyaka, grandson of Upendra, range from 949 to 973 A.D. Upendra's rule, therefore, must have been between c. 900–925 A.D. Paramāras were in the beginning very probably feudatories of the Gurjara-Pratihāras; at their instigation Upendra seems to have attacked Govardhan in Nasik district at the beginning of Indra's reign. Indra defeated him, compelling the Paramāras to transfer their allegiance to his own house. The Harsola grant attests to the fact that the Paramāras were professing allegiance to the Rāshṭrakūṭas subsequent to Indra's conquests.[42]

The defeat of the Paramāra chief Upendrarāja was only a preparatory step to the contemplated invasion of northern India. After the death of Mahendrapāla in 908 A.D., there were troubles of succession at Kanauj; his son Bhoja II could retain the throne only for about two years. His younger brother Mahīpāla wanted to oust him. The Chedi ruler Kokkala had espoused his cause[43] and was for a time successful; but Mahīpāla soon managed to get the throne, probably with the assistance of some feudatories. The dissensions in the Imperial family must have divided the feudatories also into two camps, rendering the task of an outside invader the reverse of difficult. The time of the invasion of Indra III was thus very opportune; he had not to break any formidable confederacy as Govinda III had to do, when he attacked Nāgabhaṭa, nor had he to cross swords with two powerful claimants for the supremacy in Northern India, as Dhruva and Govinda III had to do. The achievements of Indra III were, however, more dramatic than those of his predecessors.

Unfortunately we have no detailed information about this campaign. From the Cambay plates we learn that he first

42. Report of the third Oriental Conference, Madras, pp 303–308.

43. Cf. भोजे वल्लभराजे श्रीहर्षे चित्रकूटभूपाले ।
शंकरगणे च राजनि यस्यासीदभयद: पाणि: ॥ E. I., II, pp 306–7.

attacked Ujjayinī,(44) then crossed the Jamuna and finally captured Kanauj itself. Mahīpāla, the Gurjara-Pratihāra emperor, became a fugitive and was pursued by Chālukya Nārasimha, one of the generals of Indra. The poet Pampa, a protege of Nārasimha, informs us that his patron "plucked from Gurjara king's arms the Goddess of victory, whom, though desirous of keeping, he had held too loosely. Mahīpāla fled as if struck by thunderbolt, staying neither to eat nor to rest, nor to pick himself up, while Nārasimha pursuing bathed his horses at the junction of the Ganges and established his fame."(45) Mahīpāla seems to have been pursued upto Allahabad.(46) The testimony of the southern records as to the defeat and flight of Mahīpāla is confirmed by a fragmentary Chandella inscription from Khajuraho,(47) from which we learn

44. Cf. यन्मायाद्विपदन्तघातविषमं कालप्रियप्राङ्गणम् ।
व
तीर्णा यत्तुरगैरगाधयमुना सिन्धुप्रतिस्पर्धिनी ॥
येनेदं हि महोदयारिनगरं निर्मूलमुन्मीलितम् ।
नाम्नाद्यापि जनैः कुशस्थलमिति ख्यातिं परां नीयते ॥

Agreeing with my predecessors I have assumed in the text that "काल-प्रियप्रांगण" in the above verse refers to Ujjayinī. It may be, however, pointed out that Ujjain is not on the way leading from Malkhed to Kanauj; and it is not improbable that the first line refers to Kalpi, where also there still exists a temple of Kālapriya. Kalpi is situated on the way to Kanauj. If the crossing of the Yamunā referred to in the second line took place immediately after the halt in the courtyard of Kālapriya, then it will follow that Indra did not pass through Ujjain.

45. कर्नाटकभाषाभूषण, introduction, p. XIV.

46. The junction of the Ganges referred to in the text above must be with the Jamuna and not with the sea; for there is no evidence to show that Indra III had come into conflict with Rājyapāla. It is, however, likely that Mahīpāla may have fled, not towards Allahabad, for that would have brought him closer to the Chedis, who were Indra's allies, but towards Gorakhpur. Nārasimha may have pursued him for a while, and then proceeded to Allahabad on his way back to the Deccan.

47. E. I., I, p. 122.

that Mahīpāla was reinstated on the throne, probably by Harsha. The northern campaign of Indra thus produced a more dramatic result than was ever achieved by his predecessors Dhruva and Govinda, neither of whom had succeeded in occupying the Imperial capital Kanauj. More tangible and substantial results would probably have followed if Indra's career had not been cut short by his premature death, which must have necessitated the retirement of his army to the south.

While Indra was himself engaged in the north, his generals in the south were equally active. A record of one of them, Srīvijaya, has been discovered at Danavulapadu in Cudappah district. Although a pious Jain, Srīvijaya was a powerful general and claims to have defeated his master's enemies.(48) Another record from the same locality informs us that this general was also a poet. We must not, however, confound this poet-general Srīvijaya with Srīvijaya quoted in *Kavirājamārga* ; for the latter flourished at least a centurv earlier than the general of Indra.

Indra III was thus a very capable and brilliant general. During his short reign he succeeded in shattering the prestige of the Imperial Pratīhāras, and the Rāshṭrakūṭa army again became a terror in the north.

Before passing to the next king I propose to give a genealogical table showing the intimate family relationship that existed between the Rāshṭrakūṭas and the Chedis. Indra himself, his younger brother Amoghavarsha, and the latter's son Kṛshṇa III, as also the father and grand-father of Indra III had all taken wives from the Chedi family of Tripuri. This matrimonial alliance must have been of considerable help to Indra III and Kṛshṇa III in their northern campaigns.

48. A. S. R., 1905–61 pp. 121–2.

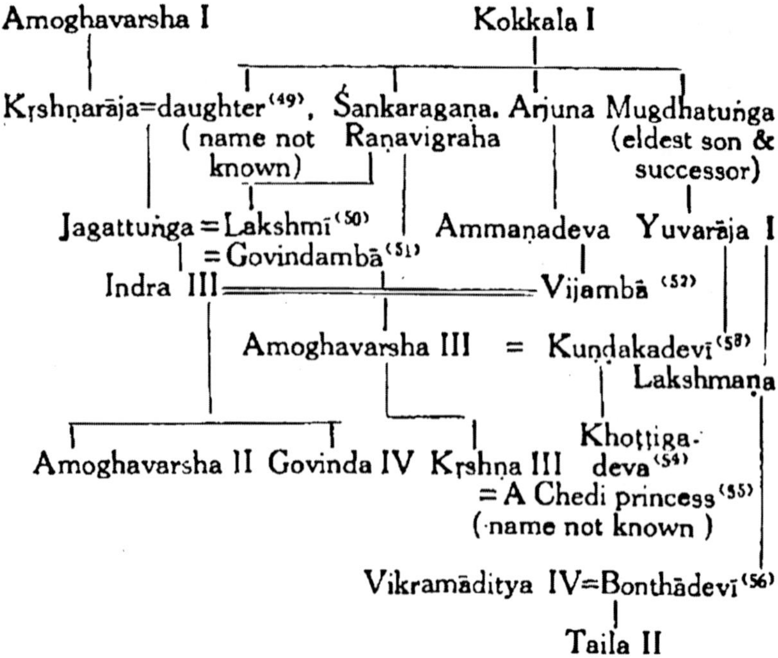

49. कोक्कलस्समभूच्च तस्य तनया या सङ्कुलस्यानुजा ॥ तस्मात् कृष्णनृपात्.........
जगत्तुङ्गाभिधान: सुत: ॥ I. A , XII, p. 265.

50. चेदीश्वरशङ्करगणदुहितरि लक्ष्म्यां ततो जगत्तुङ्गात् । सूनुरभूदिन्द्रनृप:... *Ibid.* Sangli plates say कोक्कलसुतरणविग्रहजलधेर्लक्ष्मी: समुत्पन्ना । (I. A., XII, p. 247), showing that S'ankaragaṇa of the Karda grant is the same as Raṇavigraha. Jagattunga had thus married his maternal uncle's daughter, a custom recognised as legal in the Deccan.

51. *Ibid.* Govindambā was a younger sister of Lakshmī. Jagattunga married her when he was staying with the Chedis, while out on an expedition in the north. R. G. Bhandarkar's objections to the theory that Govindambā was another wife of Jagattunga have been answered by Fleet. See B. G., I., ii, p. 414, n. 5. It may be noted that Vikramāditya II of the Western Chalukya dynasty had married two uterine sisters, Lokamahādevī and Trailokyamahādevī.

52. Sangli plates of Govinda IV, I. A., XII, p. 249.

53. Cf. युवराजदेवदुहितरि कुंडकदेव्याममोघवर्षनृपात् । जात: खोट्टिगदेव: नृपतिरभूत् । Kadba plates I. A. XII, p. 265.

54. Ditto.

55. The name of this princess is not known; the Deoli plates simply

P. T. O.

Amoghavarsha II and Govinda IV

Indra died in c. 917 A.D. and was succeeded by his eldest son Amoghavarsha II. Fleet's view that Amoghavarsha II did not reign[57] cannot be accepted. The Bhadan plates of Aparājita Silāhāra, issued within 80 years of the event in question, distinctly say that Amoghavarsha II ruled for a year; and their testimony is confirmed by the Deoli and Karhad plates of Kṛshṇa III, which also distinctly say that he did rule. The evidence of these plates is particularly cogent because, with reference to a prince like Jagattuṅga, who did not ascend the throne, they expressly mention the fact of his having not ruled.

The omission in the Sangli plates of Govinda IV of the name of Amoghavarsha II, and the statement there, that the former meditated upon the feet of Indra Nityavarsha and not upon those of Amoghavarsha, his immediate predecessor, show that the two brothers were on inimical terms. The phrase '*tatpādanudhyāta*' does not necessarily indicate that the two kings immediately followed each other. Some of the Chālukya grants assert (I. A., VI, pp. 184, 194) that Durlabha meditated on the feet of Chāmuṇḍa though Vallabha was his immediate predecessor. Amoghavarsha II was a youth of only about twenty five[58] at the time of his accession and his

Continued from the last page

say of Kṛshṇa III that the Chedis were the elderly relations of both his wife and mother, showing that he had taken a Chedi princess for his wife. Whether Kuṇḍakadevī was his mother as she was of his brother Khoṭṭigadeva, is not known.

56. I. A., VIII, pp. 11 ff. For facility of reference, the relationship with the later Chalukyas also is shown in this table.

57. B. G., I, ii., p. 416.

58. Amoghavarsha I was born in 808 A.D.; his son Kṛshṇa in c. 830,; his son Jagattuṅga in c. 850; his son Indra in c. 870, and his son Amoghavarsha II in c. 890; Amoghavarsha's age at the time of his accession thus works out to be about 25, supposing that all his ancestors were born when their fathers were only 20.

death within a year could not have been entirely due to his deep love for his father prompting him to go to heaven as soon as possible, as the Karhad plates of Kṛshṇa III would make us believe. The Cambay and the Sangli plates of Govinda IV state that he neither treated his elder brother cruelly,—though he had power to do so,—nor acquired ill-fame by committing incest with his brother's wives. That Govinda should go out of his way in refuting these charges shows that there must have been ugly rumours current about his treatment of his elder brother and his wives; that these rumours had some foundation is made clear by an unpublished grant of the S'ilāhāra ruler Chhadvaideva, now in the Prince of Wales Museum, Bombay. This S'ilāhāra ruler was a contemporary of Kṛshṇa III and his grant says that Govinda IV, who was overthrown by Amoghavarsha, was himself guilty of injustice.(59) It thus becomes clear that Govinda was suspected of having dealt unfairly with his brother. He may have peacefully superseded him, sparing his life, or may have brought about or hastened his death. 836 S'aka or 916–17 A.D. is the latest known date of Indra(60) and S'aka 840 or 918–19 A.D. is the earliest date of Govinda IV.(61) So the short reign of about a year of Amoghavarsha II probably took place in 917–18 A.D.

The reign of Govinda IV, who succeeded Amoghavarsha II, was one of the least glorious ones. He was a youth of about 20, and his Sangli plates inform us that he was as beautiful as God of Love. Most of his time he spent in the pursuits of pleasures; Kharepatan plates of Raṭṭarāja state that he was the abode of the sentiment of love and was surrounded by a

59. तत्रासा श्रीन्द्रराज: प्रथितपृथुयशास्सार्वभौम: प्रजात: ॥
श्रीमानमोघवर्शो भ्रातास्य सुतं समूलमुन्मूल्य ।
गोज्जिगमन्यायकृतं सामोघमयमशात् पृथ्वीम् ॥
Dacunha collection of copper plates in the Prince of Wales Museum, Bombay.

60. Hatti Mattur inscription, I. A., XII, p. 224.

61. *Ibid*, p. 223.

bevy of dancers.[62] Deoli and Karhad plates also describe him as the very essence of love and its pleasures, and state that he took to evil ways, which led to disaffection of ministers and that he eventually perished. He, however, enjoyed life for about 15 years. He probably found no time to look after foreign affairs; a line in his Sangli record says that the Gaṅgā and the Yamunā served his palace,[63] suggesting that Allahabad was still in his possession. This, however, may have been perhaps the case at the beginning of his career, when the Rāshṭrakūṭa armies may have been still in the north. Govinda IV, however, had neither the ability nor the inclination to try to hold the provinces conquered by his father. Some time during Govinda's reign, Mahīpāla reoccupied Kanauj and the Rāshṭrakūṭa forces were either driven back or had to retire.

Bhīma II of the Eastern Chālukya dynasty, who was a contemporary ruler, claims to have defeated a great army sent by king Govinda.[64] This Govinda is almost certainly Govinda IV. The defeat of the Rāshṭrakūṭa army must have taken place towards the end of the reign of Govinda, since. Bhīma II ascended the throne in c. 934 A.D. This reverse may have hastened Govinda's fall.

The Deoli and the Karhad plates of Kṛshṇa simply state that the vicious life and lascivious ways of Govinda IV ruined his constitution, alienated the sympathies of his subjects and feudatories and led to his destruction. The manner of his losing his kingdom is described by Pampa in his *Vikramārjuna-vijaya* where he praises his patron Arikesarin II under the title of Arjuna. In the 9th Āśvāsa of the above work, in a prose passage after v. 52, we read:—

" How can a thought of ill-will occur to you on seeing and hearing the greatness of that ocean of suppliants (sic.

62. E. I., III, p. 298.
63. यदनिन्दितराजमन्दिरं ननु गङ्गा यमुना च सेवते ।
64. E. I., VIII, p. 128.

Arikesarin) who, when Govindarāja was wroth with Vijayāditya, the ornament of Chālukya race, unflinchingly laid him behind and protected him, the valour of this crest-jewel of the feudatories, who drove into retreat and conquered the great feudatories, who came at the command of the universal emperor Gojjiga– the strength of arm of Arikesarin, who bringing to ruin the emperor who confronted him in hostility, fittingly conveyed the universal empire to Baddegadeva, who came trusting him."

Pampa was out to glorify his patron, and so we must accept this version with a grain of salt ; but it is quite clear from this account that the feudatories of Govinda rebelled against him, and eventually offered the crown to his uncle Amoghavarsha II *alias* Baddegadeva. Deoli and Karhad plates also confirm[65] the version of Pampa ; they state that Amoghavarsha was pressed by the feudatories to accept the throne to ensure the preservation of the Rāshṭrakūṭa glory. Amoghavarsha III does not appear to have prompted the rebellion himself ; even when the crown was offered to him he seems to have consulted an oracle before accepting it, if we are to trust the Deoli plates.[66] He was at this time advanced in years and he had, during his nephew's reign, led a life of retirement, mostly devoted to religion. The Karhad and Deoli plates style him as the foremost among the thoughtful, the Bhadan plates of Aparājita refer to his austerities,[67] a verse[68] in an unpublished grant of Chhadvaideva describes how Amoghavarsha purified his wealth, along with his soul, by the sacred waters of coronation. The last mentioned statement makes it clear that Amoghavarsha III actually ascended the throne and ruled.

Though Amoghavarsha III may not have himself prompted the rebellion, it is quite probable that his ambitious son

65. Cf. सामन्तैरथ रट्टराज्यमहिमालम्बार्थमभ्यर्थित: ।

66. Cf. देवेनापि पिनाकिना हरिकुलोल्लासैषिणा प्रेरित: । 67. E. I, III, p. 271.

Kṛshṇa and other partisans may have worked hard to exploit the situation in order to secure the crown for him. Both Amoghavarsha III and Kṛshṇa III had married Chedi princesses as shown already. We may, therefore, well accept the statement of the spurious Sudi plates that Amoghavarsha was staying at Tripuri, when Būtuga II married his daughter.[69] It is, therefore, not unlikely that the Chedi ruler Yuvarāja I, who was Amoghavarsha's father-in-law, may have helped his son-in-law, who was an exile at his court, by joining the confederacy that aimed at placing Amoghavarsha upon the Malkhed throne. In the *Viddhas'sālabhañjikā* of Rājaśekhara, who was late in his life residing at the Chedi court,[70] we seem to get an echo of this confederacy. The drama is a love story of the usual type, but it is fairly certain that its hero Karpūravarsha Yuvarāja is the same as Keyūravarsha Yuvarāja I, who was the father-in-law of Amoghavarsha III. In Act II of this drama we are told that a king of Kuntala, Chaṇḍamahāsena by name, was residing at the Chedi court as an exile from his own kingdom, and towards the conclusion of the IVth Act, we are informed that the Chedi forces, which were espousing the cause of the exile king of Kuntala, were successful against the enemy in a battle fought on the banks of the Payoshṇī, a tributary of the Tapti, and that the exile prince was crowned king of his own country. There is some difficulty in accepting these *obiter dicta* of Rājas'ekhara as referring to Amoghavarsha's accession: Rājas'ekhara does not retain the real names of the actors in these historic events. He names the exile Kuntala chief once as Vīrapāla (Act IV) and once as Chaṇḍamahāsena (Act II). Keyūravarsha's marriage with Vīrapāla's daughter

68. अभिषेकजलेन समं तपश्रियु: (?) मेयते समुच्छ्रित्य ।
येन धनानीव मलावर्नायतात्मा परां शुद्धिम् ॥

Dacunha collection of copper plates in the Prince of Wales Museum, Bombay.

69. E. I., III, P. 166. 70. Konow, *Karpūramañjarī*, pp. 181–2.

would seriously go against the view that Vīrapāla stands for Amoghavarsha III. But it is not unlikely that the last mentioned episode may have been a poetic invention intended to complicate the love affairs in the drama, and not a historic fact. Amoghavarsha III was a devotee of Siva and the title of Chaṇḍamahāsena, given to him by Rājas'ekhara, is thus appropriate. We would not be far wrong in assuming that Keyūravarsha espoused the cause of his son-in-law, and that one of the decisive battles, which ended in the overthrow of Govinda IV, was fought in Khandesh on the banks of the Payoshṇī. We do not know who were the allies and supporters of Govinda IV. An unpublished Silāhāra grant, once in the possession of Prof. H. D. Velankar, Wilson College, Bombay, but now untraceable, after referring to the accession of Amoghavarsha III went on to observe:—

श्रीमत्कर्कराष्ट्रकूटकटके सद्वंशसंहर्पतो ।
रौद्रद्रोहदवप्रतापशमनं निस्त्रिंशधाराजलैः ॥
येनाकारि समुद्भूतेन्द्रधनुषा भूपाश्मभिर्विद्युता ।
भाति श्रीमदमोघवर्षसुघनोऽसङ्कृतिविध्वंसनात् ॥

This verse would suggest that Karkara, a relative or feudatory Rāshṭrakūṭa chief, fought on the side of Govinda, but was overthrown by Amoghavarsha III and his allies.

The latest known date of Govinda IV is 934 A.D.,[71] and the earliest known date of Amoghavarsha III is the 7th of September, 937 A.D.[72] The rising against Govinda IV and the subsequent accession of Amoghavarsha III must have taken place some time during these three years. Honale inscriptions Nos. 21–23, dated 934 A.D., refer to Suvarṇavarsha as the overlord,[71] whereas Shikarpur inscriptions Nos. 194 and 322, coming from the same district, Shimoga, but dated in the next year, do not refer at all to the rule of Govinda. It would thus appear that the combination against Govinda was

71. E. C., VII, Honale, Nos 21–23.
72. E. C., XI, Chitaldurg No. 76.

formed in 935 A.D. and the accession of Amoghavarsha III may be placed in the next year, since from an inscription from Isamudru[73] we learn that he had ascended the throne earlier than the 7th of September 937 A.D. It is very likely that Kṛshṇa, the son of Amoghavarsha, may have taken a leading part in putting his father upon the throne ; he was an ambitious prince and may have induced his aged father to accept the crown.

CHAPTER VI

Last four Rulers

Amoghavarsha III

The reign of Amoghavarsha III, which commenced in c. 935 A.D., was a short one of about four years : for his son Kṛshṇa III was already upon the throne in May 940 A.D., when the Deoli plates were issued by him.[1] Being himself a man of religious temperament, he must have presented a strong contrast with his vicious predecessor. Actual administration was very probably entirely in the hands of the crown prince Kṛshṇa.

Revakanimmaḍi, a daughter of Amoghavarsha III and an elder sister of Kṛshṇa III, was married to a Ganga prince, named Permadi Būtuga II. Since the first child of this union Maruḷadeva was born while Amoghavarsha III was upon the throne, and since the mother of Būtuga II was active enough in 974 A.D. to supervise the administration of the village Pattu Pebbala, the statement of the Hebbal inscription,[2] that Revakanimmaḍi's marriage took place during the reign of Kṛshṇa II, does not seem to be correct. The statement of the same record that at the time of the marriage of his great-grand-daughter, Kṛshṇa II gave away as dowry Banavasi 12,000,

73. E. C., XI, Chitaldurg No. 76.

1. E. I., V, p. 190. 2. *Ibid.* IV, p. 351.

Belvola 300, Purigere 300, Bagenad 70, and Kinsukad 70 to his great-grand-son-in-law seems to be equally unreliable, for the Atkur inscription informs us[3] that these districts were given by Kṛshṇa III to his brother-in-law, as a reward for his bravery in killing the Chola crown prince Rājāditya.

The Sudi plates inform us[4] that Amoghavarsha was staying at Tripuri when this marriage took place. These plates are no doubt spurious, but for reasons discussed already in the last chapter, we can well believe that statement. Būtuga also was then not the ruling Ganga prince, for Ereyappa was at that time ruling at Talkad.

The crown prince Kṛshṇa undertook the task of putting his brother-in-law upon the Ganga throne. He killed Dantiga and Vappuga, who were probably Noḷamba princes[5] and feudatories of Rāchamalla, the Ganga ruler then upon the throne. Then he attacked and killed Rāchamalla himself, and put his brother-in-law upon the Ganga throne. Isamudru[6] inscription, which was inscribed on 7th of September 937 A.D., refers to Amoghavarsha as the ruling emperor and concludes as follows:—

"In Paleyar Deva attacked and smote and slew the Pande king in Srīpura; Indra's son smote a Pallava king... This Kannara of great might slew Ganga Permadi and gave

3. E. I., VI, p. 55. 4. E. I., III, p. 176.

5. Ayyapadeva Nanninga was the Noḷamba chief in c. 919 and he was an ally of Ereyappa, whose successor Rāchamalla was killed by Kṛshṇa. The name of Nanniga's son was Anniga. [E. I., X., pp. 54 ff.] The names of Dantiga and Vappuga bear a family resemblance to Nanniga and Anniga, hence the conjecture in the text.

Fleet notices a record at the Mahākūṭa temple of Badāmi, dated October 934 A.D., which refers to Mahāsamanta Bappuvarasa, who was a very Bhairava on a minor scale to the enemies of the brave Gopāla (B. G., I. ii. p. 417 n. 3). This Bappuva could have been assumed to be the same as Vappuga killed by Kṛshṇa, were it not very improbable that such an enemy could have challenged the authority of Amoghavarsha III in the very heart of the empire. 6. E. C., XI. Chitaldurg 76.

the throne to Bhūvallabha. Thus did those of the Rāshṭrakūṭa line slay and gain renown." The first two incidents, here referred to, have yet to be definitely identified, but the last one is obviously the same as the overthrow and destruction of Rāchamalla by Kṛshṇa and the enthronement of his brother-in-law, Būtuga.

Kṛshṇa then marched northwards and defeated the Chedis, though his mother and wife had been born in that family. The forts of Kālanjara and Chitrakūṭa, situated in the very heart of Chandella country, were occupied by the Rāshṭrakūṭa army,[7] and the Gurjara-Pratihāra emperor lost all hope of capturing them. An inscription,[8] recently published, confirms the testimony of the Deoli plates. This inscription was found at Jura in the Maihar State of the Baghelkhand Agency. It is written upon a stone and contains a eulogy of Kṛshṇa III in Canarese. That a Canarese eulogy of Kṛshṇa should be discovered in Baghelkhand can be explained only on the assumption that the claim to the conquest of Chitrakūṭa and Kālanjara is well founded. The Rāshṭrakūṭas continued to hold these forts for about ten years; they were reconquered by the Chandella king Yaśovarman some time before 953 A.D.

I have assumed here that the exploits of Kṛshṇa described above were performed while he was yet a Yuvarāja, and not subsequent to his accession. In this respect, I differ from previous writers; an analysis of the Deoli plates, however, supports my reading of the situation. These plates were issued in May 940 A.D. After mentioning the accession of Amoghavarsha III, verse 19 of this record says that his son

7. It is not possible to argue that Kṛshṇa assisted his Chedi relations in holding these places against the Chandella; for the Deoli plates, issued in May 940 A.D., soon after the capture of Kalanjara, state that Kṛshṇa III had conquered the elders of his wife and mother. This shows that Kṛshṇa was not co-operating, but fighting with the Chedis.

8. E. I., XIX, p. 287.

Kṛshṇa proved his strength even while a *Kumāra* or a prince. Vv. 20-25 then mention the killing of Dantiga, Vappuga, and Rāchamalla and the capture of Kālanjara and Chitrakūṭa. V. 26 then observes that all the feudatories between the Eastern and Western ocean obeyed the commands of Kṛshṇa, who himself, however, was always obedient to his father. V. 27 then informs us that his father died, happy to have seen his son embraced by the damsel fame. Then follows a description of the coronation of Kṛshṇa III.

The above analysis of the Deoli plates makes it absolutely clear that the restoration of Būtuga to the Gānga throne, and the capture of Chitrakūṭa and Kālanjara were the achievements of Kṛshṇa while yet a crown-prince. It may also be pointed out that Amoghavarsha was alive on the 3rd of December 939 A.D.[9] and that all the above campaigns in southern and central India could not have been physically possible within a period of four months. And yet we shall have to assume that such was the case, if we are to hold that these campaigns were subsequent to his accession; for the Deoli plates, issued by Kṛshṇa in May 940 mention all these achievements of his. The title Paramabhaṭṭāraka Parames'vara-mahārājādhirāja given by the Jura record to Kṛshṇa III would not go against my hypothesis. The *pras'asti* may have been composed and inscribed a few years later, and in the meanwhile Kṛshṇa may have succeeded his father and conquered Tanjore and Kanchi. It is also possible that Kṛshṇa may have undertaken a second expedition in Baghelkhand after his accession, when the Jura inscription may have been inscribed.

A record from Sravan Belgola[10] refers to a battle between Rakkasa-mane and Koneya Ganga when Bogya, a servant of Ganga-Vajra, rallied his retreating forces and made the whole forces of Vaḍḍega and Koneya Ganga flee with

9. E. C., XI, Chitaldurga No. 77, dated उत्तरायण संक्रांति, शके ८६१ पौष.
10. E. C., II, No. 138 (New Edition numbering).

terror. Although it cannot be proved at present that Koneya was another name of Būtuga and Vajra of Râchamalla, the record shows that the forces of Amoghavarsha III, who was also known as Baddega, were operating against the Gangas, showing thereby that it was in his reign, and not in that of his son, that Būtuga was put on the Ganga throne. Kṛshṇa, therefore, was clearly a crown-prince when he performed the above-mentioned exploits.

Amoghavarsha died some time after the 3rd of December 939 A.D. and before May 940 A.D., happy to see that his son had proved himself an able and successful general.

Krishna III

Kṛshṇa III ascended the throne some time in December 739 A.D.[11] He had already established the reputation of his arms while still a crown-prince; still he seems to have waited for a while after his accession before undertaking further campaigns. His accession seems to have been a peaceful one; the spurious Sudi plates of Būtuga II no doubt state that Būtuga secured the kingdom for Kṛshṇa on the death of Baḍḍega *i. e.* Amoghavarsha III.[12] So far, however, there is no evidence forthcoming to show that there was any trouble at the accession of Kṛshṇa III. His prestige was already very great and it does not seem likely that any serious claimant may have challenged his accession. The only possibility that we can conceive of is that if Kṛshṇa were absent at the time of his father's death in northern India on his military expedition, there may have arisen some trouble, which Būtuga may have put down before the return of Kṛshṇa. The invasion of Chola kingdom by Kṛshṇa III did not take place earlier than the 3rd year of his reign, and we know of no military conquests earlier than that date.

11. Sorab No. 476 (E. C., VIII) supplies 939 as the earliest date for Kṛshṇa as emperor. His father was alive in December of that year (E. C., XI, pp. 29–30). Hence the statement in the text. See *supra*, pp. 122–3, foot-note No. 39.

12. E. I., III, p. 176.

Kṛshṇa first turned his attention to the south. In Gangavadi his brother-in-law Būtuga was upon the throne; the Bāṇa prince Vikramāditya III was an ally of his, since he calls himself a dear friend of Kṛshṇarāja.[13] The Chola king Parāntaka was an ambitious ruler; he had conquered Bāṇavādi and put the Ganga-Bāṇa prince, Pṛthvīpati II Hastimalla in its charge. Kṛshṇa decided to attack the Chola kingdom, apparently to reinstate Vikramāditya III, but really to annex as much of the south as possible to his empire.

The Kanyakumari inscription of Parāntaka states that the Chola king had himself fought with Kṛshṇarāja and defeated him, earning thereby the title of Vīrachola.[14] The time and place of the defeat are not stated; but the record, if not an empty boast, must be referring to some engagements that may have been fought before 944 A.D., wherein he may have scored some local successes. But these were minor ones and did not affect the main issue; for, we have overwhelming evidence to show that Kṛshṇa III was occupying Tondai-Maṇḍalam from c. 944 to the end of his reign. Siddhalingamādam inscription from South Arcot district, dated in the fifth year of Kṛshṇa's reign, refers to the conquest of Kanchi and Tanjai or Tanjore;[15] the Solapuram inscription from North Arcot district is dated in Śaka year 871 or 949-50 A.D., the year in which the emperor Kannaradevavallabha, having pierced Rājāditya, entered Tondai-Maṇḍalam;[16] an inscription from the Ukkala Vishṇu temple in the North Arcot district is dated in the 16th year of his reign and mentions him again as the conqueror of Kanchi and Tanjore.[17] The same is the case

13. Udayendiram grant of Vikramāditya III, E. I. XI, p. 232. Hultzsch has himself abandoned his earlier view that this Kṛshṇa was Kṛshṇa II and quite rightly; for, the great grand-father of Vikramāditya was alive in 909 A. D. E. I., VIII, p. 3.

14. Travancore Archaeological Series, III, p. 143, v. 48.

15. Madras Epigraphical Collection for 1909, No. 375.

16. E. I., VII, p. 195.

17. Referred to at E. I., IV, p. 82.

with two inscriptions from Tiru in Chingleput district, dated in the 17th and 19th year of Kannaradeva.[18] The Karhad plates[19] were issued in 959 A.D., when Kṛshṇa was encamped at Melpati in North Arcot district, engaged in parcelling out the territory there among his servants, and accepting heavy tributes from the lords of Maṇḍalas. An inscription from Vellore[20] district is dated in the 26th year of his reign. The very fact that so many inscriptions hailing from the territory usually governed by the Cholas and Pallavas are dated in Kṛshṇa's reign shows, especially when considered in the light of the Karhad plates, that the whole of Tondai-Maṇḍalam was directly administered by Krshna III throughout the major part of his reign.

According to the Siddhalingamadam inscription, we have seen that Kṛshṇa had already conquered Kanchi and Tanjore before the fifth year of his reign. His accession took place either in 939 A.D., or perhaps in 940 A.D., and, therefore, his occupation of Tondai-Maṇḍalam may be placed in c. 945 A.D. T. A. Gopinath Rao's view[21] that Tondai-Maṇḍalam could not have been occupied before the battle of Takkolam ignores the possibility of that battle itself being the result of a counter-move on the part of Parāntaka to oust the invador. The entry referred to in the Sholapuram inscription would be recording the further advance of the Rāshṭrakūṭa army after the victory at Takkolam.

The decisive battle in the war was fought at Takkolam in North Arcot district in 949 A.D. The Chola army was led into the battle by the crown-prince[22] Rājāditya, while the

18. E. I., III, p. 285. 19. E. I., IV, p. 278.

20. E. I., III, p. 81. 21. E. I., XV, p. 51.

22. The earlier view that Rājāditya had already ascended the throne before the battle of Takkolam had to be abandoned in view of the discovery of inscriptions dated in the 45th and 46th years of Parāntaka. See E. I., XIX, p. 83, for further information. The earlier view is defended by T. A. Gopinath Rao in E. I., XV, p. 51, but his arguments are not convincing.

Rāshṭrakūṭa forces were strengthened by a contingent under the Ganga ruler Būtuga II. The Cholas fought stubbornly, and the Atkur record[23] admits that for a time the Rāshṭrakūṭa forces were overwhelmed; none dared to counter-attack. But Maṇalera and Būtuga succeeded in making a rally; the latter dashed against the crown-prince, killed the elephant he was riding, got into the howdah and killed him there. The earlier view that Būtuga killed Rājāditya treacherously, while embracing him or taking a walk with him, was based partly upon a wrong meaning ascribed to the term '*bisugeye*' and partly upon the mistake of reading '*Kaḷḷa-age* for *Kaḷān-age*.[24] The death of Rājāditya in the battle of Takkolam is confirmed by the Chola records themselves; the large Leyden grant[25] states that Rājāditya died during the battle with Kṛshṇa, while seated on the back of an elephant. It will be noticed that this record also supports the view that treachery played no part in the death of the crown-prince.

The Sudi plates[26] of Būtuga II are no doubt spurious but their statement that after the defeat of Rājāditya's forces Būtuga besieged Tanjapuri or Tanjore under orders from Kṛshṇa, may well have been a historic fact. The epithet 'Tanjaiyunkoṇḍa' or the conqueror of Tanjore has been given to Kṛshṇa III, as we have seen already, in so many records found in Tondai-Maṇḍalam, that the conclusion becomes inevitable that he had conquered and occupied the Chola capital at least for some time. The statements in the Karhad plates that Kṛshṇa defeated the Pandyas and the Keralas, exacted tributes from the king of Ceylon and planted the creeper of his fame at Rāmeśvara may all of them be true ; they receive an unexpected corroboration from Somadeva, who finished his *Yaśastilaka* about two months later than the issue of the

23. E. I., VI, p. 56.

24. J. R. A. S., 1909, pp. 443 ff. Fleet, who was responsible for the earlier mistake, has admitted the accuracy of the new reading.

25. A. S. S. I., IV, p. 201.

26. E. I., III, p. 183.

Karhad plates of Kṛshṇa III, *i. e.* in May 959 A.D. At the end of this work the author speaks of Kṛshṇarāja as a glorious monarch, who had subdued the Pandyas, the Cholas, the Cheras, and Sinhala.[27] After the overthrow of the Chola army and the capture of Tanjore, march to Rāmeśvara could hardly have presented any insurmountable difficulties. Kṛshṇa was not content with merely defeating the Cholas; the fact that so many inscriptions from Toṅdai-Maṇḍalam are dated in the reign of Kṛshṇa III makes it clear that the northern portions of the Chola kingdom were annexed by him to his empire. The statement in the Karhad plates that Kṛshṇa was encamped, at the time when the plates were issued, at Melpati in North Arcot in order to parcel out livings *i. e.* territories among his dependents and receive tributes from feudatories, also shows that part of the Chola kingdom was annexed and placed under the charge of Rāshṭrakūṭa officers. The territory to the south of Tondai-Maṇḍalam could not be annexed, as we do not come across any records from that area recognising the sovereignty of Kṛshṇa III. The Ganga ruler Būtuga II, who had acquired the throne with the help of Kṛshṇa, was his right-hand man in this campaign; in recognition of his valuable services Kṛshṇa conferred upon him Banavasi 12000, Belvol 300, Kinsukad 70, Bagenad 70 and Purigere 300.[28] The latest known date of Būtuga is April 953 A.D.[29] He died a few years later while his brother-in-law was still upon the Rāshṭrakūṭa throne, and was succeeded by his son Noḷambāntaka Mārasiṁha, born not of Revakanimmaḍi, the sister of Kṛshṇa III, but of another wife named Kollavarasi. The new ruler continued to be as intensely loyal to the Rāshṭrakūṭa connection as his father, and helped Kṛshṇa in his military campaigns.

Kṛshṇa's commitments in the south affected, in the latter part of his reign, his position in the north. He had committed

27. P. 419 (Nirṇayasāgara edition).

28. Atkur Inscription, E. I., VI, p. 57. 29. *Ibid*, p. 180.

the blunder of alienating the sympathies of his Chedi relatives by attacking them in his campaign in the north while a Yuvaraja; and the Chandellas rose to power under Yaśovarman and Dhanga. The Khajuraho inscription[30] shows that the fort of Kalanjar was recaptured by the Chandellas before 953-4 A.D., and Chitrakūṭa could not have remained much longer under the Rāshṭrakūṭa control. The Marathi C. P., however, continued to be under the rule of Kṛshṇa; Deoli plates grant a village in the district of Chhindwara, and in the same district two fragmentary inscriptions of his have been discovered.[31]

We have already seen how the Paramāra chief Kṛshṇarāja or Upendra was defeated by Indra III, sometime in c. 915 A.D. The Paramāras continued to be the feudatories of the Rāshṭrakūṭas down to the time of Kṛshṇa III, for the recently published copper-plates from Harsola,[32] issued by Sīyaka in 949 A.D., referred to Akālavarsha Pṛthivīvallabha, the son of Amoghavarshadeva, as the feudal lord of the Paramāras. We find that the Harsola plates refer to villages in Khetaka division *i. e.* modern Kaira district in northern Gujrat, as being under the immediate government of the Paramāras. Southern Gujrat was reconquered by Kṛshṇa II; it would seem that it was handed over to the Paramāra feudatories by the successors of Indra III for administrative purposes.

In the latter half of his reign Kṛshṇa had to undertake expeditions to the north. S'ravana Belgola epitaph of Mārasiṁha[33] states that he conquered the northern regions for Kṛshṇa III and thereby acquired the title of the King of the Gurjaras. It is thus clear that Kṛshṇa had to attack some ruler, who had risen to eminence and was defying his authority in Gujrat. Konow thinks that the Gurjara king, who was defeated by Kṛshṇa and Mārasiṁha may have been

30. E. I., I, p. 124.
31. Hiralal, *List of Inscriptions in C. P. and Berar*, p. 81.
32. E. I., XIX, pp. 236 ff. 33. E. I., V, p. 179.

Mūlaraja.[34] It is, however, more likely that Sīyaka, the Paramāra feudatory of the Rāshṭrakūṭas, governing Mālva and northern Gujrat, may have been the ruler defeated by Mārasiṁha and Kṛshṇa III. Holkeri inscriptions Nos. 23 and 33, dated 968 and 965 A.D. respectively, refer to two of Mārasiṁha's captains, Sūdrakayya and Goggiyamma, as Ujjenībhujangas.[35] These captains were appointed to rule over Kadambalige 1000, probably as a reward for their services in the expedition against the Ujjain ruler. Since Sīyaka's dominions included northern Gujrat in 949 A.D., we can well understand how Mārasiṁha II became known as Gurjarādhirāja by his victory over that ruler. We have seen how Sīyaka was a Rāshṭrakūṭa feudatory in 949 A.D.; his sack of Malkhed in 972–3 may have been a revenge for the defeat that was inflicted upon him by Kṛshṇa III.

We have seen already how the Jura inscription refers to Kṛshṇa's conquest of Kanchi and Tanjore.[36] The inscription is unfortunately not dated, and therefore the question, whether Kṛshṇa had led another expedition in the north after his accession, cannot be definitely settled. It is possible that after the defeat of the Paramāras, the army of Kṛshṇa may have once more overrun Bundelkhand. But this is not very likely, since the Chandellas had grown powerful by this time, and reconquered Kalanjar before 953 A.D. Kṛshṇa also was very busy in the south. Under these circumstances it seems most likely that there was no second expedition against the Chedis and the Chandellas, but that the Jura *Pras'asti* was inscribed subsequent to the conquest of Kanchi and Tanjore in c. 946 A.D.

The recently published Arumbaka plates of Bādapa[37] inform us that the Eastern Chalukya king, Amma II, was

34. E. I., X, p. 78. 35. E. C., XI. 36. E. I., XIX, p. 287.

37. Cf. आश्रित्य कर्णराजाख्यवल्लभं बाडपाधिप: ।
विनिर्गमय्य तं देशादम्मराजाख्यमूर्जितम् । E. I. XIX, p. 137.

driven out by Bāḍappa, son of Yudhāmalla II, with the help of Karṇa. Since the epithet Vallabha is added to the name of Karṇa, it is almost certain that Karṇa is the same as Kṛshṇa III, the form Karṇa being a wrong Sanskritisation of Kannara, the Prakrit name of Kṛshṇa. It would thus appear that Kṛshṇa completed his mastery over the whole of the peninsula to the south of the Narmadā by putting his own ally on the throne of Vengi. This he must have accomplished at the fag end of his reign.[38]

An inscription from Kollagallu, dated Sunday the 6th day of the bright half of *Kshaya* Phālguna of Śaka 889 A.D. *i. e.* 17th February 968 A.D., states that Kṛshṇa had died in that year and that Khoṭṭiga had succeeded him. His death, therefore, may be placed early in 968 A.D.[39]

38. The usually accepted period for the reign of Amma II is from c. 945–c. 970 A.D. and, Kṛshṇa seems to have died before February 968 A.D. But the eastern Chālukya dates are not very rigidly fixed, and a difference of a couple of years is, therefore, not an insurmountable difficulty in identifying Karṇavallabha with Kṛshṇa III.

39. Madras Epigraphical Collection for 1913 No. 236. There is some difficulty in determining the exact beginning and end of the reign of Kṛshṇa III. The latest known date of his father is 3-12-939 A.D. (E. C., XI, pp. 29–30). The earliest known date for Kṛshṇa himself is the one supplied by Sorab No. 476 (E. C., VIII), which is also 939 A.D. It is a pity that the month and the day of the year should not have been given in this record. Kṛshṇa's accession may be, therefore, placed in December 939 A.D. or Mārgasīrsha S'aka 861. Now quite a large number of his inscriptions have been found dated in the 28th year of his reign, (*e. g*, Nos. 125 of 1906, 364 of 1902 of the Madras Epigraphical Collection) and one hailing from Kilur Virattanes'vara temple in south Arcot district is dated in the 30th year of his reign [No. 232 of the Madras Epigraphical Collection for 1902]. Now supposing Kṛshṇa ascended the throne in December 939 A.D. or Mārgas'īrsha S'aka 861, the 30th year of his reign will begin in December, 968 A.D. of Mārgas'īrsha, S'aka 890. But from Kolagallu stone inscription in Bellary Taluka, we know that Kṛshṇa had died before the 6th day of Kshaya

P. T. O.

Kṛshṇa was the last able monarch in the Rāshṭrakūṭa dynasty. None of his predecessors had so completely dominated the Peninsula as he could do. Even Govinda III could not bring under his direct administration territories of the Pallava kings. Nor could he put upon the Vengi throne a friend or nominee of his. In the north, Kṛshṇa's policy wa first successful, but later on he had to relinquish his advance positions in the Chandella country. He could not counteract the influence of Yaśovarman and Dhaṅga, and committed a great mistake in allowing his Paramāra feudatories to rise to great power on the northern frontiers of his kingdom. But it must be admitted that what he lost in the north was more than compensated by his solid gains in the south. He must have been an able ruler and skilful general; otherwise his achievements would not have been possible.

Continued from the last page

Phālguna of S'aka 889 *i. e.* before the 17th February 968 A.D. (No 236. of 1913): It is possible to argue that the death of Kṛshna took place between the 5th and 15th day of Chaitra of S'aka 890; for, Holkere No. 23 (E. C. XI), dated Chaitra S'ūddha *Panchamī*, refers to Kṛshṇa as sovereign ruler, while Sorab No. 53f (E. C., VIII), dated Chaitra S'ūddha *Paurnimā*, refers to his successor Khoṭṭiga as the ruling emperor. But the mention of Kṛshṇa as the ruling emperor in Holkere No. 23 was very probably due to the fact that the news of his death had not travelled till then to Simoga district. Kṛshṇa's death, therefore, took place before February 968 A.D. or Phālguna 889 S'aka. Now since Kṛshṇa ascended the throne not earlier than December 939 A.D., his 30th year, referred to in Kolagallu inscription mentioned above, could not have commenced before December 968 A.D. But Kṛshṇa had died at least ten months before that date and therefore the 30th year of his reign was impossible. This discrepancy can be explained on the supposition that Amoghavarsha III, being mostly preoccupied with religious practices, his son was the *de facto* ruler even in his father's life-time. His regnal years may have been counted in some localities from a date earlier than his formal coronation or his father's death. This overlapping of dates is similar to that of the reigns of Amoghavarsha I and his son Kṛshṇa II. The causes in both cases were probably the same.

Khottiga Nityavarsha Amoghavarsha IV[40]

Kṛshṇa III had a son, who was the father of Indra IV. But he seems to have predeceased his father, and his son being too young, Khoṭṭiga, a younger brother of Kṛshṇa III, succeeded to the throne early in 968 A.D. The Deoli grant of Kṛshṇa III was made in 940 A.D. for the spiritual benefit of Jagattuṅgadeva, a younger brother of Kṛshṇa, who was dearer to him than his own life. It is possible that this Jagattuṅga may be the same as Khoṭṭiga; for the Deoli plates state that Jagattuṅga was extremely beautiful and we know from the Adargunchi inscription[41] that "Raṭṭakandarpa" was one of the epithets of Khoṭṭiga. If Jagattuṅga was not the same as Khoṭṭiga, he may have been another brother of Kṛshṇa III.

It was in the reign of Khoṭṭiga that the Rāshṭrakūṭa power began to decline. The first blow was given by the Paramāras from the north. Arthuna inscription of Paramāra Chāmuṇḍarāya, dated 1079 A.D.,[42] refers to king Śrī Harsha's wars with the lord of the Karṇātas. That the opponent of Harsha was not Tailapa or Karka III is proved by the Udaipur *pras'asti* of the kings of Malva[43], which distinctly says that Harshadeva captured the royal glory and splendour of Khoṭṭigadeva. The first land grant of Vākpati II, the successor of Sīyaka or Srī-Harsha is dated in 974-75 A.D., and that of Karka III, the successor of Khoṭṭiga, in September 972 A.D. Harsha and Khoṭṭiga were thus contemporary rulers, and the statement of the Udaipur *pras'asti*, therefore, may be accepted as correct. It is further corroborated by Dhanapāla, the author of *Pāiyalachchhī*, who informs us in v. 276 that his work was written at Dhārā in *Vikrama Saṁvat* 1029 *i. e.* 972-73 A.D., when Mānyakheṭa was plundered by the king of

40. Kyasnur records show that Khottiga had very likely the epithet of Amoghadeva, See E. I., XVI, p. 284. 41. I. A., XII., p. 256.

42. E. I., XIV, p. 299.

43. Cf. श्रीहर्षदेव इति खोट्टिगदेवलक्ष्मीं जग्राह यो युधि... । E. I., I, p. 235.

Malva.[44] Śravaṇa-Belgola epitaph of Mārasiṁha II states that the scenes of his victories were the banks of the Tapti, the Vindhya forests, Mānyakheṭa, etc. The victory at Mānyakheṭa presupposes the presence of an enemy in that place. This record, therefore, indirectly confirms the statements in the Paramāra records that the Rāshṭrakūṭa capital was plundered by Sīyaka.

We have seen that Khoṭṭiga was alive early in 972 A.D., when Mānyakheṭa was sacked ; he seems to have died during the war with the Paramāras, for we find his successor issuing the Kharda plates[45] in September of the same year. Sorab inscription No. 455 is dated in 972, and refers to Karka as the ruling emperor. We may, therefore, place the death of Khoṭṭiga and the accession of Karka II, in the middle of 972A.D.

Karka II

Karka II was the son of Nirupama, a younger brother of Kṛshṇa III and Khoṭṭiga. It cannot be said definitely whether this Nirupama is the same as or different from Jagattuṅga, who is mentioned as a younger brother of Kṛshṇa III in the Deoli plates. It would appear that either Khoṭṭiga, like Kṛshṇa III, left no male issue, or that Karka managed to usurp the throne after his uncle's death.

The Kharda grant of Karka II describes his glory and exploits in glowing terms; we are told that he was a terror to the Pandyas, had fought with the Hūṇas with an untrembling mind, and had defeated the armies of the Cholas and the Gurjaras. But all these exploits seem to be more imaginary than real; for he was hardly 18 months upon the throne, when he was defeated and ousted from it by Taila II. The Gadag inscription[46] of Vikramāditya VI states that the Śaka year in which the Rāshṭrakūṭas were overthrown was Srīmukha; so it must be Saka 895. The overthrow of Karka then took place sometime between March 973 and March 974. A.D. But since the

44. E. K., XIII, pt 180; 45. E. I., XII, p. 263; 46. I. A., XXI, p. 167.

latest known date[47] of Karka is July 973, we may reasonably conclude that he was defeated in the autumn or winter of 973 A.D.

The fall of the mighty Rāshṭrakūṭa empire was indeed dramatic. In December 967 Kṛshṇa III was the master of practically all the territories to the south of the Narmadā; in December 973 his nephew was overthrown and the Rāshṭrakūṭa empire remained only in memory. The causes of this dramatic downfall are not far to seek. The forward and aggressive policy of Kṛshṇa III must have caused a severe drain on the treasury, and alienated the sympathies of his feudatories and neighbours. His commitments in the south left him no time to control the north. To permit the Paramāras to rise to power was a great tactical blunder. A still greater one was the war with the Chedies, who were so closely connected with the Rāshṭrakūṭas and seem to have helped the accession of Amoghavarsha III. The sympathies of the Chedies were alienated; Taila II was a nephew *i. e.* sister's son of Yuvarāja II, the reigning Chedi monarch,[47] and therefore the Chedi court probably must have actively helped Taila against the Rāshṭrakūṭas. The cession of the Banavāsi 12,000, Belvola 300, Purigeri 300, Kinsukad 70 and Bagenad 70 to the Gangas must have seriously impoverished the Imperial treasury, as the Ganga ruler thus obtained control over most of the territories to the south of the Krishṇā.[48] The territories under the direct Imperial administration further diminished in extent by the rise to semi-independence of the Silāhāras of Konkana, the Raṭṭas of Saundatti and the Yādavas of Seuṇadeśa.[49] These were young, growing and ambitious states, only awaiting an opportunity to throw off the imperial yoke.

47. Gundur inscription, I. A., XII, p. 272 (Āshāḍha month).

48. Hebbal inscription, E. I., IV, p. 355.

49 Bhillama II, grand-father of Bhillama III, who had issued the Kalas-Budruk plates in 1025 A.D., was probably a contemporary of Karka. He had married a daughter of Rāshṭrakūṭa Jhanjha (E. I., XII, p. 212) who probably belonged to the Rāshṭrakūṭa faction opposing Karka. Bhillama II, therefore, may have joined the confederacy to oust Karka.

Karka's councillors were vicious,[50] and his own character was probably not much different. This must have alienated the sympathies of his subjects and feudatories. Some of the Rāshṭrakūṭa kinsmen must have espoused the cause of his enemy Taila, because the latter's wife Jākavvā was the daughter of Bhammaha or Brahmahara, who was a Rāshṭrakūṭa chief. The prestige of the Rāshṭrakūṭa arms was besides completely shattered by the occupation and plunder of the capital by the Paramāras a couple of years before.

Taila II, who eventually overthrew the Rāshṭrakūṭa empire, is claimed by later records to have descended from an uncle of Kīrtivarman II of the early Chalukya dynasty. The genealogy as given in the Kauthem, Yewur, Nilgund and Miraj grants is as follows:—

Vijayāditya

Vikramāditya II — A brother (described *Bhīmapapākrama*. Name not given.)

Kīrtivārman II (son of Vikramāditya II)

Kīrtivarman III (son of the brother)

Taila I

Vikramāditya III

Bhīma

Ayaṇṇa = Krishṇanandanā

Vikramāditya IV = Bonthādevī (daughter of Lakshmaṇa, the Chedi king)

Taila II = Lakshmī, daughter of Rāshṭrakūṭa Brahmahabha.

50. The Nilgund inscription thus describes the two principal advisors and generals of Karka. E. I., XII, p. 150.

The above genealogy seems to be suspicious. It claims for the later Chālukyas a descent from the early Chālukyas of Badāmī, but, as pointed out by R. G. Bhandarkar, no record of theirs claims for them Mānavya Gotra and descent from Hāriti, as is invariably the case with all the records of the earlier Chālukyas. Kīrtivarman III of the above genealogy was a contemporary and cousin of Kīrtivarman II, who was overthrown by Dantidurga. His time, therefore, must be c. 750–c. 770. The next five generations of the genealogy will thus cover a period of about 200 years, giving an average of 40 years per generation, which is obviously extremely improbable. The genealogy may be correct upto Taila; Kīrtivarman III and his unnamed father seem to be imaginary personages. The genealogy makes Kīrtivarman III a cousin of Kīrtivarman II, but it is well-known that contemporary cousins in Hindu families do not usually bear the same names. Further, if the connection of the house of Taila II with the earlier Chālukyas were really genuine, it is strange that the secretariate of Taila II should know the names of all the ancestors, but that its information should fail just in the case of the founder of the house, who, it is alleged, was a brother of the Chālukya king Vikramāditya II. It is, therefore, clear that the genealogy beyond Taila I is not above suspicion. The question, therefore, whether Taila II was really connected with the Chālukyas of Badāmī must be left an open one.

There is nothing to enlighten us as to where the ancestors of Taila were living or 'ruling'. We have seen already that Yas'ovarman, a Chālukya feudatory, son of Balavarman, was holding some petty Jahagir in Dharwar district in the time of Govinda III[51]; but in the ancestry of Taila II neither of these names appear. Chālukya *mahāsāmantas* Mārasimha and Goggi are referred to in a few records from Mysore State; but they also do not figure among the known ancestors of Taila II.

51. Kadba plates, E. I., IV. p. 340.

Chālukya Arikesarin II, who had taken part in the dethronement of Govinda IV, also cannot be connected with Taila II; Pampa in his *Vikramārjunavijaya* gives the genealogy of his patron for as many as eight generations,[52] but we nowhere find any of the ancestors of Taila II in it, as a glance at the genealogy given below will show:—

Yudhāmalla Chālukya (who ruled over Sapādalaksha)
|
Arikesarin I (who with the ministers of Bengerivishaya penetrated into the kingdom of Nirupama. See *ante.* p. 51 n. 10)
|
Nārasimhabhadradeva
|
Dugdhamalla
|
Baḍḍega (who had captured Bhīma)
|
Yudhāmalla II
|
Nārasimha (who defeated Mahīpāla during the campaigns of Indra III; see *ante.* pp. 102.)
|
Arikesarin II (Patron of Pampa : helped the accession of Amoghavarsha III; see *ante.* p. 102.)

Finally we have to consider the case of the Chālukya chief Vijayāditya, who was shielded by Arikesarin II, against Govinda II.[53] The name of this person also does not figure in the known genealogy of the house of Taila II. It seems that the ancestors of Taila were too insignificant; for even the title 'Rājan', which in our times did not convey invariably even the status of a feudatory, is not given to them by their powerful and illustrious descendants. It is therefore extremely unlikely that the daughter of Kṛshṇa, whom Ayyaṇdeva had married, could have been a daughter of Kṛshṇa II of the Rāshṭrakūṭa

52. J. R. A. S., 1882, p. 19. 53. See *ante.* pp. 107-8

dynasty,[54] especially since neither Ayyaṇdeva nor Kṛshṇa is given even the courtesy title 'Rājan.' The place where they were living is also unknown; it might perhaps be suggested that since Taila was a son-in-law of the Chedi ruler Lakshmaṇa, and since the northern parts of the Rāshṭrakūṭa dominions first passed under his control, he may have been living somewhere in the northern portion of the state of Hyderabad.

How Taila II suddenly became strong enough to challenge the mighty Rāshṭrakūṭas, and who his allies were, is still a mystery. We have already seen how it is very likely that the Yādava ruler Bhillama II of Seuṇadeśa may perhaps have been one of his allies.[55] Pampa states[56] that his patron Arikesarin II had put to flight Bappuva, a younger brother of Karka. But Arikesarin II was dead before 959 A.D. when his son Vadyagarāja (Baḍḍega II?) was ruling, and therefore Bappuva, the younger brother of Karka whom he put to flight, may have been a brother of Rāshṭrakūṭa Karkara who was a partisan of Govinda IV. Baḍḍega II may have possibly sided with Taila II. Since Taila's father had married a daughter of the Chedi ruler Lakshmaṇa, whose son was ruling that kingdom at the time of his accession, it is possible that he may have derived some assistance from his maternal uncle, especially since Kṛshṇa II had committed the blunder of alienating the sympathies of that house by wantonly attacking its territories in his northern campaign. It has to be observed, however, that no Chedi records mention any such help given to Taila.

54. This was Fleet's suggestion made with some hesitation at p. 427 of his *Dynasties*. At p. 379 of the same work he had proposed to identify this prince with Ayyapadeva, a general of Vīramahendra, who was killed in a war with Ereyappa. This is also a conjecture which would require further evidence before it can be accepted.

55. See *ante*, p. 126, n. 49. 56. *Yaśastilakachampū*, p. 419.

The struggle between Taila II and Karkka II was an intense one; for, the Managoli inscription[57] admits that it was with an exceedingly great effort that Taila acquired the sovereignty of the land. Karkka was supported by two of his Rāshṭrakūṭa kinsmen, who were his generals, and who are described in the records of the conquering dynasty[58] as cruel, insolent and overbearing, and are compared to the moving feet of Kali incarnate. These two generals were killed in battle: but the fate of Karkka himself is not known with certainty. If he also were killed in the war, there is no reason why the Chālukya records should have kept silent over that incident. It would seem that he managed to fly to the south; two inscriptions from Sorab Taluka, Nos. 476 and 479, dated about 991 A.D., mention Mahārājādhirāja Parameśvara Paramabhaṭṭāraka Srī-Kakkaladeva as the lord of the world. It is not unlikely that this Kakkala may have been the same as Karkka II, who may have managed to hold some local sway in the south of his empire for a few years, and may have been presumptuous enough to use his former imperial titles, even when he was the ruler of a petty state.

The main task of Taila II was accomplished after the defeat of Karkka II; he had, however, to fight with a number of other Rāshṭrakūṭa claimants for the vacant throne for some time. The powerful Ganga feudatory, Noḷambāntaka Mārasimha, espoused the cause of Indra IV, a grandson of Kṛshṇa III and the son of his own sister. He crowned him king[59] but his protégé, who was perhaps too young and inexperienced, could not maintain his own. His epitaph at Sravana Belgola[60] no doubt describes him as 'hero among brave men', 'the bravest of the brave', 'a marvel among those who take by force (the glory of the enemies)'; but these are all conventional adjectives.

57. E. I., V, p. 20. 58. Kauthem plates, E. I., XII, p. 152.

59. Rice, *Inscriptions from Sravana Belgola* No. 59, (second edition).

60. *Ibid* No. 57.

A *virgal* from Dasarhalli in Bangalore district[61] refers to Indra as the ruler of the place. If we assume with Rice that the probable date of this record, which is not dated, is about 980 A.D., then it will follow that Indra continued to hold some authority for a couple of years. But the effort to reinstate Indra IV soon failed; his maternal uncle Mārasiṁha died by the *Sallekhanā* vow before August 975 A.D.; and we find Indra IV doing the same on the 20th March 982 A.D.

When it became clear that Indra IV could not maintain his own against Taila II, Pāñchāladeva, the successor of Mārasiṁha, set himself up as emperor in opposition to Taila. His Mulgund inscription,[62] dated February 975 A.D., claims that he was governing, without any disorder, his kingdom which was bounded by the eastern, western, and southern ocean and by the great river (*i. e.* the Krishna) on the north. This is an obviously exaggerated statement, but it shows that he was sufficiently powerful. The epithet Chālukya-Pañchānana given to him in this record further shows that he was fighting against Taila II. The expedition against him was led by Nāgadeva, a general of Taila. The battle between the two was a sanguinary one, and the Chālukya forces had actually begun to flee away from the battle when the situation was saved by Bhūteyadeva, who made a counter-attack wherein he decapitated Pāñchāladeva. For this exploit Taila II conferred upon him the title of Āhavamalla and made him a Mahāmaṇḍales'vara.[63] The overthrow of Pāñchāladeva must be placed before 977 A.D.; for in that year his successor Rāchamalla II was already upon the Ganga throne.[64]

Taila II was thus able to retain the throne against all the claimants that arose to fight for it after the overthrow of Karka II. It must have required some time for him to compel all the Rāshṭrakūṭa feudatories to recognize his overlord-

61. E. C., XI, Bangalore No. 37.
62. E. I., VI, p. 260.
63. Torgala inscription, I. A., XII, p. 98.
64. Peggu-ur inscription, I. A., VI, p. 102.

ship. Sāntivarman, the Raṭṭa chieftain of Saundatti, is seen ignoring his sovereignty in 980 A.D.; his successors, however, are all of them seen professing allegiance to the new imperial house. The Silāhāras were deeply attached to the Rāshṭrakūṭa house as would appear from the mention in their records of their Rāshṭrakūṭa overlords even when they had been overthrown long ago. They also were compelled by Taila to transfer their allegiance to his family. The Yādava king Vaḍḍiga became a zealous supporter of Taila and participated in his wars against the Paramāra king Muñja. It is needless for the historian of the Rāshṭrakūṭas to follow further the career of Taila II.

PART II

A COMPARATIVE STUDY IN THE RASHTRAKUTA ADMINISTRATION

CHAPTER VII

Political Divisions

In order to understand properly the administrative machinery of the Rāshṭrakūṭa empire, it would be necessary to recall to memory its wide extent. The empire usually extended over southern Gujarat, Marathi districts of the Central Provinces, Konkan, the whole of Maharashtra, practically the whole of the state of Hyderabad, Karnatak, and portions of the state of Mysore. Its northern boundary extended from Cambay to Houshangabad; the eastern boundary, which is rather difficult to determine precisely, probably ran through Houshangabad, Nagpur, Chanda, Warrangal and Cudappah. The southern boundary was formed partly by the Northern Pennar, beyond which extended the Bāṇa and the Noḷamba principalities, and partly by an imaginary line starting from the sources of the Northern Pennar and passing through Chitaldurg to the Arabian sea. The western boundary was, of course, the Arabian sea. Sometimes, as under Govinda III and Kṛshṇa III, the empire embraced wider areas, but the annexation of territories beyond the boundaries above indicated was temporary, for the Rāshṭrakūṭas did not succeed in permanently amalgamating them with their empire. It should not be supposed that all these areas were directly governed and administered by the imperial government from Malkhed; for there were numerous feudatories enjoying various powers of internal autonomy. How these were controlled by the imperial government will be indicated in a later chapter of this part.

This wide empire must obviously have been divided into several provinces for administrative purposes. The Rāshṭrakūṭa land-grants usually refer to *Rāshṭrapatis, Vishayapatis* and *Grāmakūṭas* in the stated order. The almost invariable precedence given to Rāshṭrapatis makes is quite clear that *Rāshṭra* was the largest administrative unit and *Vishaya* was its subdivision. Under the Kalachuris and the early Chālukyas, who preceded the Rāshṭrakūṭas in northern Maharashtra, *Vishaya* was the larger and *Rāshṭra* the smaller administrative unit;[1] but the Rāshṭrakūṭas seem to have reversed this nomenclature, giving the name *Rāshṭra* to the larger and *Vishaya* to the smaller unit. The term *Maṇḍala* was used at this time in the neighbouring provinces to denote the territorial unit corresponding to *Rāshṭra*; thus southern Gujarat was known as Lāṭa-*Maṇḍala*[2] and the Vengi kingdom as Āndhra *maṇḍala*.[3] The Rāshṭrakūṭa documents, however, do not mention any *Maṇḍala* divisions in the home provinces.

It is rather strange that our records, which invariably refer to Rāshṭrapati officers, should nowhere mention any specific *Rāshṭra*. Specific *Vishayas* like Puṇaka *vishaya* or Karahāṭaka *vishaya* are mentioned, but no specific *rāshṭra* is ever referred to. It is, therefore, difficult to determine its extent precisely; but since *vishayas* roughly corresponded, as will be presently shown, to modern districts, it is very probable that the *rāshṭra* or *maṇḍala* was about the size of a modern division in charge of a Commissioner.

The dimensions of the next territorial unit *vishaya* can be determined fairly accurately. Our records refer to Puṇaka 1,000, Karahāṭaka 4,000, as *vishayas*. Nasik, Karṇapurī (corresponding to Bijapur district) and Mahisha are also described by the same term. It is, therefore, fairly clear that

1. Vadner inscription of Budharāja, E. I., XII, p. 130.
2. Baroda plates of Karkka, I. A., XII, p. 160.
3. I. A., XV, p. 172.

a *vishaya* roughly corresponded to a modern district, usually consisting of about 2,000 villages and hamlets.

The next territorial division was a *bhukti*. The officer in charge of its administration was called a *bhogapati* or *bhogika*. Our records do not refer to him along with Rāshṭrapatis and Vishayapatis, probably because he did neither come into direct contact with the grantees of the land grants like the *grāmakūṭa*, nor possessed considerable revenue powers like the *rāshṭrapatis* and *vishayapatis*. The Samangad plates of Dantidurga refer to Koppārakapañchaśatabhukti, and the Konnur inscription of Amoghavarsha I mentions Majjantiya-saptati-grāma-bhukti. The Paithan plates of Govinda III show that Pratishṭhāna-*bhukti* contained several groups of 12 villages. It is, therefore, clear that the *bhukti* division contained about 100 to 500 villages and hamlets. It thus corresponded sometimes to the modern Taluka or Tahsil, and sometimes to the subdivision of a district under the present British administration.

It is not to be supposed that the above conclusions about the dimensions of the units referred to, hold good universally. The use of the terms used to denote territorial divisions differed from province to province and age to age. Thus *bhukti*, which was a sub-division of a *vishaya* in the Deccan and Kathiawar, was used to denote a territorial unit larger even than a *maṇḍala* in the contemporary Gurjara-Pratihāra empire of the north, as is clear from the Dighva-Duboli grant of Mahendrapāla.[4] The term denoting a territorial division corresponding to a modern district, current in Kathiawar, was *āhāra* or *āharaṇī* and not *vishaya*, as was the case in the Rāshṭrakūṭa empire. The fact that the Wani-Dindori plates should refer to Nasik as a *des'a* and the Dhulia plates of Karkka Pratāpaśila, issued 29 years earlier, should describe it as a *vishaya* shows that these terms were sometimes used even in

4. I. A., XV, p. 105.

official documents with a certain amount of looseness. The fact that Karhāṭaka is called a *vishaya* both in 768 A.D. when it comprised 10,000 villages and hamlets and in 1054 A.D. when it consisted of only 4,000, shows that the old nomenclature continued even when the units in question had changed in extent. The conclusions above mentioned are, therefore, only of a general nature.

The villages in each *bhukti* were divided into smaller groups, each group being named after its principal village, coupled with the number of villages contained in it. Thus, Sārākachchha-dvādaśa-grāma, Vavulalla-dvādaśa-grāma, Ruridha-daśaka, Sihari-dvādaśa and Sebli 30 were the subdivisions of Pratishṭhāna, Uppalikā, Karpaṭavāṇijya, Vaṭapadraka, and Purigeri talukas or sub-divisions respectively. This peculiar way of nomenclature was not confined to small divisions only; terms like Harshpura-ardhāshṭa-śataka, Padadore-dvi-sahasra, Alatage-sapta-śata, Aṅkoṭṭaka-chaturaśīti, show that in many localities this kind of nomenclature was used in preference to terms like *vishaya* and *bhukti*. This would show that the dicta in the Mahābhārata,(5) Manu(6) and Vishṇu(7) Smṛitis that government should group together 10, 20, 100 and 1,000 villages for administrative purposes was based on actual practice, and not on imaginary calculations.

The next territorial unit was the village. Sometimes small hamlets contiguous to a big village were amalgamated with it for administrative purposes, though they otherwise retained their individual corporate character. Villages were, however, very jealous of their distinctive existence; when king Nandivarman wanted to amalgamate Kumāramangala and Vennatturakotta villages into one and name the new group as Udayachandramangala, the change had to be ratified by the villages concerned(8).

5. Sāntiparvan, 87, 3-5.
6. VII, 115.
7. III, 4-6.
8. E. I., III, p. 144.

Important towns and cities formed administrative units by themselves and were under the charge of special officers known as Purapatis or Nagarapatis. Since early time this custom prevailed; Arthaśāstra of Kauṭalya, II 36, and Manusmriti, VII 121, both lay down that towns and cities were to be under the jurisdiction of separate officers. Jaugada special edict No. 1 of Asoka mentions *nagaravoharakas* who were in charge of town government in his administration. Under the Gupta administration cities like Koṭivarsha[9] and Girinagara[10] were under the charge of officers specially entrusted with their control, supervision and government.

The numerical figures attached to some of our territorial divisions mentioned above require further discussion. It has been stated that these represent the number of villages and hamlets included in the divisions concerned; but there are several other interpretations in the field. Rice had proposed to regard these figures as indicating the revenue in gold coins of the divisions concerned.[11] The use of these figures in such a sense is not unknown; the fertile Ashte group of villages in Satara district is still popularly designated as "Ashṭe-lakh-and-a-quarter," because it used to yield a revenue of that amount when the other groups were paying much less. There are, however, several difficulties in accepting the theory that these figures in the vast majority of cases denote the revenue of the units concerned. It is difficult to imagine how the revenues of Banavasi 12,000, Gangawadi 96,000, Nolambawadi 32,000 etc. continued to be the same throughout, since these figures are almost invariably associated with them in different centuries. The figures, if interpreted as the revenue amounts, are besides too small even if we proposed to regard them as referring to Kaḷanju, the usual gold coin current in the locality. It was not an unknown practice in our period to

9. E. I., XV, pp. 130 ff. 10. C. I. I., III, No. 14.

11. *Bhandarkar Commemoration Volume*, pp. 238–9.

indicate the revenues of a division by giving its figure after it, but the method followed was different. A concrete case of such a use is supplied by the Mudiyanur Bau inscription,[12] which describes Āndhramaṇḍala as '*dvādas'a-sahasra-grāma-sampādita-saptārdhalaksha-vishaya*', a country with a revenue of seven and half lakhs accruing from 12,000 villages included in it. None of the numerous expressions occurring in our records is similarly worded. Another difficulty in accepting this theory is the fact that the larger part of government revenue in our period was collected in kind and not in cash. If the government revenues were entirely collected in cash, then nomenclature of divisions after the amount of the revenues collected in them was likely to be current. There is also a further difficulty. Srī-Budhavarsha was a feudatory of Sikharikā-dvādaśa in southern Gujrat in 813 A.D.[13]; Bankoya, the viceroy of Banavāsi, had appointed his son Kundate as the officer over Nidgundige 12.[14] If we accept the theory of Rice as universally applicable, we shall have to suppose that Mahāsāmanata Budhavarsha was the ruler over a state he revenues of which were 12 golden coins, and that the mighty governor of Banavāsi, a favourite of the reigning emperor Amoghavarsha, had appointed his son as an officer over a division the revenue of which was the same amount 12 golden coins. Could a person have acquired the feudatory status if his income were so small? Could the mighty Banavāsi governor have appointed his son to a post less im portant than that of a village patel or accountant?

Nor does it appear very likely that the figures could have stood for the population of the divisions concerned. We have a solitary expression referring to Gangawadi as *Shaṇnavati-sahasravishayaprakṛtayaḥ*,[15] but this expression is used while mentioning the witnesses to the document in which it occurs

12. I. A., XV, p. 172.
13. E. I., III, p. 54.
14. E. I., VII, p. 214.
15. I. A., XV, p. 172.

and, therefore, means that the transaction is known to or attested by the whole population of the province of Gangawadi 96,000. The population theory further presupposes that census was regularly taken during our period. No evidence can, however, be adduced to prove that such was the case. The view that was once advanced that the Khandagiri inscription of king Kāravela mentions the population of Kalinga was based upon a wrong interpretation of the expression '*Paṇatīsāhi satasahasehi pakatayo rañjayati*' occurring in that record. 35,00,000, however, represents not the number of the subjects of Khāravela but the sum he spent in promoting their welfare. This interpretation will be further absolutely inapplicable and absurd with reference to small units like Śikharikā 12 mentioned above. The view that these figures do not represent the entire population of the divisions, but the fighting force that could be mustered from them or the number of house-holds that were comprised in them is open to a similar objection. It may be further pointed out that the inapplicability of these views in not confined merely to the cases where the figures are small; for it is extremely unlikely that Banavasi 12,000, Gangawadi 96,000 and Nolambavadi 32000, which together comprised an area greater that the modern state of Mysore, had a population of only 1,40,000.

As against the interpretation here advocated that these figures refer to the villages and hamlets comprised in the divisions concerned Rice contends that the figures in many cases are too large to admit of that interpretation. He points out that Gangawadi 96,000 could never have comprised 96,000 villages, even supposing that its area was entirely covered by villages only and by nothing else. The same is the case with Noḷambawadi 32,000 and Banavasi 12,000. Dr. Pran Nath, in a recent work of great interest, seeks to get over this difficulty by proposing a new interpretation for the term *grāma*. He contends that in the time of the Guptas and even much earlier it appears that the word *grāma* was used in official records for an estate and in poetical and literary works for a village or settlement.(16) He interprets the figures after the names of the divisions as referring to estates contained in them; thus Konkana 14,000, Banavasi 12,000 etc. meant that these units comprised of so many estates.

With reference to the theory that *grāma* in our inscriptions means an estate and not a village, it has to be confessed that the arguments adduced to support it do not bear close examination. The passage quoted from *Abhidhānarājendra* does not mean that in the remotest period of Indian history the word *grāma* was used in ten different meanings, *viz*. (1) cows (*gāvah*); (2) grass (*trināni*); (3) boundaries (*sīmā*); (4) pleasure-gardens (*ārāma*); (5) well (*udapāna*); (6) servants (*cheta*); (7) fences (*bahih*); (8) temple (*devakula*); (9) an estate (*avagraha*); (10) owner (*adhipati*).(17) A glance at the commentary, relevant passages from which are quoted below,(18) will show that the word never conveyed such

16. Pran Nath: *A Study in the Economic Conditions of Ancient India*, p. 26. 17. *Ibid*, p. 28.

18. गावो तणाइ सीमा आरामुदपाण चेटरूपाणि
वाही य षाणमन्तर नुग्गह ततो य आहिपती

अथ भावार्थ उच्यते। प्रथमो नैगमः प्राह। यावन्तं भूभागं गावश्चरितुं व्रजन्ति तावान् सर्वोऽपि ग्राम इति व्यपदेशं लभते। ततो विशुद्धनैगमः प्रतिभणति।

गावो वयन्ति दूरं पि जं तु तनकट्ठहारगादीया।
सुरुढिते गता एन्ति अत्थ सन्ते ततो गामो॥

परिस्थूरमपि परग्राममपि चरितुं गावो व्रजान्ति ततः किमेवं सोप्येक एव ग्रामो भवतु? अपि च एवं ब्रुवतो भूयसामपि परस्परमतिदवीयसां ग्रामाणामपि एकग्रामतेव प्रसज्जति। न चैतावदुपपन्नम्। तस्मान्नैतावान् ग्रामः। किन्तु यावन्मात्रं क्षेत्रं तृणहारककाष्टहरकादयो सूर्ये उतिथते तृणद्यार्थं गताः सन्तः सूर्येऽस्तं यति...पुनरायान्ति एतावत्क्षेत्रं-ग्रामः। . शुद्धतरो निगमो भणति। यद्यपि गवां गोचरक्षेत्रात् आसन्नतरं भूमाग तृणकाष्टहारका व्रजन्ति तथापि ते कदाचित् परसीमानमपि व्रजान्ति तस्मान्नतावान् ग्राम उपपद्यते। अहं ब्रवीमि यावत् स्वात्मीया सीमा एतावान् ग्रामः। ततोपि विशुद्धत्तरः

[P. T. O.

diverse meanings. The verse in question refers to ten different theories about the extent of area that was denoted by the term *grāma.* The first theory maintained that it could comprise not only the area of settlement, but also the territory upto the limits of which the cows go out while grazing. The second theory contended that *grāma* could not denote so extensive an area, since cows often go out for grazing in the fields of contiguous villages. It maintained that only that much area which is traversed by the grass and fuel gatherers in the course of the day can be comprised in the meaning of the term in question. The third view maintained that even this interpretation is open to a similar objection and, therefore, *grāma* denotes only the area included in the boundaries of the village in question. The fourth view reduced even this extent and prefered to regard *grāma* as comprising only the area upto the village well. The subsequent views go on curtailing the extent of *grāma* still further till the climax is reached when it is contended that *grāma* means that temple or village-hall which was first built in the village, and around which the settlement subsequently grew. The commentator further observes that *grāma*, in the opinion of some, meant the individual houses of the speakers; the last view cited by him is that the term can be used to denote the headman of the village as well. It may be pointed out that the sense of the landed estate is nowhere advanced by any of the schools referred to in the Kosha.

(*Continued from last page*)

प्राह । यावत्तस्यैव ग्रामस्य सम्बन्धी कूपस्तावद् ग्राम: । ततोपि विशुद्धतर: प्राह । यावत् क्षेत्रमभ्यकानि चेटरूपाणि रममाणानि गच्छान्ति तावद् ग्राम: । ततोपि विशुद्धतर: प्रतिवक्ति । यावन्तं भूभागं अतिलघीयांसो बालका उत्क्रीडन्तो प्रयान्ति तावान् ग्राम:।... सर्वविशुद्धनयस्य यावान् वृतिपरिक्षेपपरिवृतो भूभागस्तावान् ग्राम: ।

जं वा पथम काउं सेसगगामो निवसई स गामो ।

तं देउलं सभा वा मज्झिमगोट्ठि पवा वा वि ॥

यत् प्रत्येकमात्मीयकमात्मीयानुग्रहरूपमेकैकं गृहं तद् ग्राम: ।

The second passage relied upon to prove that *grāma* can mean an estate is a sentence in Nasik cave inscription No. 5. The passage in question runs as under:—

'*Ahmehi pavajitānaṁ bhikhūnaṁ gāme Kakhaḍīsu puva khetaṁ dattaṁ; ta cha khetaṁ (na) kasate ta cha gāmo na vasati.*'

Senart, who has edited the inscription, translates the passage as follows: 'We have here on mount Tiraṇhu formerly given to mendicant ascetics dwelling in the cave, which is a pious gift of ours, a field in the village of Kakhadi; but this field is not tilled nor is the village inhabited.' It will be seen from the original passage and its translation by Senart that it can hardly support Dr. Pran Nath's conclusion that 'a *kshetra* could be described as a *grāma* and that the word *vasati* was used in the sense of cultivation as well as that of habitation.' As a matter of fact the passage differentiates a *kshetra* or field from a *grāma* or village in the clearest possible way.

Further, it can hardly be advanced that in chapters 171 and 173 of the *Arthas'āstra* of Kauṭalya, the word *grāma* has been used in the sense of an estate. The passage clearly refers to the devastation of ordinary villages. But there is no room for doubt as to the sense in which the term *grāma* has been used in the *Arthas'āstra*; for while describing the colonisation of new areas the book says, 'Villages, consisting each of not less than a hundred families and not more than five hundred families of agricultural people of Sudra caste, with boundaries extending as far as a *krosha* or two, and capable of protecting each other shall be formed.'[19] This passage can hardly be consistent with the view that Kauṭalya uses the word *grāma* in the sense of an estate.

With reference to the objection raised by Rice against the view that these figures cannot be possibly interpreted as the number of the villages comprised in the divisions concerned, it may be pointed out that it may be a valid objection

19. *Arthas'āstra*, Dr. Shamasastri's translation, p. 49.

only with reference to large numbers like those associated with Banavasi or Gangawadi and not with reference to smaller figures associated with *vishayas* and *bhuktis* in the inscriptions hailing from Gujarat, Maharashtra and northern Karnatak. India is a fairly vast country and the usage may have quite conceivably differed province by province and century by century. Whatever may be the difficulties that may be presented by the figures associated with the divisions in other provinces, there can be no doubt that the theory, that they represent the number of villages, not only does not encounter any difficulties in the provinces just mentioned, but is actually supported by the wording of several documents. Compare, for example, the following expressions :—

(१) साराकच्छद्वादशग्रामाभ्यन्तरे लिंबारिकाग्रामः[20]

(२) मजन्तियसप्तति-ग्राम-भुक्त्यन्तर्गतताल्युरग्रामः[21]

(३) पुरीप्रभृतिचतुर्दशशत-ग्राम-समन्वितां समस्त कोंकणभुवम्...[22]

(४) कर्मान्तरपुरप्रतिबद्धषोडशोत्तर-ग्रामशत-विषयान्तःपाति[23]

(५) मत्प्रसादेन संलब्धान् वनवासिपुरस्सरान् ।
ग्रामांस्त्रिंशत्सहस्राणि भुनक्त्यविरतोद्यतः ॥[24]

The express mention of *grāma* in association with the numbers mentioned in the above passages makes it fairly obvious that we have to interpret these numbers, even when the term *grāma* is not immediately used after them, as indicating the numbers of villages and hamlets included in the divisions concerned. Nor can it be argued that the *grāmas* mentioned in this connection are mere estates or fields and not ordinary villages consisting of village-settlements, the cultivable land, pasture and waste land, if any, that lay round the settlement. For, in a large number of cases the *grāmas* mentioned in our records can be actually identified and they are found to be ordinary villages of the above description. Thus Kantāragrāma, above

20. E. I., III, p. 109. 21. Konnur inscription, E. I., VI, p. 31.
22. I. A., IX, p. 35. 23. I. A., X, p. 284. 24. E. I., VI, p. 31

referred to, mentioned in the Surat plates, is the village of Kattargam near Surat.[25] Villages of Vilavade, Paragava, and Aitavade mentioned in the Samangad plates of Dantidurga still exist, occupying the same relative positions, and bearing names which are hardly different from those given in the plates in question. All these are villages of the ordinary type and none of them is an estate. The village of Vaṭapadraka given in the Baroda plates of Karkka is modern Baroda, the villages of Jambuvavikā, Aṅkoṭṭaka, and Vaghachha which are stated to be to the east, west and north of Vaṭapadraka are the same as modern villages of Jambuvāda, Akoṭa and Vaghodia which are to the east, west and north of Baroda None of them is an estate, all of them are villages of the ordinary type. Talegaon plates of Kṛshṇa[26] record a gran of Kumārigrāma along with the adjoining hamlets of Bhama ropara, Arulava, Sindigrama and Taravade which was situated to the west of Khambagrāma and Vorigrāma and to the east of Alandiyagrāma and Thirugrāma. Most of these villages still exist and have been identified by Dr. D. R Bhandarkar. Kumārigrāma is Karehgaon, Bhamaropura is Bhowrapur, Arulava is Uruli, Sindigrāma is Seedoneh Taravade is Turudi, Khambagrāma is Khanegaon, Vorimagrāma is Boree, Alandiya is Chorachi Āḷandī, and Thirugrāma is Theur. The Konur inscription of Amoghavarsha grants a *grāma* or village called Taleyur situated in Majjantiya *bhukti* The inscription adds that the king also granted 12 *nivartanas* of land in each of the 30 villages of that division, the names of which are given. Out of these 30 villages, 13 can be identified and they are within a radius of 7 or 8 miles from Kolanura where the Jain temple, which was the assignee of these lands, was situated. They are all villages of the ordinary type and cannot answer the description of an estate. Now one and the same document cannot be using the term *grāma* in two different senses. If the term *grāma* used in the expression

25. E. I., XIII, p. 278. 26. I. A., XIX, p. 270.

'*adbhuktivartishu trins'ātsvapi grāmeshu*' means a village of the ordinary type, it must mean the same thing in the expression *Majjantiyasaptatigrāmabhukti.*

Another difficulty in accepting the view, that the figures we have been discussing indicate the numbers of estates comprised in the divisions concerned, is the fact that sometimes the *grāma* included in a division is situated miles away from the headquarters. Thus the village of Kannaḍige granted in the Honwad inscription of Someśvara I is in Bijapur Taluka, about a hundred miles from Karhāṭaka or Karad, the capital of Karhāṭaka 4,000 in which it was situated. It must be confessed that if Karhāṭaka 4,000 meant a division of 4,000 estates situated round about Karhad, it is almost impossible to explain the existence of one of these estates nearly a hundred miles from Karhad, unless we assume that big Zemindaris existed in the Deccan of our period, about which, however, there is no evidence yet forthcoming. A *grāma* in the Karhāṭaka 4,000 can be found in Bijapur district, only if we assume that the term indicated a village and not an estate.

The figures associated with the territorial divisions of the Deccan in our period are small, and we have seen that they can be interpreted as referring to ordinary villages comprised in the divisions concerned. But how are these figures to be interpreted with reference to Gangawādi, Noḷambawādi and Banavāsi, where, as pointed out by Rice, they are too large to admit of that interpretation? It may also be confessed that we do not usually come across the inclusion of the term *grāma* after these figures, as is the case with a number of records from the Deccan, as pointed out before.

It may be pointed out that in our period the average village was much smaller and the number of hamlets included under it was much greater than is the case now. We get concrete evidence on the point from Inscriptions Nos. 4 and 5 at the Rājarājeśvara temple[27] inscribed towards the beginning of the 11th century. These two records mention the grant of about 35 villages made to the temple by king Rājarāja. Out of these, only one has an area of more than about a thousand acres, four have an area of 500 to 1,000 acres, three, an area of 300 to 400 acres, seven, an area of 200 to 300 acres, six, an area of 100 to 200 acres, three, an area of 50 to 100 acres, six, an area of 25 to 50 acres and, two, an area of even less than 25 acres. The village (*grāma*) of Gonturu, granted by Amma I, had 12 hamlets (*grāmaṭikās*) attached to it.[28] In 887 A.D. the village of Beli-ur had also 12 hamlets under it, and the revenue of all these put together was only 80 coins, presumably Kaḷanjus, and 800 measures of paddy.[29] It is quite clear from the amount of revenue, that the village in question, as well as the hamlets included under it, must both have been very small. It may be further observed that these small villages cannot satisfy the description of estates or fields. Inscriptions Nos. 4 and 5 from the Rājarājeśvara temple make it clear that even villages with an area of 50 to 100 acres are described as having their village sites, threshing floors, temples, tanks, burning grounds for high caste men, the same for the pariahs, etc. Only two of these villages, Kanjaranagar and Nagarakarkurichchhi, whose areas were about 42 and 20 acres respectively, can be called estates; for, they included only cultivable land and no village sites. Another inscription from north Arcot district mentions the grant of a certain piece of land by the citizens of Melpāḍi, the eastern boundary of which is stated to be Pulikkuran, which is described as one among the villages that were acquired and belonged to the grantor city as hamlets (*Pīdāgai*), and which was not divided into house sites. These three hamlets can certainly be described as estates or fields rather than villages, and they would support the theory of Dr. Pran Nath that *grāma* meant an

27. S. I. I., Vol. II. 28. S. I. I., I, p. 40. 29. I. A., VI, p. 103.

estate and not a village. It must, however, be pointed out that these are the only instances where we have a clear case of the term *grāma* being used in that unusual sense. In all other cases which are almost innumerable, we have the word used in the ordinary sense. To conclude, in the extreme south of India the average village in our period was very much smaller than the present typical village. It is, therefore, not impossible that the numbers associated with Gangawadi, Noḷambawadi etc. may represent the villages and hamlets included in them, if we assume that the numbers were exaggerated to a certain degree.

The theory of exaggeration of numbers is, however, based on an unproved assumption, and it is quite likely that the figures occurring after these divisions may mean something else. It may be pointed out that the figures associated with the divisions in southern Karnatak and Tamila country are all in thousands. In this respect they pointedly differ from those associated with small territorial divisions in the Deccan, where they are usually small and precise. Rice has observed that Nāḍs were often called 'thousands' in Karnatak.[1] It is, therefore, not unlikely that Banavasi 12,000, Gangawadi 96,000, Noḷambawadi 32,000, Toṇḍai 48,000 etc. were so designated, not because they contained so many villages, but because they consisted of 12, 96, 32, and 48 divisions or *nāḍs*. This seems to be the most likely explanation of these figures that can be thought of at present. Why a *nāḍ* should have been popularly called a 'thousand' is a question that remains to be answered. Perhaps in theory a *nāḍ* was popularly supposed to consist of a thousand villages, though in actuality it may have had many less. It is also not unlikely that the term *nāḍ* was first applicable only to bigger divisions actually containing about a thousand villages, but that later on it came to denote much smaller divisions. The precise interpretation of these thousands associated with *nāḍs* is at present not possible.

CHAPTER VIII

Central Government: King and Ministry

King-in-ministry was the normal form of the government in the Rāshṭrakūṭa empire. Feudatory administrations were also governed by the same principle. Neither literature, nor epigraphical records, nor accounts by foreign travellers disclose the existence of a non-monarchical form of government anywhere in the Deccan of our period. This is natural, for even in the north, governments were all monarchical at this time, as we know from the account handed down by Yuan Chwang. Tribal or republican forms of government, which are known to have been persisting in northern India down to the 4th century A.D., cannot, however, be traced in the south, even in the earlier period. This is rather strange when we remember that the village council was more democratic and elective in the south than was usually the case in the north. This may be due to the dearth of historical material relating to the earlier period of the history of the Deccan, or to the possibility of democracy not having extended beyond the scope of the village government.

Kingship at this period was hereditary throughout India. We nowhere come across any elective type of monarchy in our period, either in the south or in the north. We get only one clear case of the election of a king which is referred to in the *Rājataraṅgiṇī*. This case occurred in 939 A.D., when at the death of S'ūrvarman there was no heir of the Utpala dynasty to succeed him. Kamalavardhana, who had actually become the *de facto* king, requested the Brahmanas to elect a king, anticipating that none but himself would be elected by them. After considering the claims of several claimants, the Brahmana assembly decided to elect Yaśaskara. This, however, is the only known case of the genuine election of a king by a section of the general population as distinguished from ministers or feudatories ; but the observations of Kalhaṇa on the occasion show that a person who resorted to such a course was regarded as qualifying himself for admission into a lunatic asylum.[1] Feudatories and ministers had sometimes a determining voice in deciding as to who should be offered the crown, as when Govinda II was deposed in c. 780 A.D., or Amoghavarsha III installed in c. 936 A.D. But statements made even with reference to these occasions like

Sāmantairatha Raṭṭārājyamahimālambārthamabhyarthitaḥ 'He was requested by the feudatories to accept the throne for supporting the glory of the Rāshṭrakūṭa empire,' are more figurative than real. For we have already seen that Amoghavarsha III and Dhruva owed their elevation to the throne more to their own exertions than to the votes of the feudatories. The kingship was thus hereditary in our period and the crown passed usually to the eldest, and sometimes to the ablest son, as in the case of Govinda III.

In the Rāshṭrakūṭa administration, the advice of the Smritis that an heir-apparent should be selected in the life-time of the ruling king was usually followed. Sulaiman's statement, that the princes in India name their own successors,[2] refers to this practice of the nomination of the

1. राजतरंगिणी V. 456, ff. cf:—

प्राक्कर्मभिर्मोदितो वा प्रेरितो वा कुमन्त्रिभिः ।
नाभ्युत्सिंहासनारूढो मूढः कमलवर्धनः ॥ ४५६ ॥
एकाकिनीं रहःक्षीबां लब्ध्वा कुलभयोषितम् ।
अप्रौढोऽनुपभुज्यान्यदिने दूत्यार्थयेत यः ॥ ४५९ ॥
बिभर्ति रभसावासां यश्च संत्यज्य तत्क्षणम् ।
नीत्या कामयतेऽन्येद्युः शोच्यस्ताभ्यां परोस्ति कः ॥ ४६० ॥
अशुंगोक्षनिभा विप्रास्समगंसत गोकुले ॥ ४६१ ॥
वैमत्येन मिथस्तेषां नान्यः कोप्यभ्यषिच्यत ॥
कूर्चा भाषणनिष्ठ्युतैः स्वकूर्चष्ठीवनैः परम् ॥ ४६३ ॥

2. Elliot I, p. 6. Election as a possible means of getting a kingdom was unknown also to Somdeva, a contemporary writer on politics; cf. राज्यस्य मूलं क्रमो विक्रमश्च । नीतिवाक्यामृत V. 26.

Yuvaraja. Usually the choice fell upon the eldest son, but he was not recognised as a Yuvaraja before he was formally annointed as such. Thus in the Talegaon plates of Kṛshṇa I[3] his eldest son is simply referred to as Govindarāja, whereas in the Alas plates issued two years later he is described as a Yuvaraja. Since the village in the Talegaon plates was granted at the request of Govindarāja, it is clear that he must have been a major by that time. And though the eldest son, he had not at that time received the coronation as an heir-apparent. It would appear that the heir-apparent had to attain a certain age, probably 24, before he could be formally annointed. If the king had no son, or if the one he had was a minor and the times were troubled ones, sometimes the younger brother was made the Yuvaraja. Thus a Palase Kadamba grant[4] refers to Bhānuvarman, the younger brother of the ruling king, as *Kanīyān nṛpaḥ* or Yuvaraja. While the Ganga ruler Śivamāra was rotting in the Rāshṭrakūṭa prison, his younger brother Vijayāditya was made Yuvaraja, and the Gattavadipur plates tell us that he refrained from enjoying the earth, knowing her to be his elder brother's wife.[5]

The Yuvaraja had the status of a *Pañchamahās'abda-Sāmanta* and was invested with a necklace which was the insignia of his office, as would appear from the observation of Govinda III to his father, that he was quite content with the necklace with which he was invested by the latter at the time of his appointment as an heir-apparent.[6] He was a member of the ministry, according to the Nīti-śāstra writers of the period, and we find him exercising the royal prerogative of granting villages.[7] When the ruling emperors were old and of a retiring or religious disposition like Amoghavarsha I or Amoghavarsha III, the heir-apparents exercised

3. E. I., XIII, p. 275. 4. I. A., VI, p. 28.
5. E. C., III, Nanjangad No. 129.
6 E. I., IV, p. 242. 7. Alas plates, E. I., VI, p. 210.

almost all the powers of the ruling kings. We have already seen how this was responsible for the overlapping of the reigns of the kings just mentioned and their sons, who succeeded them.[8] The Yuvaraja usually stayed at the capital. He was hardly ever deputed as a viceroy to an outlying province under the Rāshṭrakūṭa administration. The reasons were obvious; if the Yuvaraja were absent from the capital his chances of succession were likely to be affected by the machinations of other aspirants to the throne. This was a real danger in the Rāshṭrakūṭa dynasty, whose records are too full of the wars of succession. The Rāshṭrakūṭa practice was to depute younger princes and cousins as provincial governors. Thus Dhruva was a governor at Dhulia in 779 A.D., before he rebelled against and ousted his elder brother Govinda II; Dhruva's cousin Sankaragaṇa was a governor in Berar in 793 A.D., Indrarāja of the Gujarat branch had appointed his younger son Govinda as a provincial governor.[9] These examples can be multiplied almost *ad infinitum.* The only case of the eldest son being a provincial viceroy is that of Stambha; but his viceroyalty of the newly conquered province of Gangawadi was rather an exile than an appointment. He was sent there by his father who had superceded his claims in the Yuvaraja selection.

When a king was a minor, usually a male relative was appointed to act as the regent. During the minority of Amoghavarsha I his cousin Karkka was appointed to carry on the administration on behalf of the emperor. The claims of Indra IV were being pushed forth by his maternal uncle Mārasiṁha, who was his regent. It is interesting to note that we nowhere come across queens or princesses as regents or governors in the Rāshṭrakūṭa administration. Under the Western Chalukyas queen governors were not unknown; thus Vijayabhaṭṭārikā, the senior wife of Chandrāditya, the

8. *Ante.* pp. 89 and 122. 9. Torkhede Inscription, E. I., III, p. 53.

elder brother of Vikramâditya I was a governor, if not a regent.[10] Under the later Chālukyas of Kalyani also, we have several examples of queens being appointed to important government offices. Thus Mailādevī, one of the wives of Someśvara, was the governor of Banavasi 12,000 in 1053 A.D. Ketalādevī, another wife of the same monarch, was the governor of the *agrahāra* of Ponnavada.[11] Akkādevī, an elder sister of Jayasimha III, was governing Kinsukad 70 in 1022 A.D. Kumkumadevī, an elder sister of Vijayāditya was administering Purigere 300 in 1077 A.D.[12] Lakshmidevī, the chief queen of Vikramāditya VI, was in charge of 18 *agrahāras* in 1095 A.D. That lady governors should have been so common under the Chālukyas and altogether unknown under the Rāshṭrakūṭas is indeed strange. Can we explain this fact on the assumption that the latter Chālukyas, unlike the Rāshṭrakūṭas belonged to a stock which was considerably under the influence of matriarchy ?

The regency must have lasted during the minority. The writers on politics like Śukra lay down that the king must be a major before he assumes the control of administration. That the injunction was observed in practice is clear from the statement of Al-Masudi that no king could succeed to the throne before he was 40.[13] The age given by this traveller seems to be wrong, but his statement may be taken as corroborating the Smriti view that minors could not be entrusted with the administration. Khāravela, we know, could not assume the reigns of government before he was 24.

A few words may be said about the Rāshṭrakūṭa court. We have no detailed description of the pomp and splendour of the royal court in any contemporary document, but a few hints given by our records can be utilised. The access to the court was regulated by the royal chamberlain and his

10. I. A., VII, p. 163.
11. I. A., XIX, p. 274 and p. 271.
12. I. A., XVIII, p. 37.
13. Elliot I, p. 40.

staff; a verse in the Sanjan plates of Amoghavarsha I says that even feudatories and foreign potentates had to wait outside the portals till they were called for audience. It would thus appear that Rāshṭrakūṭa kings transacted their business systematically; only those were admitted in the audience hall whose business was about to be considered. The court was surrounded by regiments of infantry, cavalry and elephants; these were intended partly to secure safety and partly to show off imperial pomp. Very often the elephants and horses carried from the defeated enemies were exhibited outside the royal court along with other valuable booty.(14) Abu Zaid, a contemporary of the Rāshṭrakūṭas, has observed that the kings of India were accustomed to wear earrings of precious stones, mounted in gold, and necklaces of great value formed of pearls and precious stones. In the Rāshṭrakūṭa court also very probably the king must have appeared on ceremonious occasions in rich dress and ornaments. He was attended, as was the case with almost all the kings in contemporary drama and fiction, by courtesans and dancing girls; this custom was so common in our period that even Somadeva, the Jain writer of our period, is compelled to countenance it.(15) Al-Idrisi records its prevalence in the Chālukya court of Aṇahilapaṭṭaṇa,(16) and the Nilgund inscription confirms the same conclusion when it informs us that Amoghavarsha I had covered all the territories of the numerous chieftains and hostile kings with thousands of courtesans. It would appear that the sovereign rulers used to compel their feudatories to accept some imperial courtesans in their courts. These used to be in immediate attendance on the kings and, therefore, must have served as ideal spies. The gifts given by a concubine of the Chālukya king Vikramāditya II just before the rise of the Rāshṭrakūṭas(17) would show that many of

14. Sanjan plates, E. I., XVIII, p. 235 ff.

15. *Nītivākyāmṛta*, XXIV, 29, 51.

16. Elliot, I, p. 88 17. E, I., VI p. 102.

these courtesans must have been fairly rich and may have wielded considerable power and influence. Al-Idrisi tells us that the Chāḷukya rulers of Gujarat used to go out once a week in state, attended only by women, one hundred in number, richly clad, wearing rings of gold and silver upon their hands and feet, and engaged in various games and sham-fights,—a description which reminds us of the Second Act of Śākuntala, where we read of king Dushyanta being followed by amazon archers, while out on hunting. The statement in Kadba plates[18] that the moon-faced damsels of the court of Kṛshṇa I used to delight the ladies of the capital by the movements of their lotus-like hands, which could skilfully convey internal emotions, might perhaps show that a similar custom prevailed in the Rāshṭrakūṭa court also. It is a little unlikely that all the ladies of the capital could have been admitted in the royal court; in that case they may be seeing these dances in some processions. It is true that the British Museum plates of Govinda III[19] do not refer to any Yavanīs or courtesans accompanying the king when they describe the boar-hunting of the king. But the king was at that time out on expedition and, therefore, the Yavanīs or courtesans may not have figured in the hunting party.

The Yuvaraja and other princes of the blood royal, members of the ministry, the chamberlain and his assistants, military officers and other high dignitaries of state were the most prominent members of the royal court. Poets also were there, for the Rāshṭrakūṭas were liberal patrons of literature, as will be shown in chapter XV. By the side of the poets, we might imagine, were sitting the astrologers. There is definite evidence to show that astrologers were maintained at the court of the Gujarat Rāshṭrakūṭas,[20] and when we remember the great hold of astrology on the popular mind

18. I. A., XII, p. 13. 19. I. A., XI, p. 126. 20. I. A., V, p. 145.

during our period we may not be wrong in assuming that the astrologers figured in the Malkhed court also. It may be pointed out that the *Kāmandaka–nīti–sāra*, a work probably written at about our period, lays down that a royal astrologer should be always maintained at the court.[21] The doctor is known to have been one of the court officers of the Gahadwalas;[22] for obvious reasons he could hardly have been absent from the Rāshṭrakūṭa court as well. Merchants, presidents of guilds, and other notables of the capital were prominent among the non-official members of the royal court.

The character of the Rāshṭrakūṭa monarchy,–whether it was limited or arbitrary, would be a question of great interest to the present-day reader. It may be pointed out that the Hindu monarchy was in theory always limited, but the constitutional checks thought of in our period by the theorists on the subject were of a different nature than those to which we are accustomed in the present age. Spiritual sanctions, effects of careful and proper education, force of public opinion, division of power with a ministry, supremacy of established usage in the realm of law and taxation, devolution of large powers to local bodies whose government was democratic in substance if not always in form,–these were the usual checks on monarchy relied on by the Hindu political writers. Though it is not possible to agree with all that Mr. K. P. Jayaswal says about *Paura* and *Jānapada* bodies serving as constitutional checks upon the king, it is clear that in some cases at least these bodies did exist. Deccan records, however, prove that the terms *Paura* and *Jānapada* were not used to denote popular representative bodies in the Rāshṭrakūṭa period. Among the officers and bodies enjoined not to interfere with the enjoyment of landed property given to the donees, *Pauras* and *Jānapadas* do not figure in the period we are studying with the solitary exception of the Deoli grant of

21. IV, 33 22. E. I., XI, p. 24

Kṛshṇa III.[23] But that record omits all officers usually mentioned in such connection like Râshṭrapatis, Vishayapatis, Grāmakūṭas, Yuktas, and Niyuktas and substitutes the expression '*Sarvāneva svajānapadān*' in their place. It is clear, therefore, that *Jānapada* here stands for subjects in general and not for their representative assemblies. The expression '*Janapadān*' in the expression '*Rāshṭrapati-vishayapati-nagarpati-grāmapati-niyuktāniyukta-rājapurusha-janapadān*', occurring in a S'ilāhāra record of 1026 A.D.,[24] also refers to the subjects of the realm in general and not to any popular assembly.

Although the term *Jānapada* was not used in the sense of a popular representative council, it is not to be supposed that non-official bodies possessing administrative powers did not exist in our period. Such bodies certainly existed in villages, and probably in districts (Vishayas) and provinces (Rāshṭras) as well; their members were known as *Grāmamahattaras*, *Vishayamahattaras*, and *Rāshṭramahattaras* respectively. It has been already shown by me elsewhere[25] that the expression *Grāmamahattara* denoted a member of the non-official village council. Analogy would, therefore, show that *Rāshṭramahattaras* and *Vishayamahattaras* may have, very probably, constituted a body of the notables and elders in the province and district respectively. Some kind of divisional popular bodies seem to have existed in Tamil country also,[26] and there is no wonder if we found them in the Deccan proper during our period.

Members of the district council, *Vishayamahattaras*, are referred to in the Kapadwanj grant of Kṛshṇa II,[27] and those of the provincial council, *Rāshṭramahattaras*, in the Dhulia

23. E. I., V, p. 195. 24. I. A., V, p. 278.

25. Altekar, *A History of the Village Communities in the Western India*, pp. 20-21. (Humphrey Milford, 1927).

26. R. C. Majumdar, *Corporate Life in Ancient India*, pp 211-13.

27. E. I., I, p. 55.

plates of Karkka, son of Dhruva.[28] These bodies were not innovations of the Rāshṭrakūṭas, for the Vadner plates of Kalachuri king Budharāja, dated 609 A.D.,[29] also refer to *Rāshṭramahattarādhikāriṇaḥ*.

It must be, however, admitted that out of the numerous Rāshṭrakūṭa grants, mentioning various officers and bodies, only the above two records mention the members of the district and provincial councils. This circumstance can, however, be explained on the assumption that these councils were not normally expected to interfere with the enjoyment of the lands granted to the donees, rather than by the hypothesis that they did not exist except under Govinda II and Kṛshṇa II. There is nothing improbable in the evolution of the bodies of *Vishaya*- and *Rāshṭramahattaras* on the analogy of the council of *Grāmamahattaras* which existed almost everywhere in the Deccan from c. 500 to c. 1300 A.D. The Rāshṭrakūṭa charters may be mentioning *Grāmamahattaras* and omitting *Vishaya* and *Rāshṭramahattaras*, because the first mentioned councillors, being the members of local village bodies, were, unlike the last-mentioned ones, directly concerned in the matter.

Our records, however, do not give any clue as to what were the powers of these councils of the district and provincial notables or representatives, whether they were elected, if so, by whom, how frequently they met and how they transacted their business. Considering the means of communication in our period, it would appear very probable that the meetings of these bodies could not have been very frequent. Their powers, therefore, must have been considerably less than those of the village councils. If they were as powerful as the village councils, one would have heard much more about them than is actually the case at present. An officer called '*Mahattamasarvādhikārin*' is mentioned in the Begumra plates

28. E. I., VIII, p. 186. 29. E. I., XII, p. 130.

of Kṛshṇa II as the *dūtaka* of the grant.[30] It may thus appear that the *Vishaya*- and *Rāshṭramahattaras* had an accredited officer of theirs, probably their president, who was perhaps acting for them when they were not is session. Gaṇapati, the chief councillor of Bankeya, the Banavasi viceroy of Amoghavarsha I, was a *mahattara*;[31] he may have been probably selected from among, or elected by, the *Rāshṭra-mahattaras* of Banavasi. In Śaka 991[32] one of the ministers of the Yādavas of Seuṇdeśa was Mahattama Srī-Amāditya. It is possible to conjecture that some of the members of these bodies were selected for some of the posts in the ministry.

Whether corresponding to these nebulous provincial councils of *mahattaras*, there existed in the capital a grand council of the empire we do not know. Such a body is nowhere referred to in our documents but there is nothing impossible in its having existed. It could not have probably met frequently, if it existed at all, and it must have been eclipsed at the capital by the king, his ministers, and other high officers. Its powers could not, therefore, have been very substantial.

Ministry

All the writers on the Hindu political science hold that ministry is the most important wheel of the administrative machinery, and evidence can be adduced to show that real-polity included that institution since very early times. The Rāshṭrakūṭa administration is no exception to the general rule. Ministers under this administration were very important and influential members of government. Nārāyaṇa, the foreign minister of Kṛshṇa III, has been described in the Salotgi inscription [33] as another hand, as it were, '*Pratihastaḥ*' of the emperor, as dear to him as his own right hand. The Pathari Pillar inscription of the feudatory Rāshṭrakūṭa chief

30. I. A., XIII, p. 66. 31. E. I., VI, pp. 29 ff. 32. E. I., II, 225.
33. तस्य य: प्रतिहस्तोऽभूत्प्रियो दक्षिणहस्तवत् । E. I., IV, p. 60.

Parabala states that he used to regard his premier as worthy of salutations by his own head.[34] A record of king Kṛshṇa of the Yādava dynasty compares his minister to his own tongue and right hand.[35] Another record of the same king states how his premier's feet were brightened by the crest-jewels on the head of the feudatories. It is, therefore, no wonder that the ministers sometimes possessed feudatory titles and were entitled to the *Pañchamahās'abdas.* Dalla, the chief foreign minister of Dhruva, was a *Sāmanta* entitled to the use of the five great musical instruments.[36] Kālidāsa, the war minister or commander-in-chief of the Chālukya king Jagadekamalla, is described as entitled to the Pañchamahāśabdas in a record of his hailing from Badami.[37] Consultations with the ministry before embarking on a particular course or policy are rarely referred to in our records, probably because there was no occasion to do so. But the above evidence regarding the influence of the ministry would show that ministerial consultations are not mentioned simply because the copper-plate grants are not treatises on constitutional theory and practice. It may be, however, pointed out that a record of the Yādava dynasty, which succeeded the Rāshṭrakūṭas in the northern portions of their dominions, states while recording the grant of some shops for certain religious objects, that the king had consulted his ministers before making the grant in question.[38]"

It must be, however, pointed out that there may have existed some rulers in our period who may have ridden rough-shod over the heads of their ministers. Naturally the majority of our records would pass over such cases. A perusal of the *Rājataraṅginī* shows that side by side with ministers who ruled wisely and ably, there existed others who were worth-

34. E. I., IX, p. 254. 35. I. A., XIV p. 69. 36. E I., X. p 89.
37. I. A., VI, p. 140.
38. Cf. श्रीसेउणाख्येन नृपेण प्रधानयुक्तेन विचार्य हट्टद्वयं दत्तम् । I. A., XII, p. 127.

less puppets in the hands of their tyrant masters. The same may perhaps have been the case under some of the Rāshṭrakūṭa rulers like Govinda II or Govinda IV, who were notoriously licentious. But the power, influence and utility of a ministry vary with the capacity, nature and temperament of the king and the ministers even in the limited monarchies of our present day. The same may have been the case in a slightly aggravated degree in the past, when the constitutional checks of the modern types were unknown. But these occasional exceptions do not disprove the proposition that under normal conditions abler ministers exercised a great influence on the administration in the age of the Rāshṭrakūṭas. How the weal of the kingdom was regarded as very intimately connected with the ministry may be seen from the following verse in a grant of Govana III of the Nikumbha feudatory family of Khandesh which, though belonging to a slightly later time than our period, may be regarded as embodying the views of the Rāshṭrakūṭa age as well:—

राष्ट्रस्य पुष्टिस्स्वजनस्य तुष्टिः ।
धर्मस्य वृद्धिस्सकलार्थसिद्धिः ॥
नन्दन्ति सन्तः प्रसरन्ति लक्ष्म्यः ।
श्रीचंगदेवे सति सत्प्रधाने ॥[39]

'When Changadeva was the good premier, the nation flourished, subjects and allies were content, religion (*i. e.* virtue) increased, all aims were attained, the wise were happy and prosperity was visible everywhere.'

Our records being usually copper plate grants do not dilate upon the merits and qualifications of ministers. The Salotgi inscription of Kṛshṇa III, however, shows that ministers were expected to be learned and well-versed in the science of politics.[40] Some of them, like Nārāyaṇa of this record,

39. I. A., VIII, p. 41.
40. Cf. पारगो राजविद्यानां कविमुख्यः प्रियंवदः । E. I., IV, p. 60.

were also poets, as was the case in the age of the great Guptas as well.[41]

Arthaśāstra, book I, chapter 3, Śāntiparvan, chapters 82, 83 and 85, Kāmandaka-Nitisāra IV, 25–31, Nitivākyāmṛta X, 5, Sukra II, 52–64, Bārhaspatya Arthaśāstra II, 42, etc., lay down in great details the qualifications of ministers. But a perusal of these passages does not leave the impression that ministers were expected to be military leaders or generals. Kāmandaka and Somadeva observe in passing that ministers should be brave and Somadeva adds that he should know the use of missiles but even such general statements are not made by any of the remaining writers on the topic. In the Deccan during the period under review we, however, find that ministers were very frequently military leaders and were accustomed to take a leading part in the warfare of the times, Thus Chāmuṇḍarāya, a minister of Noḷambāntaka Mārasiṁha who was a feudatory of Kṛshṇa III, had won for his master the battle of Gonur by defeating the Noḷambas;[42] in 1024 A.D. the minister of records and the director-general of registration in the administration of the later Chālukyas had the title of '*Mahāprachaṇḍadaṇḍa-nāyaka*', showing that he was a high military or police-officer. If we travel a century more, we find a reference to ministers being chased in battle in the Teridal inscription.[43] This record further shows that all the five ministers of Kalachuri Bijjaladeva were military leaders or *Daṇḍanāyakas*. Recruitment of ministers from military officers was fairly common in the Deccan of our period. It may be also pointed out that the great Shivaji had insisted that all his ministers, with the exception of the Pandit, should be competent military leaders. It is possible to conjecture that most of our theoretical writers do not include military ability among the qualifications of the ministers because they hailed from the north, where the

41. S'āba, a minister of Chandragupta II, was a poet as well. C. I. I. III, No. 6.

42. E. I., V, p. 173. 43. I. A., XIV, p. 26.

recruitment of ministers from the military ranks does not seem to have been very common.

The charters issued by the Śilāhāras, who were the feudatories of the Rāshṭrakūṭas in Konkan, frequently describe the whole administrative machinery, naming all the ministers and their respective portfolios. Thus under the S'ilāhāra prince Chittarājadeva, the ministry consisted of five members in 1024 A.D.[44] 61 years later under king Anantadeva of the same dynasty it was reduced to four.[45] The Yādavas of Chandor, who were ruling over a petty state, had a ministry of seven in 1069 A.D.[46] It is to be very much regretted that the Rāshṭrakūṭa secretariate did not follow the practice of the Konkan feudatories and name the various ministers and their portfolios in the copper plates grants. We have, therefore, very little information about the actual strength of the Rāshṭrakūṭa ministry and the various portfolios of its members. A perusal of the provisions upon the subject in the Nīti and Smriti works shows that there were no hard and fast rules about the strength of the ministry. The number varied from 8 to 20; some predecessors of Kauṭalya preferred very small ministries of 2 to 4. In actual practice the Hindu king seems to have remembered the saying of Kauṭalya that the strength of the ministry should vary with the needs of the situation and acted accordingly. Considering the extent of the Rāshṭrakūṭa empire, we may well presume that the ministry at the capital must have been fairly large, since those of the smaller contemporary feudatory states consisted of as many as 5 to 7 members. Unfortunately very few of the ministers are actually mentioned in our epigraphical records; their number and portfolios will have, therefore, to be inferred from the practice of the contemporary dynasties in the south.

The Sukranīti, which is a fairly late work, gives prominence to Pradhāna or the premier whom it describes as

44. I. A., V, p. 278. 45. I. A., IX, p. 35. 46. E. I., II, p. 225.

sarvadars'in or general superintendent over the members of the ministry.[47] Jīyanta, who is called *sarvasya anushṭhātā* or the person in charge of all administration in a record from Halasi belonging to the 6th century A.D.,[48] Babhīyaka, who is styled as a *mahāpradhāna* or the prime-minister in the Vaghli inscription of Seuṇachaṇḍra, dated 1069 A.D.,[49] and the premier of the Yādava ruler Kannara, who is designated as *sarvādhikārin* or the officer with powers over the whole administration,[50] were all of them occupying the status corresponding to that of the *Sarvadars'ī Pradhāna* of S'ukra. Bhadravishṇu, who was a *Purāṇāmātya* under Kapardin, a feudatory of Amoghavarsha I,[51] and Kṛshṇambhatta, who was a *mahāmātya* under Dantivarman of the Gujrat Rāshṭrag kūṭa branch in 867 A.D.,[52] were also holding similar positions in the respective administrations. Since earlier contemporary and subsequent administrations are seen to be having the post of the premier in the ministry, it may be regarded as almost certain that the Rāshṭrakūṭa administration could have formed no exception to the general rule. As in modern times so in our period too, the premiers often used to take some particular portfolio as well. Thus the premier of the Śilāhāra ruler Anantadeva was also the Lord High Treasurer in 1085 A D. [53] and that of the Yādava king Seuṇachandra II was also in charge of the revenue administration.[54]

Owing to his exalted position the premier often enjoyed the status of a Mahāsāmanta entitled to the Pañchamahās'abdas; he was also saluted by the feudatory chiefs of the Imperial power.[55] It is no wonder then that we sometimes find feudatory chiefs making grants at the dictation of the premiers of their overlords. When the king was temporarily absent from the capital or was unable to attend to duty owing

47. II, 82. 48. I. A., VI, p. 24. 49. E. I., II, p. 225.
50. I. A., VII, p. 304. 51. I. A., XII, p. 136.
52. E., I., VI, p. 287. 53. I. A., IX, p. 35.
54. I. A., XII, p. 127. 55. See *ante*. p. 160.

to illness or some other similar reason, the administration was entrusted to the premier, as would appear from an anecdote narrated by Mahmud Ufi.[56] Such, of course, would have been the case when the heir-apparent was too young to assume the responsibility of the administration.

The designation of the Foreign Minister, who has been invariably called a *dūta* in the works on politics like the Arthaśāstra, Rājadharmaparvan and Manusmṛti (chapter VII) etc., seems to have undergone a change by this time throughout India. Most of the epigraphical records use the more pompous and expressive title of *Mahāsandhivigrāhaka* to denote the person who held that responsible office in the ministry. This minister figures several times in the Rāshṭrakūṭa record, and we see him usually entrusted with the drafting of the copper plate charters creating alienated holdings. One expects the Revenue Minister to draft such charters, but the work was usually entrusted to the secretariate of the foreign minister, probably because the charters had to describe the genealogy and the exploits of the grantor and his family and the foreign office had the most reliable and up-to-date information on the point. It would be interesting to note that there is an agreement in this respect between the epigraphical practice and the dicta of the contemporary Smritis on the point. An anonymous text quoted in the *Mitākshārā* on Yājñavalkya I 319—20 states:—

संधिविग्रहकारी तु भवेद्यस्तस्य लेखकः ।
स्वयं राज्ञा समादिष्टस्स लिखेद्राजशासनम् ॥

'The drafter (of the copper plate charter) should be the person who is the foreign minister; he should draft the charter as dictated by the king himself.' The *Mitākshara* itself adds that the charter should be caused to be drafted by the foreign minister and by no one else.

56. Elliot. II, p. 163.

Rāshṭrakūṭas had several feudatories and neighbours. Mahāsandhivigrāhaka or the chief foreign minister must, therefore, have had several ordinary Sandhivigrāhakas under him. This inference, suggested by the formation of these two words, is confirmed by the Bhandup plates of Chhittarājadeva from which we learn that among the members of that king's ministry Sihapeya was the principal Sandhivigrāhaka and S'rī-Kapardin was Karṇāṭaka-Sandhivigrāhaka or the foreign minister for Karnatak. If the small feudatory kingdom of the S'ilāhāras required two foreign office officials both of the status of a minister, the ministry of the big Rāshṭrakūṭa empire must have had at least about half a dozen foreign ministers, bearing titles like Gurjara-Pratihāra-mahāsandhivigrāhaka, Gauḍa-mahāsandhivigrāhaka, Pallava-mahāsandhivigrāhaka etc. The post of the foreign minister was an important one; the well-being and prosperity of the kingdom depended upon his skill and ability. It is, therefore, natural that he should have often enjoyed the dignity and status of a Sāmanta entitled to the Pañchamahāśabdas under the Rāshṭrakūṭa administration.[57] As he had to draft foreign despatches, he was expected to be skilful in penmanship.[58]

A third member of the ministry figuring in Rāshṭrakūṭa records is the chief justice who is mentioned in the Sanjan plates of Amoghavarsha I as the drafter of the grant. The chief justice is mentioned as a member of the ministry in almost all the works on administration and he was the final appellate authority for cases coming from the lower courts, except when the king decided them himself.

Since many of the ministers and governors were military leaders, it is obvious that the commander-in-chief must have been a member, and an important one, of the ministry. *Nītivākyamṛta*[59] no doubt lays down that commanders of the army should not be members of the council, but S'ukra

57. E. I., X, p. 89. 58. *Nītivakyāmṛta*, XXXII, 2.
59. Chapter X, 101-102.

includes the commander-in-chief in the ministry and the Deccan administrations are seen to be following the view of S'ukra, rather than that of the Deccanese Somadeva. The war-minister is called *Sachiva* by S'ukra,[60] *Kampana* by Kalhaṇa[61] and *Mahāprachaṇḍa-daṇḍanāyaka* by a Yādava record. The Gahadwala records use the prosaic title of *Senāpati*. It is extremely probable that in the Rāshṭrakūṭa ministry there may have been several war-ministers like the foreign ministers. The empire was a large one and constantly engaged in warfare with its neighbours; hence this inference seems to be most natural and almost certain. The status of generals and war-ministers was very high. Kālidāsa, the commander-in-chief of the forces of Jagadekamalla, was also his premier as already shown. The Kalas inscription of Govinda IV[62] informs us that generals were supplied with palatial buildings, were permitted to use elephants for riding, were invested with brilliant robes, and cunningly worked staffs, which were the insignia of their office, and were authorised to use a multitude of curiously made parasols. They had, like the Mahāsāmantas, the great musical instruments of their own office. These privileges are no doubt mentioned in connection with generals. But we have seen already that even civil ministers were generals and, therefore, the war-minister could hardly have been a civilian; hence he must have enjoyed similar, if not higher, honours and privileges. Similar previleges were continued under the later Chālukyas, one of whose generals, Kālidāsa, was the supreme chief of great feudatories and entitled to the Pañchamahāśabdas.[63] Examples are not unknown of grateful monarchs commemorating the memory of their successful generals by granting them villages renamed after them.[64] When it is remembered that during our period the successful general of to-day had every chance of becoming a king or even an emperor to-morrow, the privileges

60. II. 90. 61. VII, 365. 62. E. I., XIII, p. 334.
63. I. A., VI, p. 139. 64. I. A., VIII, pp.279–80.

associated with the office of a general or war-minister need not cause any surprise.

Purohita, who was since early times an important member of the ministry,[65] seems to have ceased to belong to that body in the period we are studying. In the S'ilāhāra records he is differentiated from *Mantrins* and *Amātyas*,[66] and in the *Nitivākyāmṛta*[67] and Gahadwala records from the *mantrins*.[68] We do not possess any evidence about the Rāshṭrakūṭa administration, but it is not improbable that here too he may have been an officer of the royal household rather than a member of the ministry. The place of the *Purohita* was taken in our period by an officer whose business it was to excercise general superintendence over religion and morality. *Paṇḍita*, the minister of morality and religion in the *S'ukranīti*, seems to embody the tradition of the *Dhammamahāmātyas* of Asoka, *Samaṇa-mahāmātas* of the Āndhras[69] and the *Vinayasthitisthāpakas*[70] of the Guptas. The tradition was continued in the north by the Chedis, one of whose records mentions *Dharmapradhāna* in addition to *Mahāpurohita*.[71] The office existed under the early Rāshṭrakūṭa ruler Nannarāja in 708 A.D.,[72] and the officer bore the significant title of *Dharmāṅkus'a*. It is not unlikely that the descendants of Nannarāja may have continued the office when they rose to the imperial position in the Deccan. One may be reasonably certain that at least under kings like Amoghavarsha I and Amoghavarsha III, who were more interested in matters

65. Cf. Gautama, II, 2. 12. 17. Budhāyana Dharma-Sūtra. I. 10. 7. Arthas'āstra I Chap. 10; Kāmandaka IV, 32. S'ukra III, 78.

66. Bhadup plates, I. A., V., p. 277. 67. XI, 2.

68. E. I., XI, p. 24. 69. Nasik Inscriptions, E. I., VIII, p. 91.

70. A seal of this officer was discovered at Vaisali by Bloch: A. S. R., 1903-4, p. 109.

71. Kumbhi plates of Vijayasimha, J. A. S. B. XXXI, p. 116.

72. Multai plates, I. A., XVIII, p. 230.

spiritual than temporal, the office must have been revived, if it had been allowed to lapse under their predecessors.

Amātya or the Revenue Member figures in a record of the Yādavas of Chandor, belonging to the 11th century.[73] It is obvious that a similar portfolio must have existed under the Rāshṭrakūṭas as well. The functions of this minister must have been similar to those described by writers like S'ukra (II 103-5) and Somadeva (XVIII). In the Malkhed administration he must have had a very big staff and secretariate under him, for, as will be shown in the next chapter, the central administration of the Rāshṭrakūṭas had hardly left any revenue powers in the hands of the provincial governors and the district officers. In our grants we no doubt find the king making the grants and the foreign minister usually drafting them; but the officer who must have been principally consulted by the king must obviously have been the Revenue Member or Amātya, whose office used to keep the necessary records connected with land tenures and ownership. The Inspector General of Records must have been working under the supervision and control of the Revenue Minister. He is not mentioned in Rāshṭrakūṭa records, but documents of contemporary dynasties refer to him and mention his designation sometimes as '*Mahākshapaṭalika*' and sometimes as *S'āsanādhikārin.*' From the Miraj plates of Jagadekamalla[74] we learn that this officer had a big clerical establishment under him; when his *Mahākshapaṭalika* interviews Harsha we find him accompanied by a number of *Karaṇis* or clerks. There is ample evidence to show that revenue records were carefully preserved in the Rāshṭrakūṭa administration. One instance may suffice. Dhruva I of the Gujarat branch had alienated a village named Trennā in favour of a Brahmana. We find the grant renewed by his grandson Dhruva II when he ascended the throne. When Gujrat branch came to an end by the annexation of its dominions by the Malkhed house, we find

73. E. I. II, p. 225. 74. I. A., VIII, p. 11.

the descendant of the previous donees approaching Indra III to get his title confirmed by the new administration.[75] The history of this village makes it graphically clear that the secretariate of the governments of our period used to preserve careful records bearing upon land-ownership. The originals of the copper plates were preserved at the district head-quarters; the Bhadana plates of Aparājita,[76] issued in 997 A.D., expressly declare that the original draft of the copper plates in question was preserved at Sthānaka or modern Thāna, which was the head-quarter of the division. The copper plates were carefully compared with the original draft when they were inscribed by the smith; the Surat plates of Karka, which I am editing, state at the end that the chief of the imperial secretariate had certified that the contents of the plates, as they were engraved on copper, were identical with the original draft. From the Daulatpura plates of Bhoja[77] we learn that if the copper-plates granted by the grantor were lost by the donee, government used to enquire into his claims by a reference to its secretariate.

Treasurer, who is stylled as *Samāhartā* by Kautalya and *Sumantra* by S'ukra, was another member of the ministry. *Saṁgṛhītṛ* who figures in the list of the *Ratnins* of the Vedic period was discharging similar functions. We do not find this minister mentioned in the records of the Rāshtrakūṭa dynasty, but he figures in S'ilāhāra records bearing the title of *Bhāṇḍāgārika*. A large part of government revenues in our period was collected in kind and so this title given to the minister in charge of the treasury is significant. In 1094 A.D., S'ilāhāra king Anantadeva had a small ministry of only 3, and yet Bhāṇḍāgārika was included in it. This would show that the office was regarded as very important; Mahābhārata, (S'āntiparvan 130, 35), Kāmandaka (XXI, 33), Nītivākamṛta (XXI, 5) etc. declare that the treasury was the very root of the state and must be properly looked after. The treasurer figures

75. E. I., IX, p. 24. 76. E. I., III, p. 271. 77. E. I., V, p. 208.

invariably in the Gahadwala copper plates and his omission in our records must be due to the fact that the Rāshṭrakūṭa secretariate was not following the practice of mentioning all the ministers and their different portfolios in the copper plate charters.

Pratinidhi is the only minister mentioned by Sukra whom we miss in our epigraphical records. His function was to act for the king and S'ukra gives him a status inferior only to that of the heir-apparent.[78] His absence in our records may be due to the fact that kings of our period were accustomed to attend to the administration either themselves or through their heir-apparents, but not through a *Pratinidhi*. Palitana plates of S'ilāditya, dated 574 A.D.[79] mention an officer called *Rājasthānīya*, immediately after Rājaputra and before Amātya; he may, therefore, be possibly occupying the position of the Pratinidhi of S'ukra. The Antroli-Chharoli plates of Rāshṭrakūṭa Karkka,[80] however, use the term *Rājasthānīya* to denote royal officers of a very low grade. It would, therefore, appear that Pratinidhi or Rājasthānīya was not a usual member of the ministry in our period. It may be pointed out that among the writers on political science only S'ukra includes him in the ministry.

Our records supply us with very little information about the manner in which the daily business of administration was carried on at the capital. The secretariate at Malkhed must have been a big one; it must have been divided into several branches, each supervised over by its chief. S'ukra lays down that each minister was to be assisted by two secretaries,[81] but in big empires like those of the Guptas, the Rāshṭrakūṭas and the Gurjara-Pratihāras, the actual number of secretaries must have been obviously greater. The same writer lays down that ministerial orders were to be approved by the king before they were issued;[82] this practice, too, we may well presume

78. II. 71. 79. E. I. XI, p. 115. 80. J. B. B. R. A. S., XVI, p. 108.
81. II, 109-10. 82. II. 363-9.

was followed in our period, especially since towards the end of the Surat plates of Karkka, we find the king expressly stating that he had perused the document. Some of the Chola records show that royal orders, when drafted by the secretariate, were countersigned by the Chief Secretary;[83] in our documents, however, we come across the royal sign-manual, and the names of the composer of the grant and the person who conveyed it to the grantee. Ministers and Secretaries are conspicuous by their absence. It is, however probable that daily routine orders may have been issued by the ministers with the counter-signature of the king or the heir-apparent.

CHAPTER IX

Provincial, District, Divisional and Town Government

As shown already in Chapter VII, the Rāshṭrakūṭa empire was divided into several provinces or *rāshṭras* which were approximately of the same size as the modern division consisting of about 5 or 6 districts. The number of the *rāshṭras* included in the empire is not known, but to judge from its extent, it could not have been less than about 20 or 25. Some of the governors of these provinces were royal princes, as we have seen already;[1] others were appointed in recognition of their distinguished military services as shown, for instance, by the appointment of Bankeya to the viceroyalty of Banavasi 12,000 under Amoghavarsha I. The provincial governors had their own courts at their capitals which were replicas of the imperial court on a smaller scale. They were usually of the status of the *Mahāsāmanta* or the *Mahāmaṇḍaleśvara* and often bore the title of king (*Rājā* in Sanskrit or *Rasa* in Canarese). Thus the governor of Banavasi under Dhruva was called Mārakka-rasa and the one under Govinda III,

83. S. I. I. III, Nos. 151, 205. 1. *Ante* p. 153

Rājāditya-rāja-paramesvara.[2] Bankeya and his descendants, who were ruling the same province from about 850 A.D., were hereditary *Mahāsāmantas*. It will be soon shown that the feudatory status was enjoyed even by lower officers like *vishayapatis*. The reason why these district and provincial governors were allowed to use the feudatory titles seems to be that some of them were the descendants of the local kings who were once independent, but were subsequently conquered by the imperial power, and continued in the government of their patrimony as its own officers or governors This practice, recommened by Manu,[3] was followed in practice on many occasions in Ancient India.

In the Rāshṭrakūṭa administration the provincial governors had considerable powers over their subordinates. Some idea of this control may be had by a few concrete cases. In 912 A.D., when Mahāsāmanta Kaḷaviṭṭarasa was the governor of Banavasi, a subordinate of his, who was the Mamlatdar or Tahsildar (Nāḷgāvuṇḍa) of Giduvalge 70, became disaffected and was about to escape to the neighbouring kingdom of Gangawadi. While attempting to do so, he was arrested in Kumbise district by the orders of the governor.[4] When Chitravāhana, the Commissioner of Alurakheda 6,000, became insubordinate in c. 797 A.D., the governor of Banavasi had to lead an attack against him.[5] These instances would make it clear that the provincial governors had large military forces under them, which were used in times of peace for controlling local officers and feudatories and for preserving internal peace and order. In times of war with the neighbouring kingdoms these forces were requisitioned by the imperial government to fight its own battles; this is made clear by the Konnur inscription of Amoghavarsha I,[6] where we find the Banavasi governor now fighting with the Gangas, then running up to the capital

2. E. C., VIII, Sorab Nos. 40 and 22. 3. VII, 202.
4. E. C., VIII, Sorab No. 88. 5. *Ibid*, Nos. 10 and 22.
6. E. I., VI, p. 29.

to quell an insurrection there with his own battalions, and then again joining the imperial army in its expedition against the Pallavas. The same record represents Bankeya as coming at the head of the hereditary (*Maula*) forces; this would show that military service was a normal feature of the duties of the provincial governors and that they used to maintain hereditary troops which were probably maintained, as will be shown in Chapter XII, by the assignment of entire villages to them.

Provincial governors were also at the head of the revenue administration. This would be clear from the fact that they are invariably mentioned among the officers requested not to interfere with the peaceful enjoyment of the rent-free lands and villages granted by the emperors. Revenue settlement of the villages and fields in their jurisdiction was carried out by these officers in conjunction with the local bodies; one such fresh settlement necessitated in 941 A.D. by the drying up of an old canal is referred to in an inscription hailing from the province of Banavasi.[7]

The *Rāshtrapatis* of the Rāshtrakūṭa administration were occupying approximately the position of the Rajjukas of Asoka, but they did not enjoy the same autonomy; the central government at Malkhed exercised a much greater control over them. Though often enjoying the status of Mahāmaṇḍaleśvaras or Mahāsāmantādhipatis, they had no power of making grants of villages; even Bankeya, the favourite governor of Banavasi under Amoghavarsha I, had to seek imperial permission in order to alienate a village in favour of a Jain temple.[8] In the Nidgundi inscription of Amoghavarsha I[9] we no doubt find Bankeya giving 6 mattars of cultivable land to a temple of Mahādeva at the request of his son; but it is not clear whether the land granted was government property or part of the private landed estate of the governor. Very probably the latter may have been the case;

7. E. C., VIII, Sorab No. 83.

8. Konnur Inscription, E. I., VI, p. 29. 9. E. I., VII, p. 214.

if so, the statement of Vijñāneśvara at Yājñavalkya-smṛti, I, 318, that land could be given in charity only by a king and not by a subordinate officer seems to have been based on contemporary practice in the Deccan. The Hatti-Mattur inscription from Dharwar District[10] belonging to the reign of Indra III does not really go against this conclusion; for it says that Leṇḍeyarasa, the officer over Purigeri 300 *caused to be allotted* the village of Vattavur. The construction of the sentence becomes explicable only on the assumption that Leṇḍeya did not himself make the grant, but only procured the imperial sanction for the alienation of the village in favour of the temple.

The patronage under the control of the Rāshṭrapatis does not seem to have been extensive. In the Imperial Gupta administration, the *uparikas* or provincial viceroys could appoint *vishayapatis* or district officers and *nagarapatis* or town prefects in the territory under their jurisdiction.[11] Under the Rāshṭrakūṭa administration, however, the posts of *Vishayapatis* and even *bhogapatis* or Tahsildars were filled by the emperor himself. From the Nilgund inscription[12] it is evident that the governor of Belvola 300 was appointed by the emperor Amoghavarsha I himself. Only petty offices like those of the supervisors over very small units, consisting of 10 or 12 villages, seem to have been filled by the *Rāshṭrapatis*, since we find these appointments very often going to their own relatives.[13]

As observed already, the *Rāshṭrapatis* seem to have been assisted in their administrative work by a council of *Rāshṭra-mahattaras*. The probable nature and powers of this council have been already discussed in an earlier chapter.[14]

Vishayapatis

District officers were a replica on a smaller scale of the *Rāshṭrapatis*. We have seen just now how even small Tahsil or Taluka officers had to be suppressed by military force

10. I. A., XII, p. 225. 11. E. I., XV, p. 130. 12. E. I., VII, p. 214.
13. See E. I., VI, p. 102, and VII, p. 214. 14. *Ante* pp. 159-60.

when grown insubordinate; it is, therefore, clear that all the officers like the district, subdivisional and Taluka officers had some military forces under their command. Some of the district officers or *Vishayapatis* enjoyed the feudatory status like the provincial governors; thus Kundama-rāja, the governor of Kuntala vishaya in 1019 A.D., was a *mahāmaṇḍaleśvara* entitled to the Pañchamahāśabdas.(15) Whether all the district officers enjoyed this status is doubtful.

Vishayapatis exercised considerable revenue powers, since they are invariably mentioned in the copper plates among the officers requested not to disturb the possession of the donees of the lands or villages granted. They must have been obviously responsible to the provincial governors or to the central government for the revenue of their districts. Remission of taxes by subordinate officers required their sanction in order to be operative,(16) but it is not clear whether they had not themselves to refer the matter to their superiors before passing their own orders on the point. In the Gupta administration the Vishayapatis had the power to sell the waste lands situated within their own jurisdiction on behalf of the central government; it is not known whether the Rāshṭrakūṭas had permitted them similar powers. The administration was highly centralised, and it would be no wonder if we discover a record proving that no such powers were delegated to them.

Vishayapatis were associated with a council of *Vishaya-mahattaras* in their administrative work. This body consisted of the notables of the district and its probable nature and powers have been already discussed on an earlier occasion.(17)

Sub-divisional and Taluka Officers

Districts or Vishayas were divided into several sub-divisions known as Bhuktis comprising of about 100 to 500

15. I. A., V, p. 17. 16. Kunihalimalli inscription, E. I., XVI, p. 280.
17. *Ante*, pp. 159–60.

villages.[18] The officers over these divisions, which roughly corresponded sometimes to modern sub-divisions of the district, and sometimes to the Talukas, were known as *Bhogikas* or *Bhogapatis*. These officers did not usually possess the feudatory status but were generally commoners; Devaṇayya, for instance, who was administering Belvola 300 and was a favourite of Amoghavarsha I, was only a commoner. We sometimes find even these officers possessing feudatory titles,[19] but these cases are exceptional and rare. These officers were appointed directly by the central government as shown already.

Bhuktis were subdivided into smaller circles comprising of about 10 to 30 villages. Officers over these seem to have been appointed, as shown above, by the provincial or district officers. Very often even these petty posts went to military captains; we find the Ganga ruler Būtuga II appointing Maṇalera to the post of the supervisor over Atkur 12 as a reward for his conspicuous bravery in the Chola war.[20]

Imperial officers appointed over the subdivisions and Talukas administered their areas with the help of hereditary revenue officers. These officers were known as *Nāḍgāvuṇḍas* in Karnatak and *Des'a-grama-kūṭas* in Maharashtra. A country headman or Nāḍgāvuṇḍa of Belvola 300 is mentioned in a record hailing from that division,[21] and the record in question makes it clear that this officer was different from the governor of Belvola 300 appointed by the central government. The Managoli inscription of 1161 A.D. enumerates among the officers assembled on the occasion 'the 16 of the 8 districts.' This expression '16 of the 8 districts' can be best understood on the hypothesis that each of these 8 districts was in charge of two officers, one hereditary and the other appointed by the central government. Purigeri 300 and Belvola 300 each

18. *Ante* p. 136. 19. I. A., XII, p. 225. 20. E. I., VI, p. 56.
21. E. I., XIV, p. 366.

possessed a headman who was different from Mārasiṁha, who was the officer appointed by the central government over those divisions.[22] The Kumonelihalli inscription of Kṛshṇa II mentions Aladitya Gova and Kalpata as the officers holding the country shṛievalty of Anniga 100;[23] appointment of joint Mamlatdars by the central government over a Taluka of about 100 villages is hardly an intelligent administrative procedure; probably one of the two officers, therefore, was the nominee of the central government and the other the hereditary Nāḍgâvuṇḍa or the country headman of the division. In 874 A.D., when Bankeya was the governor over Banavasi 12,000, his son Kundatte was the officer over the Nilgundige group of 12 villages. When Bankeya proceeded to make a grant of five *mattars* of land at his son's request to a local temple, the record informs us that he summoned his son Kundatte and Rāpa.[24] It is almost certain that this Rāpa was the hereditary headman of Nilgundige 12 in co-operation with whom Kundatte, the nominee of the central government, was administering the group of villages under his charge. Only on this assumption we can explain as to why he was summoned along with Kundaṭṭe. A *des'a-grāmakūṭa-kshetra* or the rent-free field of the district headman is twice mentioned in a spurious Ganga record from Lakshmeshvar; this would show that there existed headmen of districts who were partly remunerated by hereditary rent-free lands, as is still the case with the Deshpandes and Sardeshpandes of Maharashtra. Tuppad Kurahatti inscription of Kṛshṇa III[25] mentions a tax which the cultivators had to pay in addition to the normal government demand for the remuneration of the country gāvuṇḍas,—a tax which was as high as the king's tax, probably because the latter was low owing to the field being temple property. This record too supplies clear evidence proving the

22. I. A., XII, pp. 27 ff. 23. E. I., XVI, p. 280.

24. E. I., VII, pp. 202 ff. 25. E. I., XIV, p. 366.

existence of country headmen similar to village headmen. Like the Deshpandes of the Maratha period, these posts were hereditary; an inscription from Shikarpur informs us that when the Nālgāvuṇḍa of Nagarkhande died while fighting for Kaḷaviṭṭa-rasa, the governor of Banavasi, his wife succeeded to the office which she ably managed for 7 years. Then when she decided to perform the *sallekhanā* vow and die, she sent for her daughter and nominated her to her office.[26] This case would make it clear that the post of the country headman was, like that of the village headman, a non-official and hereditary one. He being a man of the people must have served the purpose of popularising the administration to some extent. We do not know whether there existed popular bodies of *mahattaras* to co-operate with the divisional and subdivisional officers. But since there certainly existed, as will be shown in the next chapter, such bodies in villages there is nothing improbable in the existence of corresponding bodies for these administrative units. It is, however, doubtful wheher they were more formal and definite than the councils of the *vishaya*- and *rāshṭramahattaras*.

The subdivisional and Taluka officers were under the control of the Vishayapatis and the Rāshṭrapatis; we have already seen how the Nāḷgāvuṇḍa of Jiduvalge 70 was immediately arrested by the governor of Banavasi when he was suspected of sedition and disaffection. This incident will give some idea of the rigorous control exercised over these officers by their superiors. They had no powers to alienate any revenues on their own account; the Kyasnur inscription of Kṛshṇa III[27] refers to the remission taxation given to a field of two *mattars* by the officer over the Edevola division for the purpose of the local tank; it would appear that these officers had the power of assigning some revenues for public purposes. It is, however, not unlikely that even for such remissions the

26. E. C., VII, No. 219. 27. E. I., XVI, p. 281.

previous sanction of the higher authorities may have been necessary; otherwise, the meticulous way in which the above inscription states that at the time of the grant Maharaja Kannara was the supreme lord, Maharaja Kaḷaviṭṭa was the governor of Banavasi, and the donee was the gāvuṇḍa over the Edevolal division will have hardly any significance. The Sirur inscription of Amoghavarsha I[28] states that Devaṇayya, the governor over Belvola 300, had remitted a tax on ghee levied at the locality for his own spiritual benefit on the occasion of an eclipse. This record does not invalidate the view above advanced, that these officers had no powers to alienate the public revenues under their own authority. Taxes in kind on food-stuffs, vegetables etc. formed part of the pay of the local officers in our period, and this custom persisted in the Deccan down to the British rule.[29] It is, therefore, almost certain that the tax on ghee remitted by Devaṇayya in favour of the temple formed part of his salary and, therefore, he could dispose it off in any way he liked. The question as to how the officer could assign a part of the salary of his post and thus reduce the emoluments of his successor is also not difficult to answer; the numerous resumptions even of land-grants show that the grants, even when made in favour of Brahmans and temples, were often revoked; the successor of Devaṇayya had, therefore, the power either to continue or revoke the grant made by his predecessor according to his own inclinations.

Town Administration

In the Rāshṭrakūṭa period the cities and towns were in charge of prefects who were designated as *purapatis* or *nagarapatis*. These officers are rarely referred to in the Rāshṭrakūṭa copper plate grants, but they are almost invariably mentioned in the grants of the Śilāhāras, who were the Konkan feuda-

28. I. A., XII, p. 218.

29. Altekar, *Village Communities in Western India*, pp. 10-11.

tories of the imperial power.[30] Military captains were often appointed to the posts ; thus Rudrapayya, who was the prefect of Saravatura or modern Soratur in Karnatak, was one of the body-guards of the emperor Kṛshṇa III.[31] Mahādeva and Pātāladeva, the joint prefects of Badami under Jagadekamalla in 1140, were both of them Daṇḍanāyakas or military officers. Sometimes learned men also were appointed to these posts ; the 12 officers in charge of Teridal in S. M. C. are described in 1123 A.D. as promoting the everlasting six systems of philosophy.[32] One expects active interest in art or philosophy from men of letters rather than from military generals. Kuppeya, a governor of Soratur under Amoghavarsha I, was a Mahāsāmanta; it would, therefore, appear that some of these town prefects enjoyed the dignity and status of feudatories, as was the case with some of the *Rāshṭrapatis* and *Vishayapatis*.

The city affairs were managed by the prefects with the help of non-official committees. Such committees were fairly common during the period of Ancient Indian History ; they are referred to by Megasthenes and Kauṭalya, they existed at Nasik under the Sātavāhanas,[33] in Puṇḍravardhana division and Kathiawar under the Imperial Guptas,[34] and at Bāhuloḍa, Prabhāsa and Aṇahilapaṭṭaṇa under the Gujarat Chālukyas.[35] Coming to our own period and province we find that the administration of Guṇapura in Konkan was vested in 997 A.D. in a prefect assisted by a committee of two bankers Ambus'reshṭhin and Vappaiyas'reshṭhin, a merchant called Chelappaiyu, a Brahmana named Govaneya and some.

30. See Bhadana plates of Aparājitadeva, 997 A.D., E. I., III, p. 273, Bhandup plates of Chittarāja, 1018 A.D., I. A., V, p. 278.

31. I. A., XII, p. 258.

32. I. A., XV, p. 15.

33. Nasik Inscription No. 12; E. I., VIII, p. 82.

34. Damodarpur plates, E. I., XV, p. 150; C. I. I., III, no. 14.

35. Altekar, *Towns and Cities in Ancient Gujarat and Kathiawar*, p. 54.

others.[36] The city of Aihole also had its own corporation under Kṛshṇa II, the constitution of which, however, is not described in the record. No clue is available to indicate the way in which these town committees were formed; there is no express reference to any election of these members. The statement

पौरत्रिवर्गप्रभृतीन् समाज्ञापयति ।

which occurs in the Silahāra records above referred to, probably refers to the three upper castes, rather than to three different constituencies. Apparently five wards of the town of Mulgund and their representatives, the Mahājanas, are mentioned in the Mulgund inscription of Pānchāladeva, dated 975 A.D.[37] This may suggest the inference that cities were divided into several wards for the purpose of representation on the city council; the inscription in question is, however, fragmentary and this conclusion is not, therefore, quite certain. The divisions into wards for the purpose of representation was known in Tamil land, as is clear from the famous Uttaramallura inscriptions,[38] and there is nothing impossible in a similar arrangement being in vogue in our province as well. There must obviously have been some kind of election or selection for constituting the town committees, since these members were non-officials and were usually not more than half a dozen or so. But the precise method adopted in the Deccan of our period cannot be determined at present for want of evidence.

Our records do not supply us with the information as to whom the town prefects were responsible for the administration. They may have been possibly under the control of the Rāshṭrapatis in whose jurisdiction their towns were situated, or perhaps to a special minister or officer at the capital. Our records hardly supply any information about the methods

36. E. I., III, p. 260. 37. E. I., VI, p. 260.
38. A. S. R., 1904–5 p. 140.

whereby the local, district, and provincial governments were supervised and controlled by the Central Government. The control and supervision were, as shown already, fairly rigorous and it may have been exercised partly through the regular official hierarchy, partly through periodical tours,—a principle recommended by Manu[40] and S'ukra[41] and practised by Asoka and Harsha,—and partly through direct orders from imperial secretariate carried by special messengers, who were known as *Vallabhājñāsañchāriṇaḥ* 'carriers of royal orders'. The precise nature of the postal arrangements made by the state in our period is not definitely known, but it is obvious that postal runners and mounted couriers must have been used for the purpose with relays at convenient intervals. Such arrangements were witnessed by Ibn Batūta in the first half of the 14th century[42] and it is very likely that Mahomedan administration may have borrowed the system from its Hindu predecessors.

Selection of Officers

It would be necessary to say a few words here about the selection of officers to the various posts mentioned above. The selection was governed partly by military, partly by hereditary, and partly by educational considerations. We have already seen how many of the ministers, and provincial, district, and town governors were military officers. Very probably they must have owed their appointments to distinguished service on the battlefield. In many cases offices were transmitted from the father to the son. The viceroyalty of Banavasi 12,000 had continued for three generations at least in the family of Bankeya, who had won it by his military achievements. When Kaṇṇapa, who had won the governorship of Purigeri 300 and Belvola 300 by his bravery on the battlefield died, his younger brother Sobhaṇa stepped into his

40. VII, 124. 41. I. 374-5. 42. Gibs, *Ibn Batuta*, p. 183.

place.[43] Kauṭalya, Manu and Śukra recommend this principle of preference for heredity and the recommendation was acted upon in the Gupta period as well, at least in some cases, as clearly appears from the Allahabad pillar inscription of Samudragupta[44] and Karmadanda inscription of Kumāragupta I.[45] From Al Masudi we learn that high offices in our period were often hereditary in India,[46] and the submissive Brahmanas, who were appointed to lower administrative posts by Kasim in Sindh after its annexation, were assured by him that their appointments would be continued hereditarily.[47] The *Rājataraṅgiṇī* also affords numerous examples of offices being transmitted hereditarily.[48] This principle was thus widely prevalent in our period and the Banavasi governorship was no solitary example. The Surat plates of Karka, which I am editing, show that the father of Nārāyaṇa, the chief Foreign Minister of that ruler, was also occupying the post to which his son was later appointed.[49] There may have been many more cases of this nature in the administration.

The minister Nārāyaṇa of Kṛshṇa III, who is described as a prominent poet, a skilful speaker, and a great expert in the science of polity,[50] did not belong to a family of hereditary ministers, as was the case with his namesake just mentioned; he was very probably selected for his educational qualifications. I-tsing, who had visited India just before our period, has recorded how distinguished scholars used to be appointed by the Valabhi administration to responsible posts,[51] and the same practice must have been fairly prevalent throughout India for obvious reasons.

Many appointments must have also gone to royal favourites, who possessed no other qualification than that of being

43. E. I., IV, p. 20. 44. C. I. I., III, p. 1. 45. E. I., X, p. 70.
46. Elliot, I, p. 20. 47. *Ibid* p. 103. 48. Cf. VIII, 2473, 3322 etc.
49. Being published in E. I., XXI. 50. E. I. IV, p. 60. 51. p. 181.

in the good books of the ruling king. This need not cause any surprise, for such scandalous appointments are by no means rare even in the present age. No concrete cases of unworthy favourites being raised to high offices are known from our records, but in contemporary Kashmir, many court-flatterers were often appointed to responsible posts by some of its worthless rulers,[52] and it is not unlikely that the phenomenon may have been repeated in the reigns of some of the dissolute monarchs of the Rāshṭrakūṭa line like Govinda II, Govinda IV and Karka II. Two of the generals of the last king are compared to the feet of Kali in a Chālukya record.[53]

The average officer of our period was highly attached to the throne; many cases are recorded in the Kashmir chronicle of loyal and devoted officers burning themselves on the funeral pyres of their dead masters.[54] The custom seems to have been fairly common in our period, for Abu Zaid also refers to it.[55] This writer informs us that at the time of the coronation of a king his deeply attached followers used to take voluntarily a portion of the rice prepared for the king on the occasion. All such persons were obliged to burn themselves when the king was dead or slain. The custom existed in Malbar during the 13th century, for it is referred to by Marco Polo also.[56] Epigraphical evidence of our period shows that Abu Zaid's account is no cock and bull story. Honale No. 47[57] informs us that when Taila II died, Boppana made good his vow, entered fire and went to heaven. We do not know from the record the occasion of this vow, but it is quite possible that it may have been the king's coronation. Two other records, Arkalgad Nos. 5 and 27, refer to two officers of the Ganga ruler, Nitimārga, who burnt themselves to death when their master died. From one of these records,

52. See *Rajataraṅgini* VII, 580, VIII, 183, etc.

53. E. I., XII, p. 152 Kauthem plates.

54. V. 206–7, VII, 481, 1488, 1490, VIII, 1447 etc.

55. Elliot, I, p. 8. 56. II, p. 339. 57. E. C., VII.

we learn that pensions were often provided for the bereaved families of such loyal servants.

Abu Ishtak Al Ishtakhri and Ibn Haukal state that the Rāshṭrakūṭa administration was very partial to the Muslims and that none but Muslims ruled over their coreligionists living in that empire.[58] This statement, if not exaggerated, will only show that the personal law of the Muslims was administered to them through their own Kazis.[59] The administration seems to have given them the same privileges, which were recommended to the guilds, traders, foresters etc., by the Smritis.[60] Muslim administrators nowhere figure in epigraphical records, and if they had really existed, the Muslim chroniclers would not have been content to observe that none but the Muslims ruled over the Muslims in the Rāshṭrakūṭa empire; they would have claimed that there were Muslim officers in the administration who were ruling over the non-Muslims as well. The statements of these Muslim writers are also sometimes wild and unreliable; some of them like Al Idrisi gravely inform us that in the kingdom of Balhara, *i. e.* Gujrat of the 12th century A.D., concubinage is permitted with all persons except married women, including even daughters, sisters, and aunts if they are unmarried.[61]

Remuneration of officers was sometimes by rent-free lands and sometimes by salaries, paid partly in cash and partly in kind. The principle of offering rent-free lands to state servants is recommended by a number of writers,[62] and we have seen already how the country headmen had their own service

58. Elliot, I, p. 27 and p. 34.

59. Such was the case in the Chinese Port of Khanafa in c. 850 A.D., where a number of Muslim traders had settled down for whom the Chinese government had appointed a Kazi to look after their religious and judicial affairs. See *Sulaiman Saudagar*, Hindi Translation, by Mahesh Prasad Sadhu, pp. 35–6.

60. Bṛhaspati, I, 26; Gautama, XI, 23; Manu, VIII, 39.

61. Elliot, I, 89.

62. Kauṭalya, II, i; Manu VII, 118–9.

lands known as *Des'a-grāmakūṭa-kshetra.*[63] It will be shown in the next chapter that village headmen also were paid partly by rent-free lands. The statement made above, that part of the salaries was probably paid in kind need not cause any surprise; for, a large part of the royal revenues were received in kind, as will be shown in chapter XI, and the staple corn often formed the principal medium of exchange. In some of the Chola records[64] the prices of articles like pulses, camphor, plantains, ghee, sugar, etc., are given not in money but in paddy. The salaries of the temple servants etc., are stated usually in paddy, sometimes in paddy and cash, and rarely in cash alone. A similar practice may have probably prevailed in the Deccan under the Rāshṭrakūṭas.

CHAPTER X

Village Administration

Several problems connected with the origin and development of the main aspects and institutions of the village life and village government have been discussed by the present writer in his *History of the Village Communities in Western India.* (Oxford University Press, Bombay 1927.) A discussion of all these problems in detail is not strictly relevant for the present work. In this chapter the information about the village government of only our period will be discussed; the reader is referred to the above mentioned book for its previous history and subsequent evolution.

The Village Headman

Every village in our period was usually under the charge of a village headman, whose office was a very ancient institution both in the south and in the north.[1] Like the headman of the Taluka and the district, the village headman was also

63. *Ante* p. 159. 64. S. I. I., II, 75, 129 &c.

1. Altekar, *Village Communities*, pp. 1-2.

a hereditary officer. He was more a representative of the people than a servant of the central government. The truth of this observation will be realised from the case of a headman in Shikarpur Taluka who died of broken heart, or perhaps committed suicide, in 999 A.D., on seeing the ruin of his own town.(2) During our period this officer was known as a Grāmakūṭa in Maharashtra and Gāvuṇḍa in Karnatak. Sometimes our records mention a Grāmapati in addition to a Grāmakūṭa;(3) it would seem that Grāmapati in such cases denotes the holder of a village *inām*. *Grāmabhokṭrs* figuring in some of the S'ilāhāra records(4) seems to belong to the same category. In 974 A.D. the village of Kadkeri in Karnatak had a village governor in addition to a village headman; the former is described as a hero in battlefield and a touchstone of heroes.(5) Some of the villages were, therefore, clearly assigned to military captains. There are examples of some others being assigned to scholars,(6) and the number of those alienated in favour of learned Brahmanas was considerable. The holders of these villages seem to be referred to by the expressions 'Grāmapatis' or 'Grāmabhoktris.' The unalienated village, however, had usually no officer appointed by the central government. It used to get its business done through the agency of the village headman.

Normally each village had one village headman; there are, however, several records of the Raṭṭas of Saundatti and of the later Chālukyas, which refer to several headmen of one and the same locality. From the five Raṭṭa records of Saundatti published by Fleet(7) we learn that Sugandhavati, Elerave, and Hasudi had twelve headmen each, while Hirayakummi had six. From a record belonging to the reign of

2. E. C., VIII, Sorab No. 234.
3. Salotgi inscription of Kṛshṇa III, Surat plates of Karka, etc.
4. *E. g.* Badana Inscription E. I., III, p. 273.
5. I. A., XII, p. 271. 6. E. I., IV, p. 64.
7. J. B. B. R. A. S., X, p. 283 ff.

Vikramāditya VI we find that Teridal had twelve headmen.[8] This large number of headmen, that we see in these localities, is rather unusual. It may be perhaps due to the fact that some of these places were big towns; it is also not unlikely that there may have been prevailing in these localities the custom of allowing the senior representatives of the main branches of the original headman's family to officiate simultaneously. Two headmen, representing the two main branches of the original stock, still function in several villages of the Deccan; this principle may have been possibly given an extended application in our period in some parts of the Rāshṭrakūṭa Empire.

The headman has been, since very early times, in charge of the defence of the village.[9] In the Rāshṭrakūṭa period the villages did not enjoy that amount of absolute peace, which they have under the present administration. There were constant wars going on, and every villager had then, unlike in the present time, the prospect of winning the general's parasol. The population was well trained in the use of arms; even the bangle sellers could drive back armed forces and fight to the bitter end.[10] The all-round training in the use of arms, the presence of numerous feudatories anxious to enlarge their dominions, and the ambition which the well-trained villagers must have had to show off their valour naturally led to several skirmishes between neighbouring villages usually occasioned by the desire to lift cattle. We find an echo of these village skirmishes in the *Nītivākyāmṛta*, a contemporary work on politics;[11] the Canarese country is still dotted with numerous *Vīrgal* records commemorating the death of the village heroes, who fell in these fights. Sorab inscriptions Nos. 102, 216, 326, 351, 454, 455 etc.[12] belonging to the reigns of Kṛshṇa II, Kṛshṇa III and Karkka II, refer to the deaths of

8. I. A., XIV, p. 14.
9. Altekar, *Village Communities*, pp. 45, 54–55.
10. E. C., VIII, Sorab No. 530. 11. XIX, 11. 12. E. C., VIII.

the village heroes in skirmishes caused by this cattle-lifting propensity,—skirmishes which remind us of the *Uttara-go-grahaṇa* episode of the Mahābhārata. Honali No. 13 immortalises the memory of another hero, who had died while fighting for the cows of his village.[13] Naregal inscription of the time of Dhruva is also of a similar purport.[14] These records, though short, are thrilling ones; they let us know how these forgotten village heroes used to fight fearlessly for the safety of the villages where they were born and bred up, and even lay down their lives cheerfully, if necessary, for that purpose. Sometimes these feuds led to the destruction of villages; a record from Hatti Mattur, belonging to the reign of Kṛshṇa I, immortalises the memory of Dasamma and Ereyya, who had died while bringing about the destruction of the village of Mattavura.[15] These village skirmishes were equally common in the Pallava and Noḷamba dominions.[16] The Rāshṭrakūṭa administration, which was fairly vigorous in revenue matters, does not seem to have taken effective steps to put an end to these village feuds. While admitting that many valuable lives must have been unnecessarily lost in these avoidable conflicts, it cannot be denied that the necessity of self-defence and the fighting atmosphere around him must have made the average villager a much abler and stronger man from the military point of view than he is to-day in the present absolutely peaceful atmosphere. Many Rāshṭrakūṭa officers were military leaders, and to them these military skirmishes may not have been quite unwelcome, as they must have kept the martial spirit alive in villages, from where the army used to get its recruits. It will be shown in the last chapter of this part how the average Deccanese in this period was eagerly enlisted in the armies of even the northern kings for his martial qualities.

13. *Ibid*, VII. 14. E. I., VI, p. 163. 15. *Ibid*, p. 162.

16. *E. g.* Ambur inscription of Nṛpatuṅgadeva, E. I., IV, p. 180, Muttugur inscription of Narasimhavarman, E. I., IV, p. 360.

Every village, therefore, as a rule, had its own militia in the Deccan of our period and the imperial army must have been largely recruited from that force. The village headman was at the head of the militia and was himself a good fighter. Sorab No. 445, dated c. 975 A.D., refers to a robber's attack on Kollana, a son of Gāvuṇḍa Kevase Kūḷa, when he fought, established his fame, and went to heaven.[17] Another record from the same place, No. 359, which refers to the death of a headman in a mutual skirmish among the Nāḷ-gāvuṇḍas, shows the same thing. A reference may also be made to an early Pallava record where we find the son of a headman receiving a grant for having slain the enemy and conducted with great devotion the wife of Yuvarājamalla and her guard.[18]

The invariable mention of the village headman in the land and village grants of our period shows that he was intimately connected with the revenue administration. Throughout the subsequent centuries under the Mahomedan, Maratha, and the British administrations, he has continued to be responsible for the village revenues.[19] In the extreme south in Tamil country where village councils were permanent bodies, meeting regularly and functioning methodically, we find, as will be soon shown, that the headman was mainly shouldering the revenue responsibility, even in the case of *Brahmadeya* villages where the village councils seem to have been most developed. The communiques of the Chola government in revenue matters were addressed to the village headmen when it wished to give publicity to any particular policy.[20] Owing to his position and status the headman must have taken a prominent part in the meetings of the village council convened for the purpose of the settlement of private

17. E. C., VIII. 18. I. A., VII, p. 104.

19. For detailed evidence about the assertions in this para the reader is referred to Altekar: *Village Commuuities*, Chap. I.

20. S. I. I., III, p. 289.

disputes in the village; he was also the village magistrate having powers to try petty criminal cases.[21] It was he again who organised public work committees and raised funds for them by public subscription and by securing government contribution, who entertained and looked after the officers of central government when on tour in the village, or went to interview them at the head-quarters of the division. The negotiations about the amount of the government demand were also carried on by him. The watch and wards arrangements were also under his control and supervision. The village records, which were regularly kept in our period, were also under his custody.

The headman was remunerated for his services in various ways. In our communities the dictum of Kauṭalya that he should be given rent-free land[22] and the rule of Manu[23] that the miscellaneous taxes in kind, that were payable daily to the king by the villagers, should be assigned to him were both followed. We have already seen that the headmen of the districts had their own rent-free lands;[24] the same principle was extended to the village headman. Their rent-free lands have continued to enjoy that character right up to the present day in Maharashtra and Karnatak.[25] A record of the Raṭṭas of Saundatti[26] states that the Gāvuṇḍa of Kadole gave 200 *mattars* of cultivable land, which was his rent-free service land, situated in the circle of the rent-free service lands of the headmen of the locality. It is, therefore, clear that most of the villages of our period had a portion of their cultivable lands assigned to their headmen's families. The above record shows that the rent-free service lands of the village headmen were regarded as alienable in the Southern

21. E. I., XI, pp. 224 ff.

22. II, 1. 23. VII, 118. 24. *Ante* p. 179.

25. Altekar, *Village Communities*, pp. 7–8.

26. J. B. B. R. A. S., X, p. 260.

Maratha Country during our period, but it is not improbable that the alienee may have been required to perform the duties of the office. It is further not clear whether this right of alienating the rent-free lands was universally enjoyed by the headmen of the Deccan or whether it was a special custom in the kingdom of the Raṭṭas of Saundatti. It is quite possible that the governments of our period may have put restrictions upon the alienation of service lands as recommended by Kauṭalya,[27] but it is not also impossible that the custom at Saundatti to permit alienation may have prevailed in other parts of the Deccan as well; for in the Maratha period, the rent-free lands and privileges of the headman were alienable.[28]

The headman continued to enjoy the taxes in kind, payable to the king by the villagers, down to the recent times. The sale deeds of the headman's office in the Maratha period show that they used to receive a share in most of the articles produced or sold in their villages, like clothes, shoes, *gur*, betel leaves etc.[29] These dues of the headman are referred to as *Maulika arhaṇas* 'perquisites of hereditary officers,' in a Kaḷachuri record.[30] A record from Soratur belonging to the time of Kṛshṇa III is very instructive in this respect. The Mahājanas of the place wished to assign to a local temple the amount of charcoal that they were paying as the royal tax. We find them requesting the headman and the *Pergade* (?) of the place to sanction this diversion of the revenues which they agreed to do. We have seen already how even the higher officers had not the power of alienating government revenues under the Rāshṭrakūṭa administration. In this record, however, when they were requested not to disturb the arrangement contemplated, the headman and the *Pergaḍe* (?) are seen

27. II, 1.

28. Sen, *Administrative System of the Marathas*, p. 185.

29. *Ibid*, p. 185.

30. I. A., IV, p. 276.

immediately washing the feet of the Mahājanas, granting their request and making a further donation of 12 *mattars* of land. It is, therefore, clear that like the income from the 12 *mattars* the proceeds of the charcoal tax must have formed part of the income of the headman and the *Pergaḍe* (?); otherwise they could not have alienated them. This record, therefore, shows that the rule of Manu that daily taxes in kind consisting of food-stuffs, fuel and other miscellaneous articles were to be assigned to the village headman was followed in the Rāshṭrakūṭa as in later times.

From the nature of his duties it is clear that the village headman must normally have been a Kshatriya; the same is the case to-day in the Deccan and Karnatak. His influence with the government was as great as that with the people. Kings never forget to include him among the officers requested not interfere with the enjoyment of the royal grants; we often find him escorting royal ladies to their destination.[31] It seems that he was entitled to receive a certain fee or tax on transfer of lands; even royal transactions were not exempt from his dues leviable on such occasions.[32] Sukra's observation that the headman of a village protects it from thieves, officers and aggression[33] was perfectly true in our period; he was the head of the village militia and to him the villagers looked for leading the village defence.[34] The headman was, therefore, as much indispensable to the people as to the government.

Village Accountant

Village accountants were hereditary officers all over the Deccan like the village headman till 1914 when most of them were induced to resign their rights in several districts. Their influence till then was as great as, if not greater than, that of the village headman. We find them figuring in the docu-

31. See *ante*, p. 192.
32. J. B. B. R. A. S., X, p. 257.
33. II, 343.
34. *Village Communities*, p. 5.

ments of the Maratha and Muslim periods also. S'ukra refers to him as *lekhaka*, whose duty was to keep accounts of income and expenditure, to receive and dispose of goods after making entries in the registers and to carry on correspondence.[35] Under the Chola administration this officer existed in all villages in Tamil country ; we see him writing the orders of the village assembly,[36] and measuring and recording the amount of paddy paid by the villagers on account of the land and other taxes.[37] He had in many places a sub-accountant under him and the pay of both is mentioned in several records. It is, therefore, strange that *lekhaka* or the village accountant should not figure in the Rāshṭrakūṭa records as he does in some of the epigraphs of the Āndhra period.[38] The village administration must have found the services of the accountant as indispensable in the Deccan as in Tamil country. It is, therefore, almost certain that he must have existed in our period. Most of our land grants mention *yuktas*, *āyuktas*, *niyuktas* or *upayuktas* after the *Grāmakūṭas* and before the *Grāma-mahattaras*.[39] The position of these officers in the official hierarchy makes it clear that they belonged to the village administration. If so, they could have hardly been any others than the village accountants and their assistants, who being in charge of the village records of rights and other files, could hardly be omitted from the list of officers to be requested not to interfere with the land or village grants.

The village accountants of our period must have been performing duties similar to those mentioned by *S'ukra-nīti* and the contemporary Chola documents. The headman was considerably engrossed in administrative, military and police duties; he could, therefore, have hardly found time to look to

35. II, 348. 36. S. I. I., II, Ukkal No. 10.

37. S. I. I., II., Nos. 22 and 23.

38. Nasik cave inscriptions Nos. 16 and 27. E., I. VIII.

39. Samangad plates, 754 A.D., I. A., XI, p. 112; Radhanpur plates, 808 A.D., E. I., IV, p. 242; Sangli plates, 933 A.D., I. A., XII, p. 251; etc.

the clerical work connected with the village administration, which must have been relegated to some other officer. Obviously it is these who are referred to by the terms *yuktas* or *niyuktas*. Some of the big villages may have had two officers to look to this clerical work; one of them may have been the accountant and the other the sub-accountant. *Upaniyuktas* and *Niyuktas* figure together in some records and that can be explained only on this hypothesis. Like the office of the village headman these offices were also very probably hereditary in our age as they were till recently. No *yuktas* or *upaniyuktas* figure as donors in our period; we hardly get any evidence suggesting that these officers wielded anything like the influence that was wielded by the village headman. It is, therefore, clear that the offices of the *yuktas* and *upaniyuktas* were more or less clerical, and did not carry the same privileges or prestige as that of the village headman.

Village Council

If the evidence about the existence, nature, and functions of the imperial, provincial, and district councils is meagre, that about the village councils is more than ample. These bodies existed throughout the Rāshṭrakūṭa dominions, though their nature and functions differed to some extent in different localities. There were roughly speaking three types of the village councils in our period, the Tamil type, the Karnatak type and the Maharashtra and Gujarat type. The last two did not differ very much from each other, but the distinction between the first type on the one hand and the last two on the other was considerable.

It was only for about 20 or 25 years in the reign of Kṛshṇa III that several districts in Tamil country were annexed to the Rāshṭrakūṭa dominions where the Tamil type of the village council prevailed. A detailed description of that type is not, therefore, strictly relevant in a work dealing with the Rāshṭrakūṭa administration. The subject has been, besides, discussed by a number of previous writers on the subject.[40] Attention will, therefore, be drawn here only to salient features of the village councils in Tamil country in order to facilitate comparison and contrast with these in Maharastra and Karnatak.

Village assemblies or councils in Tamil country consisted neither of the whole adult population, as was the case in Karnatak, nor of a few select gentlemen, as was the case in Maharashtra and Gujrat, but of about 20 to 30 individuals elected by a kind of selection by ballot.[41] There were detailed rules about the qualifications of the voters and the candidates; certain property and educational qualifications were insisted upon in the candidates along with a blameless character. Persons once elected were disqualified to stand again for election for three years, a rule apparently framed to afford opportunities to all qualified persons to serve on the village councils. The election took place annually and the members elected were known as the great men of the year (*Perumakkal*). They subdivided themselves into a number of sub-committees, as was the case with the corporation of Pāṭaliputra in the time of Chandragupta Maurya. Each sub-committee was in charge of a specific department like the village tank, the village temple, roads, adjudication, wet lands, dry lands etc. The account supplied by the Uttaramallur inscriptions is confirmed by several other records. Thus Sivachulamangalam inscription of the 16th year of the reign of Kṛshṇa III proves the existence of annual election of the village councils;[41a] the Solapuram inscription from North Arcot district discloses the existence of a temple sub-committee in that village in 953 A.D., when it formed part of the Rāshṭrakūṭa empire;[42] the Gudimallam Bana inscriptions

40. R. C. Majumdar, *Corporate Life in Ancient India*; R. K. Mookerji, *Local Government in Ancient India.*

41. A. S. R., 1904-5, pp. 140 ff.

41*a*. S. I. I., III, p. 12.

42. E. I., VII, p. 197.

A and B from Chittur district attest to the existence of a village corporation in that village, discharging trust duties, regulating the village crops, controlling the village revenues, and arranging for the works of public utility.[43]

The constitution of the village councils in Karnatak differed considerably from the above type. Our records, which are fairly numerous, refer nowhere to any election or selection of the members of the village councils, although they describe on numerous occasions the powers and functions of these bodies. But the absence of election or selection in Karnatak was due not to the village bodies being less but more democratic than was the case in Tamil country. *Mahājanas*, as the members of the village council were called in Karnatak, seemed to have included in that province in the vast majority of cases the heads of all the families residing in the village. The Kalas inscription of Govinda IV[44] is very important in this respect. The record first describes the attainments and scholarship of the 200 Brahmana householders of the *agrahāra* or the Brahmana settlement of Kadiyar, observing that the village could put to shame other Brahmana villages on account of the learning and stainless character of all its 200 householders. Later on in the record these very 200 Brahmana householders are described as the *Mahājanas*. It is, therefore, clear that the Mahājanas included almost all the heads of the families residing in the village.

A record from Bijapur district, dated 1022 A.D., is till more illuminating.[45] The inscription records a grant of 50 *mattars* of land for the village school given by the 500 Mahājanas of Perur. The land is further described as belonging to the 500 houses of Perur. It is, therefore, absolutely clear that each Mahājana represented a family in the village and that all the families were represented in the village council.

43. *Ibid*, XI, pp. 224 ff. 44. E. I., XIII, pp. 327 ff.

45. Belur grant, I. A., XVIII, pp. 273 ff.

Inscriptions from Hadali[46] and Behatti[47] in Dharwar district show that the same continued to be the case in the 11th and the 12th centuries as well. The first of these records, dated 1083 A.D., refers to an *agrahāra* village, each of the 420 Mahājanas of which is described as virtuous and learned. At its conclusion the record calls upon the 420 Mahājanas of the *agrahāra* colony to protect the grant. Since an *agrahāra* village consisted mostly of Brahmanas, it is quite clear that the Mahājanas in this case also included most of the householders of the village. The inscription hailing from Behatti, above referred to, is dated 1183 A.D., and contains a grant to the 1000 Brahmanas of the *agrahāra* settlement of Kukkanuru; the Canarese postscript records a further donation to the same body and adds:—'The one thousand and two shall unfailingly preserve this grant.' A Yādava inscription from the same locality, about half a century later in date, again refers to a grant to 1002 Brahmanas of the same place.[48] It is, therefore, clear that the agrahāra village of Kukkanuru consisted of about a 1000 householders all of whom were included in the body of the Mahājanas of the locality.

An inscription from Nadwadinge in Bijapur district, dated 902 A.D.,[49] seems to show that the Mahājanas often included not only all the householders or the heads of the families of the village but also all adults. The inscription is unfortunately fragmentary, but it distinctly refers to a donation by the Mahājanas of the place, headed by their own three,(?) together with the children and old men. It would appear from this record that the term Mahājanas included at least in some localities all the adult population of the village; persons too weak or young to be members of that body were alone excluded from it.

46. I. A., XIII, pp. 33–34.
47. I. A., IV, p. 274.
48. E. I., IV, p. 274.
49. I. A., XII, p. 221.

The instances above quoted were all of Brahmana settlements, and so the Mahājanas in these cases included Brahmanas alone. But in ordinary villages consisting of a population of different castes, non-Brahmana householders also must have been included among them, though Brahmanas often may have occupied a prominent position in that body. The Radhanpur plates of Govinda III, which give a village in Nagar district in charity, refer to an assembly of 40 Mahājanas that had met on the occasion, among whom the 10 Brahmanas named in the record were most prominent.[50] A record from Hatti-Mattur in Dharwar district, dated 917 A.D.,[51] refers to an assembly of 50 cultivators headed by the oilman Jayasing-ayyasetti, Jummisetti, Malisetti, Namisetti and Kamvisetti. Here the assembly, as well as its leaders, are all non-Brahmanas; for it is not very likely that the cultivators referred to may have included Brahmanas.

It is thus clear from the above instances that the village Mahājanas, whom we meet in the records of our period, included practically all the heads of the village families, and perhaps all the adult population as well. A record from Sirur in Dharwar district, dated 866 A.D.,[52] refers to 230 Mahājanas of the place, who figure as the recipients of a donation; an inscription from Nargund in the same district, dated 929 A.D.,[53] records a grant when 220 Mahājanas of the locality had assembled together; another epigraph from the same district, dated 916 A.D.,[54] mentions 220 Mahājanas of the village of Pattiya-Maltavur; two more records from Bijapur district, one from Kattegeri, dated 1096 A.D.,[55] and the other from Managoli, dated 1161 A.D.,[56] mention an assembly of 500 Mahājanas of these places. Mahājanas in all these places must be standing for the local assemblies, and since most of these places were small villages, it is quite clear in view of the

50. E. I., VI, p. 242. 51. I. A., XII, p. 125.
52. E. I., VII, p. 203. 53. I. A., XII, p. 224.
54. I. A., XII, p. 225. 55. I. A., VII, p. 138. 56. E. I., V, p. 15

evidence already adduced above that they must have included almost all the adult householders of the localities, who had not particularly disqualified themselves from being designated by that high-sounding appellation. They certainly did not represent the executive of the village assembly, firstly because an executive committee of so large a number of members is inconceivable not only for villages and towns but also for large units, and secondly because the records sometimes mention the heads or the executive committees of the Mahājanas. Thus Nadwadinge record mentions the Mahājanas and their three heads,[57] and the Hatti-Mattur inscription of 917 A.D. mentions five merchants as being at the head of the 50 Mahājana agriculturists. The Mahājanas, therefore, did not form a small body of elected or selected members in Karnatak, as was the case with the 'great men' of the village in Tamil country. They practically included the whole of the adult population of the village.

A village assembly consisting of all the householders of a village would no doubt be quite an imposing body for ceremonial purposes, but it would be thoroughly unmanageable for deliberative and quite unthinkable for executive purposes. As will be soon shown, the Mahājanas in Karnatak used to perform the functions of trustees and bankers, manage schools, tanks and rest houses, raise subscriptions for public purposes and pay village dues to the central government. And yet apart from the two instances referred to in the concluding portion of the last paragraph, there is not a single instance of any mention of the executive or the sub-committee of the village assembly formed for any general or particular purpose. And these two cases also are rather doubtful; for the Nadwadinge record is fragmentary, and the five merchants, who are mentioned as being at the head of the 50 Mahājana agriculturists in the Hatti-Mattur inscription, may have perhaps been the executive of the guild of oilmen, to which the agriculturists may

57. I. A., XII, p. 221.

have belonged, if we assume that they were following oil-pressing as a subsidiary profession. The Nargund inscription[58] records an elaborate arrangement for compulsory contributions for a local tank on the occasions like marriage, thread-ceremony (*Upanayana*) etc., but it refers to no taxation committee of the Mahājanas, whose members were entrusted with the collection of these dues. The tank and its funds were to be managed, not by a tank sub-committee, as was the case in Tamil country at this time, but by the inhabitants of a certain street of the village which was apparently most contiguous to the tank. The Soratur inscription of 951 A.D.[59] records the assignment of certain taxes for a local temple, but it does not mention either a taxation or a temple committee. All the 50 Mahājanas undertake to protect the grant. The Salotgi inscription of Kṛshṇa III[60] gives a detailed description of a local college, its boardings and professors, and the contributions the inhabitants had agreed to pay for the maintenance of the institution, but it nowhere refers to any executive committee of the Mahājanas to look after the college management or the fund collection. An inscription from Devi Hosur in Dharwar district, dated 962 A.D.,[61] mentions the agreement of the Mahājanas of Posavur to raise a sum of 55 *gadyāṇakas* from the interest of which a certain number of Brahmanas were to be fed daily, but it nowhere refers to any committee to look after the endowment, its interest and utilisation. Two Alur inscriptions from Dharwar district,[62] one dated 1091 and the other 1124 A.D. prove not only an absence of sub-committees or village council executives, but attest to the practice, prevailing in the locality, of entrusting village works of public utility, not to any sub-committee of the Mahājanas, but to the trusteeship of single individuals of known ability and character. Both these records mention certain gifts of

58. I. A., XII, p. 224.
59. I. A., XII, p. 257.
60. E. I., IV, p. 60.
61. E. I., XVI, p. 286.
62. I. A., VIII, pp. 23 ff.

money and land by 200 Mahājanas of the place and their conveyance to Sarvajña Mahādevayyanayaka and Sarvajña Permadiyarasa for village public works (*grāmakārya*). Mantrawadi inscription of Amoghavarsha I, dated 865 A.D.,[63] supports the same conclusion. In this record we find the 40 Mahājanas of Elapunase (modern Mantrawadi), the Gorava Moni and the managers of a hamlet making a grant to a local S'iva temple, conveying 85 *mattars* of land to the honourable Gokarṇapandita saying, 'He indeed is able to protect the property and to increase it.' The record is not complete but the words just quoted show that the Pandit was a trustee selected by the donors.

It is, therefore, clear that our records do not prove the existence in Karnatak of any village council sub-committees or even an executive of the Mahājanas, and still we find them discharging the duties of trustees, bankers and managers of temples, tanks and schools. We can explain this anomalous state of affairs only on the assumption that the Mahājanas used to make some informal arrangement about the discharge of these duties; influential members of the village community were entrusted with some of these duties according to mutual convenience and trust; very probably the headman may have transacted much of such business with informal consultations with the leading lights of the village, and made the necessary arrangements for the collections of the public subscriptions and government taxes, for the deposit of the trust moneys at interest and for the management of the public schools and charity houses. This may have obviated the necessity of annual elections of the executive council and its sub-committees, as we find to have been the case in Tamil country in contemporary times. On occasions of importance all the Mahājanas probably met and expressed their views in order to guide the village headman and other influential members of the locality, who were normally discharging the

63. E. I., VII, p. 202.

various functions entrusted to them. Such meetings seem to have been fairly common, since responsibility is thrown by our records not on the headman or solitary individuals but on the whole body of the village Mahājanas.

The gentlemen who constituted the village assemblies in Maharashtra and southern Gujarat were known as *Mahattaras*. This term is nothing but a paraphrase of the words *Perumakkal* and *Mahājana* that were current in Tamil and Karnatak countries respectively. These Mahattaras or their executive (*adhikāriṇaḥ*) are referred to in most of the records from Maharashtra and southern Gujarat ranging from the 8th to the 12th century A.D. The term Mahattara indicated, like the term Mahājana, the householders or the heads of families residing in the village; this interpretation, which is suggested by etymology, is further confirmed by the Sanjan plates of Salukika Budhavarsha (c. 670 A.D.) which mention *kulamahattarādhikāriṇaḥ*, 'officers of the elders of the families immediately after the Grāmakūṭa or the village headman.[64] This expression shows that the Mahattaras were the senior members of their respective families, and members elected by or selected from among them formed the village council. Most of the Rāshṭrakūṭa grants from Maharashtra and Gujarat mention *adhikārikamahattaras* or *mahattarādhikāriṇaḥ* after the grāmakūṭa. Both expressions mean the same thing; the first is a *karmadhāraya* compound (*mahattarāḥ cha amī adhikāriṇaḥ*) meaning officers who are village elders, and the second a *tatpurusha* one (*mahattarāṇām adhikāriṇaḥ*) meaning executive of the village elders. The Gujarat and Maharashtra records do not give any specific examples of the number of the *mahattaras* of any localities as the Karnatak epigraphs do; but the meaning of the term, especially in the light of the expression *kulamahattarādhikāriṇaḥ* of the Sanjan plates of Budhavarsha, would tend to show that Grāmamahattaras included the elders of all the respectable families

64. E. I., XIV, p. 150.

of the village. The Mahattaras of Maharashtra and Gujarat, therefore, must have been as numerous as the Mahajanas of Karnatak.

As observed already the Mahattaras had a regular executive of their own in Maharashtra and Gujarat, the members of which were called Mahattarādhikāriṇaḥ. The communal responsibilities in these provinces were theoretically shared by the council of the Grāmamahattaras and not by the Grāmamahattaras themselves; for our records do not mention Grāmmahttaras in such connection but usually their council—Grāmamahattarādhikāriṇaḥ. In this respect we see a contrast between the adjoining provinces. In Karnatak the general assembly as a whole is saddled with the responsibility and never its executive body, in Maharashtra and Gujarat the case is just the reverse. It is not improbable that the general body of the village elders was accustomed to meet much less frequently in Maharashtra and Gujarat than was the case in Karnatak and had allowed its functions to be usurped by the executive council.

Our records give absolutely no information as to how the executive committee of the Mahattaras was formed, what was its strength, whether it was elected by the Mahattaras, if so, how and at what intervals, or whether it was nominated by the central government or its deputies, or whether it consisted of natural leaders among the villagers, selected by a kind of informal approval. Since neither election by the general body of the Mahattaras nor nomination by government or its officers is ever referred to, the last mentioned alternative seems to be the most probable one. *Mahattara-vāsāpakas* are mentioned in two grants of the Gujarat branch.[65] This term has not yet been interpreted but it may possibly denote those families, which claimed descent from the traditional founders of the village, and may, therefore, have

65. Dantivarman's grant, E. I., VI, p. 292, Surat plates of Karkka, being published in E. I., XXI.

occupied an important position in the village community, entitling them perhaps to a seat on the village council.

In Maharashtra and Gujarat, as in Karnatak, we do not come across any departmental sub-committees of the village council to discharge its various functions, as was the case in Tamil country. It is probable that the village executive must have obviously divided itself in practice into small sub-committees, but these are nowhere referred to in our records.

The powers and functions of the village assembly and their executives were substantially the same in Gujarat, Maharashtra and Karnatak, but they differed considerably from those of the corresponding bodies in Tamil country. In the latter province the village executive was responsible to the central government for its revenues; but how and when these were to be collected, whether and to what extent remission in taxation was to be given were matters in which the village had full powers. Nay, the government had even delegated to the village assemblies its power of selling the land of the defaulters of land-revenue. The village committees there were also the owners of the village lands and could sell or assign them for village purposes.[66] Under the Rāshṭrakūṭa administration all these powers were reserved to itself by the central government and were exercised through its representatives, as shown in the last chapter. Our records supply not a single case of the Mahājanas or Mahattarādhikārins remitting any taxes or making any lands tax-free. The Kalas inscription[67] no doubt refers to the *Agrahāra* of Kadiyur assigning the tax on pedlars for a local temple, but the case is beside the point; for the village was an alienated one and so the rights of the central government had devolved upon the Mahājanas who were the alienees. In a record from Kattageri[68] from Bijapur district, dated 1092 A.D., we no doubt find the honourable 500 making over an impost due to them

66. Mujumdar, *Corporate Life in Ancient India*, p. 193.

67. E. I., XIII, p. 327. 68. I. A., VI, p. 138.

to a local temple; but the honourable 500 obviously did not represent the Mahājanas of the place, for in that case they would have been so designated, as is the invariable practice of the Karnatak records. Besides, if "honourable 500" had represented the Mahājanas of the place having sole control over the village taxation and its disposal, they need not have drawn up any document for assigning one of their imposts for the purpose of their tank. We can understand the record only if we take the honourable 500 as the members of some outside guild who assigned an impost due to them for the tank of the village. There is only one case, that of the Mahājanas of Soratur, assigning away a tax in kind to a local temple, but the record shows that they could do so only when the headman and the Governor of the place had graciously acceded to their request in that matter.[69]

With the exception noted above, the powers and functions of the village councils were similar to those in the south. They were looking after and arranging for the public works and other needs of the village community. We find them organising schools and charity houses,[70] managing temple property[71] where no sect or other organisation existed,[72] and arranging for the maintenance and repairs of the village tank.[73] They were also receiving deposits on trust from private individuals to be utilised for specific public works according to their wishes.[74] On such occasions the feet of

69. I. A., XII, p. 258.

70. Hadali inscription, I. A., XIII, pp. 93-94; Kalas inscription, E. I., XIII, p. 327; Belur grant, I. A., XVIII, p. 273.

71. Adargunchi inscription, I.A., XII, p.258; Bhadana plates, E. I., III, p. 275.

72. J. B. B. R. A. S., X, pp. 167 ff.

73. Nargunda inscription I. A., XII, p. 224; Kattageri inscription, I. A., VI, p. 138.

74. Sirur inscription I. A., XII, p. 220; Adargunchi and Soratur inscriptions, I. A., XII, pp. 256. ff.; Nilgund and Didgur inscriptions, E. I., VI, p. 102 and p. 253.

all of the Mahājanas, even when their number was 200 or 300, were washed by the donors, even if the latter were provincial or district governors, and the ownership of the property was formerly conveyed in trust to them. This procedure would incidentally show the high reverence in which they were held. The Mahājanas used to guarantee perpetual proper untilisation of the funds entrusted to them for the purposes contemplated. It is obvious that the Mahājanas must have had their own banks, for they used to undertake the payment of the agreed interest annually on the deposits received by them. It is, however, equally probable that in many cases they may not have had public village banks under their control and management, but may have invested the sums through some village money-lenders of known credit and character. They used to raise subscriptions for public works and collect voluntary contributions; steps were also taken by them to commemorate the memory of distinguished donors by engraving their donations on stone tablets. The village councils were enabled to undertake and finance these public works by the policy of the central government of reserving a part of the revenues collected in the village for its local purposes. The village revenues were divided into two parts, *Melā-vāram* or government share and *Chadi-vāram* or the inhabitants' share.[75] The latter was at the entire disposal of the village council, and it could not be alienated even by the king except with the consent of the people. I have already shown elsewhere that the people's share of the revenues of a village was usually in the vicinity of 15% of the total revenues collected in the locality even under the British administration as late as 1830 A.D.[76] This regular income was supplemented by public subscriptions, and voluntary imposts and charity induced by the Ishṭāpūrta theory which extolled to the skies the benefactors of the community, who

75. E. I., XIII, p. 35.

76. Altekar, *Village Communities*, pp. 68, 71.

obliged it by building public wells and tanks and maintaining schools and hospitals.

The village councils of our period had considerable jurisdiction over the village disputes.[77] Sulaiman, a contemporary writer, informs us that there existed popular courts in India in addition to king's courts.[78] Their criminal jurisdiction was no doubt confined to petty cases of assaults, etc., but their civil jurisdiction was unlimited. They could try and decide cases worth any big amount. King's courts did not entertain any cases at first instance; it was only when the parties felt dissatisfied with the decisions of the village councils that they could appeal to the king or his courts. Somadeva, a contemporary writer of the Deccan, expressly declares that such was the case in his times.[79] If the parties to a dispute happened to be members of a guild the case was referred to the village council, only if the guild executive could not settle the matter amicably. The judgments of the early Mahomedan and Maratha period are found to be signed by several village elders including not only Patels and Kulkarnis but also goldsmiths, carpenters, oilmen and even untouchables like Mahars and Mangs. It is, therefore, clear that the power to decide the village cases was theoretically invested in the whole body of the village elders or the Mahājanas. In practice, however, the actual examination of the parties, their witnesses etc., seems to have been delegated to a small sub-committee, the members of which used to receive a certain honorarium from the fees that were charged to the disputants. The trials were usually held in the village temple,

77. For detailed evidence in substantiation of the statements occurring in this para the reader is referred to chapter III of my *History of the Village Communities in Western India.* The statement made in that chapter about the non-existence of guilds during our period is untenable.

78. Sulaiman Saudagar, p. 81.

79. ग्रामे पुरे वा वृत्तो व्यवहारस्तस्य विवादे तदा राजानमुपेयात् । XXVII. 22.

the holy precincts of which could effectively stifle during our period any promptings to dishonesty in the mind of parties and witnesses. The judicial powers of the Panchayats were not due to prevailing anarchy ; it was the considered policy of the state not to entertain any suits except by way of appeal from the decisions of the village Panchayats. The decrees of the village court were enforced by the central government, just as the decrees of the present day British courts are carried out by the British executive. In the 15th century in Maharashtra, parties dissatisfied with the decisions of the village court had the right of appeal to Taluka Panchayats ; it is not improbable that the councils of Vishaya and Rāshṭra-mahattaras as well may have enjoyed in our period appellate jurisdiction over the decisions of the village councils. The judicial powers of Bhogapatis, Vishayapatis, and Rāshṭrapatis are nowhere referred to in our records ; very probably they enjoyed no such powers. In the king's court too the judge was assisted by Sabhyas or jurors whose duty, according to Somadeva, a contemporary writer of our period, was to find out facts and decide the cases impartially.[80] The procedure at the court of the capital considerably resembled the modern trial by jury.

The assemblies used to meet usually in the Mandap of the local temple or under the shade of an expansive tree; many of the villages like Kadiyur, however, had halls of their own.[81] An inscription from Shikarpur[82] records a number of donations for the construction of the village halls. The Mantravadi inscription of 865 A. D. refers to a meeting of the assembly, and says that Nāgadeva was its president. Since, there were no formal elections of the executive in our assemblies, it is not unlikely that different presidents may have been elected on different occasions.

80. *Nītivākyāmṛta*, XXVII, 3. 81. E. I., XIII, p. 327.

82. Shikarpur, No. 45, E. C., VI.

CHAPTER XI

Revenue and Expenditure

An enquiry will be made in this chapter into the various sources of revenue of the Rāshṭrakūṭa empire and the way in which they were utilised. Our principal sources of information in this connection are the statements made in the copper-plate grants about the immunities of the village alienated in favour of Brahmanas and temples. This information can be compared with the rules of the contemporary Smriti writers and statements in the records of other contemporary dynasties. Accounts of the Muslim traders are also, to some extent, useful.

The principal sources of revenue may be classed under five heads. These were:—

(1) Regular taxes,
(2) Occasional taxes or exactions,
(3) Fines,
(4) Income from government properties, and
(5) Tributes from feudatories.

Of the above items, the last one will be considered in detail in the next chapter where the position of the feudatories will be considered; the remaining will be discussed here.

(1) Regular Taxes

An analysis of the epigraphical evidence shows that the following taxes were regularly levied in all the villages of the empire:—

(i) *Udraṅga.*

(ii) *Uparikara.* It will be shown that *Bhāga-bhoga-kara*, mentioned in some of our records, is the same as the items Nos. i and ii mentioned here.

(iii) *Bhūtotpātapratyāya* or *s'ulka* or *siddhāya.*
(iv) *Vishṭi.*
(v) Miscellaneous taxes.

(2) Occasional exactions

These were principally of three kinds:—
(i) *Chāṭabhaṭapraves'adaṇḍa.*
(ii) *Rājasevakānām vasatidaṇḍaprayāṇadaṇḍau.*
(iii) Emergency demands of the State.

(3) Fines

This item requires no explanation.

(4) Income from Government properties

Under this head were included :—
(i) Sheri or crown land, waste lands and trees.
(ii) Mines and salt.
(iii) Treasure trove and property of persons dying without any heirs.

(5) Tributes from the feudatories

This item will be discussed in the next chapter where the position of the feudatories will be considered in detail.

(1) Regular Taxes

(i and ii) *Udraṅga* and *Uparikara*

These taxes are mentioned very frequently not only in the grants of the Rāshṭrakūṭas but also of the earlier dynasties like those of the Parivrājakas, Maitrakas and the later Guptas of Magadha. It must be, however, confessed that modern scholarship has not yet succeeded in ascertaining satisfactorily their exact meaning; nor do Sanskrit dictionaries help us much. This latter fact is rather surprising and perplexing; for these expressions are very common in the numerous records of our period and yet are unknown to most of the Kosha writers. It is only in *S'ās'vata Kosha* that we come across a sense that can be reasonably considered in connection with the present enquiry; the work gives *Uddhāra* or *Udgrāha* as a synonym of the term.[1] The only other Kosha where the word is mentioned at all is the *Trikāṇḍa s'esha-kosha*, according to which *Udraṅga* is the name of the celestial city of Harischandra moving in the air.[2] This meaning which has been copied from this Kosha by some of the modern Sanskrit and English dictionaries, can be hardly considered in connection with the present enquiry. Since the word is very common in the epigraphical literature and almost unknown to the Koshas, can it be possible that the word is a Sanskritised form of some non-Indo-European word? The term *Udraṅga* cannot be also connected with the word *draṅga* which means a frontier town in the *Rājataraṅgiṇī*; it is not possible to argue that the expression *sodraṅgaḥ* might mean 'along with the octroi duties', for then the form would have been *sadraṅgaḥ* and not *sodraṅgaḥ*. As it is, though we get several variations of the fiscal terms occurring in epigraphical records, the form of the term *sodraṅgaḥ* is constant; not even once do we get *sadraṅgaḥ* as an alternative form.

What etymology or dictionaries cannot explain can be attempted to be elucidated by the method of analysis. An analysis of the Rāshṭrakūṭa records shows that the terms *sodraṅgaḥ* and *soparikaraḥ* do never figure along with the expression *sabhāgabhogakaraḥ* in one and the same grant. In the Samangad plates of Dantidurga[3] and the Kapadwanj plates of Kṛshṇa II[4] the term '*sabhāgabhogakaraḥ*' is used, but the expressions *sodraṅgaḥ* and *soparikaraḥ* are missing. In all other records of our dynasty the latter terms are figuring, but the former one is absent. There is not a single record where neither set of taxes is mentioned. It is, therefore, clear that *bhāga* and *bhoga* are nearly synonymous with *udraṅga* and *uparikara* and stand for taxes that were universally levied.

1. Referred to by Buhler at I. A., XII, p. 189 N. 30. 2. II., 79.
3. I. A., XI, p. 111. 4. E. I., I, p. 52.

What then could have been these universally levied taxes ? The Smriti literature invariably uses the term *bhāga* or its synonym *aṁs'a* for denoting the land tax.[5] In the Sanskrit literature the king is very often described as subsisting on *s'ashṭhāns'a i. e.* the 6th part of the produce of the land. It is, therefore, almost certain that the *bhāgakara* of the inscriptions must be standing for the land tax.

Bhogakara represents the petty taxes in kind that were to be paid to the king every day. From the very nature of the case, these taxes in the form of betel leaves, fruits, vegetables etc., could have been exacted by the king only when he was on tour; they were, therefore, usually assigned in practice to local officers as part of their incomes, as shown already in the last chapter. Every day these taxes in kind were seen being enjoyed by the local officers and, therefore, the term *bhogakara* used for them was quite appropriate. In this connection attention may be drawn to Manu VIII, 307, where the expression *pratibhāgam* has got a v. l. of *prītibhogam* which has been explained by the commentator Sarvajña Nārāyaṇa as '*Phala-kusuma-s'ākhātṛṇādyupāyanam pratidinagrāhyam*' 'daily presents in the form of fruits, flowers, vegetables, grass etc.' The interpretation proposed for *bhāgakara* is, therefore, supported by the usage that was known to some of our commentators. Sometimes, however, Government used to impose additional taxes for the salaries of some of its officers. We have already seen how the village of Tuppad Kurahatti had to pay an additional tax in money for the remuneration of the district officers in the reign of Kṛshṇa III.[6] Contemporary Ganga–Pallava and Chola records also mention fees for the district and village officers that had to be paid by the villagers.[7] This additional tax on land may also have been included in the term *bhogakara*.

5. Cf. Gautama, X, 24–7; Manu, VIII, 130; Kauṭalya, V, 2; etc.
6. *Ante*, p. 179.
7. S. I. I., II, pp. 530–1; III, p. 391.

We have already seen that the terms *udraṅga* and *uparikara* are very nearly or identically the same as the expressions *bhāgakara* and *bhogakara*. The two Gadyāṇas, which the villagers of Tuppad Kurahatti had to pay for the remuneration of the country *gāvuṇḍa*, was a tax on land which had to be paid over and above (=*upari*) the normal land tax. *Uparikara*, therefore, was quite an appropriate term to denote it, since it was an additional impost. *Bhogakara*, therefore, becomes identical with *uparikara*, either term denoting taxes, normal or additional, in kind or cash that were imposed for the part payment of the salaries of the mofussil state officers. Fleet was inclined to hold that *uparikara* may have been the tax on temporary tenants who had no proprietory rights in the village soil.[8] There is, however, no independent evidence to show that the government used to impose any extra or special taxation on such tenants. There was besides no reason why state records should distinguish the tax paid by the permanent tenants from that obtained from temporary cultivators. The theory, therefore, that *udraṅga* was a tax on permanent and *uparikara* on temporary tenants yet remains to be proved and is not likely to be correct.

Since *udraṅga* and *uparikara* have been shown to be nearly identical with *bhāgakara* and *bhogakara* and since *bhogakara* is further shown to be identical with *uparikara*, it follows that *udraṅga* has to be equated with *bhāgakara*, which has been shown to stand for the normal land tax of the government. It has to be confessed that no etymological derivation of the term can be suggested, which will explain this interpretation; but the word itself is practically unknown to dictionaries in its fiscal sense, and may have been derived from some non-Aryan stock; hence the difficulty of properly deriving it.

It is not easy to determine the exact incidence of the taxation on land in our period. The Smriti and Nīti writers lay

8. C. I. I., III, p. 98.

down that the state demand should vary between 8% to 16%.[9] The Arthaśāstra would advocate a levy of 25%[10]. Śukra, a medieval writer, permits land taxation between 25% to 50% in the case of irrigated lands, but adds that the taxation on ordinary dry lands should be such that the net produce should be twice the cost of production, the latter term including the government dues as well.[11] Chaṇḍeśvara, another medieval writer, states that the expression '*shadbhāga*' with reference to land tax is merely figurative, and means that the king should take such amount as is necessary for the needs of government and may not be felt as oppressive by the subjects.[12] Since the theory writers differ so greatly and allow so wide an option to the state we may take it that the land tax in the Rāshṭrakūṭa dominions must have varied with the quality of the land and the needs of the state.

Let us now try to determine the actual amount of the land tax that was levied by the governments of our period. The paucity of records throwing any light on the subject, the vagueness of their statements when available, and the difficulty of interpreting the technical terms used in them are the main reasons that have so far deterred an enquiry in this direction; but it is high time that an effort at least should be made. Let us consider a few concrete cases that are available in this connection.

(1) Bevinahalli inscription from Chitaldurg district[13] of Mysore State, belonging to the time of Khoṭṭiga, informs us that the revenue of two villages Madlur and Malagavadi was 50 *gadyāṇas*, petty taxes in kind being excluded. A *gadyāṇa* was equal to two *kalanjus* and the latter was a gold coin weighing about a quarter of a tola[14] or about 45 to 50 grains. The revenue of these two villages was thus about 25 tolas of gold

9. E. g., Manu, VIII, 130. 10. Book V, Chap. 2.
11. IV, ii, 110 ff. 12. Chap. XII, p. 62. (Jayaswal's edition).
13. E. C., XI, Chitaldurg No. 74.
14. Elliot, *Coins of South India*, p. 47.

or 375 tolas of silver, since the ratio between the prices of the two metals in our period was about 1:15.[15] Making allowance for the alloy, 25 tolas may be roughly equated to Rs. 500.

(2) The second of the three Kongu inscriptions, edited by Kittel,[16] gives us some idea of the taxation under the Gangas, who were for some time the feudatories and for some time the neighbours of the Rāshṭrakūṭas. The record informs us that Beli-ur, which consisted of 12 hamlets, used to pay 80 golden coins and 800 measures of paddy. Since the inscription hails from Coorg, the gold coins were probably *Kalanjus* and the measure of paddy a *kalam*. The latter measure differed in different localities from about 36 to 72 maunds.[17] The Government tax on Beli-ur and its 12 hamlets amounted to 20 tolas of gold or 300 tolas of silver and about 4000 maunds of paddy *i. e.* 1600 maunds of rice. It will be shown in chapter XVI that ten *kalams* of paddy measuring about 400 seers used to cost about a *kalanja* or a quarter of atol a of gold. If the *kalam* of this place was of the same measure, the total government demand would have amounted to 40 tolas of gold or 600 tolas of silver. In modern figures this may amount to about Rs. 800.

(3) In the Cambay plates of Govinda IV, dated 930,[18] we have got the following passage:—

'Brāhmaṇebhyashshaṭśatāni agrahārāṇam suvarṇalaksha-traya-sametāni......devakulebhyo grāmāṇāmashṭaśatāni suvarṇalakshachatushṭayam drammalakshadvātrinśatam cha dadatā.'...

15. Sukranīti gives the ratio of the prices of the two metals as 1: 16 (IV, ii, 98). Tavernier, writing in 1660, says that one golden rupee was equal to 14 silver ones during his times [p. 13]. We may, therefore, well assume that the ratio of the relative prices of the two precious metals was somewhere in the vicinity of 1:15 during our period, though no epigraphical record from the Deccan of our period is at present available to support that statement.

16. I. A., VI, p. 103.

17. See chapter XVI.

18. E. I., VII, p. 36.

In connection with the temples, 32 lakhs of *drammas* were paid in addition to the assignment of 800 villages, and therefore, the text uses the particle *cha*. In the clause referring to the donations to the Brahmanas this particle does not figure and, therefore, the expression *suvarṇalakshatrayasametāni* must be taken as referring, not to an additional gift of that amount, but as an adjective of *shaṭsatāni*, indicating that the government revenue from the 600 villages granted was three lakhs of *suvarṇas*. It, therefore, follows that the expression *grāmāṇam ashṭas'atāni suvarṇalakshachatushṭayam* is intended to indicate that the revenue of the 800 villages granted to the temples was 4 lakhs of *suvarṇas*; *suvarṇalakshachatushṭayam* is a mistake for *suvarṇalakshachatushṭayasametāni*. In both the cases the average revenue of one village works out to be 500 *suvarṇas*. *Suvarṇa* is not to be taken here as the gold coin of that name, referred to by Manu as weighing 80 *raktikas* or about 146 grains, and introduced into currency by Skandagupta in the latter half of his reign. In South India the normal gold coin of our period was *kalanju*, weighing about a quarter of a tola. It is this *suvarṇa* or golden coin that is obviously referred to in the Cambay plates. The revenue of an average village in the time of Govinda IV was thus 500 *suvarṇas i. e. kalanjus*; it thus amounted to 125 tolas of gold or 1875 tolas of silver; we may equate it to about Rs. 2,500.

(4) In the Bāṇa principality, which was sometimes on the border of the Rāshṭrakūṭa empire and sometimes included in it, the revenue of the village Viprapīṭha, which is the same as modern Guddimalam in Kalahasti Zemindari in Arcot and Nelore districts, was 10 *kalanjus* of gold and 500 *kādis* of paddy.[19]

In the above 4 cases we have no doubt the actual amount of the revenues collected in the villages concerned, but they do not enable us to determine the incidence of taxation, since the acreage under cultivation is not given in a single case.

19. E. I., XVII, p. 7.

Nor does the Tuppad Kurahatti inscription of Kṛshṇa III[20] help us in this connection. This record states : Tondayya, the country *gāmunda* of Belvola 300, and six *gamuṇḍas* granted in concert to the temple constructed by Aychayyā 50 *mattars* (of land) by king's measure and one *mattar* for a garden. On this for the share of the king the fixed revenue shall be 2 *gadyāṇas* and for the revenue of the country *gāmundas* the fixed revenue of two gold *gadyāṇas*. The total taxation for this field of 50 *mattars* and the garden of 1 *mattar* would be only 4 golden *gadyānas i. e.* 2 tolas of gold or 30 tolas of silver. Unfortunately the precise dimensions of a *mattar* are not known, and there is ample evidence to show that the measure varied with localities. The grants made by the Śilāhāra prince Gonakarasa on one and the same occasion but in three different localities were by *mattar* of three different dimensions, prevailing in the places concerned.[21] The Mangoli inscription of Bijjala, dated 1161 A.D.,[22] assigns eight *mattars* to the four Brahmanas whose households constituted the Brahmana house-hold of the deity. It would thus seem that a Brahmana family required two *mattars* of dry land for its subsistance. A *mattar* therefore, may have been equal to about 4 or 5 acres of land at Mangoli, and its dimensions in other localities could not have been very much different. The tax of eight *kalanjas* of gold that was levied from about 50 *mattars* of dry land in the time of Kṛshṇa III at the village of Tuppad Kurahatti would thus be from a piece of about 200 acres. The taxation per 100 acres is thus found to be only one tola of gold. This may have been, however, due to the fact that the permanent assessment for that piece of land was not the normal government demand, but only a kind of quit-rent, since the land was given to a temple as a *devadāya* grant. There is evidence to show that the temple

20. E. I., XIV, p. 366.
21. Salotgi Pillar inscription, C. E. I., IV, p. 66.
22. E. I., V, p. 22.

lands were taxed on a lower scale. It will be soon shown that the average demand of government under the Cholas was 100 *kalams* of paddy per *veli*; but an inscription from Konerirajapuram informs us that 12 *velis* of temple land in the locality were charged a tax of only 600 *kalams* of paddy, before it was altogether exempted from taxation. The average taxation on temple land in this case is thus found to be only half of that on ordinary lands. Even then the taxation amount per acre at Tuppad Kurahatti would be too low, for it would be only 2 tolas of gold per 100 acres. It is possible that the quit-rent in this case was only nominal, or that the land was very poor in quality.

A record from Honawad in Dharwar district, dated 1054 A.D.,[23] refers to an allotment of ordinary dry land to a temple by king Somes'vara 'at the payment of half a *paṇa* as the payment for a *mattar*.' The rate referred to here must be obviously of taxation and not of the price of the land in question. The record, however, does not mention whether the *paṇa* mentioned was intended to be a gold, or silver, or copper coin. If we assume it to be a gold *paṇa*, weighing 80 *raktikas* or about a 3/4 tola, the rate of government taxation per *mattar*, which seems to have been equal to about 4 or 5 acres as shown above, was about 3/8 tola of gold or about 6 tolas of silver. But, it is possible that the *paṇa* may have been intended to be a silver or even a copper one; for Somes'vara may have decided to charge only a nominal quit-rent on the land he had given to a temple for his spiritual benefit.

The effort to determine the incidence of actual taxation on the agricultural land in the Deccan of our period cannot succeed in the present state of our knowledge. But inscriptions Nos. 4 and 5,[24] engraved in the Rājarājes'vara temple at Tanjore in 1014 A.D., give us a good idea of the land taxation

23. I. A., XIX, p. 272.
24. S. I. I., II.

towards the beginning of the 11th and the end of the 10th century A. D. The incidence of the land taxation under Kṛshṇa III in the portions of Tamil country annexed by him to the Rāshṭrakūṭa empire, towards the middle of the 10th century, could not probably have been much different; hence the utilisation of these inscriptions cannot be regarded as unjustifiable for the purpose of the present work.

These two valuable records give us the precise area of 35 different villages, stating in each case what area was actually taxed and what area was exempted from taxation. In the case of 5 villages the taxation was levied in cash and the rate works out to be 10 gold *kalanjus* per *veli i. e.* $2\frac{1}{3}$ tolas of gold or about 37 tolas of silver for about $6\frac{1}{3}$ acres. In the remaining 30 villages the tax was collected entirely in paddy, and the average is seen to be about 100 *kalams* per *veli*. Dr. S. K. Krishnaswami Aiyangar informs me that a *veli* in Tanjore district yields at present an average crop of 200 to 250 *kalams* of paddy (by the Tanjore measure) and that two crops on the average are grown in the course of the year, except in the narrow belt on both the sides of the Kaveri, where as many as three are possible. If we assume that the rainfall in our period was the same as it is now and that the present yield is not far different from that in the 10th century A.D., the government demand would be about 100 *kalams* from the gross produce of about 500 *kalams*; for in the villages given by Rājarāja only 2 crops are possible, and the modern *kalam* of Tanjore district is nearly the same as the *kalam* of our period. Land taxation at 20 per cent of the gross produce is fairly high, but it may be pointed out that about 15 per cent of this revenue was returned to the village for its own needs,[25] and that there were no further demands as Water cess or Local Fund cess or Road cess. The records give the entire amount of the revenues paid by the villagers. All the revenues that were collected in our period remained in the country and no

25. Altekar, *Village Communities*, p. 70.

part was exported to any country outside India in the form of pensions or recruitment charges.

The land taxation under the Rāshṭrakūṭas was probably equally high. The empire was almost continuously engaged in incessant warfare, and its opponents were also powerful rulers like the Gurjara-Pratīhāras, the Pālas and the Cholas. The military expenditure, therefore, must have been very heavy and the taxation, therefore, could not have been light. Al Idrisi, apparently relying on earlier writers, expressly declares that the subjects of the Rāshṭrakūṭa kingdom were paying heavy taxes, and that, as a result, the king was immensely rich.[26] The land taxation, therefore, under the Rāshṭrakūṭas may have been as high as 20 per cent of the gross produce. Since the Rājarājeśvara temple inscriptions Nos. 4 and 5 give the total demand realisable by the state from the farmers, we may reasonably presume that this 20 per cent taxation included all the miscellaneous dues like the *uparikara* or *bhogakara*. It may be pointed out that Sher Shah and Akbar used to claim 33% of the gross produce from the peasant,[27] and that in Vijayanagar, the incidence of taxation seems to have been still higher.[28]

The lands which were charged this high percentage are situated in the fertile district of Tanjore, and it may be presumed that less fertile lands were charged a lower percentage. Contemporary Chola inscriptions refer to 3 or 4 different classes of land, classified according to their quality, and it is quite probable that the taxation may have varied with each class. The same procedure was probably followed in the Deccan as well. It may be pointed out that the S'ukranīti[29] lays down that the government revenue demand should vary with the nature of the irrigation of the soil.

26. Elliot, I, pp. 85–6.
27. Moreland: *Agrarian System of Moslem India*, pp. 76 ff.
28. Moreland: *India at the Death of Akbar*, p. 98.
29. IV, ii, 115–6.

To conclude, it seems fairly clear that the states in our period were not following the advice of Gautama or Manu, who lay down a land tax varying between 8 to 16 per cent, but of Kauṭalya and S'ukra who permit a much higher taxation. It may further appear as probable that the percentages referred to in the Dharmaśāstra and Nīti works refer to gross produce and not to net produce.

In the case of some special tenures, the taxation was either very low or non-existent. *Mānya*, *Aradhamānya*, *Namasya* and *Baḷagachchu* are the principal tenures to be noted in this connection. In the case of *Mānya* tenures, the land was entirely free from all taxes; neither *Mel-vāram* (Governmen's dues) nor Cūdi–vāram[30] (inhabitants' dues) had to be paid. We sometimes find the holders of this tenure paying voluntary cesses for works of public utility; an 11th tcentury record refers to a voluntary cess of 1 Paṇa on all the rent-free lands at Tavargere for the maintenance of a Pujari in a local temple.[31] In the case of the *Ardha-mānya* tenures, the inhabitants' dues (*Cūdi-vāram*) had to be paid. The lands, assigned to public servants as their salaries, either in full or in parts, may have belonged to one of these categories. *Namasya* tenures consisted of lands alienated in favour of the temples and Brahmanas; they were sometimes fully and sometimes partially free from the taxes usually levied on landed property. Lands, granted to military officers for distinguished bravery were known as Baḷagachchu or swords-washing grants;[32] these too may have paid only a light tax, if at all they had to pay any, as the inhabitants' share.

Let us now consider the question whether the land tax was permanently fixed or periodically revised. Tuppad Kurahatti inscription of Kṛshṇa III[33] states that *the fixed revenue* for the king's share on the land in question shall be two Gadyāṇas. The expression 'fixed revenue' may quite

30. E. I., XIII, p. 35.
31. I. A., V, p. 345.
32. E. I., VI, p. 57.
33. E. I., XIV, p. 366.

possibly point to a permanent settlement of the government demand; it seems not unlikely that when lands were given to Brahmanas or temples, their assessment may have been permanently fixed, if they had not been altogether exempted from taxation. Whether other lands were similarly permanently settled is a question on which our records throw no light. We have, however, seen that the writers of Smritis and *Niti* works allow a wide option, and permit the demand to vary between 8 and 50 per cent. It is, therefore, not unlikely that the government may have periodically revised its taxation demand in view of the changed circumstances or its own needs. This inference is supported by an inscription from Banavasi, dated 941 A.D.,[34] which seems to refer to a fresh settlement necessiated by the drying up of an old irrigation canal.

Kauṭalya recommends[35] a remission of land tax in case of the failure of crops due to famines, pestilences, and wars. We get no evidence about the practice in this respect from the epigraphical records of our period, probably because there was no reason to enunciate such a principle in documents creating rent-free tenures. The case of a revision survey rendered necessary by the drying up of a village canal, referred to in the last para, would suggest that the principle of remission, recommended by Kauṭalya, may have been acted upon by some states. It may be further pointed out that when the land tax was collected in kind, as was usually the case in our period, and was fixed as a certain share of the actual crop that was produced in the field for the year in question, detailed rules about remissions were not necessary; if on any account whatsoever the yield was less, the share of the government also would automatically diminish.[36] Ukkal

34. E. C., VIII, Sorab, No. 83. 35. II, 1.

36. Cf. 'Under the original Indian (i. e. Hindu) system, in which the produce was divided at the harvest, the peasant and the state shared the risk of the enterprise.' Moreland, *India at the Death of Akbar*, p. 100. Some of the records mentioned in the text above, show

inscription No. 9[37] shows that if under normal circumstances the land tax was not paid for three years the lands were sold by the village communities to the exclusion of the defaulting landholders.

The land tax was collected usually in kind and rarely in cash; inscription Nos. 4 and 5 at the Rājarājes'vara temple show that in the vast majority of the villages, the tax was realised in paddy in Tamil country. Coming a little to the north we have the instance of the actual taxation of a village in Gangawadi which used to pay a tax of 20 Kalunjus and 2000 Kadis of paddy.[38] It is very likely that the taxes in kind were those realised from lands and those in cash from other sources. Beli-ur, another village in the same province, is known[39] to have been paying a revenue of 80 gold coins and 800 measures of paddy in 887 A.D. Here also the same explanation might hold good. The Cambay plates of Govinda IV no doubt state that the Emperor had given 1400 villages to temples and Brahmanas, each of which yielded an average revenue of 500 Suvarṇas;[40] but it is not very likely that the entire revenues in all these villages were collected in cash alone. It is probable that the plates give the cash equivalent of the revenues collected in these villages, so that the imperial charity may appear imposing and magnificent. It must also be remembered in this connection that the Dharmas'āstras laud to the skies gifts of gold and land but not of corn; that may have been another reason for stating the revenues of

that this system of sharing was superceded as early as our period by that of assessment based on averages at least in some cases; but this latter system does not seem to have become common or popular. Down to the time of Sher Shah and Akbar, sharing of the actual crops produced in the season was the more common method of assessment even under Muslim administrations in Northern India, p. 41. (See Moreland). *The Agrarian System of Moslem India*, p. 44.

37. S. I. I., III.
38. *Ibid* p. 94.
39. I. A., VI, p. 141.
40. E. I., VII, p. 26.

these villages in gold rather than in corn. In some cases the payment of the tax may have been entirely in cash in the Deccan, as was sometimes the case in some of the Chola villages; the Begumra plates of Kṛshṇa II[41] refer to one such village, which seems to have been paying its entire taxes in *drammas.* It is, however, very likely that in the vast majority of cases the land tax in the Rāshṭrakūṭa dominions was paid in kind, as was the case in the Ganga and Chola dominions.

The collection of the land tax in kind, the amount of which was to vary with the actual produce of the year, must have necessitated a large supervising staff to prevent the farmers from removing surreptitiously a portion of the crop with a view to evade the full share of the government demand. The commentator on the Kurundhama Jātaka[42] refers to the case of a scrupulous Setthi, who regretted his having plucked a handful of corn from his own field before the king's share was paid, and the Arthas'āstra prescribes[43] fines for the purchase of field products like grass, corn and vegetables direct from the fields, since such a procedure was prejudicial to the interests of the government, as it was thereby deprived of its legitimate share of the produce. S'ukra[44] draws the attention of the king to the necessity of preventing the contents of his treasury being destroyed by the depradations of insects; the treasury department had thus to take a good deal of care lest the corn should be destroyed; old corn used to be sold away, and new one purchased, so that the contents of the granary may always have the best market value.

The land tax was collected in several instalments. From the Begumra plates of Kṛshṇa of the Gujrat branch dated 888 A.D.,[45] we learn that it was collected in three instalments, one in Bhādrapada or September, one in Kārtika or November and one in Māgha or March. It is interesting to note that

41. I. A., XIII, p. 68. 42. No. 276 43. II, 22.
44. IV, ii, 28. 45. I. A., XIII, p. 68.

this record partially confirms the statement of Bhattasvāmin, the commentator of the Arthas'āstra, that the *kara* or the land tax was paid in the months of Bhādrapada, Chaitra and the like,[46] and that of Kullūka[47] that the tax was gathered every year in Bhādrapada and Pausha. It would, therefore, seem that government permitted the farmers to pay the tax in at least three instalments. Such an arrangement was also inevitable since the tax was usually collected in kind and not in cash.

(I, iii) Bhūtopāttapratyāya

This tax has been almost universally mentioned in all the grants of our period, and the same is the case with the documents of the earlier and later centuries. This expression has so far defied the efforts of scholars to discover its meaning. It was proposed to explain the term as a tax for protecting those who have come into existence, or as a tax for spiriting away ghosts;[48] Dr. Ghosal proposes to translate it literally as 'a revenue derived from the elements and the wind,'[49] but admits that the precise meaning of the expression is uncertain.

Our records give several readings of this term. *Sambhṛtopāttapratyāya*,[50] *bhūtapātapratyāya*,[51] and *bhūtavātapratyāya*[52] are the main ones. Of these *bhūtapāta* occurs only twice and may be a mistake for *bhūtavāta* or *bhūtopātta*.

46. Arthas'āstra, II, 15.

47. On Manu, VIII, 307.

48. It is no doubt true that a 10th century record from Banavadi mentions an offering of boiled rice which the villagers had to pay for the ghosts of the village, (E. I., XI, p. 6) but as no other record mentions such a tax it is almost certain that it was not a universal one. It is also unlikely that Brahmana donees would have ever consented to receive for themselves such a tax.

49. Ghosal, *Hindu Revenue System*, p. 217.

50. *e. g.* in Konnur inscription of Amoghavarsha I, E. I., VI, p. 29.

51. *e. g.* in Baroda plates of Karkka, I. A., XII, p. 161.

52. *e. g.* Kavi plates, I. A., V, p. 145.

The remaining three readings signify more or less the same thing. The term *Bhūtopāttapratyāya* means a tax (*Āya*) on (*prati*) what has been taken in *i. e.* imported (*upātta*), and what has been produced (*bhūta*) in the village. The reading *Sambhṛtopāttapratyāya*, if not a mistake for *Sabhūtopātta-pratyāya*, would indicate a tax upon articles (manufactured and) stored (*sambhṛta*) and goods imported. *Bhūtavātapra-tyāya* is more enigmatical, but the expression *vāta* may refer to articles imported (*vā*, III conj., to wish to gain, to invite, to invoke) into the villages. It is, therefore, clear that these expressions refer to the general excise and octroi duties that were collected at the villages. This interpretation is further supported by the fact that the expression *Bhūtopāttapratyāya* does not figure along with the term *sas'ulka* in any of our records; Karda plates of Karkka II, dated 973 A.D.,[53] Kauthem plates of Vikramāditya, dated 1008 A.D.[54] and Miraj plates of Jagadekamalla dated 1024 A.D.[55] describe the respective grants of the villages as *sas'ulka*, but they omit the expression *sabhūtopāttapratyāya*; the remaining records use the latter term but omit the former. It is thus clear that the *s'ulka* tax is nearly the same as the *bhūtopāttapratyāya* one.

The Sirur inscription of Amoghavarsha I[56] and the Soratur inscription of Kṛshṇa III[57] mention a tax on clarified butter and charcoal respectively; the government's right to claim, apparently from the herdsmen and cattle-breeders, the best bull and she-buffalo is mentioned in some of the records of the Vākāṭakas and the Yādavas of the Deccan, and of the Cholas of Tamil country,[58] a copperplate of the S'ilāhāras of Konkan, who were administering the coastal territories

53. I. A., XII, p. 264.

54. I. A., XVI, p. 24.

55. I. A., VIII, p. 18.

56. E. I., VII, p. 203.

57. I. A., XII, p. 257.

58. *E. g.* Chammak plates, C. I. I., III, p. 238; Behatti inscription of Kṛshṇa, J. B. B. R. A. S. IV, p. 48; Tandontottam plates, S. I. I., II, pp. 530–1.

of the Rāshṭrakūṭas, mentions a customs duty of one golden Gadyāna from every ship arriving from a foreign country and of one silver *dharaṇa* from every one coming from coastal ports.[59] Some of the inscriptions of the Cholas[60] mention a tax on potters, shepherds, weavers, oilmen, shopkeepers, stall-keepers, brewers and gardeners. *Siddāya* tax, *i. e.* a tax on articles manufactured, was levied at Badami in the 12th century.[61] All these taxes will fall under the category of *Bhūtopāttapratyāya*. Some of the taxes mentioned above do not figure in the records of the Rāshṭrakūṭas, but most of them, and others also of a similar nature, may have very probably been levied by them also. The general expression *Sabhūtopāttapratyāya* being used in the plates there was no further necessity to specify them individually. It may be pointed out that most of these taxes have been advocated in standard books on polity and Dharmaśāstra.[62]

Octroi and excise duties were collected sometimes in kind and sometimes in cash. The taxes on butter and charcoal at Sirur[63] and Soratur[64] were collected in kind, but the octroi duties at Badami[65] and the customs dues at Kharepatan were collected in cash. The taxes collected in kind were very often assigned to local officers as shown already; this was inevitable, for the central government could hardly have managed to have at the capital a store of shoes, flowers, betel-leaves etc. that were paid as taxes in the distant villages of its empire. Even if a store had been opened there, most of these articles would have been rendered useless before they reached the depot. Epigraphical records do not supply any information about the percentage of the taxes we are discussing, but a number of writers like Manu, (VII, 131-2) Vishṇu, (III, 33) Gautama (II, i, 30) and Kauṭalya (II, 21) lay down that the excise duty to be levied should be 16% in case of articles like fish, meat, honey, medicines, fruits,

59. E. I., III, p. 286 60. S. I. I., III., p. 391.
61. I. A., VI, p. 141. 62. Manu VII, 131 ff.; Vishṇu, III, 29 ff.

pottery, fuel, etc. The taxation may have varied in practice with different articles to some extent, but the average may have been in the vicinity of 16%. From Ibn Batuta we learn that the octroi duties in the first half of the 14th century A.D. were 25%. The percentage of customs duties seems to have varied between 5 and 10%. Vishṇu (III, 30) and Gautama (II, i, 26) prescribe 5%. Śukra (IV, 2, 110) recommends a duty varying from 3% to 6% and Baudhāyana (I, 10, 15) permits a levy at 10%.

(I, iv) Vishti or forced labour

This tax has been referred to in most of the records of our period. The Hindu polity has laid down the proposition that every citizen ought to pay something by way of taxation to the state in return for the protection that he gets, howsoever poor he may be. Taxation, whether in cash or in kind, was both impracticable and cruel in the case of the poorer classes. The state therefore[63] levied a tax in labour from them. Manu and other writers have laid down that artisans, labourers etc. should be made to work for one or two days in the month for the state. It was obviously impossible for the central government to collect this tax in labour in its central treasury. It was, therefore, realised partly during the tours of the king and the officers of the central government, partly for the routine government work in the village like the cleansing of the government granary, weighing or measuring the land-tax paid in kind etc., and partly when public works in villages like the excavation of village tanks or wells had to be carried out. On such occasions the headman could compel the artisans and the labourers to work for the state or the village community.

(I, v) Miscellaneous Taxes

Under this head may be included several miscellaneous dues. First may be mentioned a tax on houses, the exis-

63. VII, 138.

tence of which is proved by an inscription from Hebbal, dated 975,[64] which records a grant of 12 sites of houses for a temple *with complete exemption from taxes.* The existence of a ferry tax, which is recommended by most of the Smriti writers, is proved by the Torkhede plates of Govinda III, dated 813 A.D.,[65] which expressly mention this impost. It is difficult to say whether the tax on marriage, which is mentioned in some Chola records,[66] and the duty leviable at the festival of attaining puberty, which is referred to in an inscription of Vinayāditya,[67] dated 680 A.D., were universal taxes or imposed only by some whimsical rulers. The last mentioned inscription also mentions a tax on men dying without a son, and a 13th century Yādava document[68] attests to the existence of a tax levied on persons, who were not blessed with a son.

The tax on persons having no son or dying without a son seems at first sight a strange one. Some might imagine that it was levied by the Hindu state in its desire to see that its subjects discharged the religious duty of procreating a son. The tax, however, was due to no such desire, nor could it have appeared to our age as an unjust imposition. Its imposition as a matter of fact marked a great concession to the subjects. To understand its genesis, we shall have to cast a glance at the history of the widow's right to inherit her husband's property. This right was recognised late in the history of the Hindu society, as was also the case elsewhere. S'atapatha Brāhmaṇa,[69] Maitrāyaṇīya Saṁhitā,[70] Āpastamba,[71] Baudhāyana[72] and Vasishṭha[73] Dharmasūtras do not recognise this right, which Yājñavalkya seems to have been

64. E. I., IV, p. 355. 65. E. I., III, p. 53.
66. *E. g.* Tandontottam plates, S. I. I., III, p. 531.
67. I. A., XIX, p. 145. 68. Pool, *Kolhapoor*, p. 333.
69. IV, 4, 2, 13. 70. IV, 6, 4. 71. II, 14, 2-4.
72. XI, 2, 53. 73. XVII, 62.

the first writer to advocate vigorously. He was later followed by Nārada, Kātyāyana and S'ankha.[74] When the widow was not recognised as an heir, at the death of her husband living separately from other collaterals, the property would have either escheated to the crown as heirless or devolved upon distant collaterals, who it may have been thought, ought to pay to the state a portion of the wealth they had got as wind-fall. Some of the states seem to have continued the tax even when the widow was recognised as her husband's heir as a partial compensation for the loss they had to sustain by the new theory that the property could devolve upon the widow as well. This tax in the Deccan will have to be pronounced as humane, when compared to the practice of some of the earlier and contemporary states of confiscating all the property of a person dying without a son on the plea that it was heirless, even when the widow was surviving. We shall discuss this theory in detail under the item 'Income from government properties.'

Some of the taxes mentioned under the present head do not figure in the Rāshṭrakūṭa records, but it would be rash to say that they did not exist in our period, since they are mentioned in the inscriptions of the earlier, contemporary and later dynasties.

(2) Occasional Exactions

(2. 1) *Chāṭabhaṭapraves'adaṇḍa* :—' Exactions at the time of the arrival of regular and irregular military and police forces.' Most of the village grants are stated to be free from this exaction. Chāṭas and Bhaṭas were the members of the police and military forces of the state, and when they were quartered in a village while on the march, the villagers had to meet a number of demands of their unwelcome guests. S'ukra lays down that soldiers should encamp outside a

74. Quoted in the Mitākshara on Yājnavalkya II. 135–6.

village and should not enter it except on official business.[75] It would thus appear that 'good governments of our period were trying to minimise the exactions of the soldiery by preventing it from entering into villages, except with the permission of the higher authorities. S'ukra's rule would, however, minimise only individual high-handedness. That the military authorities would call upon the villagers to meet their various needs is made clear by a record from Davangiri belonging to the 10th century A.D.[76] This inscription states that when Mahāsāmantādhipati S'āntivarman of Banavasi 12,000 came in to due course to Palarur, he sent a summoner to the Mahājanas to say:—'A supply of grass is wanted for our troops of horses and elephants'. Thereupon, the cutters said, 'Right well we cut.' The king was pleased and set free the offering of boiled rice for the ghosts. It is obvious that the inhabitants must have been required to subsidise the troops and officers with many commodities besides grass. The tax *Senābhaktam* mentioned in the Arthas'āstra[77] corresponds to this exaction.

(2, ii) *Rājasevakānām vasatidaṇḍaprayāṇadaṇḍau.*' Fines or dues leviable at the time of the halt or departure of the royal officers'. These are mentioned in a Yādava grant[78] but may have been common in our period as well. Tandontottam plates of Vijayanandivikramavarman[79] mentions a fee for the man, who used to bring the royal orders to the village. This fee would also come under the present category.

Customary presents to the king and higher officers on occasions of festivity like the birth of a son, or marriage may also be mentioned here. The *utsaṅga* tax mentioned in the Arthaśāstra[80] has been interpreted in this sense by the commentator Bhaṭṭasvāmin. Such presents were made in

75. V. 84. 76. E. I. XI, p. 6. 77. II, 15.
78. I. A., XIV, p. 319. 79. S. I. I., II, p. 531. 80. II, 15

the Indian States till recently and may have been common in our period as well, when some persons were so enthusiastically loyal as to offer their heads to deities in order that the king may have a male issue.[81]

(2. iii) Emergency demands of the State

The modern system of public debt was practically unknown in ancient times and the states were, therefore, compelled to levy extra taxation in case of emergency, in order to tide over the difficulty. This procedure is countenanced by the Mahābhārata[82], Arthaśāstra[83] and S'ukranīti[84] and may have very probably existed in our period too, since Somadeva, a contemporary Deccanese writer, permits the state to tax even the temples, Brahmanas and the wealth collected for sacrifice on such occasions.[85] Emergency taxation does not figure in the copper plates because the donees were not invested with the powers of levying it.

Exemption from Taxation

Exemption from taxation has been claimed as a privilege of the learned Brahmanas in most of the Smritis. It was conceded in practice only to a very limited extent. This question will be discussed in detail in chapter XIV where the position of Brahmanas will be considered in detail.

(3) Fines

The income from fines formed in our age, as in modern period, one of the items of the state income. Fines could hardly have formed any appreciable fraction of the total income of the state, and a considerable portion of them must have been consumed by the expense of the judiciary. When villages were alienated, the right to receive the fines imposed upon the delinquents was also usually transferred to the donees. The usual expression in this connection is *sadaṇḍa-*

81. E. C., VII, Sorab No. 479 82. XII, 87, 26–40.
83. V, 2. 84. IV., 2, 10. 85. *Nītivākyāmṛta*, XXI, 14.

das'āparādhaḥ; sometimes the more expressive terms like *daṇḍāya* or *pratishiddhāya* are used.[86] These alternative forms will show that Dr. Ghosal's view that the expression confers upon the donee the right to be exempted, at least in part, from the ordinary penalties for the commission of some of the traditional offences[87] is hardly sound. The incorrectness of this view will be at once manifest when it is remembered that the expression figures not only in grants given to Brahmanas, but also in those given to temples. Most of the village disputes were tried in the villages themselves; it was customary to impose a fine even in civil cases on the unsuccessful litigants. A part of these fines was spent in meeting the expenses connected with the trial of the case before the Village Panchayat; the balance, which normally went into the state treasury, was diverted to the donees in the case of the alienated villages.

(4) Income from Government Properties

(4, i) Crown lands; Waste lands and Trees.

Stray plots of cultivable lands in several villages, waste lands, lands awaiting cultivation, forests and some specific trees formed government property. The Rāshṭrakūṭa administration did not claim proprietary right in all the land under cultivation within its jurisdiction. The numerous copperplate grants, giving villages to temples and Brahmanas, assign to the donees the government's right to the taxes derived from the land and other sources; there is not a single case where the proprietary right in the entire land under cultivation in any village has been transferred to a donee. The plate uses a long series of expressions specifying the rights accruing to the donees, but not a single expression is used in any of our grants, suggesting that the donees acquired the proprietary rights in the cultivable lands in the village. Even the right

86. *E.g.*, I. A., XIX, p. 165.
87. Ghosal, *Hindu Revenue System*, p. 220.

of ejection is nowhere mentioned. It is, therefore, clear that in our period the state did not lay any claim to the ownership of the entire soil situated in the realm. Nay, there are actual cases of previous purchase when land, and not the revenue rights, were assigned to the donees. Tirukkoyalur inscription[88] of the 21st year of the reign of Kṛshṇa III (c. 961 A.D.) states how a Vaidumba king purchased about 3 *velis* of land from the local assembly in order to assign it to a temple in the village. Some of the Chola records, granting land and not the right to the revenue, expressly refer to the previous purchase of the rights of the former owners and hereditary proprietors.[89] It is further worth noting that when the proprietary right in the soil is given to the donee, the grant is usually of a few acres and not of an entire village. In this connection the Konnur inscription of Amoghavarsha I[90] is very important. The record states that, at the request of his favourite general, Bankeya, Amoghavarsha I gave to a Jain temple

(1) the village of Taleyur,

(2) a flower garden, 500 × 150 cubits in dimension, situated in the same village, and

(3) 12 *Nivartanas* of land, situated in each of the 30 villages included in the sub-division in which the village of Taleyur was situated.

Now there was no necessity of specifying the precise dimensions of the flower garden, situated in the village Taleyur, if the grant of the village meant the grant of the entire land within its boundaries. The separate mention of this garden and of its precise dimensions shows that the proprietary rights in the soil were transferred to the temple only with reference to this small plot of land. Item No. 3 above further shows that when it was the case of transferring

88. S. I. I., III, pp. 104–6. 89. *Ibid*, II, Nos. 22 and 23.
90. E. I., VI, p. 29.

proprietary rights in soil, the state could usually give only small pieces scattered over different villages, and not entire villages themselves.

A number of other records support the same conclusion. The Atkur inscription, belonging to the middle of the 10th century, records a grant of land to a temple by Būtuga II, the brother-in-law of Kṛshṇa III; the piece given is one yielding an income of two Kaṇḍugas (3 Khaṇḍis) only. In an inscription from Mulgund, we find a king named Kanna granting

(1) a piece of 12 Nivartanas situated in the *S'īvaṭa* of that village,

(2) that portion of land which was situated between two tamarind trees to the south of that village, and

(3) six *mattars* in Pareyaloku to the west of the boundary of Sugandhvatī or modern Saundatti.[91]

The fact that this king should find it necessary to give only detached pieces of cultivable land situated in the different corners of the village shows that the state was not, and did not claim, to be the proprietor of the entire land of the realm. This conclusion is quite in harmony with the views on the subject prevailing in the Hindu period proper. Jaimini distinctly says that the king is not the owner of the soil and his commentator S'abara agrees with him. The same is the view of Kātyāyana.[92] Nīlakaṇṭha[93] refers to the text of Jaimini and asserts that a king cannot grant in charity the proprietary right in the soil in the realm, because it does not belong to him but to various individual proprietors. The view of Mādhava [94] and Mitramis'ra[95] is the same. It is only Jagannātha, who advocates the view that the king is the

91. J. B. B. R. A. S., X, p. 199.

92. Quoted in Vīramitrodaya, Rājanīti, p. 271.

93. *Vyavahāramayūkha*, Svatvanirūpaṇam, p. 56.

94. Nyāyamālā, p. 358. 95. See No. 91 above.

owner of the soil and the subjects are mere lessees, and that the former's right of ownership arises out the fact of his being the first occupant of the country.[96] But Jagannātha is a very late writer and his testimony is contradicted by the almost unanimous views of both earlier and later writers. It may be observed that Manu[97] also does not support the state-ownership of land as is sometimes contended by some authors. The topic discussed in the verse in question is about the ownership of the treasure-trove and not of land. Some of the Greek writers suggest that the theory of the state-ownership of the land existed in the days of Chandragupta Maurya, but hardly any value can be attached to their statements since they are contradicted by others.[98]

Though the state was not the owner of the entire cultivable land in the kingdom, it used to own some pieces in most of the villages situated in the realm. These may have been lands which had lapsed to it as heirless property, or which had been confiscated by it for offences committed by their former owners or which were actually purchased by it for state purposes. In some cases these state lands may also have been waste lands brought under cultivation by government. The examples given above show how the state owned stray pieces of lands in many villages and more can be quoted. The Silāhāra ruler Govunarasa is known to have granted 206 *mattars* of land to the Salotgi College;[99] the Raṭṭa prince Snātivarman had given 150 *mattars* in the field of his own *S'īvata.*[100] The meaning of this word *S'īvata* is not definitely known, but it seems to stand for the crown lands. Honawad inscription of Someśvara[100] shows that when actual pieces of land were granted away they were not always free from the land tax. Either its full amount or a certain quit rent was charged.

96. Quoted in Sen's *Hindu Jurisprudence*, p. 27.
97. VIII, 39.
98. MacCrindle, Megasthenes, p. 48.
99. E. I., IV, p. 56.
100. I. A. XIX, p. 275.

Forests were government properties in our period. A Pallava record[101] falling within our period mentions a grant of four pieces of forest land in the vicinity of Kanchi, showing thereby that the state used to claim ownership in the forest lands situated within its jurisdiction. Most of our records granting villages use the expression *savṛkshamālākulaḥ*. It is very likely that the expression refers to the transfer of the state's right in the forest lands that may be situated within the boundaries of the village. It must be, however, admitted that another interpretation of this term is possible. Some of the Indian states of the Deccan still claim the right of ownership in certain trees like sandal, *hirḍa* etc, even when they may be growing on private soil. The same was the case with many of the states in the Punjab.[102] The records of the Gahadwar dynasty show that its rulers claimed proprietary rights in mango and Madhuka trees growing in the kingdom.[103] It is, therefore, not unlikely that the expression *savṛkshamālākulaḥ* may be referring to the state's ownership of some such trees as well. There is, however, no evidence belonging to our period to prove that the Rāshṭrakūṭas used to claim this right. The expression can be interpreted as referring to the state's ownership of the trees growing in the forests or by the roadsides, or on the village waste lands.

Ownership of the waste lands was naturally vested in the state. Specific evidence to prove this theory is afforded by the two Ganga records in the Bangalore museum[104] which record the grant of uncultivable waste lands situated in Guladpadi and Berapur 12 to two soldiers for their distinguished bravery in war. That the Gupta administration also claimed this right is proved by the Damodarpur plates,[105] where we find government officers disposing off waste lands by sale.

101. I. A., VII, p. 169.
102. Punjab States Gazetteer, VII, A. p. 16.
103. *e. g.* E. I., XI, p. 24.
104. E. I., VI, p. 44.
105. E. I., XV, p. 130.

The first part of the expression *sakāshṭhatṛṇakūpataḍāgopetaḥ*, which occurs in many of our records[106] transfers to the donees the right to utilise grass, fuel etc., growing on the waste lands included in the boundaries of the village concerned. It must be, however, noted that the Smriti writers lay down that a certain portion of the village waste lands should be set apart as pasturage[107] and most of the Deccan villages still possess them. In our period, too, the same must have been the case. The ownership of the pasture lands was vested in the village Mahājanas.

(4. ii) Mines and Salt

In ancient as in modern times the state was the owner of the mines in the realm. The expression *sahābhyantarasiddhi*, which occurs in most of our grants, transfers to the donees the state's right to the mineral wealth in the interior of the earth. *Vāchaspatya-bṛhadadhidhāna* and *S'abdārthachintāmaṇi* both give *nishpatti* or production as a synonym of *siddhi*; according to *Dharaṇi* the word also means *sampatti* or wealth. Macdonell and Apte state in their dictionaries that the word has also the sense of payment or recovery. *Abhyantarasiddhi* would, therefore, mean 'realisation of whatever is in the interior (of the soil)' or 'wealth in the interior (of the earth)' or recovery of whatever is in the interior (of the earth)' It is, therefore, clear that the meaning, which is here ascribed to this term for the first time, is the correct one and the expression proves that the state was the owner of the mines and minerals.

Mineral wealth included salt mines as well, the ownership in which was expressly claimed by the Gahadwals and the Cholas.[108] The Rāshṭrakūṭa records nowhere expressly

106. *e. g.* E. I., I, p. 53.

107. *e. g.* Manu, VIII, 237, Vishṇu V, 147.

108 *e. g.* Saheth Maheth plates of Govindachandra, E. I., XI, p. 24; Tandonotottam plates of Vinayanandivikramavarman, S. I. I., II, pp. 531-2.

claim this right for the state. That may be perhaps due to its not having claimed any royalty in the salt manufacture; it is, however, also possible that the expression '*sahābhyantara-siddhi*' having included that right as well, it was not deemed necessary to specify it separately. It is, however, rather strange that even the records of the S'ilāhāras, whose dominions included the coastal districts where salt must have been manufactured on a large scale, should not be specifically claiming this right. That might perhaps show that the Rāshṭrakūṭas and their feudatories did not claim the salt monopoly like the Cholas and the Gahadwals.

(4, iii) Treasure-trove and the property of heirless persons

This is the last item to be considered under this head. Our copper plate grants usually transfer to the donees the right to the treasure-troves that may be discovered in the villages or lands granted. The expression used in this connection is *nidhinikshepasametaḥ*[109] 'along with the right to treasures and buried wealth'; there is no ambiguity whatsoever about its meaning. Most of the Smriti writers[110] also state that the king was entitled to a fairly large share of the treasure-troves, except when the discoverer was a Brahmana.

Gautama,[111] Vasiṣṭha,[112] Vishṇu[113] and Manu[114] lay down that the heirless property of the non-Brahmanas was to escheat to the state. The interpretation of the term 'heirless' seems to have differed with different times. It is true that the widow was not recognised as an heir for a long time as shown already; but the Dharmaśāstras, which deny her that right, concede it to other collaterals, like the brothers,

109. Cf. I. A., II, p. 301; XIX, p. 345 etc.

110. *e. g.* Manu, VIII, 35-39; Yājnnavalkya, II, 34-5; Vishṇu IV, 1; etc.

111. XXVIII, 41-2.

112. XVII, 73

113. XVII, 13-4.

114. IX, 189.

cousins or uncles. A person who dies without a male issue but leaves behind him some collaterals cannot, therefore, be regarded as dying without an heir. It would, however, appear that some states in the ancient period regarded such persons as dying without heirs in order to claim their property for themselves. Some of the Jātaka stories disclose such a state of affairs,[115] and the 6th act of the *S'ākuntala* provides us with a most convincing case. There we find that the king stops the intended confiscation of the property of a dead merchant in order to see whether one of the widows, who was enceinte at the time of the tragedy, would give birth to a son. A similar case is mentioned in the *Mohaparājaya* of Yashaḥpāla who flourished in Gujarat in the 12th century. Kumārapāla is there grieved to learn that his subjects should be under the justifiable impression that their king always desired that rich persons should die without leaving behind any sons.'[116] The king consequently renounces this right after his conversion, and the *Kumārapālapratibodha* claims that the magnanimity of permitting the weeping widows to keep her property was not shown in the past even by kings like Raghu and Nahusha.[117] The case in the Deccan, however, was different. The tax on persons dying without a son, which has been already referred to, proves that only a fraction of their property passed to the state as a kind of succession duty. Managoli Inscription, dated 1178 A.D., further makes it absolutely clear that the property of persons dying without a male issue did not escheat to the crown, as was the case in contemporary Gujarat. The inscription states :—

115. *e.g.*, Vol. IV, pp. 485–6.

116. Cf. निष्पुत्रं म्रियमाणमाढ्यमवनीपालो हठा वाञ्छति । p. 43, Act III, v. 50.

117. न मुक्तं यत्पूर्वं रघुनहुषनाभागभरत—
प्रभृत्युर्वीनाथैः कृतयुगकृतोत्पत्तिभिरपि ।
विमुञ्चन्संतोषात्तदिह रुदतीवित्तमधुना
कुमारक्ष्मापाल त्वमसि महतां मस्तकमणिः ॥ p. 48.

If any one should die at Manigavalli without sons, his wife, female children, divided parents, and brothers and their children.........and any kinsmen and relatives of the same Gotra, who may survive, should take possession of all his property, *i. e.* bipeds, quadrupeds, coins, grains, house, and field; if none such should survive, the authorities of the village should take over the property as *Dharmadeya* property.'[118]

It would be clear from this valuable record that the property of sonless persons did not escheat to the crown but devolved on the kinsmen in an order which is very similar to that laid down by Yājnavalkya.[119] Somadeva, a contemporary writer from Karnatak, also states that the king may take a share of the property of the widow only when in difficulty.[120] This would show that normally the property was allowed to devolve upon the widow and other near heirs. It is interesting to note that the epigraphical evidence from the Deccan confirms the tradition that the widow was recognised in that province as her husband's heir since early times. This tradition is mentioned as early as in the Nirukta;[121] Yājnavalkya also, who recognises the widow as an heir and permits the king to inherit the property of the dead under no circumstances whatsoever, was most probably a southerner like his commentator Vijnāneśvara.

Government Expenditure

Epigraphical records naturally give no information in details about the various items of state expenditure during the period of Ancient Indian History, but it is strange that the Niti and Smriti works also should be silent upon the point. Most of them give in great details the various sources of revenue, but the information which only a few of them

118. E. I., VI p. 28.
119. II, 135–6.
120. IX, 5.
121. Nirukta, III, 5.

supply about the heads of the expenditure is very scrappy and unsystematic. Kauṭalya[122] enumerates 14 items of expenditure but the list is neither systematic nor exhaustive. Royal harem and kitchen are the only items of the civil list mentioned by him, the items of civil administration and judiciary are altogether omitted, only a few heads of the military expenditure are enumerated and the navy is forgotten altogether. The only work which lays down definite principles of public expenditure is the S'ukranīti.[123] The author of this interesting work very probably lived in the vicinity of our period and his dicta seem to have been based upon the actual practice of the three great military powers of the age, *viz.* the Rāshṭrakūṭas, the Gurjara-Pratīhāras and the Pālas. His view would, therefore, be particularly valuable for our present enquiry. S'ukra divides the income in six parts and lays down that one should be kept as reserve, as many as three should be assigned to the army, and half of a part should be reserved for each of the four following items, *viz.* (1) Charity, (2) Privy purse, (3) Civil administration and (4) ' People '. It is very likely that if ever the Rāshṭrakūṭa and Gurjara-Pratīhāra budgets are discovered, they would disclose a similar allocation of funds. These empires were maintaining huge military forces and it is quite possible that their military expenditure may have amounted to half of the Central revenues. It must be, however, added that S'ukra includes also the police forces under the expression *bala*. The percentage for the general administration seems to be rather small, but it must not be forgotten that many of the state officers were paid by rent-free lands. S'ukra permits only about 8 % for the king's privy purse and it is perhaps possible that in actual practice the kings for our period may have taken a little more. The percentage reserved for charity, *viz.* about 8 % seems too high. But it must be remembered that the religious outlook of the age was different from ours, and that the sums spent under

122. II. 6. 123. I, p. 315-6.

this head helped indirectly the cause of education as well. The last item 'people' seems to include the provision made in the Central budget for the general needs and improvements of the country; grants for big public works, expenses for the upkeep of the imperial roads, special grants to local bodies for works beyond their limited means etc., were probably included under this item. Education, sanitation, local roads and public works were to a great extent managed by the local bodies, which were supplied with the necessary funds by the earmarking of a certain percentage of the revenues collected in the villages for the local needs.[124] The imperial budget, therefore, had no separate provision for these various items; the central government had only to make extra special grants to local bodies for projects beyond their limited means, and the item 'people' probably denotes that provision in the Imperial budget.

CHAPTER XII

The Military and Police, and the Feudatories

Section A: The Military and the Police

There was hardly a monarch of our dynasty who had not to undertake extensive military operations either to quell internal rebellions or to carry out ambitious foreign expeditions. The military machine of the Empire must, therefore, have been a very strong and efficient one. It used to inspire terror literally from the Himalayas to the Cape Kamorin and and Kathiawar to Bengal when handled by efficient emperors and generals, and it was through its instrumentality that the Rāshṭrakūṭas compelled 'every prince,' to quote the words of Sulaiman, 'though master in his own state, to pay homage

124. *Ante* p. 209.

to themselves'.[1] The ascendancy of the military was so great that it was reflected even in civil administration; we have seen already how many of the provincial governors, district officers, and city prefects were generals or captains. The incessant wars with foreign powers and the protected feudatories had infused the military spirit in the whole population; there were local militias even in villages[2] and skirmishes among them were not infrequent.

The reputation for bravery which the Marathas and Karṇāṭas possessed in the days of Yuan Chwang was maintained if not enhanced in our period. Bengal rulers used to recruit soldiers from Karnatak and Lāṭa,[3] a procedure which will clearly show that the Rāshṭrakūṭa dominions were inhabited by races, famous all over the country for their martial qualities. In his *Viddhas'ālabhañjikā* Rājas'ekhara, a contemporary writer, pays a handsome compliment to the bravery of the Karṇāṭas when he observes that they were naturally brave.[4]

The army headquarters were at the Imperial capital, Malkhed. The Salotgi inscription of Kṛshṇa III[5] describes Malkhed as '*sthirībhūtakaṭake*' *i. e.* a place where the military forces were located. There must have been provincial headquarters as well. Al Masudi has observed about the Gurjara-Pratihārās that they used to maintain large army garrisons in the south and north, east and west in order to deal promptly with the prospective attacks on all the fronts.[6] The army arrangements of the Rāshṭrakūṭas were also similar. The army of the south was under the Banavasi viceroy and that of the north under the rulers of the Gujarat branch. The first had to carry operations against the Gangas, Noḷam-

1. Elliot, *History*, p. 7. 2. *Ante* pp. 190–192

3. Bhagalpur plates, I. A., XV, p. 305.

4. Cf. समरकर्मणि निसर्गोद्भटा एव कर्णाटाः; Act IV.

5. E. I., IV, p. 66. 6. Elliot, *History of India* 1.

bas, Pallavas and the Cholas, and the latter had to guard the frontiers against the Gurjara Pratihāras and their allies and feudatories. Though not specifically mentioned in epigraphical records, there must have been an army of the east as well to deal with the Vengi and Vanga rulers. Any corps could be summoned in any direction in times of difficulty. Thus the southern army under the Banavasi viceroy was summoned by Amoghavarsha I to quell the rebellions in the central and northern portions of the empire.(7) All these armies must have been mobilised for the memorable campaigns in the south and north of Dhruva, Govinda III, Indra III, and Kṛishṇa III.

The Indian armies in the time of the Rāshṭrakūṭas had ceased to be *chaturaṅga*, for chariot as a fighting force was not used in our time. We nowhere find any mention of battalions of chariots either in epigraphical records or in the accounts of the contemporary Muslim writers. The epigraphical documents, while describing the military victories resulting in the surrender of war materials, refer to elephants, infantary and cavalry; chariots are mentioned only in connection with the insignia of honour of distinguished generals and military officers.(8)

From contemporary Muslim writers we learn that the Rāshṭrakūṭa, Pāla, and Gurjara Pratihāra armies were famous for their infantry, elephant battalions and cavalry respectively. Al Masudi says about the Balhara *i. e.* the Rāshṭrakūṭas king:–

'His horses and elephants are innumerable but his troops are mostly infantry because the seat of his government is mostly among mountains.'

The latter part of this statement is incorrect, but it may have been probably intended to mean that the infantry was mostly recruited from the mountainous

7. E. I., VI, p. 29.

8. See the Kalas inscription of Govinda IV, E. I., XIII, p. 334.

tribes inhabiting the Vindhya and Sahya ranges, as was later the case in the Maratha Empire. The cavalry battalions in the army could not have been insignificant, for the Rāshṭrakūṭas had very often to face the Gurjara Pratīhāra armies, which were particularly strong in that arm. Govinda II was a great horseman[9] and the lightning all-India movements of Dhruva, Govinda III and Indra III presuppose a strong cavalry. The Deccan had no good breed of horse, and the Rāshṭrakūṭas were probably importing their army horses from Arabia, as was later the practice of a number of states. It may be interesting to note that most of the places mentioned in the *Nītivākyāmṛta* as famous for their breed of horse are trans-Indian and that the first variety mentioned in that work is that of the Tājika *i. e.* the Arabian horse. At the time of Marco Polo the kingdom of Thana used to import its army horses from Arabia; the traffic in horses was so great in the 13th and 14th centuries that no ship came to India without horses in addition to other cargo.[11] The Vijayanagara rulers also had to rely on Arabia for their army horses. The same, therefore, was almost certainly the case in our period as well. This dependence on Arabia for the supply of the needs of the cavalry may have been one of the main reasons that induced the Rāshṭrakūṭas to maintain friendly relations with the Muslim traders residing in their dominions.

The recruitment to the army was extended to all the classes; even the Brahmanas are to be seen in the fighting force. Bettegiri inscription of Kṛshṇa III[12] immortalises the memory of a Brahmana named Ganaramma who laid down his life while defending his village in a valliant manner. The Kalas inscription of Govinda IV[13] describes the glorious

9. Cf. निजतुरंगमैकविजयानीतलक्ष्मीसनाथः। Kadba plates, E. I., IV, p. 340.

10. XXII. 10. The reading Tārjīka is obviously a mistake for Tājīka.

11. Marco Polo, II, p. 391.

12. E. I, XIII, p. 334.

13. E. I., XIII, p. 189.

career and achievements of two Brahmana generals Revādāsa Dīkshita and Vīsottara Dīkshita who are expressly described as Somayājins and ornaments of the Brahmaṇa race. Kudarkota inscription records the erection of a building for vedic studies by a Brahmana in memory of his son Takshadatta, who had died in war. Both the father and the son are described in the record as familiar with the three Vedas.[14] The Smriti rules do not seem to have been much respected with reference to the selection of professions in our as also in the earlier periods. It will be shown in chap. XIV how even the Jains used to enlist themselves in the army and distinguish themselves on the battlefield.

A part of the army consisted of the hereditary forces and the forces of the feudatories. The Muslim writers seem to be referring to the hereditary forces when they mention the troops of the Indian kings, who came out to fight for their king though they received no pay from him.[15] The principle of heredity, which was allowed to operate to some extent in the appointments to civil offices seems to have governed to a great extent the recruitment of the army as well. *Maulabala* or the hereditary force is very often referred to in our epigraphical records as the most efficient and trustworthy arm. Amoghavarsha I particularly extols the capture of the fort of Kedaḷ by Bankeya, because it was garrisoned by hereditary (*maula*) forees. Both Sukra[16] and Kāmandaka[17] hold the *maula bala* in the highest esteem. It would seem that fighting was followed as a hereditary profession in several families or localities from where the hereditary forces were recruited. Bankeya, the viceroy of Banavasi, has been described as the leader of a hereditary force. It would thus appear that the military captains who were often hereditary, used to recruit their forces from the families of hereditary

14. E. I., I, p. 180.
15. Elliot, I, p. 7.
16. IV, 7, 8–10.
17. XVIII, 4. ff.

fighters. The Arthaśāstra[18] refers to villages enjoying exemption from land tax (*āyudhīyaparihāra*) on condition of supplying a certain number of soldiers to the army. These villages were obviously tenanted by families from among whom the *maula bala* was recruited. There may have been similar villages in our period also, which were assigned to the members of the *maula bala*. We can now well understand the apparently incredible statement of the contemporary Muslim writers that the troops in India are not paid by Indian kings but maintain themselves without receiving anything from them.

The Muslim writers, who make this statement, also add that the members of the fighting forces of the Rāshṭrakūṭas were paid regularly by their employers. It would, therefore, seem that even the *maula bala* was paid a part of its salary in cash by the Malkhed government. We have seen already how the Rāshṭrakūṭas used to exercise rigorous administrative control over their viceroys and feudatories, who had to send all their collections to the imperial exchequer. This must have enabled them, unlike many of their contemporaries, to pay their troops directly in cash or kind at the army headquarters. Direct payment must have naturally increased the efficiency of the fighting force. The Rāshṭrakūṭa administration is thus seen sharing the views of Kāmandaka, a contemporary writer, who points out that a force, which is given its wages without delay, will fight with greater enthusiasm than a force which is not promptly paid.[19]

In contemporary Kashmir the soldiers, when out on duty, were paid an additional allowance[20] as was the practice of the East India Company for some time at the beginning of its career. We do not know whether the practice in Kashmir prevailed in the Deccan of our period as well. It is, however,

18. II, 34. 19. Chapter, XV.

20. Rājataraṅgiṇī, VII, 1457, VIII, 757, 808—810 etc..

not unlikely that the soldiers may have been paid, when out on a campaign, an additional allowance by the Rāshṭrakūṭas as well, since such an allowance was calculated to infuse greater enthusiasm in the army.

Government used to pay pensions to the dependents of the soldiers killed in war; a concrete case of such a provision is contained in one of the Bāṇa records.[21] Another record of the same dynasty chronicles the death of an officer, who was successful in driving away the enemy, but who fell while pursuing him, as he was too much in advance of his column. ' His army put off their arms with which they had come, raised a lamentation, and made a gift to yield an annual income for him.' It would seem that the soldiers of this regiment felt that the death of their gallant officer was due to their negligence in not having followed him with agility in his pursuit. It is not, however, unlikely that even in such cases the central government may have paid its own pension in addition to the provision made by the members of the regiment.

The Rāshṭrakūṭa forces did not consist of untrained or half trained soldiers. Regular officers were appointed to train different units. A cavalry instructor is referred to in an inscription from Ron in Dharwar district.[22] This record, which probably belongs to the time of Amoghavarsha I, records a gift of land by the illustrious Turagavenḍega (Marvel in training horses), when he was going out to battle. The training of the recruits, however, was not as arduous a task during our period as it is now. We have seen already how most of our villages had their own militias, recruited from their own inhabitants. These militias must have been the principal recruitment fields for the regular armies. The recruits thus possessed a certain amount of military efficiency at the time of their enrolment. The Rāshṭrakūṭas could very well have afforded to set a high test for

21. I. A., XII, p. 39. 22. E. I., XIII, p. 187

admission to the army, *e. g.* requiring the recruit to show his skill in archery or riding as was done by some of the Muslim states in the 14th century.[23]

Most of the Rāshṭrakūṭa emperors were themselves distinguished soldiers and must have been, at least in theory, their own commanders-in-chief. Under them were a number of generals, who may have been in charge of the different corps. The status of the general was as high as that of a Māhāsāmanta entitled to the five great musical instruments. They were allowed to use elephants and chariots, invested with the robes of their office and assigned distinctive parasols.[24] Here again we find epigraphical evidence corroborating the statement in the *Nītivākyāmṛta*, a contemporary work on politics, that the generals were to be respected not only by the feudatories but also by the emperor, who was to invest them with insignia of honour and dignity similar to his own.[25] *Balādhikṛta*, *daṇḍanāyaka*, and *mahāprachaṇḍadaṇḍanāyaka* are the main military designations that we come across in our documents. The precise relative status of these is difficult to determine. Several other designations also must have existed. The fierce lord of the elephant force is mentioned, in the Kalas inscription[26] and cavalry and infantry also must have had their own separate officers of the different grades. These latter are not referred to in our records but are mentioned in the copper plates of the Gahadwal dynasty and in the *Nītisāra* of Kāmandaka.[27]

The army had its own commissariat office. A number of merchants were engaged by this office for the purpose of meeting the needs of the army when on march. One such merchant contractor figures in inscription No. 177 of the Madras Epigraphical Report for the year 1912. This document records a charitable gift of Narasingayan, a merchant

23. Gibbs, *Ibn Batuta*, p. 189.
24. E. I., XIII, p. 334.
25. XII, 1.
26. E. I., XIII, p. 334.
27. XIX, 32.

from Mānyakheta who had accompanied the camp of Kṛshṇa III during the southern campaigns of that emperor.

The *Rājataranginī* refers to ambulance corps arrangements made for the soldiers in the Kashmir armies.[28] It is very likely that similar arrangements must have been made by the Rāshṭrakūṭas, though so far no evidence is forthcoming to prove their actual existence. The same observation will probably be true about the Sappers and Miners corps.

The army must have been accompanied by numerous camp followers. Quite a large battalion of cooks, washermen, sweepers, watermen, cartmen, etc., must have been necessary to meet its various needs. It seems that in Northern India slaves were employed for these menial duties; Al Utbi informs us that the victory, which the Hindus had almost secured against Mahmud of Ghazni in the battle of Ohind was lost by them owing to the revolt of the slaves in the household, who attacked them in the rear while the battle was at the critical stage.[29] We do not know whether this unsound practice was followed by the Rāshṭrakūṭas in their military administration. The reputation for great efficiency, which the army possessed, and the numerous victories that stand to its credit would suggest that it was all composed of free men; slaves could hardly have found a place in it even for menial duties.

Wives and other female relatives of the emperors used to accompany them even in distant expeditions. Amoghavarsha I was born, while his father's camp was pitched at the feet of the Vindyas, during his campaign in the Central India.[30] An inscription from Tiruvurrur records a gift from the mother of Kṛshna III made to a local temple.[31] It is interesting to note that Kāmandaka has no objection against this unsound

28. VIII, 741. 29. Elliot, *History*, II pp. 33-4.
30 E. I. XVIII, p. 244.
31. Inscriptions from Madras Presidency, Chingleput, No. 1048

practice[32] and it is, therefore, not unlikely that it may have been fairly common in our period. Our records do not enlighten us as to whether officers and soldiers were allowed to be accompanied by their families when the armies were out on campaigns. In the case of ordinary soldiers this must have been an impossibility, and it would seem that only high officers and generals may have been shown this indulgence. Among the causes that contribute to the weakness of the fighting force, Kāmandaka mentions the presence of women in the camp.[33] It would thus appear that strict and efficient military administrations of our period were not permitting any officers to be accompanied by their families when out on campaigns. The only exception made seems to have been in favour of the emperors and perhaps the generals.

No evidence is available to determine the exact strength of the Rāshṭrakūṭa army. Muslim writers simply attest to its high prestige, but they are silent about its numerical strength. Al Masudi informs us that each of the four armies that were maintained in the four directions by the Gurjara-Pratihāras was seven to nine lakhs in strength.[34] The reports of the strength of the armies of the various states in India that had reached the Muslim traders and travellers were often exaggerated; Sulaiman says[35] that the elephant force of the Pālas was 50,000 strong, but Ibn Khurdadba, a contemporary of his, observes that it was only 5000 strong.[36] Al Masudi no doubt states that the Bengal elephant force was reputed to be 50,000 strong, but adds that the reports in these matters were exaggerated. He refers to the report that there were 15,000 washermen in the camp of the Bengal ruler, in proof of his contention that no strict reliance could be placed on what one heard about these matters. The statement of Al Masudi that each of the

32. XIV, 69.
33. XVIII, 45.
34. Elliot, I, p. 23.
35. *Ibid*, p. 5.
36. *Ibid*, p. 14.

four armies of the Gurjara-Pratihāras was about eight lakhs in strength may be similarly exaggerated. It is, however, quite likely that Al Masudi may have based his statement about the strength of each of the Gurjara-Pratihāra armies on the report of the strength of only one of them, which may have been strengthened in numbers by the temporary mobilisation of large forces from other fronts or armies. The total fighting force of the Gurjara–Pratihāras may have been a million or a million and a quarter. The Rāshṭrakūṭas had more than once crossed swords with them successfully and their forces too could not have been much less in numbers. Their civil administration was largely manned by military officers, and, therefore, it is not in the least unlikely, that they might have so arranged the matters as to raise easily an efficient fighting force of about a million, when critical battles had to be fought at several fronts. The Vijayanagar Empire of later period, with approximately equal resources, had an army of about a million.[37]

Forts

Writers on the Nitis'āstra devote a large space to the description of the various types of forts (*durga*) and declare that the strength of the army becomes immensely increased if it can take their shelter. The Deccan, over which the Rāshṭrakūṭas were ruling, affords ideal opportunities for the construction of mountain forts. It is, therefore, strange that neither Muslim chroniclers nor epigraphical documents should give any information about or description of the forts of the period. This silence will have to be interpreted as accidental. The Konur inscription of Amoghavarsha I[38] refers in glowing terms to the great feat of Bankeya in capturing the fort of Kedala from the enemy; it is, therefore, clear that the value of the forts was well understood by the

37. Moreland, *India at the Death of Akbar*, pp 16–17.
38. E. I. VI, p. 29.

Rāshṭrakūṭas. We may presume that they must have built several forts on the hills, which were plentiful in their dominions. The fort of Morkhind in Nasik district is one of the forts in Maharashtra, the antiquity of which goes back to our period; when the Wani-Dindori[39] and Radhanpur[40] plates were issued by Govinda III, he was encamped in that fort. Many other forts in the Deccan, which were repaired by Shivaji in his war of independence, may have been as old as our period. It is almost certain that the Rāshṭrakūṭas must have built several forts in their Empire, though unfortunately we know nothing about them at present.

Navy

Neither Muslim accounts nor epigraphical records give us any information about the navy of the Empire. Even the grants of the S'ilāhāras, the Konkan feudatories of the Rāshṭrakūṭas, give no clue to the condition or the strength of the navy. There was no necessity of the naval force to carry on the warfare with the Gangas, Pallavas, Chālukyas, Pālas, and the Gurjara Pratīhāras, who were the principal foes of the Empire. The Arabs, with whom the Rāshṭrākūṭas used to come into contact, were a maritime power, but they were always on terms of friendship with them. and this may have rendered the maintenance of a strong navy unnecessary. From Abu Zaid, a contemporary writer, we learn that some of the kings on the western coast, *e. g.* the king of Cape Kamorin, used to have their navies; it is, therefore, not unlikely that our Empire too may have had a naval force. But it is not in the least likely that its strength could have been anything like the strength of the army.

Weapons of War

It is to be regretted that the weapons of war should have been nowhere mentioned in our records in the manner

39. I. A., XI, p. 157. 40. E. I., VI., p. 242.

of the Allahabad Pillar Inscription of Samudragupta.[41] Historians of Mahmud of Ghazni mention swords, spears, bows, arrows and maces as the weapons used by the opposing Hindu forces.[42] These were also the principal weapons of fighting in contemporary Kashmir. It is, therefore, clear that these must have been the weapons mainly used by the Deccan armies of our period. Stone-throwing-machines are mentioned in the Mahābhārata ; they were used by Alexander the Great and the Muslim invaders of Sindh. But neither epigraphical records, nor Mahomedan writers refer to the use of such machines by the Hindu forces of the time. They were, however, used by the Kashmir armies, and were known as '*yantrotpala*' *i.e.* machines (to throw) stones.[43] It is, therefore, not unlikely that the use of these machines may have been known in the south as well. The rules of fighting as laid down by Manu prohibit the use of poisoned arrows ; it will be soon shown that not all these rules were observed in our period and we know that in contemporary Kashmir, arrows used to be besmeared with a certain ointment in order to set ablaze the camp of the enemy.[44] It is, therefore, not likely that the arrows used were always pure and unbesmeared. It was customary in Kashmir to supply the soldiers with heavy armours[45] to protect them while fighting; we may well presume that similar protection was available to the soldiers in the Deccan of our period.

Rules of Fighting

The rules of righteous fighting laid down by some of the earlier writers had become dead letter during our period. The war had ceased to be a concern merely of the fighters. Whole villages were often destroyed[46] and the loot of property could not be avoided. Express reference to the depredations of war

41. C. I. I., III, p. 1.
42. Elliot, *History*, II, p. 30.
43. Rājataranginī, VIII, 2530.
44. *Ibid*, VII, 983.
45. *Ibid*, VIII, 3294.
46. E. I., VI, p. 162.

is made in a Yādava Grant of the 11th century.[47] One of the articles of treaty concluded between Nayapāla and Karṇa, at the instance of the Budhist monk Atīśa, was to restore or compensate for the property seized by either side with the exception of the articles of food.[48] When Chacha captured the fort of Sikka, he killed 5000 soldiers and made the inhabitants slaves and prisoners of war.[49] This procedure was in direct contradiction of the rule in Manusmriti, VII, 92. Kiraṇapura and Chakrakoṭṭya were burn. when they were captured by the hostile forces,[50] and Mānyakheṭa was plundered when it capitulated to the Parmāra ruler S'rī Harsha.[51] Numerous examples of a similar nature are recorded by Kalhana.[52] It is, therefore, clear that the rules of humane and equitable warfare laid down by earlier writers were more often violated than observed during our period throughout the length and breadth of India. It is interesting to note that the practice of the age is in conformity with the theories to be seen in contemporary works. Kāmandaka boldly declares that one need not refrain from the destruction of the enemy even by unfair and immoral means,[53] and even the Jain ascetic writer Somadeva, is compelled to countenance crooked (*kūṭayuddha*) and treacherous (*tūshnīm yuddha*)[54] warfare.

Police Department

The policing arrangements of villages were under the supervision of the headmen. The village watchman was in the immediate charge of the work, and it was his business to detect all the crimes, especially the thefts, that may be committed in the village. If a theft or robbery was committed, he had either to find out the culprit or to trace his footsteps to

47. I. A., XII, p. 123.
48. J. P. T. S., I., p. 9.
49. Elliot, I, p. 142.
50. E, I., IX, p. 51.
51. E I., XIII, p. 180.
52. Rājataranginī, IV, 294, VI, 351, VII, 149 etc.
53. XVIII, 54.
54. XXX, 90-91.

a neighbouring village; otherwise he was compelled to compensate for the loss. His liability was, of course, limited by his means and it was based on a shrewd suspicion that he himself might be the thief or in league with him. If the watchman refused to pay, his grain-share at the time of the harvest was cut off, his service-land was transferred to his nearest relative, or he was fined, imprisoned and given corporal punishment.[55] If the stolen goods could not be either recovered or full compensation for them could not be exacted from the watchman, the whole community or the government had to compensate the victim.

This communal and government liability has been recognised by several writers. Vishṇu says that if the king is unable to recover stolen goods, he must pay their value out of his treasury.[56] The rules in the Arthaśāstra are more detailed. Kauṭalya says, 'When any part of merchandise has been lost or stolen, the headman of the village shall make up the loss. Whatever merchandise is lost or stolen in the intervening places between two villages, shall be made good by the superintendent of the pasture. If there is no pasture-land, then the officer called Chorarajjuka would be responsible. Failing him, the boundary and neighbouring villages shall make up the loss, and if the property cannot be ultimately traced, the king shall ultimately make good the loss out of his own treasury.[57] That this communal and government liability, which has been admitted even by Kauṭalya, was actually enforced in practice is shown by a 12th century inscription from Rajaputana, which embodies an agreement on the part of the townsmen of Dhalopa, that they would be responsible for any thefts that might occur in their town. The king of the place had made the arrangements about the watch and ward of the place.[58] The principle of the communal responsibility was thus recognised by early

55. Altekar, *Village Communities*, p. 59.
56. III, 67. 57. IV, 13. 58. E. I., XI, p. 40.

writers like Vishṇu and Kauṭalya, and was actually enforced in Rajputana of the 12th and in the Deccan of the 17th and the 18th centuries. It is, therefore, very likely that it was enforced in our period as well.

Manu lays down that there should be established police stations in the kingdom, one being intended for 2, or 4, or 5 villages.[59] Similar arrangements probably existed in our period. The police officers were known in our period as Choroddharaṇikas or Daṇḍapāśikas. The former are actually mentioned in the Antroli-Charoli copper plates of Karkkarāja of Gujarat,[60] and the latter in several Valabhi records.[61] That only one Rāshṭrakūṭa record just mentioned should make reference to the police officers is probably to be explained on the assumption that it was not deemed necessary to mention these officers in the copper-plate grants creating alienated villages, as these officers had no powers to interfere with the fiscal matters. There cannot be any doubt that the Choroddharaṇikas were fairly common in our period. Chola records of our period mention watchmen, whose duty it was to keep a watch over the paths;[62] it is not unlikely that similar officers may have been employed in the Rāshṭrakūṭa dominions as well.

Crimes, that could not be locally detected, must have been investigated by these Choroddharaṇika and Daṇḍapāśika officers. It is very likely that these officers worked under the directions of the Rāshṭrapatis and Vishayapatis, who being also at the head of the local troops, could have afforded military assistance to the police department, in case it was necessary for the apprehension of desperate robbers or dacoits.

Section B: The Feudatories

Feudatory states are not a new feature in the Indian polity introduced by Lord Wellesley. Since very early times

59. VII, 114. 60. J. B. B. R. A. S., XVI, p. 106.
61. E. g. Valabhi plates of Dhruvasena. dated 526 A. D. V. p. 204
62. S. I. I., II, Nos. 23 and 24.

empires in India have generally consisted partly of directly administered areas, and partly of territories under feudatory states, which were allowed a large amount of autonomy in return for their allegiance and tribute to the imperial power. Writers like Manu have laid down that even when an enemy king is conquered or killed in war, the conqueror should not annex his state, but should appoint a near relative of the former ruler as his own nominee to the vacant throne, imposing his own conditions upon him. The Mauryan, Gupta, Vardhana and the Gurjara-Pratihāra Empires show that this principle was very largely followed in practice in Ancient India. Even foreign observers have noted this peculiar feature of the Indian polity. Writing in about 850 A.D., Sulaiman says :—'When a king subdues a neighbouring state in India, he places over it a man belonging to the family of the fallen prince, who carries on the government in the name of the conqueror. The inhabitants would not suffer it to be otherwise.' The Rāshṭra-kūṭas also usually followed this principle, and as a result, the empire included a large number of feudatory states. Examples of attempts at annexation are not unknown; thus Dhruva I had imprisoned the Ganga king and appointed his eldest son Stambha as the imperial viceory over the newly annexed province.[63] Govinda III is described in the Baroda plates of Karkka[64] as the uprooter of the royal families; Karhad plates of Kṛshṇa III were issued when that king was encamped at Melpadi in South Arcot district, engaged in creating livings for his dependents out of the newly conquered southern territories, and in taking possession of all the property of the defeated feudatories.[65] It must be, therefore, admitted that some of the more ambitious rulers of our dynasty sought to set at naught the principle of non-annexation; but it has to be added that their efforts were one and all unsuccessful. Gangawadi could not be directly administered as an annexed

63. *Ante* p. 54.
64. I. A., XII, p. 157.
65. E. I., IV, p. 278.

province for more than 30 years, and the portions of Tamil country that were annexed by Kṛshṇa III were recovered by the Cholas immediately after his death.

The number of the feudatories representing the conquered royal houses was further enlarged by the creation of new ones as a reward for military service. Most of these used to be originally appointed only as governors with the feudatory privilege of the Pañchamahāśabdas, but the principle of hereditary transmission of office used to convert them soon into full-fledged feudatories.

Some of the protected states like Hyderabad, Baroda and Kolhapur, have their own feudatories at present; a similar practice prevailed in our period as well. In 813 A.D., Govinda III was the emperor; his nephew Karkka was the feudatory ruler over southern Gujarat, and S'rī-Budhavarsha of Salukika family was governing Siharika 12 as a sub-feudatory, to which position he was raised by the younger brother of Karkka.[66] The Raṭṭas of Saundatti, who were the feudatories, first of the Rāshṭrakūṭas and then of the later Chālukyas, had their own sub-feudatories.[67] Naturally, therefore the status and powers of the feudatories could not have been the same in all cases, a circumstance which reminds us of the present-day Indian polity, where also different ruling princes enjoy different powers and status. The important feudatory chiefs were entitled to the use of the five musical instruments, the names of which, according to a Jain writer, named Revākopyāchara, were S'ringa (horn), S'ankha (conch), Bheri (drum), Jayaghaṇṭā (the bell of victory) and Tammata.[68] They were also allowed the use of a feudal throne, fly whisk, palanquin, and elephants. Many of the sub-feudatories on the other hand may not have enjoyed any ruling powers at all, and may have been designated Sāmantas or Rajas only by courtesy. In many Canarese

66. E. I., III, p. 53. 67. I. A., XIV, p. 24.
68. I. A., XII, p. 96.

inscriptions even sub-divisional officers are seen having the title of *rasa* or king. It is probably on account of this circumstance that we read in the S'abara-bhâshya on the Mīmānsāsūtra II, 3, 3 that the title *rājan* was used by the Āndhras even with reference to a Kshatriya who was not engaged in ruling over a town or country, and that Kumārila, a writer belonging to our period, amplifies the statement by observing that the term Āndhra has been used with reference to the southerners in general.

Feudatory states had to entertain an ambassador from the imperial court. He exercised general powers of supervision, and control and occupied a position corresponding to that of the Political Agent or Resident of the present day. He was received, as merchant Sulaiman informs us, with profound respect that was naturally expected to be shown to the representative of the paramount power. He had under him a number of spies for fishing out information; the thousands of courtesans with which Amoghavarsha I is known to have covered the courts of hostile kings[69] must have been intended for a similar purpose, and been working under the direction of the imperial ambassador. The various kinds of spies, mentioned in the Arthaśāstra, were probably not unknown to the Deccan of our period.

The control, which the paramount power exercised, differed partly with the status of the feudatory and partly with the strength of the paramount power. General obedience to the orders of the imperial power was expected and exacted. Attendance at the imperial court was required not only on ceremonial occasions, but also at periodical intervals; otherwise we cannot understand how our literary writers and epigraphical documents should be always describing the imperial courts as full of feudatories. A regular tribute had to be paid; we find Govinda III touring about in the southern parts of his empire for the purpose of collecting the tributes

69. E. I., VI, P. 102.

due from his feudatories.[70] Special presents were expected on the occasions of festivity in the imperial household like the birth of a son or marriage.[71] As in medieval Europe, they had to supply a certain number of troops to their feudal lord and to participate in his imperial campaigns. Narasimha Chālukya, a feudatory of Indra III, had taken a prominent part in the latter's campaign against the Gurjara-Pratihāra emperor, Mahīpāla.[72] The Gujarat Rāstrakūṭa viceroyalty was created as a kind of bulwork against the Gurjara-Pratīhāras.[73] The Chālukyas of Vengi had to supply forces to the Rāshṭrakūṭas in their wars against the Gangas.[74] From a Bangalore museum Ganga record[75] we learn that Nāgattara, a feudatory of the Gangas, had to participate with his own forces, at the bidding of his sovereign, in a feud between Ayyapadeva and Vīramahendra wherein he lost his life. This practice prevailed in northern India also; Chatsu inscription of Bālāditya[76] and the Kahla plates of Kalachuri Sodhadeva[77] show that the ancestors of these feudatories had to participate in the wars of their feudal lord, Mihira Bhoja, with the Pālas of Bengal. Much of the confusion that arises, while marshalling the facts of ancient Indian history, is due to the habit of the subordinate feudatories of claiming as their own the successes which were really won by their feudal lords.

The measure of internal autonomy that was enjoyed by the feudatories was not uniform as observed already. The bigger among them like the Gujarat Rāshṭrakūṭas and the Konkan S'ilāhāras enjoyed large amount of internal autonomy. They could create their own sub-feudatories.[78] Subject to the payment of a certain amount of tribute they had full

70. I. A., XI., P. 126. 71. *Nitivākyāmṛita* XXX, 32.

72. *Karṇatakabhāshābhūshaṇa*, introduction, p. XIV.

73. I. A., XII. p. 160. 74. *Ante* pp. 91–94.

75. E. I., VI, p. 49. 76. E. I., XII, p. 101.

77. E. I., VII, p. 85. 78. E. I., III, p. 53.

powers over their revenues. They could assign taxes,[79] alienate villages,[80] and even sell them[81] without the sanction of the imperial power. The position of these feudatories was probaly as high as that of Kumārapāla of Assam and Dhruvasena of Valabhi in the court of Harsha. How slender was the control which the proud feudatories were disposed to tolerate in our period can be judged from the following extract from a letter of Akkham, the Lohana chief of Brahmanabad, to Chacha, who had called upon him to recognise his sovereignty—'I have never shown you opposition or quarrelled with you. Your letter of friendship was received and I was much exalted by it. Our friendship shall remain and no animosity shall arise. I will comply with your orders. You are at liberty to reside at any place within the territory of Brahmanabad. If you have resolved to go in any other direction, there is nobdy to prevent you or molest you. I possess such power and influence that can render you aid.'[82]

Smaller feudatories enjoyed far less autonomy. Not only could they create no sub-feudatories, but they had not even the power of alienating any villages. When Budhavarsha, a Chālukya feudatory of Govinda III, desired to give a village to a Jain sage who had made him free from the evil influence of Saturn, he had to supplicate for the permission of his feudal lord.[83] Śaṅkaragaṇa, a feudatory of Dhruva, is seen taking his sanction at the time of alienating a village.[84] The necessity of imperial permission for such alienations is proved by the records of other contemporary dynasties both in the south and north. Vīrachola and Prithvīpati II, feudatories of the Cholas, had to take imperial sanction before they could

79. I. A., XIII, p. 136.
80. See the copper-plate grants of the Gujarat Rāshṭrakūṭas.
81. Tilgundi plates, 1083 A. D., E. I., III, p. 310.
82. Elliot, I., p. 146.
83. I. A., XII, p. 15.
84. E. I., IX, p. 195.

alienate villages in charity.[85] The early Kadambas also exercised a similar control over their feudatories.[86] In the Gurjara-Pratihāra empire even the feudatories in distant places like Kathiawar had to take imperial permission for such transactions; the 'Political Agents' of the imperial power had to sanction such alienations on behalf of their suzerains by authenticating the documents by their signatures.[87] The same practice prevailed in Nepal, as is clear from a 7th century inscription of S'ivadeva.[88]

Third-rate feudatories felt the heels of the imperial shoes still more severely. In the Kapadwanj plates of Kṛshṇa II[89] we find the emperor giving away in charity a village situated within the jurisdiction of his feudatory Mahāsāmanta-prachaṇḍadaṇḍanāyaka Chandragupta. In the Kadarol inscription of Someśvara, we find a feudatory chief agreeing to pay annually five golden Gadyanakas for a certain charity, because he was commanded to do so by Someśvarabhatta, the premier of the Imperial power.[90] It would be thus seen that the smaller feudatories had to remain in the dread, not only of their emperor, but also of his ministers and ambassadors.

The feudatories were subjected to a number of indignitiest if they dared to rebel and were defeated in war. Sometimes they were compelled to do the menial work, as was the lot of the Vengi ruler who had to sweep the stables of his conqueror Govinda III.[91] They had to surrender their treasures, dancing girls, horses and elephants to the imperial power as a punishment for their disloyalty. Even their wives were sometimes put into prison and the marriage of Chacha with the widow of his feudatory Akkham would show that the less cultured princes used to subject them to further indignities and

85. E. I., IV, p. 82; S. I. I., II, p. 369.
86. I. A, VI, p. 32.
87. E. I., IX, p. 9.
88. I. A., XIII, p. 98.
89. E. I., I, p. 53.
90. I. A., I, p. 141.
91. E. I., XVIII, p. 248.

humiliations. Attempts at annexation, though rare, were not unknown.

If the central government became weak, the feudatories used to be practically independent. They could then exact their own terms for supporting the fortunes of their titular emperor; the commentary on the *Rāmapālacharit* shows how Rāmapāla of Bengal had to pay a heavy price in order to get the support of his feudatories for winning the throne.[92] Their position became still more strong if there was a war of succession; they could then take sides and try to put their nominee on the imperial throne, thus playing the role of the king-makers. On such occasions they could pay off their old scores by dethroning their old tyrant and imposing their own terms on the new successor. Dhruva, Amoghavarsha I and Amoghavarsha III had owed their thrones to a considerable degree to the support of their feudatories. The weakness of the position of Amoghavarsha I was to a large extent due to the fact that he owed his throne to his feudatories, like the cousin ruler of the Gujarat branch, who would not brook the former degree of the imperial control.

92. Banerji, *The Palas of Bennal*, p. 85.

PART III

CHAPTER XIII

Religious Condition

The Hindu revival, begun in the north under the S'unga patronage, reached its culmination in India as a whole during our period. There were a few exceptions; Sindh continued to be largely under the Buddhist influence down to the beginning of our age as the *Chachanāmā* testifies; in Bengal Buddhism continued to flourish down to its conquest by the Muslims towards the end of the 12th century. In the Deccan itself the revival of Hinduism did not in the least affect the prospects of Jainism; it continued to be the religion of a strong minority throughout our period. That sect was destined to make rapid progress in Gujarat in the 12th century under the influence of Hemachandra and his pupil and patron king Kumārapāla. In spite of this local ascendency of Buddhism and Jainism in some of the provinces of India, it must be, however, admitted that the period under review marked a distinct and decisive advance of the reformed Hinduism. The discomfiture of Buddhism can be regularly traced from a much earlier period. It is true that in spite of state patronage of Hinduism Buddhism continued to prosper in the Gupta age, as the accounts of Fa Hsien and the sculptures of the Gupta school of Buddhist art at Sarnath, which represents the indigenous Buddhist art at its best, clearly show. But the tide had turned; and its effects were to be clearly seen in the seventh century. In spite of Harsha, Yuan Chwang found that the Punjab, and the Northern United Provinces, which were definitely Buddhist at the time of Fa Hsien, had slipped back into heterodoxy. Sacred places of Buddhists like Kosambi, S'ravastī, Kapilavastu, Kusinagara, and Vaiśāli were either-wild ruins or populated by heretics;[1] even in Magadha, Buddhism was not supreme.

The new ground gained in the interval was only at Kanauj, where the number of the Vihāras increased from 2 to 100; but this was due to the temporary impetus given by the patronage of Harsha and did not represent the tendency of the age. Buddhism had realised in the days of Yuan Chwang and I-tsing that its days in India were numbered; these Chinese pilgrims record a number of superstitious beliefs current among the Buddhists themselves, about the destined disappearance of their religion from India. At Budhagaya itself the brethern believed that their faith would disappear when certain images of Avalokiteśvara in that locality would be completely buried under sand, and some of them were already more than chest-deep under that material in the seventh century A.D.[2] A garment alleged to have been worn by the Buddha himself was shown to Yuan Chwang at Purushapura or modern Peshawar; it was in a sadly tattered condition and the monks believed that the religion would perish the moment the garment was no more. I-tsing, who came in the third quarter of the 7th century, saw very clearly what way the things were moving; he emphasises the necessity of a synthesis of the various sects, if the rapid decline of the religion was to be arrested.[3] In the Deccan and Karnataka, Buddhism was never very strong; in the 1st and 2nd. centuries B.C. and A.D., as the epigraphic evidence from the Western India shows, it had several centres along the Western Coast; but they had begun to decline much earlier than our period. The pious Fa Hsien did not visit the Deccan because he was told that the people there were subscribing to bad and erroneous views and did

1. Watters, I, pp. 366, 377, II, pp. 125–6, 63.
2. Watters, II, p. 115.
3. Takakusu :—I-tsing, *A Record of Buddhist Religion*, p. 15.

not follow the Sramanas and the law of the Buddha.[4] He had heard only a hearsay report; but it could not have been altogether erroneous. The Vākāṭakas who were ruling in Northern Maharashtra were orthodox Hindus; the founder of the house had performed a number of Vedic sacrifices like *Agnishṭoma, Āptoryāma* and *As'vamedha* and his descendants were either Shaivites or Vaishnavites, but never Buddhists.[5] Earlier rulers of the Chālukya house, which subsequently rose to power, were again orthodox Hindus, who prided themselves on having performed a number of Vedic sacrifices like *Agnichayana, Vājapeya, As'vamedha, Bahusurvarṇa* etc.[6] Buddhism, therefore, naturally began to decline. Yuan Chwang records that in Konkan there were 100 monasteries, but heretics were very numerous; the case could not have been much different in Maharashtra which, though a much a bigger province, had also the same number of monasteries.[7] The number of Buddhist monks in both the provinces was only 6000. The strength of Buddhism lay in its cloistered population, for there was nothing to mark off distinctively the lay Buddhist population from the ordinary Hindus. Any one could become an *upāsaka* by reciting the triple formula; the church did not care either to prescribe a special form of recognition, or to regulate religious ideas and habits and metaphysical beliefs of the laymen, or even to prohibit them from becoming at the same time lay followers of some other church.[8] The total Buddhist population in the Deccan at the middle of the 7th century could not have been much more than 10,000, and that number may have further dwindled down by the beginning of our period.

4. Legge, Fa Hsien, *A Record of Buddist Kingdoms*, Chap. XXXV.
5. Fleet, C. I. I., III, pp. 236–7.
6. Mahakuta inscription of Mangalīs'a, I. A., XIX, p. 17.
7. Watters, II, p. 239.
8. Oldenberg: *The Buddha*, pp. 162–3, 382–4.

It is a noteworthy fact that the revival of Hinduism did not affect the fortunes of Jainism in the Deccan. This may be ascribed mainly to two causes. Firstly the religion was fortunate to acquire state patronage under the early Kadambas, Chālukyas, and the Western Gangas. Many of the Rāshṭrakūṭa kings were themselves Jains and so were many of their viceroys and generals. The second cause was the influence of the work and achievements of a number of important Jain saints and writers like Samantabhadra, Akalankadeva, Vidyānanda, Mānikyanandin, Prabhāchandra, Jinasena, Gunachandra, and Pampa.(9)

Wide and sympathetic toleration was the general characteristic of our age. There were a few persecutions here and there; in the *S'ankaradigvijaya*, a book of essentially lengendary character, S'as'āṅka is alleged to have ordered a general murder of Buddhists including women and children; in Sindh, Chacha's brother Chander is said to have compelled(10) his subjects to accept his faith under the threat of sword; Udayendiram plates of Nandivarman which record the grant of a village to Brahmanas *after the destruction of the irreligious*, (11) may suggest a kind of persecution of heterodox sects in Tamil country; the Jains for some time suffered terribly from the S'aiva fanaticism of some of the Pandya rulers. But these cases were rather exceptional and did not represent the spirit of the age. From the 5th century A.D., the Purānas were advocating the view that all the different deities were the manifestations of the same divine principle, and that their followers should not quarrel. This view had begun to be universally accepted. Kṛshṇavarmā, a king of the early Kadamba dynasty, who describes himself as the performer of the As'vamedha sacrifice, is known to

9. See Chapter XVI, section B.

10. Elliot, I. p. 153.

11. Cf. अन्यानधर्मकृत्यान् विनाश्य I. A., VIII, 276; but अधर्मकृत्यान् may mean immoral persons as well.

have given a munificent gift for the maintenance of a Jaina establishment.[12] Even when he was an avowed Buddhist, Harsha used to worship in public Hindu deities like the Sun and S'iva.[13] Karka Suvarṇavarsha of the Gujarat branch himself a staunch S'aiva, had given a field to a Jain Vihara at Naosari.[14] Amoghavarsha I was undoubtedly a follower of Jainism, and yet he was such an ardent believer in the Hindu goddess Mahālakshmī, that he actually cut off one of his fingers and offered it to her, being led to believe that an epidemic, from which his kingdom was suffering, would vanish away by that sacrifice.[15] Dantivarman of the Gujarat branch, himself a Hindu, gave a village to a Buddhist Vihara.[16] Brahmanas of Ballal family at Mulgund offered a field to a Jain Monastery in 902 A.D.[17] The records of the Raṭṭas of Saundatti are very interesting in this respect, Mahāsāmanta Pṛthvīrāma, a contemporary of Kṛshṇa II, is known to have erected a Jain temple in c. 875 A.D. His grandson was also a Jain, but the latter's grandson was a follower of Hinduism and is known to have given a grant of 12 *nivartanas* of land to his preceptor, who was well-versed in the three Vedas. His son Srīsena is known to have built a Jain temple. The Belur inscription of Jayasimha, dated 1022 A.D., is extremely interesting. The donor Akkādevī is described in this document as practising[18] the religious observances prescribed by the rituals of Jina, Buddha, Ananta *i. e.* Vishṇu and Rudra. The temple that she had erected was for Tripurusha *i. e.* Vishnu, Brahmā and S'ankara. This interesting lady had, not only made a synthesis of Hindu cults but also of all the main religious movements of the time, *viz.* Buddhism, Jainism, Vaishnavism and Saivism. Another

12. I. A., VII, 34. 13. Smith, *Early History*, p. 364.
14. Surat plates of 821 A.D., E. I., XXI.
15. Sanjan Copper-plates, E. I, XVIII, p. 248.
16. E. I., VI, p. 292. 17. J. B. B. R. A. S., X. 193.
18. I. A., XVIII, 274.

document belonging to the same century[19] opens with a laudation of Jina, followed immediately by that of Vishṇu. The inscription informs us that at the desire of the king, the Lord Nāgavarmā caused to be built a temple of Jina, Vishṇu, Iśvara and the Saints. What a clear example of wide toleration! A still more interesting case is to be found recorded in the Dambal stone inscription from Dharwar district belonging to the 11th century.[20] The donors were the followers of a S'aiva sect called Balanju; the grant drafted by them opens with a salutation to Jain *munīndras*, followed by another to the Buddhist Goddess Tārā and the purpose of the charity was to provide funds for a temple of Tārā and Buddha. The above examples will make it abundantly clear that the view of Prajāpati-smriti,[21] that a person should not visit a Jaina temple or cremating ground after partaking of a *Srūddha* feast would have found no acceptance in the Deccan of our period.

Such examples were not confined to the Deccan alone. Govindachandra, Gahadwal king of Kanauj, himself a Saivite, was married to a Buddhist princess Kumāradevī, and is known to have given six villages for the maintenance of the monks in the Jetavana of Sravasti.[22] Madanapāla of Bengal, himself a Buddhist, gave the gift of a village to a Brahmana for reciting the Mahabharata to his queen Chitramatikā.[23] It seemed as if the people had realised that there was no cultural difference between the three religions, and that a man may follow any one of them or make a combination, suitable to his own individual temperament, of the acceptable elements of any or all of them. The case seems to have been somewhat similar to that of a modern man of culture, who fails to realise any inconsistency in being a member, at one and the same time, of different societies formed for the promotion of literature, fine arts and morality. There was a certain amount of feeling

19. Belgave inscription of Somes'vara I, p. 1048. A. D., I. A., IV, p. 181. 20. I. A., X, 188. 21. V, 95.
22. E. I., XI, p. 22. 23. J. A., S. B., Vol. 69, p. 66.

exhibited in philosophical writings of the period, but even there behind the superficial clash, there was an inner movement of synthesis. It is now almost universally recognised that the scheme of Advaita philosophy, as outlined by S'ankara was largely influenced by the *S'ūnyavāda* of Nāgārjuna; many of the verses in the *Mūlamadhyamakārikā* of the latter anticipate the position later assumed by S'ankara.[24]

It need hardly be added that there was harmony prevailing among the followers of the different sects of Hinduism, since it existed even among the followers of the orthodox and the heterodox religions. The opening verse in the Rāshṭrakūṭa copperplates pays homage to both S'iva and Vishṇu. Their seal is sometimes the eagle, the vehicle of Vishṇu, and sometimes S'iva in the posture of a seated *Yogin*. The Gahadwal kings were themselves Saivites, but they used to worship both S'iva and Vishṇu at the time of making land grants.[25] There is a verse in the Surat plates of Karka stating that Indra, the father of the donor, did not bow his head even before any god, S'ankara excepted.[26] This smacks a little of the sectarian narrowness and some people may have occasionally exhibited it in our period. But it is not improbable that even in this verse the poet may have exaggerated the reality in order to develop a contrast. The general spirit of the age cannot be regarded as embodied in this verse. In the 10th century there existed at Salotgi in Bijapur district a temple constructed for the joint worship of Brahmadeva, S'iva, and Vishnu.[27] At Kargudri there

24. Cf. मायोपमं जगदिदं भवता नटरङ्गसदृशं दृष्टं ।
नात्मा न सत्त्वं न च जीवगतिधर्मा मरीच्युदकचन्द्रसमाः ॥
शून्यमिति न वक्तव्यमशून्यमिति वा भवेत् ।
उभयं नोभयं चेति प्रज्ञप्त्यर्थं तु कथ्यते ॥

25. E. g., E. I., XI, p. 24.

26. Cf. मुक्त्वा च सर्वभुवनेश्वरमादिदेवम् ।
नावन्दतान्यममरेष्वपि यो मनस्वी ॥ E. I., XXI.

27. E. I. IV, p. 66.

existed another shrine erected for the joint worship of S'ankara. Vishṇu, and Bhāskara.[28] These temples are more illustrative of the spirit of the age than the verse in the Surat plates referred to above.

The spirit of toleration was not confined to the religions of the land, but was extended to Mahomedanism as well. There were several Mahomedans in the western ports come for the purpose of commerce; they were allowed to practise their religion openly. Jumma masjids were permitted to be built for their use.[30] This permission to build mosques may be contrasted with the reply given by Mahmad Tughlagh to the request of the Chinese emperor to permit the rebuilding of some Buddhist temples sacked by the Muslims. The Sultan received the valuable gifts brought by the Chinese embassy, but wrote saying that the request could not be granted under the Islamic law as permission to build a temple in the territories of the Muslims could be given only to those who paid the Jizia tax. 'If thou wilt pay the Jizia, we shall empower thee to build a temple.'[31] Muslim officers were appointed to administer their personal law[32] to the Muslim inhabitants. This toleration is indeed surprising when one remembers the brutal treatment of the Hindus by the Muslim conquerors of Sindh, who gave no quarter to the Hindus in the warfare, demolished their temples, imposed the Jizia tax upon them, and enslaved thousands of Hindu women and sold them in the streets of Baghdad.[33] This policy of doing a good turn for an evil one may be indeed admired from the point of view of universal toleration and brotherhood, but it shows clearly that the Hinduism of our period was too blind or shortsighted to see the danger that was awaiting it from the religion it was tolerating so liberally.

28. I. A. X p. 251.
30. Elliot, I. p. 27 and p. 38.
31. Gibbs. *Ibn Batuta*, p. 214.
32. Elliot, I. p. 27.
33. *Ibid*, pp. 170, 173, 176 and 182.

The Muslims on the western coast were using Indian dress and language,[34] but a little enquiry would have shown that they were completely Persianised in Sindh, where they were under the complete sway of Persian costume, language and customs. The political alliance of the Rāshṭrakūṭas with the Arabs was not solely responsible for this toleration, for it continued under the Chālukyas of Gujarat also. Muhmud 'Ufi narrates a story of Rai Jaysing of Aṇahilapaṭṭaṇa, who personally investigated into the complaints of the Muslims of Cambay regarding the damage done to their property and mosques in a riot, punished the Parsi and Hindu ringleaders, and gave a lakh of *balotras* for the reerection of the mosques.[35] So neither the horrors of the conquest of Sindh nor the vandalism and rapine of the 20 and odd invasions of Mahmud of Ghazni could change the tolerant attitude of the Hindus towards the followers of Islam. Religious retaliation was out of question; Ibn Batuta describes how at the door of the Cathedral mosque in Delhi, enormous idols of brass were kept prostrate on the ground in order to make every visitor tread on them.[36] Hinduism of our period was in a position to inflict similar indignities, both in the south and the north, on the Muslim inhabitants of the Hindu states, but did not resort to such conduct.

The Hindu revival, which reached its culmination in our period, had three aspects, theological, philosophical and popular; let us consider them one by one.

The theological movement found its greatest exponent in Kumārila who, according to tradition, was an elderly contemporary of S'ankara, but may have really flourished a few decades earlier. Kumārila boldly stood for the pure Vedic religion, opposed the heterodox theory of Sanyāsa, and advocated the life-long performance of Vedic sacrifices involving slaughter of sentient beings. It is not to be, however, supposed

34. *Ibid*, I, 19. 35. *Ibid*, II, pp. 163-4.

that the theological movement began with Kumārila, it rather ended with him. It began with Patanjali; Pushyamitra S'unga, who was his contemporary, had performed the Aśvamedha sacrifice twice.[37] Literary activity continued under the Vṛttikāra, Śabarasvāmin, and Prabhākara and we find some of the Hindu rulers of the intervening period very enthusiastic about Vedic sacrifices. Nayanikā, the widow of the third Sātavāhana king, is known to have celebrated a number of Vedic sacrifices like Aśvamedha, Gavāmayana, Gargātirātra, Āptoryāma, etc.; Pravarasena, the founder of the Vākāṭaka dynasty of northern Maharashtra, is recorded to have performed[38] Agnishṭoma, Āptoryāma and Aśvamedha sacrifices. Two of the Gupta emperors are so far known to have celebrated the last mentioned sacrifice and one of the early Chālukya kings is recorded to have participated in several Vedic sacrifices.[39]

The arguments of the theological school, in spite of the brilliant advocacy of Kumārila who flourished just before our period, failed to carry conviction to the popular mind. The theories of *Ahinsā* and *Sanyāsa* had become so popular that a person advocating the life-long performance of Vedic sacrifices, involving slaughter, had no chance of captivating the popular mind. We hardly come across any Hindu kings of our period who cared to boast that they had performed Vedic sacrifices. We have numerous grants of the Rāshṭrakūṭa kings given to Brahmanas to enable them to discharge their religious duties, but these duties are generally of the Smārta rather than of S'rauta character. The Sanjan plates of Amoghavarshal[40] and the Cambay plates of Govinda IV[41] are the only two exceptions, where it is expressly stated that the grants were made to enable the Brahmanas to perform

36. Gibbs, *Ibn Batuta*, p. 195.
37. J. B. O. R. S., X, p. 202.
38. C. I., I., III, p. 236.
39. I. A., XIX, p. 17.
40. I. A., XVIII, p. 235.
41. E. I., VII, p. 41.

Vedic sacrifices like Rājasūya, Vājapeya, and Agnishṭoma. In all other cases the grants were made for discharging purely Smārta duties connected with *bali, charu, vais'vadeva* etc. These facts, disclosed by the analysis of the epigraphical evidence, are the most convincing proof that in spite of Kumārila's efforts, the S'rauta religion almost died down in our age. Some of the Smriti writers of our period assert boldly that *brāhmaṇya* cannot result merely by following the S'rauta religion to the exclusion of the Smārta one:[42] nay it is further declared that a man who studies and follows the Veda and its ritual and derides those of the Dharmaśāstra, ensures himself 21 births in the realm of the quadrupeds.[43] It is thus clear that both the theory and practice of the age had abandoned the Vedic sacrifices. Alberuni was informed that the Vedic sacrifices were rarely performed and practically abandoned because they presupposed a long life which was no longer vouchsafed in the present age.[44] This seems to have been another excuse invented for the non-performance of the Vedic sacrifices which had otherwise grown unpopular.

The philosophical revival had commenced about the second century B. C. when the nucleus of the present Brahmasūtras seems to have been formed. For about four centuries the Brahmasūtra school continued to expound the Hindu philosophical view and refute the heresies of the Jains and the Buddhists and others till the Brahmasūtras assumed their present form at about the middle of the 3rd century A. D. A number of writers continued the work, but it found its most powerful exponent in the great S'ankarāchārya, who flourished in our period. This great philosopher, though born in Kerala, was an all-India figure, and it would be interesting to enquire what was the influence of his teachings and activities in the Deccan of our period.

42. E. g. Atri, v. 354. 43. *Ibid*, v. II.

44. Sachau, Alberuni's India, II p. 139.

By advocating the superiority of Sanyāsa to Karmamārga and by maintaining that the Vedic sacrifices had merely a purificatory effect, S'ankarāchārya undoubtedly helped the tendency of the age to abandon the Vedic rituals; his controversy with Kumārila may or may not have been historical. It is true that S'ankara's arguments went equally against the Smārta Karmamārga, but we must not forget that people usually apply theories to the convenient and not to the logical extent. It must be also remembered that S'ankara himself was a fervent devotee of Pauranic deitiee and some of his most eloquent and appealing writings consist of prayers addressed to them. In this respect S'ankara was a powerful asset to the popular religion.

It is to be regretted that there should be so far discovered no trace of S'ankara and his work in epigraphical documents. This is rather strange, for tradition claims that he toured about preaching, discussing, controverting and founding monastic establishments throughout the length and breadth of India. There is ample evidence to show that the philosophico-literary activity enunciated by S'ankara continued ever increasing for several centuries. But the effect on popular life of the teachings and institutions of S'ankara during our period is difficult to estimate in the present state of our knowledge.

The first question to be answered is whether Sanyāsa became more popular than before as a result of S'ankara's teachngs. The answer seems to be in the negative. The negative evidence of the epigraphical records of our period is to some extent significant. The Rāshṭrakūṭas and their feudatories and contemporaries have given a number of grants, but none has been so far discovered made in favour of a Hindu Sanyāsin or his Maṭha. Buddhist and Jain Sanyāsins very often figure in our epigraphical records but Hindu Sanyāsins never. Sulaiman, who had several times visited the ports of western India during our period, no doubt refers to Hindu Sanyasins when he says :—'In India there are persons who in accordance with their profession wander in woods and mountains and rarely communicate with the rest of the mankind.' . But the presence of these Sanyāsins cannot be attributed to the influence of S'ankara, for the theory of four Ās'ramas, which had been started several centuries before the time of S'ankara, was responsible for their presence. It seems that we have to admit that S'ankara's advocacy of Sanyāsa did not produce in the society an upheaval, comparable to that produced by the Upanishadic, Jain and Buddhist movements. The reason seems to be the association of Sanyāsa with the heterodoxy in the popular mind, produced by the Jain and Buddhist monasteries, that were flourishing for several centuries.

S'ankarāchārya had founded four Maṭhas in the four corners of India and very soon subsidiary ones sprang into existence. Till recently these institutions were powers in the land; a decree (*ājnāpatra*) from them was respected by society as implicitly as the command of the king. What was the influence of these institutions over the Deccan of our period ?

It seems that these institutions did not wield any influence in our period. In the first instance we have got not a single reference to any Pīṭha or its activity in any records of our period. In the second place there are indications that down to the 12th century A. D., the term *Jagadguru*, which subsequently came to designate exclusively the occupants of the Pīṭhas funded by S'ankara, was used to denote ordinary Brahmanas of outstanding preeminence, learning and character. The Managoli inscription of 1161 A. D.[45] mentions that towards the end of the 10th century, in the Brahmadeya village of Manigavalli there flourished a celebrity, Is'vara Ghalisāsa by name, who was the Jagadguru of the world and whose feet were worshipped by Taila II, the overthrower of the Rāshṭrakūtas. There is nothing to indicate in the record that

45. I. A., p. 15.

Is'vara Ghalisāsa had any connection with the Pītha of Sringeri or its branch at Sankes'vara. Besides, were he a Jagadguru of the order founded by S'ankara, his name would have appeared in a Sanyāsin garb. He was a married man and the headship of the *agrahāra* of Managoli seems to have been hereditary in his family. His *gotra* was the same as that of the Chalukyas *viz.* Hārita, and Taila believed that it was the favour of this celebrity that had secured him the throne. It is therefore not unlikely that the title of Jagadguru may have been conferred upon him by his grateful and illustrious disciple. The record makes it clear that Is'vara Ghalisāsa was not the head of any Maṭha located at Managoli, and yet he was styled Jagadguru. If in our period the Pīṭhas founded by S'ankara had wielded the same influence as they did till recently, if there had been a branch of the Sringeri Pītha at Sankes'vara which is fairly near to Managoli, Is'vara Ghalisāsa, the head of the Managoli Agrahāra, who had no connection with any Maṭha, could not have dared to use the title Jagadguru. This record, therefore, makes it clear that the Pīthas founded by S'ankara were not exercising any appreciable influence in the Deccan till the end of our period. It must be further remembered that the claim to give the final verdict in socio-religious matters, claimed and conceded to the occupants of the Pīthas founded by S'ankara, must have appeared as preposterous in our period. In the Hindu period these matters were decided by special officers of Government who were variously known as Vinayasthitisthāpakas, Dharmānkus'as, Dharmapradhānas or Panditas. The last mentioned officer was to be a member of the ministry according to the *S'ukranīti*, a work which very probably belongs to our period with the exception of some interpolations, and it was he who was to review the realm of social and religious practices, to find out which of them, though prescribed in the S'āstras, were against the spirit of the age, which were absolutely obsolete, being countenanced neither by the S'āstra nor by custom, and to issue such orders regarding the points at dispute as may secure both this world and the next.[46] The Smritis of our and of earlier period[47] assign this function to a *parishad* or conference, composed of distinguished learned men of known character and piety. There is no real contradiction between S'ukra and these Smriti writers; for the royal officers, when and where they existed, may have presided over and been guided by the decisions of these experts. The case was similar to that of the judicial Panchayats: the judgments signed by Rama-Shastri Prabhune of the Peshva period used to embody the decisions of the Panchayats to whom the cases were referred, though the signatures of the Panchas did not appear on the judgments. It is therefore not likely that the ministers of the Hindu states and the Parishads of our period would have looked with favour upon the proposal to surrender their rights in social and religious matters to the order founded by S'ankarāchārya. It is very probable that the occupants of the Pīṭhas acquired their present powers and jurisdiction subsequent to the fall of Hindu states. With the establishment of Muslim rule the state ceased to look after the social and religious usages and the Parishads may, therefore, have gladly welcomed the idea of utilising the prestige, which was by that time acquired by the representatives of the order founded by S'ankara, for the enforcement of their decisions. As years rolled on, the prestige of the Pīṭhas increased in the Deccan and the Parishads were forgotten altogether.

Let us now proceed to consider the popular Hinduism *i. e.* the religion of the masses of our period. This religion may be described as the Smārta Pauranic religion. The

46. Cf. वर्तमानाश्च प्राचीना धर्माः के लोकसंश्रिताः। शास्त्रेषु के समुद्दिष्टा विरुध्यन्ते च केऽधुना ॥ लोकशास्त्रविरुद्धा ये पंडितास्तान् विचिन्तयेत्। नृपम् सम्बोधयेत् तत्र परत्रेह सुखप्रदैः ॥ II, 98-100

47. Gautama II, 10,47-48; Manu a XII, 110 ff; Yājanvalkya I, 9; S'atātapa 129; S'ankha, IV, 29, 63.

reform movement, which culminated in this development, had begun much earlier than our period; it had commenced with the later Smriti writers and the remodellers of the older Purāṇas and had so completely captured the imagination of the masses in our period that the advocates of the theological revival found themselves helpless before it. Unfortunately the precise chronology of these works is not yet definitely fixed, but it is generally agreed that the majority of them were composed sometime between 500 and 1000 A.D. Let us see what epigraphical evidence has got to say about the success or influence of this movement.

The Smritis had preached ths gospel of the Pancha-mahāyajnas, which were intended as substitutes for the Vedic sacrifices involving slaughter. Vast majority of the Brahmana donees of our period are described as performers of these sacrifices. During our period Smarta *agnihotra* was fairly common at least among professional priests; *Atrisamhitā*, which belongs to our period, says that a Brahmana, who does not keep *agnihotra*, is a person whose food should not be accepted.[48] The prevalence of *agnihotra* during our period is proved also by the testimony of Alberuni, who observes that the Brahmanas who kept one fire were called *Ishṭins* and those who kept three were called *agnihotrins*.[49] Some of the Nigama writers include *agnihotra* among things prohibited in the Kali age, but that view was not the view of our age.

If we compare the daily routine laid down by early Smriti writers for a Brahmana householder with that laid down by later Nibandha writers, we shall find a great change. The earlier writers like Manu and Yājnavalkya prescribe one bath and two prayers a day and lay an emphasis principally on the Panchamahāyajnas. The Nibandha writers seek to increase the Smarta ritual to such an extent that hardly any time is left for secular duties. Our period marked the transition time.

48. v. 254.

49. Sachau, I, p. 102.

The Nibandha writers definitely lay down three baths for a Brahmana, the Smriti writers of our period hesitate between one and two. Sankha is satisfied with one bath only, but Daksha, Kātyāyana, and Vaiyāghrapāda advocate two,[50] the second one being at the mid-day. That the rule of the Smritis was actually followed in practice towards the end of the 13th century,[51] is proved by Marco Polo who testifies to the fact that the Hindus of Malabar, both males and females, used to take two baths a day.[51] The theory of three daily baths had begun to appear towards the end of our period, and had not yet become popular. Alberuni notes the theoretical rule that a Brahmana should take three baths a day, but adds that in practice, the evening prayers were recited without a previous bath. He observes:—'Evidently the rule about the third bath is not as stringent as that relating to the first and second washings.'[52]

The number of prayers, *sandhyās*, was also tending to increase at about our period. As the etymology of the term *sandhyā* shows, the *sandhyā* times could obviously not have been more than two in the beginning. A third *sandhyā*, however, began to be advocated by some of the Smriti writers of our age. Atri lays down that a twiceborn should recite *sandhyā* thrice;[53] Vyāsa concurs and supplies three different names to the three different sandhyās as Gāyatrī, Sarasvatī, and Sāvitrī respectively.[54] The Nibandha writers accept this theory and prescribe three *sandhyās* universally.

It will be thus seen that the Smriti writers of our period were showing a tendency to make the simple Smārta religion as rigid and complex as the S'rauta one; detailed rules, hardly leaving much scope for individual liberty, began to be framed for *s'aucha*, *dantadhāvana*, bath, *āchamana* etc. S'rauta

50. Quoted in *Smṛtichandrikā*, *Āhnikākaṇḍa* pp. 290–291. 463.
51. II, p. 342
52. II, pp. 33, 134.
53. Quoted in *Āchāramayūkha*, p. 39. 54. Ibid.

sacrifices had died down in our period but the rigidity of ritualistic details which characterised them became a prominent feature of the Smarta religion from about the 12th century onwards. Our period was the transition period.

Another characteristic feature of the Hinduism of our period was the popularity of the *Vratas*. The theory and advocacy of Vratas was a peculiar feature of the Puranas, most of which were either composed or remodelled near about our period. Out of the 113 Vratas mentioned in the *Vratārka* of S'ankarabhaṭṭa as many as 110 are based on the authority of the Puranas. 128 Vratas mentioned in the *Vratakaumudī* and 205 described in *Vratarāja* are all of them based on Pauranic authority. Vratas offered opportunities for individuals of both the sexes of personally going through a course of religious life characterised by self-denial and austerities. There was also the bait of the fulfilment of desires intended for the ignorant. They therefore powerfully appealed to the popular mind, and are still characteristic feature of Hinduism in rural areas. In the Deccan of our period, they were probably becoming popular We do not find any reference to their popularity in epigraphical records of our period. But this fact is probably accidental, for we have ample evidence to show that the Pauranic religion, as a whole, was capturing the popular imagination.

The Nargund inscription, dated 939 A.D.[55], records some voluntary contributions from the various classes of inhabitants for the purpose of a local tank. The contribution of the Brahmanas is stated to be one golden Paṇa on the occasion of each *Prāyas'chitta* performed in the village. The Kalas inscription of Govinda IV [56] also records an assignment by the local Brahmanas of the fees they used to receive at penitential rites (*prāyas'chittas*) for the maintenance of a local college. These records will therefore show

55. I., A., XII, p. 224. 56. E. I., XIII, p. 325.

that at least some of the various Prāyas'chittas that have been prescribed in the Smritis were performed by some sections of Hindu society. Some of the later Smritis, that were written not far from our period, *e. g.* Laghu-Sātātapa Brihadyama, and Āpastamba, are almost entirely devoted to the discussion of penitential rites. These can be better described as Prāyaśchitta manuals necessitated by the general tendency of the age to perform them.

The Puranas offered new *saguṇa* and anthropomorphic nuclei for religious devotion, and the deities that were glorified in them soon became popular gods of the masses. Growth of sectional rivalry was anticipated by the doctrine that all the deities are the manifestations of one and the same Supreme Power. Our epigraphical records bear eloquent testimony to the popularity of the Pauranic deities in our period. That S'aivism and Vaishnavism were the main sects of our time is indicated by the usual opening verse in the Rāshṭrakūṭa grants, which contains a salutation to both S'iva and Vishṇu. The grant of Abhimanyu Rāshṭrakūṭa mentions a Dakshiṇa-S'iva temple, whose custodian Jaṭābhāra seems to have been a Pāśupata. At Salotgi in Bijapur district there was a temple of Kātyāyanī and another constructed for the joint worship of Brahmā, Vishṇu, and S'iva.[57] The custom of founding a S'iva temple in commemoration of a dead ancestor, and of naming the deity after the person to be commemorated, had already become prevalent in our period. Hebbal inscription, dated 975 A.D.,[58] refers to a temple of Bhujjabbeśvara built to commemorate Bhubbarasi, the grand mother of the Ganga ruler Mārasinha II. Ragholi plates of Jayavardhana[59] and the Kavi plates of Govinda of the Gujarat branch[60] attest to the prevalence of the Sun worship. The Pathari pillar inscription discloses a temple of S'auri.[61]

57. E. I., IV, p. 60.
58. E. I., IV, p. 350.
59. E. I., IX, p. 42.
60. I. A., V, p. 145.
61. E. I., IX, p. 250.

A temple of S'āradā existed in Managoli.[62] The worship of the presiding deities of the locality is mentioned in record from Saundatti, dated 875 A.D., which refers to the temple of the deity presiding over Sugandhavatī 12.[63] Whether Vithoba of Pandharpur, perhaps the most popular diety of the Deccan to-day, existed in our period is difficult to determine with certainty. An inscription from Belgaum district, dated 1250 A.D., refers to a grant made in the presence of Vishṇu at Pauṇḍarika-kshetra, which is described in the document as situated on the banks of the Bhīmā.[64] The name of the Tīrtha and its situation on the Bhīmā make it obvious that our inscription clearly proves the existence of the Viṭṭhala temple at Pandharpur in 1250 A.D. It was even then a famous centre of pilgrimage; the premier Mallseṭṭi utilised his presence at Paundarika-kshetra for making the donation. The fame of the temple was already well established by the middle of the 13th century A.D.; it is, however, difficult to say how far earlier than 1200 A.D. the worship of Viṭṭhala had commenced at Pandharpur. Since it was a famous centre at about 1200 A.D., we may reasonably presume that the worship of the God at the place was at least a couple of centuries old at that time.

In addition to the above gods the masses were worshipping a number of aboriginal deities. The worship of Mhasoba was current. Al Idrisi obviously refers to it when he says:—[65] 'Others worship holy stones on which butter and oil is poured." Tree and serpent worship is mentioned by the same writer; the serpent worshippers, we are told, used to keep them in stables and feed them as well as they could. He further says:—'Some acknowledge the intercessory powers of graven stones' This may possibly refer to the belief in inscribed talismans or it may refer to cases like that of the famous

62. E. I., VII, p. 143.
63. J. B. B. R. A. S., X, 199.
64. I. A., XIV, p. 70.
65. *Elliot*, I, p. 76.

Garuḍadhvaja erected at Vidiśā by the Greek ambassador Heliodorus, which was being worshipped as Khāmbābā at the time Dr. D. R. Bhandarkar discovered it.

The followers of all these different gods formed, or rather appeared to a foreign observer as forming, different sects.[65] Al Idrisi therefore states that there were 42 different sects in India at his time. But since the followers of the different deities shared the belief that they were worshipping the different manifestations of one and the same Supreme God, they can hardly be described as forming different sects.

The problem of the origin and prevalence of the image worship is still to be properly worked out. Dharmasūtra writers rarely refer to the duty of worshipping images of gods either at home or in public temples; nor is it mentioned by Manu. The cult of public temples seems to be later than the time of Asoka. It may have been deemed a suitable substitute for the great S'rauta sacrifices which were attended by a great number of people. Possibly the example of Buddhism with its splendid temples and monasteries may have given rise in the Hindu mind to a desire to have similar centres of public worship and congregation. Whatever the real causes may have been, temples soon became recognised centres of public worship and were characteristic of the Hinduism of our period. It must be, however, noted that the sums of money that were being spent over the temples, images, their ornaments and daily worship were tending to become excessively high in our period. Al Utbi says :—' The kings of Hind, the chiefs of that country, and rich devotees used to amass their treasures and precious jewels and send them time after time to be presented to idols, that they might receive a reward for their good deeds and draw near to their God.'[66] Not much evidence is forthcoming from the Deccan proper about the wealth unnecessarily hoarded in temples in the form of ornaments etc., but we know that in northern India temples were

66. Elliot, II, p. 34.

the places that yielded highest amount of plunder to Mahmud of Ghazni. Epigraphical evidence is available to show that large sums of money were spent in Tamil country to furnish costly gold and jewel ornaments to the deity in the Rājarājeśvara temple by Chola kings and their subjects.[67] Some of the temples in the Deccan too must have been centres of wealth; Kṛshṇa I is known to have given a number of gold and jewel ornaments to the S'iva image in the Ellora temple, which he had excavated from solid rock at great cost.[68] Specific cases of alienations of lands and villages for different temples are fairly numerous and the Cambay plates of Govinda IV,[69] dated 930 A.D., inform us that this monarch gave away 400 villages and 32 lakhs of *drammas* for the different temples in his dominions. Watchmen were essential under these circumstances for the bigger temples and we often come across provision made for their maintenance.[70]

Part of the charity that flowed into the temples was usefully utilised. It will be shown in Chapter XVI how many of the temples of our period used to maintain schools and colleges. They were very often disharging the duty of poor-relief by maintaining feeding houses. Abu Zaid refers to these when he mentions inns for travellers attached to temples.[71] Epigraphical evidence proves the existence of many such feeding houses maintained in temples; one existed at Kolagallu in Bellary district in 964 A.D.[72] and others existed at Managoli,[73] Nilgund,[74] Hesarge,[75] Bagewadi,[76] Belgamve,[77] Dambal,[78] Gadag,[79] and Behatti[80] in Kar-

67. S. I. I., II, Nos. 1–3. 68. I. A., XII, p. 159.
69. E. I., VII, p. 26. 70. E. I., V, p. 22; S. I. I., II' pp. 301–3 etc.
71. Elliot, I, p. 11.
72. *Inscriptions from the Madras Presidency*, Bellary district, No.82.
73. E. I., V, p. 22. 74. E. I., III, p. 208.
75. J. B. B. R. A. S., X, p. 256. 76. I. A., VII, p. 307.
77. I. A., V, p. 49. 78. *Ibid*, X, p. 188.
79. *Ibid*, II, p. 301. 80. *Ibid*, IV, 274.

natak and Kharepatan[81] in Konkan. Some of the records mentioning the above feeding houses do not fall strictly within our period, but they are mentioned here to give an idea of the general practice of the age.

We get some idea of the details of the daily temple life from the epigraphical records of our period. Daily worship was done three times a day,[82] and many of the Chola records specify the quantity of rice and other articles, to be used at the time of the *naivedya* at each of these worships. The richer establishments used to have a set of musicians, who used to play music at the temples at the time of worship. The provision for their maintenance figures in the Hebbal inscription of 975 A.D.[83] and in several Chola records. The worship offered was sumptuous; scented water for the bath, costly clothes, and rich *naiveaya* were provided for. These and some similar items were included under the term *aṅgabhoga* of the deity for which provision is made in some of our records. Flowers and garlands were of course indispensable; a number of our records mention grants made for flower garlands which were very often attached to the temples. Some of our records mention provision made for the *raṅgabhoga* of gods. The precise meaning of the term is difficult to determine, as it is not known even to Sanskrit Koshas. But since the term *ranga* can mean a play-house, it is permissible to conjecture that the expression *raṅgabhoga* may refer to periodical celebrations of Pauranic dramas, which may have been exhibited at the time of the annual fair at the temple. An inscription at the Rājarājes'vara temple, belonging to the beginning of the 11th century, records a provision made for the actors, who used to take part in a drama called Rājarāja.

Chariot processions were held on the occasions of fairs; an inscription from Pattadkal in Bijapur district, dated 778[84] A.D.,

81. E. I., III, p. 300.
82. *Ibid*, VII. p. 194.
83. *Ibid*, IV, p. 355.
84. I. A., XI, p. 125.

mentions the grant of a horse-chariot and an elephant chariot by a dancing girl to a local God. Two records, falling outside our proper period, *viz.* Managoli inscription, dated 1161 A.D.,[85] and the Siddhapur inscription, dated 1158 A.D.,[86] refer to *damanāropaṇa* and *pavitrāropaṇa* ceremonies that were performed in the months of Chaitra and S'rāvaṇa respectively. It is not unlikely that these ceremonies were performed in our period as well, since one of them *viz. damanāropaṇa* is mentioned by Alberuni as a popular festival in Chaitra, when Vāsudeva was swung to and fro in a swing.[87] In his *Smṛtikaustubha*, Anantadeva prescribes the celebration of *damanāropaṇa* in Chaitra and *pavitrāropaṇa* in S'rāvaṇa.[88] We thus get a proof of the actual prevalence of some of the ceremonies described by later writers in our period. The view advanced earlier in this chapter, that some of the new ceremonies and rituals that find literary recognition in the Nibandhas of later period were already getting popular in our period, is thus not altogether without a foundation.

Theoretically Hinduism no doubt regards idols as mere visible symbols of the Divine, but the great paraphernalia of idols, their worship, temples, and establishments began to engender during our period an imperceptible feeling that the visible idol was everything, and the greatest importance began to be attached to its sanctity and safety. This was rather regrettable, for very often the feeling worked against national interests. Hindus could have ousted the Muslims from Multan had they not been compelled to retire by the threats of the Muslim garrison to break the famous idol of the sun in that city, if it was beseiged.[89] If the philosophy of idol-worship were properly understood at the time, this threat could not have deterred the Hindus ; another idol could have

85. *Ibid.* 86. I. A., XI, p. 274. 87. II, p. 178.
88. p. 19. 89. Eliot, I, p. 23.

been installed in the proper religious manner to replace the destroyed one. Idol destruction by Mahmud of Ghazni would not have unnerved the Hindu opposition, if the philosophy of the idol worship were properly understood in our period.

Temple worship was usually entrusted to Brahmanas; our records very often refer to settlements of Brahmana householders near the temples to look after the temple worship. But the non-Brahmana Gurava worshipper, who is now so common in the Deccan, also makes his appearance in our period. The worship in the Ramesvaram temple on the Tungabhadra was being performed by a Gurava in 804 A.D., when Govinda III had visited the place; Shivadhāri, who is expressly described as a Gurava in the record,[90] was the recipient of a grant from the emperor. In the S'iva temple at Mantrawadi in Dharwar district there were Gurava worshippers in 875 A.D., who were required to keep unbroken the vow of chastity.[91] At present the Guravas are not required to lead celibate life anywhere in the Deccan; therefore, this information supplied by our epigraph is very interesting and important. The Guravas are also mentioned in a Soratur inscription of the time of Kṛshṇa III,[92] but their precise connection with the temple worship is not very clear from the record. The Gaṅga ruler Būtuga II had a pet dog; he was let loose at a mighty boar and the two killed each other in the fight. The affectionate master raised a tablet to commemorate his pet and appointed a Gurava for its worship. It would be noticed that the cases of Gurava worshippers, mentioned above, all pertain to S'iva temples, except the last one where he was appointed to perform the worship of a dog tablet. It would be, therefore, permissible to conjecture that the Guravas were originally non-Aryan, and very probably Dravidian priests, who continued to officiate at the temples

90. I. A., XI, p. 127. 91. E. I., VII, p. 202.
92. *Ibid*, XII, p. 258.

of deities which were originally non-Aryan. Later on they may have been allowed to be associated with Aryan temples and gods as well.

The Gṛhya-sūtra ritual requires animal sacrifices in connection with some popular deities like Vināyaka, Kshetrapāla, etc.[93] That these sacrifices prevailed in our period in northern India is proved by the statement of Alberuni, that the worshippers of some gods deities Durgā, Mahādeva, Kshetrapāla, and Vināyaka used to kill sheep and buffalos with axes and offer them as *naivedya* to the deities concerned.[94] Similar practices must have prevailed in the Deccan since early times, but it is not unlikely that the great influence which Jainism exercised in our period may have led to these sacrifices getting unpopular to a great extent. It may be also pointed out that the Muslim travellers like Al Masudi and Al Idrisi, who were mainly acquainted with the conditions of the Deccan and who describe in detail its religious practices, do not refer to this custom which is mentioned by Alberuni, who was acquainted with the conditions prevailing in the north. Animal sacrifices are even to-day rare in the Deccan when compared to their great popularity in a province like Bengal. This comparative weaning of the masses in the Deccan from them may be attributed to the great influence of Jainism during our period.

A very regrettable feature of the temple atmosphere was its vitiation by the association of dancing girls. This has been noticed by the foreign travellers of our period as well as of later times[95] and is also proved by epigraphical records. In big temples their number was often to be counted in hundreds. An inscription at the Rājarājeśvara temple, belonging to the beginning of the 11th century, records an order of Rājarāja, transferring as many as 400 dancing girls from the

93. *Mānava*, II, 14; *Āpastamba*, XX, 12-20; *Bhāradvāja*, II, 10; etc.

94. I, 120. 95. Abu Zaid, Elliot, I, p. 11; Marco Polo, II, p. 345.

various quarters of his kingdom to the Tanjore temple, and assigning to each of them one *veli* of land.[96] There is evidence to show that the custom did exist in the Deccan as well; at the Lokamahādevī temple in Pattadkal (Bijapur district) there were dancing girls by the middle of the 8th century; one of them was so rich as to give to the temple-god one horse and one elephant chariot. In the Bhujjabeśvara temple at Hebbal in Dharwar district there were five dancers in the middle of the 10th century, each one being assigned 4 *mattars* of land for her maintenance. That these dancing girls were not leading pure lives, but had degenerated into women of easy virtue, would be clear from the statement of Marco Polo[97] that a person, who desired to take to the life of a Sanyasin, was tested by his capacity to stand the blandishments of the temple girls who were specially sent to lure him. Marco Polo's testimony no doubt refers to the Malabar of the 13th century, but we shall not be far wrong in assuming that the state of affairs in the Deccan of our period was not far different. In course of time the custom seems to have spread to Buddhist establishments in Greater India. A passage on Kambodia in *Chan Ju-kwa* states:—'The people are devout Buddhists. There are serving in temples some 300 foreign women. They dance and offer food to Buddha. They are called *a-nan* or slave dancing girls.'[98]

The origin of this regrettable custom is to be traced to the desire to provide for good music at the time of divine worship and popular festivals. The precise time of its origin is still obscure. It is not mentioned by the Greek historians. The Arthaśāstra, book II, chapter 27, which gives a detailed account of prostitutes, is unaware of their connection with temples. The temple dancing girl does not figure in the Jatakas and is not mentioned by the Chinese travellers. We may, therefore, presume that the custom was not very

96. S. I. I., II, pp. 278 ff. 97. II, p. 366.

98. p. 53, quoted in Marco Polo, III, p. 115.

common till about the 6th century A.D. But at about this time the custom seems to have arisen, for it is referred to in *Matsya-purāṇa* and *Padma-purāṇa*, *Sṛshṭi-khaṇḍa*. The 70th chapter of the former and the 23rd chapter of the latter contain a discourse on the duties of harlots; 16,000 widowed wives of Kṛshṇa, when ravished by the Abhiras and thus reduced to the sad plight of prostitutes (veśyās), enquire from Dālbhya about their duties. The latter informs them that they should stay in palaces and temples.[99] It is, therefore, clear that the custom had already come into existence when the Puranas were being remodelled sometimes during or after the Gupta age. It is not to be, however, supposed that the custom did not evoke any opposition from the higher sections of the society. Alberuni's statement, that the Brahmanas would have abolished this custom if kings had not stood in their way[100] is confirmed by a contemporary inscription from Rajaputana. Sadadi inscription of Jojaladeva, belonging to the 11th century,[101] records a decree of that king regarding the fairs at local temples. It goes on to observe :—' On the occasion of the fair of a particular temple the dancing girls of all other temples in the city must attend, properly attired, and participate in the music. Our descendants should see to it that this arrangement continues in the future. If at the time of fairs an ascetic or *vadaharaka* (?) or a learned (Brahmana) seeks to interfere with this procedure, he should be forthwith stopped. The concluding sentence of this quotation makes it quite clear that the learned men and ascetics of the age had, as Alberuni has stated, realised that the association of dancing girls with temples was abnoxious and were making efforts to abolish it. The richer classes of the society, however, championed the new custom and their support made it permanent. It would appear that girls were often purchased for being dedicated to the temples.

99. Chap. 49, v. 102. 100. II, p. 157. 101. E. I., XI, p. 28.

A large space in the Puranas is devoted to the purpose of describing the importance of the various Tirthas or sacred places in the different parts of India. The cult of pilgrimage had become fairly popular in our period. Muslim writers have noted how thousands of pilgrims used to visit the Sun temple at Multan and the S'iva temple at Prabhāsa, some of whom used to crawl on their bellies during the last stage of their journey.[102] For the daily ablutions of the idol at the last mentioned place, arrangements were made to provide fresh Ganges water every day.[103] The popularity of Prayāga, Vārāṇasī and Gayā must have been still greater; long sections are devoted by several Puranas[104] for the glorification of these places. Laghu-S'ankha Smriti says[105] that many sons are to be desired because then alone there would be the possibility of at least one among them going to Gaya and performing the S'rāddha there. A number of other Smriti writers[106] of our period describe the merit accruing from consigning the bones of the dead to the holy Ganges. There is epigraphical evidence to show that the cult of pilgrimage was as popular in the Deccan of our period as it was elsewhere. Dantidurga repaired to Ujjayinī when he wanted to perform the *Hiraṇya-garbha-mahā-dāna*;[107] and a number of our records state at their end, that any person interfering with the charity described therein, would incur the sin of slaughtering a thousand cows at Varanasi and Ramesvara.[108] These holy places were obviously regarded the holiest even in the distant Deccan of our period. In those days when travelling was so difficult, costly, and dangerous, all could not visit these distant Tirthas; the doctrine of acquiring merit vicariously through some one else, by requesting

102. Elliot I, p. 67. 103. *Ibid*, p. 98.
104. E. g., Skanda Purāṇa. 105. V. [illegible]
106. E. g., Yama, I. 89–91; Laghu-S'ankha, V. 7 etc.
107. E. I., XVIII, p. 248. 108. E. g., I. A., XII, pp. 220 225 etc.

him to dip so many times more in the sacred pools on one's own account, was, therefore, bound to arise, and we find it mentioned in some of the Smritis of our period.[109]

The curse of the sin of the slaughter of a thousand cows, which has been mentioned in several inscriptions of our period referred to in the last paragraph, would attest to the immense veneration in which the cow was held in our age. Several Smritis of our period contain detailed rules about the reverence and consideration that was to be shown to the cow.[110] The term of detestation used with reference to the Muslims in our period was the cow-eaters.[111] In the 14th century capital punishment was inflicted in Hindu states upon a person who had committed the crime of killing a cow Ibn Batuta cites the concrete case of a Shaikh, who was given the lighter punishment of the mutilation of both the hands and feet for the slaughter of a cow because he was held in high veneration by the Hindus as well.[112] Beef eating was inconceivable, but in some localities like the Malabar, the pariah class was accustomed to eat it, if the cow had died a natural death. This practice was current in the 13th century at the time of Marco Polo, and it still prevails in many localities ; but whether it existed in our period we do not know. In the 17th century it was regarded a sin to allow a cow to die in one's house.[113] The Smritis of our period do not share this belief and we may well doubt whether this notion existed in our period.

In the extreme south the Bhakti movement had grown strong under the Vaishnava and S'aiva saints during our period; its traces are, however, nowhere to be found in the Deccan

109. *Atrisamhitā*, vv. 50–51; Paithīnasi and Vṛddhavasishṭha quoted in the Āchārādhyāya of the *Smṛtichandrikā*, p. 348.

110. Apastamba Smṛiti, Chap. X; Atrisamhitā, vv. 220–3.

111. Elliot I, p. 193.

112. Ibn Batuta, p. 256.

113. *Travels of Tavernier*, p. 440.

of our period. Pandharpur was a centre of Vishṇu worship in the 13th century as noted already, but whether it had then become a centre of Bhakti movement we do not know. It is not unlikely that Jnānadeva may have had several predecessors, now lost into oblivion, who may have popularised the gospel of Bhakti among the masses by vernacular poetry earlier than his time. But whether any advocates of that movement existed in the Deccan of our period is very doubtful.

The theories of heaven and hell, retribution and rebirth make their appearance almost everywhere in the epigraphical records of our period, and no chapter and verse need be quoted to prove their general prevalence. Many of the kings of our period claim credit for having restored the Dharma as it existed in the Kṛta age; this statement would show that the theory of the progressively degenerating cycles of the *yugas* or ages was well established in our period.

A verse occurring in the Manu Smriti and several other works states that *tapas* or austerities was the order of the day in the Kṛta age, quest of knowledge or truth in the Tretā, sacrifices in the Dvāpara and charity in the Kali.[114] An examination of the data belonging to our period shows that this verse represents the realities of the situation at least as far as our age is concerned. Austerities were not unknown to our period; Sulaiman refers to many ascetics that used to mortify the flesh in a variety of ways in the 9th century Deccan.[115] The quest after the truth or knowledge was also fairly serious as the new philosophical activity which commenced with S'ankara shows. The Ṣ'rauta sacrifices had practically disappeared and their place was taken by the Smārta ones. The average man of our age, however, believed in the efficacy of charity for the securing of religious merit. A verse in the Kalas-Budruk plates, dated 1026 A. D.,[116] says that neither learning nor wealth produce so much merit as

114. I. 86. 115. Elliot, I, p. 6. 116. I. A., XVII, p. 127.

charity. The gift of a piece of land was regarded as the most meritorious, the reason, as it is given in an 11th century record,[117] being that all wealth was really produced from land. The close connection between the Smriti writers and the composers of the epigraphical records of our age is shown by the fact that most of the benedictory and imprecatory stanzas in our grants are borrowed from the contemporary Smritis and Puranas, or vice versa. The verse quoted in the previous foot-note has been attributed to *S'ivadharmapurāṇa* by Hemādri.[118] Bṛhaspati Smriti verses 26, 28, 30, 32, 33, 39 & 17 correspond to the well known verses beginning with बहुभिर्वसुधा भुक्ता, स्वदत्तां परदत्तां वा, अग्नेरपत्यं प्रथमं सुवर्णं, भूमिं यः प्रतिगृह्णाति, सर्वेषामेव दानानां, गामेकां स्वर्णमेकं च। and आस्फोटयंति पितरः। respectively which occur in many of the grants of our period. Hemādri attributes most of the above verses to various Puranas.[119] It is, therefore, clear that persons who drafted our epigraphical charters were close students of Puranas and Smritis.

The influence of these works on our age is also proved by an analysis of the objects given in charity, and of the occasions when they were given. *Hiraṇyagarbhadāna*, which was given by Dantidurga at Ujjain, has been prescribed by the Matsyapurāṇa;[120] the gift of an *ubhayatomukhī* cow *i. e.* a cow in the process of delivery, which was given by a courtesan at Pattadkal in c. 770 A.D.,[121] has been recommended by the *Atri samhītā*,[122] which asserts that the merit of such a gift is equal to the gift of the whole earth; *Skandapurāṇa* adds that all considerations about the appropriateness of time are to be brushed aside when it is the question of making such a

117. रत्नान्नपानगोऽश्वाद्यं सर्वं भूमौ प्रजायते। तस्माद्भूमिप्रदानेन नरो भवति सर्वदः॥

118. Dānakhaṇḍa, p. 509. 119. *Ibid*, pp. 494–510.

120. Chapter, 274. 121. I. A., XI, p. 125. 122. V. 333.

gift.[123] Dantidurga,[124] Indra III[125] and Govinda IV[126] are known to have given the *tulāpurushadāna* (*i. e.* the gift of that much quantity of gold which is equivalent to one's own weight,) which has been prescribed in the *Matsyapurāṇa*[127] and the *Dānakhaṇḍa*[128] of Hemādri.

Most of the occasions on which our grants were made are those which have been regarded as particularly sacred by the Smriti and Purana literature of our age. Many of our grants have been given on the days of the monthly *saṁkrāntis*, the sanctity of which has been recognised by *Laghu-Sātātapa Smriti.*[129] Uttarāyaṇa and Dakshiṇāyana days on which some of our grants[130] were given were of course regarded as particularly sacred ; some of the Raṭṭa records[131] show that even the Jains regarded these days as specially holy for such purposes. The belief in the sanctity of the days of the equinox, which is attested to by the *Viddhavasishṭha Sṛmti*[132] is seen reflected in the Antroli-Chharoli record, which mentions a gift made on the day of the autumnal equinox.[133] The sanctity of Kapilāshashṭhī is attested to by the Mangoli inscription[134] which records numerous donations made on that rare *parvan.* The College at Salotgi got extensive gifts on a *sarvapitṛ-amāvāsyā* day[135] and the Nadwadinge grant of Kṛshṇa II[136] was made on the auspicious occasion of a *siddhiyoga.* The *tulāpurusha* gift of Dantidurga was given on the day of the *rathasaptamī*, which is declared to be a

123. Quoted by Hemadri, *Dānakhaṇḍa*, p. 82.
124. Samangad plates, I. A., XI, p. III.
125. Begumra plates, E. I., IX, p. 24. 126. E. I., VII, p. 30.
127. Chap. 274. 128. p. 212. 129. V, 147.
130. *E. g.*, Dantivarman's grant, E. I., VI, p. 287 ; Mulgund grant, *Ibid.* p. 260. 131. J. B. B. R. A. S., X, pp. 237 ff.
132. Quoted by Hemadri, *Dānakhaṇḍa*, p. 72.
133. J. B. B. R. A. S., XVI, pp. 112 ff.
134. E. I., V, p. 23. 135. E. I., IV, p. 355.
136. I. A., XII, p. 112.

particularly holy day in the *Bhavishyapurāṇa* and the *Kāsī Khaṇḍa* of the *Skandapurāṇa*[137]. The Torkhede grant of Govinda III[138] was given on the occasion of a *vijayā saptamī* and the charity given on this day is described in the *Bhavishya-purāna*[139] as hundredfold efficacious. This Purana describes *vijayā saptamī* as a name given to the 7th day of the bright half of a fortnight, if it falls on a Sunday and is presided over by a lunar mansion consisting of five stars. It is a pity that our inscription should not have specified the week day and its lunar mansion, so that we could have verified the statement of the *Bhavishyapurana* about the *vijayā saptamī*. The Baroda plates of Dhruva II[140] record a grant made on the day of the Mahākārtikiparvan, which is described by the *Brahmapurāṇa* as that full moon day of Kārtika which is presided over by the lunar mansion Rohinī; this is described as a particularly holy day by that Purana. [141] Kapadwanj plates of Kṛshna II record a grant given on a *mahā-vaishākhī* day. *Atri-Smṛti* describes Vaishākha full moon day as particularly holy and suitable for making donations;[142] I am, however, unable to find which particular full Vaishākha moon day was regarded as *Mahā-Vaishākhī* day. The Karhad plates of Kṛshṇa III[143] were issued on the 13th day of the dark half of the month of Phalguna, which has been described as a Vārunṇī day; an *upapurāṇa* [144] states that this day is called Vāruṇī, if it is presided over by the lunar mansion S'atatārakā, *mahavāruṇī* if the week day is Saturday, and *mahāmahāvāruṇī* if there is also an auspicious *yoga* on that day. It may be pointed out that the week day

137. Quoted in the *Nirṇayasindhu*, p. 162. 138. E. I., III, p. 54.

139. Quoted by Hemādri, *Dānakhaṇḍa*, p. 63.

140. I. A., XIV, p. 200.

141. Quoted by Hemādri, *Dānakhaṇḍa*, p. 65.

142. VI, 7. 143. E. I., IV, p. 260.

144. Quoted in the *Tithitatva* as quoted by the *S'abdakalpadruma*.

on which the Vāruṇī day of 939 A.D. fell was not Saturday but Wednesday and our record describes the *parvan* as a simple Vāruṇi day, and refrains from describing it as a *mahā* or *mahāmahāvāruṇī* day. The close connection that we thus find between the epigraphical records and the Smriti, Purana and Nibandha literature would fully justify our procedure in some places in this chapter to fill the gaps in the epigraphical records by the information supplied by these works.

The theory of charity being the most effective means of securing religious merit was no doubt in ascendency in our age, but it may be added that Brahmanas alone did not benefit by it. Part of the money spent on temples was utilised for poor relief as already shown. Part of it went to maintain schools and colleges as will be shown in Chap. XVI. It will be also shown there that the *brahmadeya* grants also served the same purpose to a great extent. Part of the charity of the age was definitely and avowedly diverted for the purpose of public works. The Smritis of our period[145] lay down that men acquire the merit of *ishṭāpūrta* by providing funds for public works like tanks, wells, gardens, temples, hospitals, poor houses, schools etc., and there are numerous records belonging to our period which show that the teachings of these Smritis did not fall on deaf ears. A tank at Nargund in Dharwar district was constructed and maintained by the donation of a private individual, and by the voluntary contributions which the inhabitants had agreed to pay for its maintenance on occasions like marriage, *upanayana*[146] etc. The College at Salotgi was also maintained by a princely gift of a local potentate and voluntary contributions of its citizens.[147] When the hall of this College needed overhauling, it was rebuilt also by a private individual.

145. *E. g.*, Yama, I, 69-70. 146. I. A., XII, p. 224.
147. E. I., IV, p. 61.

The Shikarpur inscription No. 284, belonging to the time of Kṛshṇa II. [148] records the construction of a tank and temple by a private individual, who also granted a piece of land to maintain them. Somadeva, a contemporary Jain writer from Karnatak, boldly departs from the traditional view, which is very rarely the case with him, and declares that the endowments of feeding and drinking houses, and the erection of temples and rest houses was the most important duty of the Vaishyas or the moneyed classes.[149] The theory and practice of our age, therefore, show that the doctrine that charity was the best means of securing religious merit was not entirely and exclusively for the benefit of the Brahmanas; the community as a whole also benefited by it.

It was during our period that Hinduism came into contact with Mahomedanism both in the south and in the north. In Sindh hundreds of women were forcibly ravished and thousands of men were converted during our period. Many Mahomedan travellers had come and settled down in the ports of western India where, as we have seen already, mosques had begun to raise their heads. What was the attitude of Hinduism towards the problem of reconversion of those who were forcibly converted? Devala Smriti, which was composed in Sindh after its conquest by the Muslims, is essentially a Smriti composed for prescribing the rules for reconversion; it permits reconversion of forcibly converted men within a period of 20 years. Another Smriti writer of our age, Bṛhadyama[150] lays down the general principle that a suitable *prāyas'chitta* should be prescribed for such persons. With reference to women forcibly ravished by the Mlechchhas, a number of Smritis of our period[151] lay down that such unfortunate ladies should be readmitted into theie families after a suitable penitential ceremony, even if the ravishment had resulted in conception.

148. E. C. VII. 149. *Nītivākyāmṛta*, VII, 83.

How far these theories were accepted by the society of our period is the question which the historian has to answer. There is evidence to show that the Hinduism of our period was not so conservative or short-sighted as the present day Hinduism, and was prepared to follow in practice the gospel of reconversion which was recommended to it by its thinking sages. A specific case of reconversion has been mentioned by Al 'Utbi.[152] Nawās Shāh was one of the Indian rulers who had been established by Mahmud of Ghazni as a governor of some of the districts conquered by him, in reward for his embracing the Islam. Al 'Utbi proceeds to narrate :—'The Satan had got the better of Nawās Shāh, for he was again *apostatizing towards the pit of plural worship, had thrown off the slough of Islam* and held conversations with the chiefs of idolatry, respecting the casting off the firm rope of religion from his neck. So the Sultan went swifter than the wind... and turned Nawās Shāh out of his government, took possession of his treasures ..' This account given by a Muslim himself clearly proves that Nawās Shāh repented of his conduct and was making arrangements for his reconversion which enraged Mahmud. Al 'Utbi does not state whether Nawās Shāh was actually converted back into Hinduism, but since he was so summarily dealt with by Mahmud, it is almost certain that the reconversion was not merely planned but actually carried out.

Muslim writers themselves supply further evidence to show that reconversions on a mass scale used to take place in the 8th and 9th centuries. Al Bilāduri, while describing the general condition of the Muslim power and religion in India towards the end of the 8th century, says that the Muslims were by that time compelled to retire from several parts of India and that *the people of India had returned to idolatry*

150. Vv. 5-6. 151. *E. g.*, 200–202; Devala, 36 ff.
152. Elliot, II, pp. 32-33.

except those of Kassa.'[153] The sentence in italics shows that mass reconversions had taken place in several places in the latter half of the 8th century; the advice of Devala and Bṛhadyama was actually followed in the matter.[154]

It is a pity that the lead given by these Smriti writers was not followed subsequent to our period. There is evidence to show that already in the 11th century Hinduism had begun to hesitate about readmitting the converts within its fold. Alberuni says that he was repeatedly told that when the Hindu slaves in Muslim countries escaped and returned to their country and religion, they were readmitted after an expiation; but when he enquired from the Brahmanas whether this was true, they denied it, maintaining that there was no expiation possible for such individuals. It is thus clear that towards the beginning of the 11th century the masses were for reconversion but the orthodoxy had begun to frown on the practice The main reason why the orthodoxy was seeking to interdict the reconversion was its growing notions of purity. Interdining and intermarriages among the various members of the Hindu castes had become unpopular during our period, as will be shown in the next chapter; grave difficulties about the place of the reconverts in the Hindu society, similar to those that are being experienced today, must have begun to present themselves during our period. For, Alberuni rejects the reports about reconversions and accepts the information of his Brahmana informants for very significant reason. He says:—'How should that (*i. e.* reconversion) be possible? If a Brahmana eats in the house of a Sudra for sundry days he is expelled from his caste and can never

153. *Ibid*, I, p. 126.

154. Sulaiman says that the Gurjara-Pratīhāras were the greatest enemies of the *Muslim religion*. (Hindi tran. p. 52) It is possible that the emperors of this dynasty may have actively helped the movement of reconversion by extending state help to it.

regain it'.[155] It would thus appear that the growing notions of excessive purity were responsible for the disappearance of reconversion; it was very probably first given up by the Brahmanas, and the rest of the castes may have soon followed their lead.

As to social relations between the Muslims and the Hindus, Alberuni informs us that no drinking or eating with a Mlechchha was permitted in his time.[156] In the 14th century Malabar, Muslims were not allowed to enter Hindu houses.[157] There is no evidence as to the social relations between the two communities in the ports on western India during our period; as already pointed out, the Muslims in the Deccan during our period were using Indian dress and language.[158] It is, therefore, perhaps likely that there may not have been too much exclusiveness during our period at least in the Deccan. During the 14th century, even in the distant Malabar and Bengal the Hindus had begun to worship Muslim Pirs and Shaikhs;[159] one cannot be, therefore, sure that the mosques in the ports on western India had no Hindu worshippers.

Buddhism

As stated already, Buddhism was losing ground rapidly in the Deccan of our period. The spread and popularity of Jainism may have been partly at its cost; tradition says that Akalanka, a Jain teacher of Sravan Belgol, defeated the Buddhists in c. 780 in a discussion held in the presence of king Hemaśitala of Kanchi and that the prince was converted to Jainism and the Buddhists were exiled to Candy.[160] The scene of victory is stated to be Kanchi but Akalanka belonged to the Jain establishment of Sravan Belgol, which was situated in the heart of Karnatak; the scholastic and

155. Sachau, II, pp. 162–3.
156. Sachau, I, pp. 19–20.
157. Ibn Batuta, p. 231.
158. Elliot, I, 39.
159. Ibn Batuta, p. 268.
160. I. A., VII, p. 25.

missionary activities of the Jains of that centre may have proved detrimental to Buddhist interests in Karnatak and Maharashtra as well.

Three Buddhist establishments are so far known to have flourished in our period, one at Kanheri near Bombay, the second at Kâmpilya in Sholapur district, and the third at Dambal in Dharwar district. Three inscriptions belonging to the reign of Amoghavarsha I[161] attest to the existence of a Buddhist Sangha at Kanheri. Several records of the Āndhra period[162] preserved in these caves prove that Kanheri was a centre of Buddhism in that period. The inscriptions referred to above show that in our age also the place was a famous centre of Buddhism, for we find an inhabitant from distant Bengal constructing meditation halls and making permanent endowments for the benefit of the monks of this Sangha. The endowment made provision, inter alia, for the purchase of books; it would, therefore, appear that the Sangha had a library, and perhaps a school, attached to it. It resembled in this respect the famous monastic university at Valabhi, where also there was a library, which often received grants for the purchase of books.[163] The S'ilāhāra administration, within whose immediate jurisdiction the Sangha was situated, did not look upon it with an hostile eye; for we find a premier of that state making an endowment, the interest of which was to be utilised for the purpose of supplying clothes to the monks.

Dantivarman's grant[164] records the donation of a village to a Buddhist monastery at Kāmpailya. It is tempting to identify this Kâmpilya with the capital of southern Panchāla, but it looks a little improbable that a monastery in southern Panchāla should have been assigned a village in southern

161. *Ibid*, XIII, pp. 136 ff.
162. J. B. B. R. A. S., V, p. 23; VI, pp. 10 ff.
163. I. A., VII, p. 67.
164. E. I., VI, p. 287.

Gujrat. This monastery was probably situated in Kampil, a village in Tuljapur Taluka of Sholapur district.[165]

An inscription of the time of Vikramāditya VI, dated 1095-6 A.D.,[166] proves the existence of two Buddhist monasteries at Dambal in Dharwar district. It is very likely that the antiquity of these establishments would go back at least to our, if not an earlier, period. There was a temple of the Buddha and Tārā at the place in the 11th century and the description and importance of Tārā, as attested to by our record, would suggest that the establishment was a Mahāyāna one. In the Mahāyāna system Tārā was invoked for help in distress on land and sea and our inscription also shows that similar was the conception about that deity in the Deccan of our peried. Cf. :—

हरिकरिशिखिफणितस्करविपज्जलार्णवपिशाच्चभयशमिनि ।
शशिकिरणकान्तिधारिणि भगवति तारे नमस्तुभ्यम् ॥
या ज्ञानार्णवमन्थनात् समुदिता प्रज्ञेति या कथ्यते
या बुद्धस्य विभूतिदा त्रिभुवने बोधिस्वरूपा परा ।
या हृद्व्योम्नि तथागतस्य वसति स्फीतेव चांद्री कला
सा तारा भवदुःखतापशमिनी प्राशास्तु वस्सर्वदा ॥

The above are the only known centres of Buddhism in the Deccan of our period. It is, therefore, clear that the religion had lost all hold on popular mind and was in the last stage of its decline.

Jainism

Our period was probably the most flourishing period in the history of Jainism in the Deccan. Soon after it Jainism received a set-back owing to rapid spread of the new Lingayat sect. In our period, however, the sect

165. I am indebted to the late Prof. R. D. Banerji for drawing my attention to this village in Sholapur district.

166. I. A., X, p. 185.

had no serious militant rival and was basking in the sunshine of popular and royal favour. The literary activity of the Jains was also remarkable in this age, and they seem to have taken an active part in the education of the masses. That, before the beginning of the alphabet proper the children should be required to pay homage to Gaṇes'a by reciting the formula *S'rī Gaṇes'āya namaḥ* is natural in Hindu society, but that in the Deccan even to-day it should be followed by the Jain formula *Om namassiddhebhyaḥ* shows, as Mr. C. V. Vaidya has pointed out, that the Jain teachers of our age had so completely controlled the mass education that the Hindus continued to teach their children this originally Jain formula even after the decline of Jainism. The formula can of course be interpreted in a non-Jain sense as well, but it cannot be denied that originally it had a Jain significance.

The way to the prosperity of Jainism in our period was already paved in the earlier age. Many of the Kadamba kings of the 5th and the 6th centuries were patrons of Jainism.(167) There are several spurious records at Lakshmesvar(168) really belonging to the 10th or 11th century purporting to record grants in favour of Jain establishments made by early Chalukya kings Vinayāditya, Vijayāditya, and Vikramāditya II. These kings must have been known to the tradition, at least as occasional patrons of Jainism; otherwise it is hardly possible to explain why these and no other kings, should have been selected as donors when the records were forged. Most of the Ganga kings of Talwad were either Jains or patrons of Jainism. Grants to Jain establishments made by Rāchamalla have been found in Coorg,(169) and when this king captured Vaḷhmalai hill, he commemorated its conquest by erecting a Jain temple upon it.(170) At Lakshmesvar there existed in our period buildings

167. I. A., VI, pp. 22, ff; VII, pp. 34 ff. 168. *Ibid*, VII, pp. 111 ff
169. *Ibid*, VI, p. 103. 170. E. I., IV, p. 140.

known as *Rāya-Rāchamalla vasati, Ganga-Permādi-chaityālaya*, and *Ganga-kandarpa-chaityamandira*.[171] The names of these edifices bear testimony to the patronage of Jainism by the various members of the Ganga ruling family, after whom the buildings were named. Mārasimha II was a staunch Jain; he was a disciple of Ajitasena and his firm faith in his religion sustained him through the terrible ordeal of the *Sallekhanā* vow whereby he terminated his life after his abdication in c. 974 A.D. Mārasimha's minister Chāmuṇḍarāya is the author of the *Chāmuṇḍapurāṇa*; it was he who set up the colossal image of Gommates'vara at Sravana Belgola, and his reputation as a patron and devotee of Jainism was so great, that he was regarded as one of the three special promoters of Jainism, the other two being Gangarāja and Huḷḷa who were the ministers of the Hoysala kings Vishṇuvardhana and Mārasimha I. In Noḷambawadi the religion was prospering, we have a record from that province mentioning the gift of a village by a merchant who had purchased it from the ruling king in order to bestow it upon the Jain monastery at Dharmapuri in Salem district.[172] Among the Rāshṭrakūṭa emperors Amoghavarsha I was more a Jain than a Hindu. In his *Pārs'vābhyudaya* Jinasena calls himself as the chief preceptor (*paramaguru*) of that king who used to regard himself as purified by the mere remembrance of that holy saint.[173] *Sārasaṅgraha*, a Jain mathematical work, also mentions that Amoghavarsha was a follower of the *syādvāda*.[174] Amoghavarsha's offering one of his fingers to the Goddess Mahālakshmī, in order to extricate his kingdom from an epedemic,[175] only shows that he worshipped some Hindu deities along with Mahāvīra. He seems to have taken an active interest in Jainism; some of the

171. I. A., VII, pp. 105–6.
172. E. I., X, p. 57.
173. I. A., XII, pp. 216–8.
174. Winternitz, *Geschichte*, III, p. 575.
175. E. I., XVIII, p. 248.

Jain monasteries in Banavasi attribute, as my colleague the late Prof. R. D. Banerji informed me, the authorship of some of their religious ritual to Amoghavarsha. We have seen how Amoghavarsha I had abdicated his throne more than once; that was probably due to his being a sincere Jain, anxious to observe the vow of *akiñchanatā* (possessionlessness) at least for some time. This emperor had appointed Guṇabhadra, the author of the last five chapters of *Ādipurāṇa*, as the preceptor of his son Kṛshṇa II;[176] the latter is known to have given a donation to a Jain temple at Mulgund.[177] So, if not a full-fledged Jain, he was at least a patron of Jainism. The same observation may hold good of the next ruler Indra III, for the Danavulapadu inscription[178] records that the prosperous Nityavarsha *i. e.* Indra III caused to be made a stone pedestal for the glorious bathing ceremony of Arhat S'ānti, in order that his own desires may be fulfilled. The last of the Rāshṭrakūṭas, Indra IV, was a staunch Jain; when his efforts to regain his kingdom from Taila II failed, he committed suicide by the *sallekhanā* vow.[179]

Many of the feudatories and officers of the Rāshṭrakūṭas were also Jains. Most of the Raṭṭa rulers of Saundatti were followers of Jainism, as pointed out already.[180] Bankeya, the Banavasi governor of Amoghavarsha I, was a Jain; he got the imperial sanction for the alienation of a village to a Jain establishment at his capital.[181] Bankeya's son Lokāditya is described by his preceptor Guṇachandra as the propagator of the religion founded by Jina; and S'rīvijaya, a general of Indra III, was a Jain and a patron of Jain literature.[182]

These are the kings, feudatories and officers of our period who are so far known to have been followers or patrons of Jainism. There may have been many more; for, as will be

176. J. B. B. R. A. S., XXII, p. 85.
177. *Ibid*, X, p. 192.
178. A. S. R., 1905–6, pp. 121–2.
179. I. A., XXIII, p. 124.
180. *Ante*, pp. 272–3.
181. E. I., VI, p. 29.
182. E. I., X, p. 149.

shown in Chapter XVI, our period produced a galaxy of Jain authors and preachers whose literary and missionary activities must have produced a considerable effect, helped as they were by royal patronage. It is very probable that at least one third of the total population of the Deccan of our period was following the gospel of Mahāvīra. Rashid-ud-din states on the authority of Alberuni[183] that the people of Konkan and Thana were Samanis or Buddhists at the beginning of the 11th century. Al Idrisi calls the king of Naharvala *i. e.* Aṇahilapāṭaṇa as a Buddhist, whereas we know definitely that the king he had in view was a Jain, not a Buddhist. It is thus clear that the Muslims very often mistook Jainism for Buddhism and the above referred to statement of Rashidu-d-din may be taken to prove the prevalence of Jainism rather than Buddhism in parts of the Deccan during the 10th and the 11th centuries. Subsequent to our period Jainism lost much of its ground by the rise of the Lingayat sect which grew partly at its cost.

We can get a glimpse into the life of the Jain Maṭhas of our period from our records. From the records of the early Kadambas[184] we learn that the Jains used to stay in one place during the rainy season, at the end of which they used to celebrate the well known Pajjushaṇa ceremony laid down in their scriptures. Another festival, lasting for a week, was celebrated from the 8th day of the bright half of Chaitra. This festival is still celebrated with great eclat on mount S'atrunjaya,[185] because Puṇḍarīka Gāndhāra, the chief desciple of Rishabhadeva, is stated to have obtained salvation with his 50 million followers on this day.[186] Both these festivals, which were common in the 6th century Deccan, must have been popular in our period too, since they are prescribed in the Jain scriptures and celebrated to this day.

183. Elliot, I, p. 68. 184. I. A., VII, pp. 34 ff.

185. Nahar and Ghosh, *An Epitome of Jainism*, pp. 676–7.

186. *Encyclopaedia of Religion and Ethics*, V, p. 878.

The Jain temples of our period had become replicas of the Hindu temples. The worship of Mahāvīra was just as sumptuous and luxurious as that of Vishṇu or S'iva. Epigraphical records are seen making provision for his *angabhoga* and *rangabhoga* just as they do in the case of the Hindu deities. What a commentary on the doctrine of absolute *akiñchanatā* preached and practised by him!

Food and medicine were provided for in the Jain Maṭhas and provision was also made for the teaching of the Jain scriptures.[187]

The Konnur inscription of Amoghavarsha I and the Surat plates of Karkka (E. I., XXI) record grants made for Jain establishments. Both epigraphs, however, say that the grants were made, inter alia, for the purpose of *balicharudāna*, *vais'vadeva*, and *agnihotra*. These are essentially Hindu rituals and one is surprised to find grants made to Jain temples and monasteries for the purpose of performing them. It may be that during our period Hinduism and Jainism resembled each other more closely than is the case now, or the above expressions may have been introduced in these records by the oversight of the imperial secretariat. In the Konnur record, the expression is actually misplaced and, therefore, the latter alternative seems to me more probable.

The influence of religion is estimated by the result it produces upon character. What then was the general character of the people in our period? It is gratifying to find that the Arab merchants of the age, in spite of their religious differences, pay as high a compliment to the Indian character as was paid by Megasthenes and Yuan Chwang. Al Idrisi says[188] :—

'The Indians are naturally inclined to justice and never depart from it in their actions. Their good faith, honesty, and fidelity to their engagements are welknown and they are

187. J. B. B. R. A. S., X, p. 237. 188. Elliot, I, p. 88.

so famous for these qualities that people flock to their country from every side; hence the country is flourishing and their condition prosperous.' The Marathas of Deogiri and Nandurbar are described by Ibn Batuta[189] as upright, religious and trustworthy. The travellers whose testimonies have been quoted above belong to a slightly later period than ours, but there is nothing improbable in their description holding good of our age as well.

It is very often asserted that the gospels of Ahimsā and Sanyāsa, that were popularised by Jainism and Buddhism, have ultimately resulted in the enslavement of India for the last 1,000 years. Some events, that have happened in our period, seem to support this view. When Bajhra, the nephew of Dahir, was preparing to defend the fort of Swistan against Mahmud Kasim, all the Samanis (*i. e.* Buddhists) assembled and said to him:—'Our religion is one of peace and quiet and fighting and slaying is prohibited as well as all kinds of shedding of blood. You are secure in a lofty place, while we are open to the invasions of the enemy and liable to be slain and plundered as your subjects. We know that Mahmud Kasim holds a firman from Hajjaj to grant protection to all those who demand it. We trust, therefore, that you deem it fit and reasonable that we make terms with him, for the Arabs are faithful and keep their engagements.'[190] It would be, however, a mistake to suppose that the Buddhists of Sindh were emasculated by their religion. They no doubt said that their religion forbade them from slaughter and shedding of the blood, but that was merely for cloaking their cowardice. The rapid successes of Mahmud Kasim and the brutality with which he butchered all those who opposed him had unnerved the population of Sindh. The Buddhists of Swistan were using the tenets of their religion only as a convenient excuse in order to avoid the prospect of

189. p. 228. 190. Elliot. I, p. 158-9.

being butchered or enslaved by the conqueror. It should be noted that the Hindus of Brahmanabad were equally meek and submissive, and the Brahmanas among them played the mean game of winning over the population to the side of the conqueror,[191] thereby bringing disgrace to the memory of their ancestors, who had incited the population against Alexander the Great and paid the extreme penalty for the glorious offence of patriotism.

It must be remembered that Jainism preaches the doctrine of Ahimsā in a more extreme form than Buddhism, and yet the history of the Deccan of our period shows that it had no emasculating effect upon its followers. Krishṇavarmā, an early Kadamba king, though a Jain, had the title of 'the lover of war' (*raṇapriya*).[192] The Jainism of Amoghavarsha I did not prevent him from offering a dreadful feast to the god of death on the battle-field of Vingavalli.[193] Bankeya, the Banavasi viceroy of the same emperor, was a devout Jain and yet a most active, successful and skilful general.[194] Indra III was at least a patron, and very probably a follower of Jainism; and so were his generals S'rīvijaya and Nārasimha, and yet these had fought several battles and overrun the whole of Central India and the Madhyadeśa, in order to accomplish their ambitious plans of conquest. Nārasimha II, who was such a staunch Jain as to die by the *sallekhanā* vow, was yet the hero of a hundred battles. Most of his predecessors on the Gānga throne were Jains and were yet taking part in the incessant warfare that was going around them freely and enthusiastically.

The teachings of religion are only one influence that go to form the character of a people. Christian gospels recommend renunciation and meekness as strongly as the Jain and Buddhist scriptures, and yet Christian nations have been most

191. *Ibid.* I, p. 184. 192. I. A., VII, p. 34.
193. *Ibid.* XII, p. 250. 194. E. I., VI, p. 29.

worldly-minded and agressive. What very often happens is that people seek to cover their own weakness and cowardice, which have been due to causes that have very little to do with religion, under the specious name of religion and philosophy by distorting their teachings. In the face of the achievements of the Jain princes and generals of our period, we can hardly subscribe to the theory that Jainism and Buddhism were chiefly responsible for the military emasculation of the population that led to the fall of Hindu India.

CHAPTER XIV

Social Condition

Most of the writers, who have attempted to describe the social conditions and institutions in ancient India, have relied upon the evidence afforded by the Dharmas'āstra literature. This evidence is undoubtedly very valuable; but since the dates of many of the Smriti writers are but very vaguely known, it is necessary to check and correlate it with epigraphical facts and the accounts supplied by foreign travellers. Besides the Smritis have, to some extent, been written from a certain viewpoint which may not have been always shared by the majority of society. In the following pages, the method above indicated, with which the reader of these pages must be already familiar, will be followed.

The most striking feature of the Hindu Society has been the caste system since very early times. To trace the history of this institution from its beginning is irrelevant for our present enquiry; we shall, therefore, try to ascertain its nature during our period. The usual theoretical number of the castes is four, but it is rather strange that Greek writers like Megasthenes and Strabo and Muslim writers like Ibn Khurdadba and Al Idrisi should concur in maintaining that their number was seven. The seven castes of the Muslim travellers are, however, not identical with the seven castes of the Greek ambassador : the latter does not enumerate any of the untouchables among his castes, while the former include at least two among the depressed classes. Alberuni, however, differs from the earlier Muslim travellers and maintains that there were sixteen castes, the four well-known ones, five semi-untouchables and seven untouchables. The actual number of the castes and sub-castes of our period was, however, more than sixteen; the Smritis of our period mention several subcastes, and according to Kalhaṇa, who flourished in Kashmir in the 12th century, the number was 64.[1]

The seven castes mentioned by Ibn Khurdadba, who died in 912 A.D., are (1) Sābkufrīa (spelt as Sabakferya or Samkufrīa according to some Mss), (2) Brahma, (3) Katarīya, (4) Sūdariyā, (5) Baisurā, (6) Sandālia, and (7) Lahūd.[2] The seven castes of Al Idrisi are practically identical with the seven ones mentioned above, if slight variation in spelling is ignored.[3] There is, however, one variation; the name of the 7th caste according to Al Idrisi is Zakya and not Lahūd as Ibn Khurdadba asserts. Both of them agree, however, in observing that the members of this caste were following the professions of the dancers, tumblers, and players. The order of enumeration of these castes is not according to their relative status or importance; for both mention the Vaishyas after the Sudras and the Lahūd or Zakya caste, which comes last, seems certainly not lower in status than the Chandala one, which precedes it.

It is quite clear from the details given by these writers that Brahma, Sūdariā, Baisurā, and Sandālia are the same as Brahmanas, Sudras, Vaishyas, and Chandalas. Katarīyas, who could drink three cups of wine and whose daughters could be married by the Brahmanas, are obviously the same as the Kshatriyas. Sābkufrīyas or Sabakafreyas seem to stand

1. VIII, 2407. 2. Elliot, I, pp., 16-7. 3. *Ibid*, p. 76.

for Sanskrit Satkshatriyas,[4] since we are told that they were superior to all the remaining castes and that the kings were chosen from among them. The distinction between the Katarīyas and Sābkufrīas or Satkshatriyas seems similar to the distinction between the Kshatriyas and the Rājanyas of the earlier period; the former constituted the general military order while the latter were the members of the aristocracy descended from the royal stock. This distinction between the Kshatriyas and Satkshatriyas reminds us of the distinction between the Sudras and Sachchhudras, though the former is not known to the Dharmaśāstra literature.[5]

The information of Alberuni about the caste system is more detailed and interesting, and though he was not like Ibn Khurdadba or Al Idrisi directly connected with the Deccan we cannot pass over his account as the conditions in the south were not much different from those prevailing in the north. After mentioning the four principal castes Alberuni says:—

'After the Sudras follow the people called Antyajas, who render various kinds of services and are not reckoned among the castes but only as members of a certain craft or profession. There are eight classes of them who freely intermarry with each other, except the fuller (washerman), shoemaker, and weaver; for no others will condescend to have anything to do with them. These eight guilds are :—

(1) The fuller or washerman,
(2) The shoemaker,
(3) The juggler,
(4) The basket and shield maker,
(5) The sailor,

4. Arabic letters ta and *ba* can be easily confounded in Mss. because the former differs from the latter only by the addition of two dots. The expressions Satkufriya and Satakafreya are fairly similar to the original Skt. form *Satkshatriya*.

5. See p. 333.

(6) The fisherman,
(7) The hunter of wild animals and birds, and
(8) The weaver.

The four castes do not live with them in one and the same place. These guilds live near the villages and towns of the four castes but just outside them. The people called Hādī, Domba, Chandāla and Badhatau are not reckoned among any class or guild. They are occupied with dirty work, like the cleansing of the villages and other services. They are considered as one sole class distinguished only by their occupations.'[6]

The above description of the Muslim writers raises several interesting points with reference to the position of the untouchables. Ibn Khurdadba and Al Idrisi mention only two untouchable castes, Sandālia and Lahūd or Zakya, which correspond with the Chandāla and the juggler classes of Alberuni. Were the remaining classes mentioned by Alberuni as untouchables really so, and if so, why does he divide them into two groups?

After mentioning the eight varieties of the Antyajas, Alberuni expressly adds that all these classes lived near the towns or villages of the four castes, but outside them. It is therefore clear that they were regarded as untouchables. It may be pointed out that some of the later Smritis like Angiras,[7] Brihadyama,[8] Atri,[9] and Āpastamba[10], which discuss the problem and the treatment of the untouchables, pronounce most of these classes as untouchables. Washerman, shoemaker, juggler, fisherman, Chandāla, and basket-maker of Alberuni correspond to *rajaka*, *charmakāra*, *naṭa* or *s'ailushika*, *kaivarta*, *chaṇḍāla* and *veṇujīvin* of these Smriti writers. Since early times these were regarded as untouchables and till quite recently; washermen, shoemakers, fishermen, and

6. I, pp. 101 ff. 7. Vv, 17, 20. 8. Chapters I and II,
9. Vv. 174, ff. 10. Chapters, IV and V.

Chandalas because their professions were dirty, and jugglers and basketmakers, probably because these professions were the monopoly of the non-Aryan aborigines in the beginning. One of the inscriptions on the Rajarajesvara temple at Tanjore provides, as we have seen, for the enactment of a certain drama at the time of the annual fair and states the salaries paid to the actors. A perusal of Sanskrit literature also shows that the actors who enacted the dramas of Bhāsa, Kālidāsa, and Bhavabūti were not regarded as untouchables. The Naṭas, who are pronounced as untouchables by the Smriti writers, were not obviously the members of this class; they were tumblers, jesters, and rope-dancers who are described as untouchables by the Muslim writers of our period.

We have next to consider the case of the weaver, the sailor, and the hunter of wild animals and birds, who are included by Alberuni among the untouchables of the first group. From Manu[11] we learn that members of the Mārgava and Āyogava sub-castes, who were supposed to have sprung from *pratiloma* unions, were assigned the professions of the sailor and the hunter; that would explain why they were regarded as untouchables. The weaver, however, whom Alberuni regards as untouchable, is nowhere regarded as such in the Smriti literature, and if we follow Alberuni, we shall have to suppose that the famous weaving industry of ancient India was a monopoly in the hands of the untouchables. There is no evidence, however, to show that such was the case. According to Bṛhadyama Smriti[12] it would appear that the Hindus of our period regarded it as sinful to touch a person who was dealing in red cloth and, according to Āpastamba Smriti,[13] it was extremely undesirable to touch or wear blue cloth or colour. It would seem that notions like these were responsible for the theory that persons, who produce or deal in red or blue cloth, were impure. If Alberuni's information

11. X, 34, 48. 12. III, 52. 13. Chapter VI.

about the weavers being regarded as untouchables is correct, we shall have to suppose, as the Smriti literature leads us to believe, that it refers only to a section of that class engaged in producing red or blue cloth which was losing in the estimation of the orthdoxy. It may be pointed out that at present the tailors are divided in Maharashtra into two castes; the members of one caste are called Shimpis (ordinary tailors) and those of the other Nīli Shimpis (*i. e.* tailors dealing with blue cloth). The latter are held by the former in low estimation, and no interdining or intermarriages are possible between the members of these two sub-castes. It is clear that the Nīli Shimpis are regarded as degraded because they had not tabooed blue cloth tailoring in middle ages. It is possible that weavers also in our period may have formed two similar classes. It is, however, difficult to say whether the section dealing with the manufacture of red and blue cloth was actually regarded as untouchable, as Alberuni would have us believe, or whether it was merely held in lower estimation. The probability seems to be that the latter was the case.

Hāḍī, Domba, and Badhatau now remain to be considered. What section of the untouchables is called Hādī by Alberuni is not clear; he tells us that of all the classes below the castes, the Hāḍīs are the best spoken of, because they keep themselves free from everything unclean, though their work was the cleansing of the villages etc. That the Dombas were regarded as untouchable is proved also by the Rājataranginī: King Chakravarman went outside the court hall when he had to see a troop of Domba dancers.[14] It is true that he subsequently began to share his bed with some of the Domba dancing girls, but he was all along conscious of having committed a grievous sin thereby. The term Badhatau of Alberuni is an *apabhrans'a* of *vadhaka* or the

14. V, 354.

executioner, who is untouchable even according to the Dharmaśāstra literature.

The distinction which Alberuni draws between the eight untouchables of the first group, and the four ones of the second one, is unknown to the Smriti literature. Alberuni himself says that the shoemaker, washerman, and weaver were regarded as lower than themselves by the rest of the untouchables of the first group, who while intermarrying among themselves, would have nothing to do with the members of these classes. It would be, therefore, clear that all the Antyajas were not on the same level in our age; the juggler, basketmaker, sailor, fisherman, and hunter seem to have constituted in our period a class of semi-untouchables. The reason why Alberuni separates the Chandala, Domba, Hādī and Badhatau from the Antyajas of the first group seems to be that these latter had no guild organisations of their own, like the Antyajas of the first group. This inference is supported by the fact that he refers to the Antyajas of the first group as castes or guilds and adds that the Antyajas of the second group were not reckoned among any such castes or guilds.

Our epigraphical records and foreign travellers do not enable us to realise the intensity of the notion of untouchability of our period. Kalhaṇa's chronicle, however, throws a flood of light on the actual condition during our period, and since the Kashmirian historian is supported by the Smriti literature, we may well assume that similar notions prevailed in the contemporary Deccan as well. The feeling of untouchability was so deep-rooted that we find a Chandala sweeper refraining from touching a foundling on the road, lest it should be polluted, and requesting a Sudra lady to pick and rear it up.[15] The untouchables could not enter the audience hall; the kings used to see them in the outer courtyard when necessary

15. Rājataraṅgiṇī, V. 77.

as did Chandravarman when he had to hear a shoemaker's complaint.[16] Even conversation with the untouchables was regarded as polluting by some sections of the society; when Chandrāpīḍa began to talk with the shoemaker, the courtiers became agitated, which led the latter to enquire whether he was inferior even to a dog.[17]

Let us now discuss the position of the higher castes. Ibn Khurdadba and Al Idrisi, who were acquainted with the conditions prevailing on the western coast, observe that the members of the remaining six castes, Brahmanas included, paid homage to the members of the Sābfukrīya caste from among whom kings were selected.[18] This would support the contention of the Jains and the Buddhists that the Kshatriyas were superior to the Brahmanas and not vice versa. It must be, however, noted that the Sābkufrīa caste is distinguished by these Muslim writers from the Katarīya or the Kshatriya caste and that their testimony would, therefore, show that not all the Kshatriyas but only the Sat-Kshatriyas, *i. e.* the actual princes and their descendants, were held superior to the Brahmanas and reverenced by them. And this is quite natural; for, the actual rulers and their descendants, who in many cases in our period were not even Kshatriyas, must have been obviously treated with respect by the Brahmanas. The average Kshatriya, however, did not enjoy a status superior to that of an average Brahmana, for from the *Chachanāmā*[19] we learn that the principal inhabitants of Brahmanabad supported the contention of the Brahmanas that they were superior to the rest of the population. Kassim accordingly maintained their dignity and passed orders confirming their preeminence.

The Brahmana community of our period followed a number of professions, besides those that were theoretically permitted to it. A section of course followed the scriptural

16. *Ibid*, IV, 62.
17. *Ibid*, IV, 67.
18. Elliot, I, p. 16 and p. 76.
19. *Ibid*, p. 183.

duties; Al Idrisi describes Brahmanas as dressed in the skins of tigers and other animals and addressing crowds around them about God and His nature.[20] Our epigraphical records also make it clear that some of them were maintaining the sacred fires and performing the various Smārta sacrifices prescribed for them. According to Alberuni,[21] these Brahmanas were called *isṭins.* Many others were discharging, as will be shown in chapter XVI, their scriptural duty of teaching and conducting schools and colleges, where they used to impart education without stipulating for any fees. Jurists, astrologers, mathematicians, poets and philosophers were, as Abu Zaid informs us, mostly members of this class.[22] Administrative civil posts seem to have been largely filled from among the Brahmanas; the *Chachanāmā* informs us that Kassim appointed Brahmins to hereditary administrative posts following the practice of his predecessors; it is also shown already how many of the ministers and officers of the Rāshṭrakūṭas were Brahmins by caste. From I-tsing[23] also we learn that towards the end of the 7th century A.D. the scholars of the Valabhi university used to proceed to the royal courts after their education was over in order to show their abilities and talents with a view to be appointed to practical government. These scholars, we are told by I-tsing, used to receive grants of land or government service. We may presume that the scholars trained at the famous centres of education in the Deccan like Kalas, Mangoli, Salotgi etc., may have received similar treatment from the Rāshṭrakūṭa emperors and their feudatories. Government service was largely manned from among the Brahmanas even during the Mauryan period, as the testimony of Megasthenes shows.[24] Smriti writers no doubt say that Brahmanas should not take up service, but they had probably non-govern-

20. *Ibid*, p. 76.
21. Sachau, I, p. 102.
22. Elliot, I, p. 6.
23. p. 176.
24. Maccrindle, *Megasthenes*, pp. 47–48.

ment service in view when they made this statement; for, they themselves lay down that Brahmanas alone should be appointed as a rule to the ministry and the judicial posts.[25]

The observation of S'ankarāchārya,[26] a contemporary writer, that the castes were no longer following their prescribed duties and functions is supported by historic evidence. It has been already shown how some of the Brahmanas of our period were enlisting in the army both as privates and captains.[27] From Alberuni[28] we learn that some of the Brahmanas in the 11th century were trying their fortunes in the trades of clothes and betel nuts, while others preferred to trade indirectly by employing a Vaishya to do the actual business for them. These last mentioned Brahmanas were following the advice of Gautama-Dharma-Sūtra which lays down that Brahmanas may live upon agriculture, trade etc., if they apppoint agents to carry on the business.[29] According to Manu, a doctor was never to be invited for a dinner in celebration of a *havya* or *kavya* ritual; but from Arabian travellers we learn that the physicians were honoured equally with learned men, and we find a Brahmana physician among the donees of an *agrahāra* village given by a Pallava king in the 8th century.[30] This would show that the medical profession was not treated with contempt by the society, as the Smriti writers would make us believe. Its disparagement by Manu and others is probably due to their theory that medicine was the profession of a mixed caste called Ambashṭha, a view which does not seem to have been founded on the actual state of affairs in the society. Puritanical notions of purity may also have been partly responsible for the ban placed on the doctor at the Śrāddha dinner.

25. Manu, VII, 37, 58; VIII, 20.

26. इदानीमिव कालान्तरेऽप्यव्यवस्थितप्रायान्वर्णाश्रमधर्मान् प्रतिजानीते । ब्रह्मसूत्रभाष्यम्, १, ३, ३३.

27. *Ante*, pp. 249-50.

28. II, 132.

29. X, 5 and 6.

30. I., A. VIII, p. 277.

Trade, agriculture, banking, fighting etc., were permitted to Brahmanas only in times of difficulties by earlier writers on the Dharmaśāstra. As time began to roll on, these became quite normal avocations for the first caste. We therefore find the Smritis of our period boldly withdrawing the ban on these professions and permitting them to the Brahmanas. Banking (*kusīda*) has been praised as an ideal profession for the Brahmanas by Brihaspati[31] and the same writer along with Hārita, Parāśara and the author of *Kūrmapurāṇa* boldly differs from Manu in declaring that agriculture could be followed as a normal profession by the Brahmanas.[32] *Āpastamba Smriti*[33] also declares that agriculture, cattle breeding etc., were necessary and normal avocations for the Brahmanas and not their *Āpaddharmas*.

Exemption from taxation and the capital punishment are two of the main privileges claimed for the Brahmanas by the Smritis and the Puranas. It must be, however, noted that it is only for the S'rotriya or the learned Brahmana that these privileges were originally claimed; the S'ānti Parvan expressly states that the Brahmanas, who followed trade and industry, were to be fully taxed. It is quite clear from the numerous Rāshṭrakūṭa charters that the donees of the *Brahmadeya* grants, who were as a rule learned Brahmanas, used to receive all the taxes payable by the inhabitants to the king; they themselves had to pay nothing to the latter. But whether ordinary Brahmanas of our period enjoyed similar exemption from taxation is extremely doubtful. The Tuppad Kurahatti inscription of Kṛshṇa III,[34] the Honawad inscription of Someśvara[35] and numerous Chola records make it quite clear that even lands granted to temples by kings were not entirely exempted by them from the Government taxation; a quit rent,

31. As quoted in the *Smṛti Chandrikā* Āchārakāṇḍa, p. 473.
32. *Ibid*, 454.
33. Chap. 76 v. 22.
34. E. I., XIV, p. 366.
35. I. A., XIX, p. 272.

sometimes as high as 50 per cent of the normal demand, was charged. If *Devadeya* grants were thus not exempted from taxation, it is extremely unlikely that ordinary Brahmanas following a number of secular professions, could have enjoyed in our period complete exemption from taxation. Somadeva, a contemporary writer, lays down that when the king had to make a capital levy in order to tide over a difficulty, he could take a portion of the property of Brahmanas and temples, taking the only precaution that money absolutely necessary for the performance of the sacrifices and worship was left with them.[36] This again would suggest that not all the Brahmanas could have enjoyed complete exemption from taxation in our period. There is no epigraphical evidence to support such a general claim. An inscription from Gujarat, dated 1230 A.D.,[37] no doubt says that king Somasimha had exempted Brahmanas from taxation. But this statement is made in the course of that king's eulogy, and may not be more reliable than the assertion, immediately following, that he had defeated a host of enemies. It is further not clear whether all the Brahmanas or only a section of them was exempted from taxation.

There existed in our period, as in earlier ones, a number of learned and pious Brahmanas who were given grants of land or money in recognition of their erudition and public service in educating students without any stipulation for fees. These seem to have been exempted from taxation as far as the lands that were assigned to them were concerned. This reality in the body politic is reflected in the Dharmaśāstra literature when it lays down that a S'rotriya or learned Brahmana was not to be taxed.

Exemption from the capital punishment is another privilege claimed for the Brahmanas by a number of Smritis, and

36. *Nītivākyāmṛta*, XXI, 14.

37. Cf. मुक्त्वा विप्रकरानरातिनिकरान्निर्जित्य । E. I., VIII, p. 211.

the claim is corroborated by Alberuni[38] and Bouchet[39] from whom we learn that Brahmanas were not given the extreme penalty of the law in northern India in the 11th and the southern India in the 17th century. In ancient times the sin of *Brahmahatyā* (the killing of a Brahmana) was regarded to be the most heinous one, and it seems that the Hindu state tried to avoid it, even if it was to result indirectly by way of judicial punishment, especially as it could achieve its object in another and more effective way. *Āpastamba Dharma-Sūtra*[40] lays down that a Brahmana was to be blinded and banished for the offences that involved capital punishment for the other castes. That the advice of this Dharma-Sūtra writer was followed in our period is proved by the statement of Alberuni that though the Brahmana was above the death sentence he could be banished and his property confiscated, and that if he was guilty of stealing a precious and costly article he was blinded and his right hand and left foot were cut off.[41] It may be pointed out that the sentence for the theft of a precious article referred to by Alberuni is not to be found in the Smriti literature. It would, therefore, appear that the Hindu state of our period normally refrained from inflicting the capital punishment on the Brahmana, probably because the alternative punishment permitted by the Dharmaśāstra or custom was sufficiently deterrent. The life of a Brahmana blinded and banished or blinded and maimed in the right hand and the left foot was hardly better than a living death. We may, therefore, conclude that it must have been on rare occasions that the capital punishment was inflicted on the Brahmana during our period. That it was sometimes inflicted is clear from the Arthaśāstra of Kautalya where it is laid down[42] that a Brahmana guilty of treason should be punished with drowning, and from the *Rājataranginī*,

38. Sachau, I, p. 162. 39. J. R. A. S., 1881 p. 227.
40. II, 27, 16. 41. I, p. 162. 42. Book IV, Chap. 11.

where we sometimes come across the cases of Brahmanas being executed by haughty tyrants.[43] But as against these rare cases of executions, we have several cases of even tyrannical rulers like Diddā[44] and Bhikshāchara[45] being compelled to accede to the requests of Brahmanas, because they had threatened to commit suicide by fasting.[46] Here again the fear of the sin of Brahmahatyā seems to have been working on the minds of the rulers, who yielded to the demands of the Brahmanas, who in many of the cases above referred to, it may be pointed out, were deputed by the oppressed subjects to get their grievances redressed through the threat of suicide by fasting. The privilege of immunity from taxation was conceded, as we have seen, only to the learned and pious Brahmanas; one cannot be, however, certain that the immunity from the capital punishment was similarly restricted. It is, however, clear that Brahmanas who had joined the army could not have claimed the privilege of *avadhyatva*, and it is not unlikely that others, who violated the scriptural rules by following a number of prohibited professions, may have been treated as ordinary persons.

Let us now proceed to consider the position of the Kshatriyas. Those among them who were actual rulers or their relatives enjoyed the highest status in the land, as has been shown already. It is probably these, and not all the ordinary Kshatriyas, who enjoyed immunity from the capital punishment as reported by Alberuni.[47] This privilege is not extended to the Kshatriyas by the Dharmaśāstra literature, but since it is mentioned by Alberuni, who was a fairly close student of Sanskrit literature, we may presume that it was actually claimed by and conceded to the elite among the Kshatriyas. It may be further noted that according to the

43. VIII, 1013, 2060. 44. VI, 307. 45. VIII, 908.

46. See also VII, 400, 773, VIII, 2076, 2221 for further cases of *prāyopaveśanas*. 47. Sachau, II, p. 162.

testimony of Alberuni, a Kshatriya guilty of theft, was merely maimed in the right hand and left foot and not blinded in addition like the Brahmana. It would thus follow that in actual practice the privileges of the Kshatriya were by no means less than those of the Brahmana, though they do not all of them figure in the Smriti literature.

It may be noted that during our period, as in earlier times, not all the fighters were Kshatriyas and not all the Kshatriyas were fighters. The army consisted of a number of non-Kshatriyas as pointed out in chapter XII. A number of Kshatriyas also must have taken to professions theoretically not their own. In the 17th century such was the case, for Travernier expressly states that the Rajputs were the fighters, whereas the remaining Khatris, *i. e.* Kshatriyas, had degenerated from their ancestral military profession and taken to trade.[48] This tendency may have very probably made its appearance during our period.

Among the Indian kings who were Yuan Chwang's contemporaries and whose castes are mentioned by him, five were Kshatriyas, three Brahmanas, two Vaishyas, and two Sudras. It is therefore clear that kingship had ceased to be an exclusive monopoly of the Kshatriyas even earlier than our period. We can, therefore, well understand how the imaginary opponent of Kumārila, who flourished just before our period, should have assumed the position that kingship and Kshatriyahood were not coextensive terms,[49] since the members of all the four castes were to be seen ruling in contemporary times.

Now let us consider the religious position of the Kshatriyas. The queens and kings of earlier periods like Nayanikā, Samudragupta, Pṛthvīsheṇa, who were presumably Kshatriyas, are known to have performed several Vedic sacrifices. In our period these sacrifices had become unpopular, as shown already in the last chapter; so we do not find any kings

48. *Travels in India*, pp. 387-8. 49. *Tantravārtika*, on II, 3, 3.

celebrating them. The Kshatriyas, however, were still permitted to study the Vedas, for Alberuni tells us that they could read and learn them in his times.[50] He, however, immediately adds:—'He (*i. e.* the Kshatriya) offers to the fire and acts according to the rules of the Puranas.' All the Hindus of our period were following the Puranic rather than Vedic rules and rituals, as shown in the last chapter. It is, however, not unlikely that Alberuni's statement refers to the Kshatriyas performing their rituals and sacraments with the help of the Puranic rather than the Vedic Mantras. If so, it would follow that the Kshatriyas were rapidly going down to the position of the Vaishyas and Sudras, as far as the religious privileges were concerned. The absence of the mention of their *gotras* by the kings of our period in their copper-plate grants would also show that they were getting more and more dissociated from the orthodox Vedic atmosphere.

The Vaishyas were losing their position among the Traivarṇikas much earlier than our period. S'rikrishṇa enumerates them along with Sudras as persons who were backward or suffering from religious disabilities.[51] *Baudhāyana Dharma-Sūtra*[52] points out that the Vaishyas were practically of the same status as the Sudras, as both were marrying indiscriminately and following similar professions like service and tilling. In our period there was no very great difference between the positions of these two castes, for Alberuni expressly says so.[53] He further informs us that[54] if a Vaishya or Sudra was proved to have recited the Veda, his tongue was cut off. There are many clear indications in Alberuni's works to show that he was well acquainted with the contents of the Dharmaśāstra literature; if, therefore, he makes such a statement which goes directly against the rules of the Smritis

50. Sachau, II, p. 136. 51. *Gītā* IX, 32. 52. I, 11, 4.
53. Sachau, I, p. 101. 54. *Ibid*, II, p. 136.

on the point, the reason may be well presumed to be that the position of the Vaishyas was actually reduced in practice to that of the Sudras, in spite of the rules of the Smritis. It is, therefore, certain that at the end of our period the Vaishyas were levelled down to the position of the Sudras throughout the whole of India. To discuss the causes of this phenomenon is beyond the scope of the present work.

The Smriti writers permit the Vaishyas to follow the military profession when in distress. A number of the Deccan guilds of our period were maintaining their own militias, as will be shown in chapter XV; even the Jains were among the martial races of the Deccan during our period, as has been shown in the last chapter. 17th century travellers like Tavernier note that the Vaishyas would rather die than kill the smallest animal and had, therefore, no fighting value.[55] The case, however, was entirely different in the Deccan of our period.

The unanimous opinion of the Vedic and Smriti writers that the Sudras were not to be permitted to read the Vedas is supported by Alberuni from whom it appears that the rule was actually enforced in practice.[56] A number of later Smritis like Baijavāpa,[57] Jātūkarṇya,[58] Aus'anas, and Laghuvishṇu[59] distinguish a pious Sudra (*Sachchhūdra*) from an ordinary one (*Asachchhūdra*), and extend to the former the privilege of *Srāddha*, *Sanskāras* and *Pākayajñas*. Somadeva, a Jain writer of the Deccan of our period, confirms the testimony of these Smritis when he observes that internal and external purity qualifies even a Sudra for spiritual duties connected with gods, Brahmanas, and ascetic life.[60] There is no epigraphical evidence to show that these privileges were actually enjoyed by the Sudras of our period, but it is not

55. *Travels in India*, p. 386. 56. II, p. 136.
57. Quoted in the *Vīramitrodaya*, *Paribhāshā*, p. 135.
58. V. 50. 59. V. 105. 60. *Nītivākyāmṛta*, VII, 12.

likely that the Brahmanical writers would have enunciated religious privileges not countenanced by the society. We may, therefore, take it as certain that the respectable among the Sudras used to perform the S'rāddhas, Sanskaras, and other Smārta rites throughout India, of course through the medium of the Brahmanas and with Pauranic Mantras.

Much earlier than our period had the service of the twiceborn ceased to be the only profession of the Sudras. A number of Smriti writers like Bṛhadyama,[61] Us'anas, and Devala[62] declare that trade, crafts and industries were the ordinary and not the exceptional avocations of this caste. In the 17th century, infantry was largely recruited from this caste[63] and the same was the case in our period. The military career naturally brought the throne within the reach of the Sudra, and we have already seen how two of the kings ruling at the time of Yuan Chang were Sudras.[64] The theory that the Sudra could not own any property was a dead letter long before our period; Medhātithi, who flourished in our period, declares that even a Chaṇḍāla had proprietory rights and that his stolen property, when recovered, ought to be restored to him by the king.[65]

Our epigraphical records prove that during our period, Brahmanas of one province were freely going to permanently settle in another. The donees of the Alas plates of Yuvarāja Govinda[66] and the Wani-Dindori plates of Govinda III[67] were immigrants from Vengi in Kalinga country, and since they were assigned villages in Maharashtra, it is clear that they had permanently domiciled in that province. The donees of the Begumra plates of Indra III[68] and the Sangli plates of

61. I, 5. 62. Quoted in the *Smṛtichandrikā Āchārakaṇḍa*, p. 455.

63. Tavernier, p. 328. 64. *Life*, p. 79.

65. Cf. सर्वग्रहणेन चाण्डालेभ्योऽपि चोरहृतं द्रव्यं देयमिति। On Manu, VII, 40.

66. E. I., VI, p. 208. 67. I. A., XI, p. 157.

68. E. I., IX, p. 24.

Govinda IV[69] were immigrants respectively from Pataliputra and Pundravardhana (in northern Bengal). It is, therefore, clear that provincial barriers of castes had not arisen in our period. Indra III and his religious advisers did not share the view of the *Atrisaṁhitā*[70] that a Magadha Brahmana was not to be honoured even if he was as learned as Brihaspati; for, in that case the donee of the Begumra plates would not have been a Brahmana from Pataliputra. Nāgamārya, the donee of the Cambay plates of Govinda IV,[71] was an immigrant from Kavi in Gujrat settled in Malkhed. It is obvious that the present-day prejudice in the Deccan, that a Brahmana from Gujrat is inferior to one from the Deccan, does not go back to our period; for Gujrat Brahmanas were settling down in Karnatak and were being honoured with *brahmadeya* grants. In no records of our period are the donees described as Gauḍa, Kanoji, Nāgara or Drāviḍa Brahmanas. In later records, however, such provincial denominations become the order of the day. Thus in Bahal (Khandesh district) inscription of the Yādava king Singhana, dated 1222 A.D.,[72] the composer of the grant describes himself as a Nāgara-Jñātīya-Brāhmaṇa. Though the provincial castes had not arisen in our period, the way to their formation was being paved. Smritis like the *Atrisaṁhitā* were helping the fissiparous tendency by dubbing as worthless the Brahmanas of certain provinces; their teachings had no effect on the Deccan of our period, but they were being gradually followed in the north in the 11th century. For, Alberuni notes that in his time it was regarded as sinful for a Brahmana to cross the Sindhu or the Chambal and enter the territories beyond them.[73] The time was, therefore, at hand when provincial barriers were to introduce further ramifications in the caste system.

69. I. A., XII, p. 248. 70. I, 388. 71. E. I., VII, p. 26.
72. E. I., III, p. 123. 73. Sachau, II, pp. 134–5.

Let us now proceed to consider the attitude of our age towards the question of the intercaste marriages. These marriages, if *anuloma*, have been permitted as legal by most of the Smriti writers, both old and new; the *Nītivākyāmṛta*, which was composed in the Deccan of our period, concurs with the Smritis.[74] That they were once common in the Hindu society is proved by the rules of *ās'aucha*,[75] and partition,[76] where detailed provisions are given as to the liabilities, duties, right, and privileges of the children born of intercaste *anuloma* marriages These intercaste unions could not have been numerous, for society usually prefers marriage alliances with the equals. They, however, did exist and served the useful function of rendering the caste system flexible to a great degree. Historical examples can be cited to show that these intercaste marriages were actually taking place. The father of the famous Sanskrit poet Bāṇa had married a Sudra lady in addition to a Brahmana one; for in the 2nd Ulhāsa of the *Harshacharit* Bāṇa mentions a *pārās'ava* brother (*i. e.* a brother born of a Brahmana father and Sudra mother) of his, Chandrasena by name.[77] Since Chandrasena was the first to report to Bāṇa the arrival of the messenger from Harsha, it may be presumed that the Sūdrā and the Brāhmaṇī mothers and their children were living together under the same roof. Bāläditya, the last king of the Gonanda dynasty in Kashmir is known to have given his daughter in marriage to a Kāyastha.[78] The Jodhapur inscription of Pratīhāra Bāuka concurs with the Ghatiyala inscription of Kakkula in stating that the founder of the house, Harischandra, had two wives, one of the Brahmana

74. XXXI, 28.

75. Baudhāyana, as quoted by Haradatta at Gautama, II, 5, 4.

76. Gautama II, 3, 33: Vishnu, X etc.

77. About 3 pages from the beginning of the Ulhāsa.

78. *Rājataraṅgiṇī*, IV, 489.

and the other of the Kshatriya caste.[79] Ghaṭotkacha cave inscription of Hastibhoja, a minister of the Vākāṭaka king Devasena, informs us that Hastibhoja's ancestor Brahmana Soma had married a Kshatriya lady 'in accordance with the precepts of the revelation and tradition.'[80] While most of the ancestors of Lokanātha, the grantor of the Tipperah copper plates,[81] (c. 650 A.D.) are described as good Brahmanas, his mother's father is called Pārāśava *i. e.* sprung from a Brahmana father and a Sudra mother. It is therefore clear that the father of this gentleman had at least two wives, one a Brāhmaṇī and the other Sūdrā. Coming down to our own period, we find that Rājaśekhara had married a Kshatriya lady, and she seems to have been his only wife. Ibn Khurdadba writing about the state of affairs in western India during our period, states that the *anuloma* intercaste marriages used to take place.[82] These marriages were, however, getting more and more unpopular towards the end of our period. Alberuni, after laying down the theoretical rule that *anuloma* intercaste marriages were permissible, adds that in his time the Brahmanas did not avail themselves of this liberty and were invariably marrying women of their own caste only.[83] Sangrāmarāja, an 11th century king of Kashmir had married his sister to a Brahmana; the notions of decency of the 12th century historian Kalhaṇa were outraged by this union. The historian deplores that the king should have courted infamy by this intercaste marriage and exclaims, 'What a great disparity between the princess fit to be the consort only of a powerful king and the Brahmana bridegroom of small mind with his hand always wet with the libation water poured at the time of the receipt of gifts.'[84] It is

79. J. R. A. S., 1894, p. 1 and 1895, p. 576.

80. A. S. W. I., IV, p. 140.

81. E. I., XV, p. 301.

82. Elliot, I, pp. 16.

83. Sachau, II, pp. 155–6.

84. VII, 10–12.

therefore fair to conclude that the intercaste *anuloma* marriages ceased to take place soon after our period. It is true that a Dutch clergyman of the 17th century, Abraham Roger by name, observes that Brahmanas used to marry girls of all the four castes, though their marriages with Sudra girls were disapproved.[85] Another 17th century European observer, Bernier, however contradicts this statement asserting that the intermarriages between the four castes were forbidden.[86] Abraham Roger had lived in the southern presidency, and he had probably the Nambudri Brahmanas in view when he refers to the unions of the Brahmanas with the girls of the lower castes. We may therefore conclude that Kalhaṇa was the spokesman of the 12th century view and that soon thereafter the intercaste marriage became obsolete.

A number of earlier writers like Gautama,[87] Āpastamba,[88] and Baudhāyana (Dharma-Sūtrakāra)[89] permit freely intercaste dinners; the custom had begun to fall into disrepute in our period, for a number of later Smritis either restrict or condemn it. Angiras[90] prohibits the dinner with a Sudra and permits one with a Kshatriya only on days of religious festivity and with a Vaishya when in distress.[91] Yama and Vyāsa[92] declare that a Brahmana should beg cooked food only in the houses of the members of his own caste. That these writers faithfully reflect the feeling of our period, to which in all probability they belonged, is proved by the statement of Alberuni that a Brahmana was permanently expelled from his caste, if he was found guilty of having eaten the food of a Sudra for a certain number of days.[93] Alberuni does not attest to the cessation of interdining among the three

85. J. R. A. S., 1881, p. 221. 86. *Travels in India*, p. 325.
87. Chap. XVII. 88. II, 3, 4. 89. II, 3, 14. 90. Vv, 55, 57.
91. Quoted by Haradatta at Gautama, III, 5, 8.
92. Quoted by *Smritichandrikā Sanskārakāṇḍa* p. 109.
93. Sachau, II, p. 13.

higher castes, but the Smritis of our period, as shown above, had begun to frown upon the practice. The cessation of the intercaste marriages, and the difference in diet that soon manifested itself, were further making interdining impracticable. Brahmanas of an earlier age were non-vegetarians, but from Al Masudi and Al Idrisi we learn that in Western India they had become thorough vegetarians during our period. Kshatriyas on the other hand, were then as now non-vegetarians, and were besides, not total abstainers from wine like the Brahmanas; they were permitted in theory three cups of wine.[94] This disparity in diet and drink must have made interdining between the Brahmanas and the Kshatriyas an impracticable and, therefore, an unpopular practice. This difficulty need not have stood in the way of the intercaste dinners between the Vaishyas and the Brahmanas of the Deccan during our periods, for the influence of Jainism had weaned away a large mass of the traders and agriculturists from non-vegetarianism.[95] But the Vaishyas had by this time degenerated to the position of the Sudras as shown already, and this fact was making interdining between them and the Brahmanas impracticable.

Let us now consider the family system of our period. Joint families were the order of the day, but cases of separation in our period were not as rare as is sometimes supposed. Some of our records, which mention the specific shares of the cosharers of *agrahāra* villages, prove that in many cases fathers and sons were living separately. In the Torkhede inscription of Govinda III,[96] separate shares are assigned to two brothers showing that they were no longer members of a joint family. In the Chikka-Bagevadi inscription, dated 1149 A.D.[97] Lalla and his brother Jajjuka were assigned different

94. Elliot, I, pp. 16–7.

95. Al Kaziwini has noted that most of the Hindus at Saimur were vegetarians; Elliot, I, p. 97.

96. E. I., III, p. 54.

97. I. A., VII, p. 303.

shares as also Naiva and his brother Gona. In the Bendegiri grant of Kṛshṇa, dated 1249 A.D.,[98] there are eight cases of brothers and two of sons being given separate shares from their brothers and fathers respectively. The Paithan plates of Rāmachandra, dated 1271 A.D.,[99] mention the case of a father living separately from his six sons, and four cases of brothers who were no longer following the joint family system. Epigraphical evidence thus shows that though the Smritis had disapproved partition in the life-time of the father, such partitions were not rare in practice. Some of the above records do not strictly belong to our period, but they can be utilised to indicate the general state of affairs in our period as well, since nothing is known to have happened in the next two centuries to revolutionise the notions of the society in this respect.

A record from Managoli in Bijapur district, dated 1178 A.D., observes:—'If any one in the village should die at Mamgavalli without sons, his wife, female children,[100] divided parents, brothers and their children, and any kinsmen and relatives of the same Gotra who might survive, should take possession of all his property, *i. e.* bipeds, quadrupeds, coins, grains, house and field. If none such should survive, the authorities of the village should take the property as Dharmadeya grant.'[101] The record reveals the actual order of succession in the Deccan of the 12th century, and it is very probable that the same may have been the case in our period. It is noteworthy that this order of succession agrees sub-

98. *Ibid*, XIV, p. 69. 99. *Ibid*, XIV, p. 315.

100. The expression 'female children' is probably intended to include the daughter's son. It may be pointed out that the text of Yājnavalkya also uses the word *duhitaraschaiva* only. Vijnānes'vara maintains that the particle *cha* is intended to denote the daughter's son as well. Historically, the contention is justifiable, since the daughter's son was recognised as heir fairly early.

101. E. I., V, p. 28.

stantially with that given by Yājñavalkya and his commentator Vijñāneśvara.[102] The inscription does not mention like Yājñavalkya the *bandhus*, disciples, and fellow students among the heirs; but it may be pointed out that the inscription was not intended to be a text-book in a law college, and its drafters may have omitted disciples, fellow students etc., because the cases of property going to persons who were not even *sagotras* were very rare in practice. The epigraphical evidence, therefore, shows that the theory of succession advocated by the Mitākshārā school was substantially based on the actual practice as it was prevalent in the Deccan. In contemporary Gujarat the law of succession was different; property of persons dying without sons used to escheat to the crown till the conversion of Kumārapāla to Jainism. The credit of permitting the widow to inherit her husband's property has been claimed for that king.[103] That a widow in the Deccan could inherit her husband's property is made further clear from the case of a country Gavunda, who was succeeded in his office by his widow.[104] That daughters were heirs on the failure of sons is further proved by a Saundatti record[105] which informs us that when Mādirāja II of Kolara family was killed in battle, Gaurī, his only daughter, was married to a Banihaṭṭi chief, who consequently became heir to the fiefdom of the Kolara family as well.

Now let us consider the position of women. We have seen already how widows and daughters were recognised as heirs. The *Strīdhana* rights, we may presume, were also recognised. They have been conceded in the Hindu society since very early times and even the Smriti writers, who refuse to recognise the widow as an heir, permit women to have

102. Yājnavalkya, II, 135-6.
103. *Mohaparājaya*, Act III, See *ante*, p. 243.
104. E. C.; VII, No. 219.
105. J. B. B. R. A. S., X, p. 177.

undisputed proprietary rights over certain varieties of *Strīdhana* property.[106] A 12th century record from Kolhapur seems to refer to the case of a daughter selling landed property.[107] The record is unfortunately fragmentary and so we do not know whether the land that was sold by this lady was sold with the consent of the reversioners, or whether it was a piece of property that had devolved upon her as a daughter or as a widow. In any case the record shows that the women in the Deccan could sell landed property under certain circumstances.

Alberuni says that the Hindus of his time used to arrange the marriages of their sons, because they used to take place at a very early age.[108] In another place he informs us that no Brahmana was allowed to marry a girl above 12 years of age.[109] That Alberuni's observation was true of the Deccan of our period as well, is proved by the *Nītivākyāmṛta* from which we learn that boys were usually 16, and girls not above 12, at their marriage.[110] It may be pointed out that as early as the time of the Dharmasūtras, *i. e. c.* 300 B.C. – *c.* 100 A.D., pre-puberty marriages were regarded as preferable to post-puberty ones; almost all the Smritis that were composed at about our period pronounce most frightful curses upon the guardians who fail to marry their female wards before they attain puberty.[111] We may, therefore, safely conclude that during our period pre-puberty marriages of girls were the order of the day at least among the Brahmanas. There seem to have been some occasional cases of post-puberty marriages among the ruling families; the marriage of Samyogitā, with the famous Pṛthvīrāja, for example, took place

106. E. g. Vasishṭha, XVII, 43, Baudhāyana II, 2, 49; Āpastamba II, 6, 14, 9 recognise this right though they do not admit widow as an heir.

107. E. I., III, p. 216.

108. II, p. 154.

109. *Ibid*, p. 131.

110. XI, 28; XXX, 1.

111. E. g. Bṛhadyama III, 22; Samvarta I, 67; Yama I, 22; S'ankha XV, 8; Laghus'ātātapa 65.

when she was quite grown up. But such cases were exceptions and not the rule.

Several law writers from Baudhāyana downwards observe that the custom of marrying the maternal uncle's daughter prevailed among the inhabitants of the Deccan. Inscriptions of our period refer to a number of cases of such marriages. Jagattunga, the predeceased son of Kṛshṇa II, had married a daughter of his maternal uncle S'ankaragaṇa.[112] The same was the case with Indra IV. Such marriages are recognised as valid by the Dharmas'āstra literature for the Deccanese and are still not unknown. They may have been fairly in vogue in our period.

There is no Purda system even today in the Deccan, except in the case of a few royal families who are known to have imitated it from the north. We may, therefore, well presume that the custom was unknown in our period. Abu Zaid says :—'Most princes in India allow their women to be seen when they hold their Court. No veil conceals them from the eyes of the visitors.'[113] The statement in the Kadba plates that the moon-faced damsels in the court of Kṛshṇa I, who were skilful in exhibiting internal sentiments by means of the movements of their hands, used to give delight to the ladies of the capital, would support the testimony of Abu Zaid that no Purda was observed in the Deccan of our period.

Merchant Sulaiman says :—Sometimes when the corpse of a king is burnt, his wives cast themselves upon the pile and burn themselves ; but it is for them to choose whether they will do so or not[114]. It will, therefore, appear that the Sati custom was not so common in the Deccan of our period even in the royal families as it was in Kashmir, where we find even unchaste queens like Jayamatī compelled to ascend the

112. Sangli plates, I. A., XII, p. 265. 113. Elliot, I, p. 11.
114. *Ibid*, I, p. 6.

funeral pyre by the force of the public opinion.[115] Nay, Kalhaṇa records the cases of concubines, servants, and sisters-in-law burning themselves along with dead kings.[116] The inference that the Satī custom was not so common in the Deccan as it was in the north is further supported by the fact that though there are several inscribed *vīrgals* of our period, scattered all over Karnatak commemorating the deaths of village heroes who had died for their communities, mention of Satīs in these records is hardly to be seen. The only known case of Satī belonging to our period is that of Gundamabbe, one of the wives of Nāgadeva, a minister of Satyāśraya, who had no issue and who is known to have burnt herself with her husband when the latter was killed in war.[117] Alberuni's statement that wives of kings had to burn themselves whether they wished it or not[118] seems to have been based on the events in contemporary Kashmir and does not hold good of the Deccan. The statements of Sulaiman and Alberuni would further show that the custom was still mainly confined to the royal families and that it had not yet spread to the masses, as was the case in the later centuries.[119]

The custom of tonsuring widows is not referred to by any Muslim traveller of our period. Alberuni describes in detail the hard lot of the widow but nowhere mentions her tonsure. The Smritis of our period describe in minute details the various rules to regulate the life of the widow, but they nowhere lay down that she was to shave her entire head periodically. *Vedavyāsasmṛiti*[120] alone lays down that a widow should part with her hair at the death of her husband,

115. Rājataranginī, VIII, p. 366.
116. *Ibid*, VII, pp. 724, 858; V, 206; VII, 481, 1488, 1490, 1486.
117. Rice; Karnāṭakabhāshābhūshaṇa, Introduction p. XVII.
118. II, p. 155.
119. See Marco Polo II, p. 341, Ibn Batuta p. 191, Bernier p. 30. Tavernier p. 414.
120. II, 53.

but this is a solitary exception. Epigraphical evidence also shows that tonsure was not in vogue in our period: Pehoa *pras'asti* of Mahendrapāla, while describing the exploits of a feudatory named Pūrṇarāja, states that he was the cause of the curly hairs of the wives of his enemies becoming straight.[121] Another expression, that is frequently used in our epigraphs to describe heroes, is '*ripuvilāsinīsīmantoddharaṇa-hetuḥ*' 'the cause of the cessation of the parting of the hairs of the damsels of the enemies.' This expression will show that queens, when widowed, used to refrain from decorating their hair; the hair, however, was allowed to grow and was ample in quantity as the expression quoted in the last foot-note will show. The tonsure system, we may therefore conclude, was not in vogue in our period. It was, however, well established some time before the 17th century, for Tavernier informs us that Hindu widows of his time used to shave off their hair a few days after the deaths of their husbands.[122]

There is a difference of opinion among the Smriti writers of our period as to whether virgin widows should be married or not. Parās'ara[123], Nārada,[124] and Laghu-S'ātātapa[125] permit remarriages in the case of such widows, bu Angiras,[126] and Laghu-As'valāyana[127] prohibit the marriage with a bride, even when she was merely accepted by, but not married to, another previously. It is, therefore, difficult to say whether virgin widows in the higher classes were remarried or not in our period. The present writer has shown elsewhere[128] that the Gupta Emperor Chandragupta II had married his brother's widow Dhruvadevī, but that is a much earlier case. Inscriptions, accounts of foreign travellers and the literature of the period nowhere refer to widow

121. सरलितप्रचुरालकजालकः । E. I., I. p. 246. 122. p. 406.
123. IV, 26. 124. XII, 97. 125. V, 44.
126. V, 110. 127. XXI, 6.
128. J. B. O. R. S., XIV. pp. 223 ff.

re-marriages.[129] Later Nibandha writers are unanimous in declaring that such marriages are illegal in the present age. We may, therefore, conclude that widow remarriages were getting unpopular in our period. It must of course be remembered that the question of widow marriages never troubled the lower classes, among whom they were and are fairly common.

Ibn Khurdadbā, who writes about the Deccan of our period, states :—"The kings and people of Hind regard fornication as lawful and wine as unlawful. This opinion prevails throughout Hind, but the king of Kumar (*i. e.* the territory round the Cape Kamorin) holds both the fornication and the use of wine as unlawful".[130] This is an astounding statement, since fornication has been unanimously regarded by all the Smriti writers, both old and new, as one of the most heinous crimes. A still more astounding assertion has been made by another Muslim merchant, Al-Idrisi, who states that in the country of Balharā (*i. e.* Gujarat of the 12th century A.D.) concubinage is permitted with all women except the married ones, and that a man may have intercourse with his daughter, sister or aunt, provided they are unmarried.[131] Both these statement have to be classed under the category of the travellers' tales.[132]

It has been shown already in the last chapter how women, who had the misfortune of being dishonoured, were admitted back into their families and castes, during our period. The theory that such a procedure is not permitted in the present Kali age had not yet attained popularity.

Our epigraphs supply us with some interesting information about a few legal points. Land transfers and similar transactions were done in writing, and the title deeds were

129. It may be pointed out that Alberuni observes that death by *sati* and life-long widowhood full of misery were the only two alternatives before the Hindu widow. II, p. 155.

130. Elliot, I, p. 13. 131. *Ibid*, p. 89. 132. *Ante*, p. 304.

regularly attested. Two of the three Kanheri inscriptions,[133] which record grants in favour of the local Buddhist Sangha, are attested to by two witnesses each. In the 3rd inscription there are no witnesses, probably because the donor was the premier of the kingdom. The spurious Ganga grant of Vīra-Nolamba is attested to by four witnesses.[134] Sometimes the principal officers and the whole population of a district are mentioned as witnesses of a transaction, as in the Kadba plates of Govinda III.[135] If the debtor was a man of good status and well known character, loans were sometimes advanced on personal security; a Raṭṭa inscription informs us that Rudrabhaṭṭa, the founder of the Banahatti house, had raised a loan of 100 golden coins on the security of a letter of his name. He had agreed to call himself Rudraṭa and not Rudrabhaṭṭa, as long as the debt was not paid.[136]

Government documents of transfers of lands or villages were not always attested, but their originals were carefully preserved in the state archives for future reference. The Bhadan plates of Aparājita, dated 997 A.D., expressly states that their originals were kept in the state archives at Thana.[137] At the time of the renewal of old grants, these originals must have been consulted in order to see whether the claims advanced were justifiable or not. Nevertheless, governments used to insist upon the possession and production of the copper plates on the part of the grantee or his successors in title. We come across cases of lands being fully assessed on the plea that their owners could not support the claim for exemption by the production of the *tāmrapaṭṭa*, creating the privileges claimed.[138] On the other hand, we

133. I. A., XIII, pp. 133 ff.
134. I. A., VIII, p. 96.
135. E. I., IV, p. 340.
136. J. B. B. R. A. S., X, p. 25
137. E. I., III, p. 275.
138. Chikka-Bagewadi plates, I. A., VII., p. 303. Nidhanpur p. 74. E. I., XIX, p. 118.

sometimes find owners recovering the possession of their lands by the production of the copper plates.

During our period adverse possession was regarded as creating a substantive title, if it extended continuously for three generations. A verse to this effect occurs at the end of the Kadba plates of Govinda III,[139] and the theory of adverse possession advocated therein agrees entirely with the dictum of Nārada that even an illegally acquired estate cannot be recovered by its rightful owner, if the adverse possession had extended over three generations. This epigraphical confirmation of the view of the *Nārada Smṛti* will show that the portions dealing with the civil law in the Dharmaśāstra literature were usually based on actual practice, as Nilakaṇṭha maintains.[140]

The Hindu dress of our period does not seem to have required much tailoring. Towards the end of the 7th century A.D., the Hindu male dress usually consisted of two unstitched cloths, one worn round like the present *dhoti*, and the other used as an upper garment.[141] Nārada confirms the above statement of I-tsing, for he informs us that a witness might be presumed to be a perjurer if he continuously goes on shaking the upper garment, wherewith his arm is covered.[142] This again would suggest that an upper garment was used instead of a stitched shirt. Two travellers of the 13th and the 14th centuries, Marco Polo and Ibn Batuta, show that down to the 14th century the dress in the Deccan continued to be of the same kind. Marco Polo states that in the whole of Malabar no tailor could be found who could cut or stitch a coat,[143] and from Ibn Batuta we learn that even the Zamorian of Calicut was wearing only a loose unstitched upper garment which was fluttering in the air. Women were,

139. I. A., XII, p. 18.
Vyavahāramayūkha, Introductory chapter.
130. I-tsing, p.68. 142. I, 194. 143. II, p. 338.

however, using stitched petticoats, as would appear from the references in the contemporary literary works.

The paintings in the Ajanta caves show[144] that men were wearing large turbans in the Deccan in the 5th and 6th centuries. In this respect the southern practice differed from that in Kashmir, where down to the 11th century no one could wear a turban except the king.[145] It seems that the practice of growing beard was more common in our period than is the case now.[146] From I-tsing, we get an interesting description of the umbrellas in vogue towards the end of the 7th century A.D.[147] The umbrella was woven with bamboo skin and was made as thin as possible. It was about two or three feet in diameter. Sometimes it was woven with reeds instead of bamboo products; paper was inserted in the weaving and the whole was varnished with lacquer. This umbrella probably belonged to Bengal where I-tsing had spent most of his time: but we may presume that the Deccan umbrella was not much different from the one described by the Chinese traveller, since umbrellas of the type were quite common in Konkan till quite recently.

We come across no surnames of Brahmana donees in the inscriptions of our period. Only their personal names and the names of their fathers and *gotras* are given. The custom of surnames, however, soon came in vogue after our period: for in the Chikka Bagewadi[148] and Bendegiri[149] inscriptions of the Yādava king Kṛshṇa, we find surnames making their appearance. It is interesting to note that many of the surnames given in these records survive in the Deccan to the present day, *e. g.* Pāṭhaka, Dvivedi, Upādhyāya, Dīkshita, Paṇḍita, Paṭṭavardhana, and Ghalisāsa. Vedārthada, Prasan-

144. Codrington, *Ancient India*, p. 26.
145. Rājataraṅgiṇī, VII, 926.
146. Sulaiman Saudagar, Hindi edition, p. 81. 147. p. 74.
148. I. A., VII, p. 305. 149. I. A., XIV, p. 69.

nasarasvatī, and Prauḍhasarasvatī are some of the surnames that have not survived in the struggle for existence. The reason seems to have been that they were too cumbrous for daily use. It will be easily perceived that most of the surnames above mentioned are really titles, descriptive of the literary achievements of the various individuals. Later on they crystallised into hereditary surnames.

Some of our inscriptions supply us interesting information about the sports and amusements of the age. Dancing was a favourite amusement. The Kadba plates support the inference in this respect to be derived from the contemporary dramas, when they observe that the ladies of the capital used to be charmed by the skilful dance of the dancers in the court of Kṛshṇa I.[150] The presence of the dancing girls at the temples is also indicative of the same fondness. Inscription No. 67 at the Rājarājeśvara temple at Tanjore records the provision made for the actors who took part in the drama at the time of the annual fair;[151] a number of the Deccan records also mention the provision made for the *raṅgabhoga* of deities.[152] The expression *raṅgabhoga* probably refers to the provision for Pauranic dramas, that used to be performed at the time of the annual fairs in the Deccan till quite recently. Such plays were organised also on occasions like Dasara, Holi, Rāmanavamī and Gokula-ashṭami. Kauṭalya refers to popular dramas organised by the villagers,[153] and we may well presume that they were fairly common in our period.

Animal fights were also not unknown in our age. One of the Ganga records refers to a fight between a boar and a favourite hound of Būtuga II wherein both the animals were killed.[154] The death of this hound was certainly a great

150. I. A., XII, p. 13. 151. S. I. I, II, p. 11.
152. E. g., Managoli inscription, E. I., V, p. 23.
153. II, 1. 154. E. I., VI, p. 56.

historic event; had it not died, inscribed commemorative tablet at Atkur would never have come into existence; and we may have been still groping in the dark about the circumstances leading to the death of the Chola crown-prince Rājāditya.

Hunting was one of the favourite pastimes of the Rāshṭrakūṭa rulers. One of the inscriptions of Govind III[155] informs us how he speared the boars preserved for his sport, when he returned to Rāmesvaram on the Tungabhadrā. This inscription would show that there were game preserves in the various centres of the empire for the use of the emperors and courtiers.

The sciences of astronomy and astrology were remarkably developed in our period, and epigraphy supplies ample evidence to illustrate the hold which the latter had over the popular mind. From the Kadba plates of Govind III [156] we learn that even the Jains had taken to astrology; for, the record states how a grant was made in favour of a Jain Matha because its head had removed the evil influence of Saturn from which a feudatory Chalukya prince was suffering. Saturn was indeed tremendously dreaded in our period; the Śilāhāra prince Aparājitadeva[157] and Mahāmaṇḍaleśvara Govuṇarasa[158] are seen taking with pride the title of 'Sanivāravijaya, 'one who is successful (even) on Saturdays'. The time when Dahir started to fight with Kasim was carefully selected by his astrologers; and in order to counteract the advantage which the Muslim opponent enjoyed by the presence of Venus behind his back, Dahir had fixed on his back a golden image of that planet.[159] Unfortunately this golden Venus did not perform her duties faithfully, and poor Dahir was defeated and slain. What Marco Polo has said about the people of Gujarat and Malabar, *viz.* 'They pay greater

155. I. A., XI, p. 126.
156. E. I., IV, p. 340.
157. E. I., III, p. 269.
158. E. I., IV, p. 66.
159. Elliot, I, p. 169.

heed to signs and omens than any other people that exist.'[160] seems to have been substantially true of the Deccan of our period.

Besides astrology, there were a number of other superstitious beliefs current in the society. It was believed that if certain vows and conditions were observed, gods could be compelled to do the needful; we sometimes come across devotees threatening the poor god with non-co-operation. From one of the Raṭṭa records from Saundatti we learn that Kesirāja of Banahatti had sworn to the Unborn :—If disease and trouble should ever manifest themselves among those whom I protect, I will come to you no more.'[161] Catching a serpent alive was regarded as a signal proof of chastity; Sugalādevī, the wife of Maṇḍalaśvara Varma, had caught a serpent alive in her hand and a temple was built in her honour as the chastest lady of the land.[162] Spells and enchantments against serpent bites were current, but evidence is available to show that their futility was often realised.[163] Many women were induced to administer herbs and medicines to their husbands, which were supposed to be efficacious in keeping them under their control, but which very often ruined their health and hastened their death.[164] Sometimes some loyal subjects used to take the vow that they would offer their own heads, if their king were to be blessed with a son. Sorab No. 479 informs us that in c. 991 A.D. Katega took a vow to offer his head to the goddess Gundabbe of Hayve, if his king Sāntivarman got a son; a son was soon born and then Katega allowed the royal soldiers to cut off his head, and of course went to heaven.[165] There were others who used to vow to offer their own heads in case a son was born to them, cases are on record to show that such

160. II, p. 365.
161. J. B. B. R. A. S., X, p. 281.
162. I. A., XII. p. 99.
164. J. B. B. R. A. S., X, p. 279.
165. E. C., VIII.

vows were actually kept.[166] Ibn Khurdadbā informs us that persons who had grown very old and weak very often used to commit suicide in holy places, either by drowning or by burning themselves on auspicious days.[167] This custom may have prevailed to some extent, since the famous Chandella king Dhanga is known to have courted death by allowing himself to be drowned at Prayāga, when he had grown very old.[168]

It is not to be supposed that the above practices were universal; they were confined to certain sections of the society. They are simply mentioned here in order to give an idea of the superstitions of the age as they can be ascertained from epigraphy.

CHAPTER XV

Economic Condition

An enquiry into the economic conditions of our period is beset with several difficulties. Sources of information, both indigenous and foreign, are scanty and their interpretation is rendered difficult by the uncertainty as to the precise meaning to be attached to the technical terms used therein. It is proposed to utilise in this chapter some of the records hailing from Tamil country. A part of that province was under the Rāshṭrakūṭa occupation for nearly a quarter of a century in the reign of Kṛshṇa III, many of whose records hail from that province, which can be interpreted only with the help afforded by other Chola records. It would be therefore both necessary and useful to supplement our information from other contemporary Chola records.

166. E. C., IV, introduction, p. 9.
167. Elliot, 1, p. 10.
168. E. I., I. p. 164.

Let us first enquire into the wealth of the country. This is primarily derived from its natural products and industries, and secondarily from its commerce and conquests. The natural products of the Deccan under the Rāshṭrakūṭas could not have been much different from those of the present day as far as the produce of the soil is concerned, since no considerable climatic changes are known to have taken place during the last 1000 years. Cotton was produced in large quantity in southern Gujarat, Khandesh, and Berar; cotton yarn and cloth are mentioned among the articles of export from Bharoch by the Periplus in the 1st century A.D., by[1] Marco Polo in the 13th century[2] and by Tavernier in the 16th century.[3] It is obvious that in our period too the regions referred to must have been producing cotton, as they do even today. Gujarat cotton in Marco Polo's time was a rough variety suitable for stuffing only, the same probably was the case in our period too. Indigo is known to have been extensively exported from Gujarat and Thana in the 17th[4] and 13th[5] centuries A.D. and the crop was probably raised in our period too. Incense and perfumes were exported in large quantity from Saimur and Thana in the 12th and 13th centuries[6] and the same may have been the case in our period too. The chief crops in Maharashtra must have been *jawari*, *bajri* and oilseeds and Karnatak must have produced cotton in addition. Konkan was rich in coconuts, betelnuts and rice; the western ghats and parts of Mysore yielded large quantities of sandal, teak, and ebony wood. It may be pointed out that the timber of these trees was exported from western Indian ports since pre-historic times.

1. Schoff. *periplus*, p. 39 2. II, p. 393. 3. p. 52.
4. Moreland, *From Akbar to Aurangzeb*, p. 160.
5. Marco Polo, II, pp. 393 and 398.
6. Elliot, I, p. 87; Marco Polo, II, p. 393.

The fertility of the Deccan soil compares unfavourably with that of the alluvial plains of Bengal or the United Provinces, but the comparatively meagre wealth, that was available from this source, was supplemented by the metallurgical products in a much greater degree than is the case at present. Copper is mentioned as an article of export from Bharoch in the Periplus[7] and since northern India depended almost entirely on the produce of the local copper mines down to the beginning of the 17th century A.D.,[8] we need not suppose that the copper exports in the first century A.D., were merely of the nature of re-exports. But it was not only in northern India that this metal was worked out; traces of more or less extensive workings of copper mines have been discovered in the districts of Cudappah, Bellary, Chanda, Buldhana, Narsingpur, Ahmadnagar, Bijapur and Dharwar.[9] Some of these mines are known to have been worked up right up to the time of Hyder Ali. It is, therefore, very likely that the wealth of the Deccan of our period must have been to some extent increased by the yields of these copper mines. We should not forget in this connection that copper was a much costlier metal than it is now. In the 17th century it was five times costlier than now,[10] and at about our period silver was only 3 times dearer than copper and 14 times cheaper than gold. The relative ratio of prices of gold and copper, as given by Brihaspati, is 1 : 48.[11] The present ratio of the prices of these metals is about 1 : 1500.

Far more valuable than the mines of copper were the mines of precious stones, that were actively worked with

7. Schoff, *Periplus*, p. 36.
8. Moreland, *From Akbar to Aurangzeb*, p. 183.
9. Ball, *A Manual of the Geology of India*, Part III, Chap. V; La Touche, *A Bibliography of Indian Geology and Physical Geography*, pp. 113–137.
10. Moreland, *India at the Death of Akbar*, p. 147.
11. Dr. D. R. Bhandarkar *Carmichæl Letcures*, 1921, p. 189.

great profit during our period. Cudappah, Bellary, Karnul, and the Krishna valley near Golconda, continued to yield rich harvests in diamonds till a much later time, as we know from Marco Polo,[12] Ibn Batuta[13] and Tavernier[14]. At the time of Ibn Batuta Deogiri, which was then till quite recently the capital of the Deccan, was a famous centre of the jewelry trade;[15] during our period Malkhed, the Rāshṭrakūta capital, which was much nearer the diamond fields, must similarly have been the main market for the precious stones unearthed in the mines mentioned above. Tavernier, writing in the 17th century, says that the port of Goa had formerly a large export trade in jewelry; but whether this former period mentioned by him can go back to our age is doubtful.

Contemporary documents do not give any adequate idea of the industries of the period; but we can get a fair notion from the accounts of foreign merchants of the earlier and later periods. Cloth industry was the principal one. From the Periplus we learn that cloth was largely exported from Bharoch and Damarike *i. e.* Dravid country.[16] The principal centres in the Deccan were Minnagar, Gujarat, Ujjain, Paithan and Tagara.[17] Most of these continued to be centres of cloth industry down to the 17th century A.D. Marco Polo states that Gujarat, Thana and Warangal used to manufacture and export considerable quantities of cloth in the 13th century,[18] and Tavernier notes that prodigious quantities of clear and white calicos were manufactured in Burhanpur and Berar, and were transported thence to Persia, Turkey, Poland, Arabia and Cairo.[19] It is therefore but fair to conclude that during our period, which is almost midway between these two, the industry may have been equally thriving. Paithan and Warangal were, and still are, particularly famous for their muslins. About the

12. II, p. 360. 13. p. 217. 14. p. 319. 15. p. 227. 16. p. 34
17. Pp. 34, 42, 43. 18. II. pp. 393, 395 and 361. 19. p. 40

cloth manufacture at these places, Marco Polo says,—'These are the most delicate buckrams and of the highest price; in sooth they look like the tissue of spider's web. There can be no king or queen in the world but might be glad to wear them.'[20] *Paiṭhaṇī*, the name given to the high class silken *saries* of ladies in the Deccan, is significant in this connection.

From Marco Polo we learn that southern Gujarat and northern Maharashtra were great centres of tanning industry in the 13th century. Leather was exported in large quantities from Thana;[21] in Gujarat the quantity of hide dressed was so great that several shiploads could be exported to Arabia and the Persian Gulf.[22] This tanning industry of the Deccan and Gujarat is not mentioned in the Periplus, but since it was in full vigour in the 13th century, and had captured a number of foreign markets, it is reasonable to infer that it must have begun its career during our period.

Ibn Batuta compliments the Marathas of the region round Daulatabad and Nandurbar on their skill in arts; but what particular arts he was referring to is difficult to ascertain, as he does not mention them. Marco Polo refers to the mat industry flourishing in southern Gujarat and northern Maharashtra in the 13th century when beautiful mats in red and blue leather, exquisitely inlaid with figures of birds and beasts and skilfully embroidered with gold and silver, used to be exported in large quantities from these provinces.[23] It is not improbable that this industry too, which was prospering in the 13th century, may go back to our period.

Mysore was very rich in elephants and we may therefore well presume that it may have been a centre of ivory industry.

Contemporary records do not give any detailed account of the commerce of the period, but the accounts given by the Periplus, Alberuni, Al Idrisi, Marco Polo and Ibn Batuta can give us some idea in this respect. Bharoch, which was

20. II, p. 391. 21. II, p. 395. 22. II, p. 393. 23. II, pp. 393–4.

an all-India port since very early times, continued to be so in our period. From Al-Idrisi, who is slightly later than our period, we learn that it was a port for vessels coming from China as well as for those coming from Sindh and the Persian Gulf.[24] Its inhabitants were rich and principally engaged in trade; they used to engage freely upon speculations and distinct expeditions. Merchandise from every country was found there, and was sent on from there to other countries. The Gujarat Rāshṭrakūṭas must have derived considerable revenues from the import duties at this port. The prosperity of Bharoch may have been, to some extent, affected in our period by the rise of the port of Cambay and its inclusion in the Gurjara Pratīhāra empire. This must have diverted to the new port a portion of the northern trade which formerly flowed to Bharoch, as Cambay was nearer to the Gurjara-Pratīhāra capital Kanauj.

Kalyan which was a natural port of export for the northern Deccan was the next port of importance. In the 6th century at the time of Cosmos Indicopleustes, it was one of the five important ports trading in cloth, brass, and black-wood logs; the same was very probably the case in our period too. Naosari, Sopara, Thana, Saimur, Dabhol, Jayagad, Devagad and Malvan were other ports of minor importance, engaged chiefly in coastal trade. The revenues from all these ports must have been fairly extensive. From the Kharepatan plates of Anantadeva it wood seem that the import duties on the coastal trade were less than those on the foreign trade.[25]

The above description of the natural resources and industries of our period can enable us to complete the list of the articles of export. Cotton yarn and cloth, both rough and fine, muslins, hides, mats, indigo, incense, perfumes, betel nuts, coconuts, sandal and teak wood, sesame oil, and ivory

Elliot, I. p. 87. 25. E. I., III, p. 286.

must have been the principal articles available for export; most of these have also been actually enumerated among the articles of export by the Periplus, Al Idrisi, Marco Polo, and Ibn Batuta. Bharoch used to export a number of products from northern India as well in the time of the Periplus, and the same probably continued to be the case, at least to some extent, in our period too. Diamonds were available for export, but it is not known whether the Rāshṭrakūṭas had put any embargo on the trade in that commodity. From some of the later writers like Tavernier,[26] we learn that some of the kings of later days would not permit the export of the bigger diamonds; it is not impossible that the same restriction may have been imposed by the governments of our period.

Among the articles of imports at the port of Bharoch, the Periplus mentions inferior pearls from the Persian Gulf, dates, gold, slaves, Italian wine, but in small quantity, copper, tin, lead, topaz, storax, sweet clover, flint glass, antimony, gold and silver coins, and singing boys and girls for kings.[27] With some exceptions these must have continued to be imported even in our period, as they were not procurable in India and were required by her people. From Marco Polo we learn that Thana used to import gold, silver, and copper in the 13th century.[28] Import trade in horses was extensive. Marco Polo says that every vessel visiting the Deccan and Gujarat ports invariably carried horses in addition to other cargo. This trade must have been even brisker in our period; for, the needs of the mounting department of the Rāshṭrakūṭas and their feudatories must have been very great.

The principal means of transport in our period was the bullock cart. Al Idrisi says that there was no other means of travelling in Gujarat, except chariots drawn by oxen under

26. II, chap. 9, 21. 27. Pp. 40, 42. 28. II, p. 395.

the control of a driver.[29] The same was probably the case in our period. Horses were fairly dear and were therefore not available for transport purposes. The bullock carts were, however, fairly comfortable; Tavernier, writing in the 17th century, says that they were more commodious than anything that has been invented for ease in France and Italy.[30] This compliment is of course paid to the conveyance of the 17th century, but when we remember how conservative the Hindu artisan is, it would appear very probable that the bullock carts of our period too were equally good.

We have no contemporary records which throw light upon the condition of the roads. The author of the Periplus complains[31] that goods from Paithan, Tagara and other places in the Deccan had to be brought to Bharoch in waggons through great tracts without roads, and the picture drawn by Tavernier about the state of affairs in the 17th century is no more flattering.[32] About the Deccan he says that wheeled carriages do not travel there, the roads being too much interrupted by high mountains, tanks, and rivers. These reasons assigned by Tavernier would show that the roads were bad mainly in the ghats and hilly areas. The military necessities of the empire must have compelled the Rāshṭrakūṭas to keep the roads in a fairly good condition. It is not very likely that in our period, even the roads over the ghats and hills were as bad as they were in the times of the Greek and French traveller.

Besides the bullock cart, the oxen and pack horses of an inferior breed must have been used for transport, especially in the hilly tract, or when it was desired to have a speedy transport. In the Muslim period several subcastes used to follow the caravan's profession, transporting merchandise from one place to another. Individuals used to own as many as 100 bullocks; they used to move along with their wives,

29. Elliot, I. p. 87 30. p. 30. 31. P. 43. 32. I. Chap. 11.

children, and priests, and had no houses of their own.[33] A similar mode of transport was probably in vogue in the Deccan of our period where roads were too hilly to admit of cart transport.

Problems connected with land revenue and the incidence of taxation have been discussed already in chapter XI; some other agrarian topics will be considered here. The prevailing tenure of the Deccan of our period was Rayatwari, but a zemindar class, the members of which were assigned royal revenues, did exist to a limited extent. The mention of *grāmapati* along with *grāmakūṭa* in some of our records shows that the former was a village holder. Some of the officials were assigned revenues of villages and towns, as shown already, and these probably are referred to as *grāmapatis*. There is no evidence, however, to show that whole districts or Talukas were being assigned to revenue farmers.

A record belonging to the middle of the 10th century hailing from Tirukkalavur states that the village assembly had taken on trust for cultivation a piece of land, the proceeds of which were to be utilised, apparently, for some charity.[35] The members of the assembly had agreed to have the land cultivated (on the terms) *two to one*. The expression in the Italics obviously refers to the lease condition determining the shares of the owner and the tiller, but unfortunately there is nothing in the record to indicate whether it was the owner or the cultivator who was entitled to two shares. Nor do we know whether the produce was to be divided in the gross or after the government dues had been paid. In the Deccan at present sometimes the owner receives three shares and the tiller two, sometimes the owner two and the tiller one and sometimes the division is equal. It is, therefore, difficult to state whether the assembly in the above case received two shares or only one. The former alternative seems probable.

33. I., pp. 31–33 34. *Ante*, p. 189. 35. S. I. I., III, No. 10.

Let us now consider the question whether the land was freely transferrable or not. There is sufficient evidence to show that the transfer of land was not an affair in which only the seller and the purchaser were concerned. A record from Saundatti,[36] which is unfortunately fragmentary, records a gift of land to a Jain temple, which was made with the consent of fifty agriculturists. It seems very probable that these agriculturists were the Mahajanas of the locality; if so, it is clear that the sales of the land required the consent of the village community. An inscription from Belgaum district records that when the Raṭṭa ruler Kārtavīrya gave 800 *kammas* of land to a temple at Nesarge, the six headmen of the place received a gift of money 'like that which was customary to give at the time of buying.'[37] It would therefore seem that even when the rulers of the land were alienating landed property, they had to pay a certain duty to the village headman. This customary gift to the village headmen seems to have been due to the necessity of getting the consent of the village community, whose spokesmen they were. This record belongs to the 13th century and since it does not refer to the consent of the Mahajanas for the transaction, like the 10th century record from the same locality referred to above, it would appear that the consent of the village community was gradually becoming a more or less formal affair. Here again we find epigraphical evidence supporting the Smriti literature. In his lengthy introduction to the Dāyabhāga section, Vijñānes'vara quotes an anonymous text, declaring that transfer of land can become effective only with the consent of the village community, castemen, neighbours and kinsmen. He, however, maintains that the consent of the village community was merely intended for the publication of the transaction; it does not mean that the transaction becomes ultra-vires if no such consent was obtained previously. The con-

36. J. B. B. R. A. S., X., p. 208. 37. *Ibid*, p. 257.

sent of the neighbours also was merely to avoid any quarrel about the boundaries.[38] It would therefore appear, both from the epigraphical and Smriti evidence, that the consent of the village community was becoming a more or less formal affair at the end of our period.

There is evidence to show that if a village or land was owned by several cosharers, no new owner could be introduced except with the consent of the whole body. The Sivapur inscription of Mahās'ivagupta, belonging to c. 800 A.D., assigns $\frac{1}{4}$ share of 5 villages to 15 Brahmanas. The grant was hereditary, but on the condition that the grantees and their descendants continued to be men of learning and high moral character. The record expressly adds that if a sharer died heirless, or was ignorant, or immoral, his share was to be assigned to some other relative by the remaining coshares, and not by the king.[39]

The village artisans like the carpenter, the smith, the potter, etc., were maintained by the community by the assignment of a certain grain-share from each farmer, in return for which the artisans were to supply his needs during the year. This system has been very ancient in the Deccan and continues to the present day.[40]

Let us now proceed to consider the means of exchange. A number of Chola records, to which attention will be drawn later, show that during our period barter was extensively practised in Tamil country. It has been shown in Chapter XI how the Rāshṭrakūṭas and their feudatories used to receive

38. यद्यपि 'स्वग्रामज्ञातिसामन्तदायादानुमतेन च । हिरण्योदकदानेन षड्भिर्गच्छति मेदिनी ॥' इति तत्रापि ग्रामानुमतिः......व्यवहारप्रकाशनार्थमेवापेक्ष्यते न पुनर्ग्रामानुमत्या विना व्यवहारासिद्धिः ॥

39. E. I., XI, p. 192.

40. For a detailed history of this system in the Deccan, see Altekar, *A History of the Village Communities in Western India*, pp. 92–97.

their revenues sometimes wholly and sometimes partly in kind. The government transaction under these circumstances must have been at least partly by barter. We shall not therefore be far wrong in assuming that in our province, as in Tamil country, the barter system was fairly in vogue.

A number of coins of gold and silver are mentioned in our records, but it is strange that so far not a single coin, belonging indisputably to the Rāshṭrakūṭa dynasty should have been discovered. Silver coins of Kṛshṇarāja bearing the legend *Paramamahes'vara-mahādityapādā (or mātāpiṭṛpādā)-nudhyāta-S'rīKṛshṇarājaḥ*, which have been discovered in large quantities in the district of Nasik and in Marathi C. P. were first attributed with some hesitation to the Rāshṭrakūṭa king Kṛshṇa I, but that view does not seem to be correct. As Rapson has pointed out, these coins imitate too closely the latest Gupta coins of the locality to permit the assumption that they belong to Kṛshṇa I.[41] They are besides undated; Rāshṭrakūṭa silver coins bore the dates of issue.[42] Our notions of the Rāshṭrakūṭa coinage have therefore to be based, not on first hand evidence but on a number of *a priori* considerations.

Dramma, *Savarṇa*, *Gadyāṇaka*, *Kaḷanju* and *Kāsu* are the principal coins mentioned in our period. Dramma is the Sanskritised form of the Greek term *drachme*. The silver coins of the Indo-Baktrian kings, weighing about 65 grains, were known by that name and we may presume that the weight of the *drammas* mentioned in our records was more or less the same. One of the Kanheri inscriptions belonging to the time of Amoghavarsha I mentions golden *drammas* and distinguishes them from ordinary *drammas* mentioned a little earlier.[43] It would thus appear that the name *dramma* was

41. Rapson, *Indian Coins*, p. 27. For further discussion on these coins, see I. A., XIV, p. 68.

42. Sulaiman Saudagar, p. 50.

43. I. A., XIII, p. 133.

given to both silver and golden coins in the northern provinces of the Rāshṭrakūṭa empire. Our four anna silver piece weighs about 48 grains ; silver *dramma* was thus about one-third bigger than this coin.

Cambay plates of Govinda IV mention a gift of 1400[44] villages yielding an annual revenue of seven lakhs of *Suvarṇas*. The value and weight of this Suvarṇa coin is difficult to determine. According to several well known authorities like Kauṭalya, Manu, etc., the term Suvarṇa denotes a golden coin weighing 80 *raktikās* or about 146 grains. Suvarṇa coins of this description of early dates have not been discovered, but it is well-known that the Imperial Guptas tried to restore this national unit towards the middle of the 5th century A.D. The Suvarṇa coins mentioned in the Cambay plates, however, did not very probably weigh so much as 146 grains. Most of the golden coins of southern dynasties of our period vary in weight from 45 to 55 grains; no golden coins weighing about 146 grains have so far been discovered belonging to the Deccan of our period. It is not improbable that the term Suvarṇa has been used in the Cambay plates to denote, not the technical *Suvarṇa* coin weighing about 146 grains, but the current golden coin weighing like the *dramma* about 65 grains.

The epigraphical records from Karnatak and Tamil provinces usually mention Kaḷanju, Gadyāṇaka and Kāsu as the current coins of the land. These were all golden coins. Kaḷanju is really the name of a prickly climbing species of Cæsalpina, the weight of whose seed varies between 45 to 50 grains. The average weight of the early punch-marked golden coins of the south also varies between 45 and 50 grains. The normal weight of a Kaḷanju coin of our period may therefore be presumed to be more or less the same. It was

44. E. I., VII, p. 26.

therefore about a quarter of a tola in weight.[45] It must be, however, remembered that there were some local variations in its weight; thus an inscription[46] refers to a gift of 25 Kaḷanjus for a perpetual lamp weighed by the balance used in the case of charitable edicts. A record of the time of Parāntaka I mentions Kaḷanjus weighed by a stone called after Vedelvidugu, which was the surname of the Pallava king Tellarareinda Nandipottaraiyar.[47] Since the actual weight of the Kaḷanju seed varied by a few grains, it would seem that the standard was specifically determined by the state from time to time. The variation could not have been of more than a few grains.

The coin Gadyāṇaka was equal to two Kaḷanjus and thus weighed about 90 grains. It was a gold coin equal to the modern eight anna piece. 7 Kaḷanjus were equal to 20 Kāsus: a Kāsu thus weighed about 15 grains of gold.

Other coins occasionally mentioned are Manjāḍi and Akkam. Manjāḍi was one-twentieth of a Kaḷanju and thus weighed only about $2\frac{1}{7}$ grains. Akkam was one-twelfth of a Kāsu and was thus about half the size of the Manjāḍi.

The coinage, above referred to, was almost all in gold, *dramma* being the only exception. Silver coins from the southern India, belonging to the first millennium of the Christian Era, are very rare. We shall therefore experience some difficulty in converting the prices in gold of our age into corresponding prices in rupees of the present day, as we do not know the precise ratio of prices of these two metals during our period. Dr. D. R. Bhandarkar has pointed out[48] how the Nasik cave inscription No. 12 shows that the ratio between the prices of these two metals was 1 : 14. The record expressly equates 35 Kārshāpaṇas to 1 Suvarṇa, and since the ratio of copper to gold was never so high as 1 : 35, we have to

45. Elliot, *Coins of Southern India*, pp. 46 ff.
46. S. I. I., III, No. 191. 47. S. I. I., III, p. 228.
48. *Carmichael Lectures*, 1921, p. 191.

conclude that the Kārshāpaṇas of the record were silver and not copper coins each one weighing 32 ratis, *i. e.* two-fifths of a golden *Suvarṇa*: the ratio between the prices of the two metals thus becomes 35 × 32 : 1 × 80 *i. e.* 14 : 1. *S'ukranīti*, which was probably composed not much later than our period, gives the ratio as 1 : 16.[49] Tavernier, writing in the middle of the 17th century, says that the golden rupee was equal to 14 silver ones.[50] It would thus seem that the relative prices of these two metals were fairly constant from the 1st to the 17th century, and we may, therefore, presume that in our period they were somewhere in the vicinity of 1 : 15. The ratio before the recent rise in the price of gold was about 1 : 30.

The following table of the values of the various coins may be useful to the reader for ready reference.

Name.	Metal.	Approximate weight	Approximate present value.
(1) Dramma.	silver.	65 grains or $\frac{1}{3}$ tola	about 6 as.
(2) Dramma.	gold.	,,	about Rs. 7.
(3) Kalanju.	,,	48 grains or $\frac{1}{4}$ tola.	about Rs. 5.
(4) Gadyāṇaka.	,,	96 grains or $\frac{1}{2}$ tola.	about Rs. 10.
(5) Kāsu.	,,	15 grains.	about Re. 1 10 as.
(6) Manjādi.	,,	$2\frac{1}{2}$ grains.	about 4 as.
(7) Akkam.	,,	$1\frac{1}{4}$ grains.	about 2 as.

Commerce and industry, that were described a little while ago, presuppose not only currency, but also banking facilities. These latter were provided in our period by guild organisations. These organisations have been, since early times, a conspicuous feature of the Hindu trade and industry. As early as the Āndhra period, the whole of the Deccan was spread with a network of guilds,[51] which used to regulate trade and industry, train apprentices, and do the banking business, not only for their members but also for the public.

49. IV, 2, 98. 50. P. 13. 51. I. A., 1919 p., 82.

The guilds continued to flourish in our period too. In c. 775 A.D. there was a guild of weavers at Laxmesvar, the headman of which had agreed to make a certain contribution for a certain religious object.[52] An inscription from Mulgund, dated c. 880 A.D., records a gift by four heads of a guild belonging to 360 towns.[53] The precise import of this description of the guild is not easy to determine, but it looks very probable that the description is intended to indicate that its membership was spread over 360 towns and villages. The record immediately proceeds to record a gift, made by some local Brahmanas, with the consent of 2000 merchants. The context of these two passages in this inscription would suggest that these 2000 merchants were connected with the guild, or were perhaps its members. It is, therefore, not unlikely that the members of the guild were spread over 360 different localities.

The absence of more numerous references to guilds in records, strictly falling within our period, must be regarded as merely accidental, for we get several references to them in the epigraphs of the succeeding centuries. An inscription from Belgamve, dated 1083 A.D.,[55] refers to a guild which apparently ruled over or had its offices in 18 cities; another from Managoli, dated 1161 A.D.,[56] refers to several grants made by the guilds of oilmen, weavers, artisans, basket-makers, mat-makers and fruit-sellers. Recently two inscriptions have been published, one from Kolhapur, dated S'aka 1058, and the other from Miraj, dated S'aka 1066 A.D.,[57] which give interesting information about a guild of the Vira-Balanjus, the membership of which had extended over four districts. A record from Saundatti, dated 1205 A.D.,[58] refers to an assemblage of all the people of the district, headed by all the guilds of the place. The names of the guilds are not given in this record, but they

52. E. I., VI, p. 166. 53. J. B. B. R. A. S., X, p. 192.
54. *Ibid.* 55. I. A., V, p. 344. 56. E. I., V, p. 22.
57. E. I., XIX, p. 33. 58. J. B. B. R. A. S., X, p. 238.

were in all probability similar to those at Managoli. It is, therefore, quite likely that the guild organisation in our period was not quite so negligible as the references occurring in the inscriptions, strictly belonging to our age, may perhaps lead us to conclude.

Some of our records give us a glimpse into the working of these guilds. The weavers' guild at Laxmesvar had only one head, the Mulgund guild, with a probable membership of 2000, had four heads, while the one at Belgamve, which is described as ruling over 18 cities, had an executive of 9. The Vīra Balanju guild mentioned in the Miraj inscription had an executive of 15, belonging to the different localities of the districts, over which its membership had spread. It would thus seem that every guild had an executive, the strength of which varied with its membership and activities. It is interesting to note that these executive committees of the guilds, which we discover in inscriptions, should be also found in literary works like the *Yājñavalkyasmṛti*,[59] and *Nītivākyāmṛta*.[60] Meetings of the general body were convened when general policy had to be discussed or grants from guild properties or requiring recurring contributions from individual members were contemplated.[61]

A number of records above mentioned, *e. g.* those from Managoli, Miraj, etc., record contributions from members of guilds towards religious objects on a certain scale; it would thus appear that the guild acted as a corporate unit and that the resolutions, probably passed by a majority, were binding on all the members. The guild at Belgamve had its 500 edicts; this fact may show that they could frame bye-laws binding upon its members. Here again we find epigraphy corroborating the Smriti literature, for Manu[62] and Yājñavalkya[63] lay down that the rules and regulations of the guilds

59. II, p. 189. 60. XXIX, p. 9. 61. I. A., X, p. 185.
62. VIII, 41. 63. II, 187-8.

were to be respected by the king, if they were not against public interest.

While describing the guild members who had come to witness the wrestling between Kansa and Kṛshṇa, *Harivans'a*[64] refers to their banners bearing upon them the representations of the implements of their different industries. That the association of particular banners with particular devices mentioned in the *Harivans'a* is not fictitious is proved by the Belgamve and Kolhapur inscriptions referred to above, which refer to the banner of the Vīra-Balanjus, and describe it as bearing the device of a hill. These banners were probably carried at the head of the caravans or militias of the guilds, as was later the custom of the European companies in India.[65]

An inscription from Dambal states that a guild of the locality had its own umbrellas and *chauris*.[66] The umbrellas and *chauris*, which this guild was using in 1095 A.D., were obtained by a royal charter from Jagadekamalla (c. 1018-1040 A.D.) It would thus appear that some of the bigger guilds used to receive royal charters determining their powers and privileges. The above record further describes the Dambal guild as the lord of Aihole, the best of towns. This may perhaps show that some of the big guilds were often entrusted by the state with the government of towns and cities. The reason for such a step may have been the loans advanced to the state by the guild banks; as a security for these loans towns like Aihole may have been handed over to the creditor guild by the debtor state. Maintenance of troops was a natural corollary of the overlordship of towns and cities; members of guilds must have either formed or officered their own militias, otherwise it would be difficult to justify their description in the Dambal and Kolhapur records as ' persons whose breasts were embraced by the goddess of

64. Chap. 86, 5. 65. Tavernier, p. 36. 66. I. A., X, p. 188.

perfect impetuosity and bravery'. It may be pointed out that the Mandsor inscription, belonging to the middle of the 5th century A.D., also describes some of its members as experts in archery, and bold in forcibly uprooting the enemy in battle.[67] Another reason why guilds had to maintain their own militias was to safeguard their goods, while being transported from one place to another. From Tavernier we learn that in the Muslim period each cart in the caravan had to be protected by four soldiers, each of whom had to be paid Rs. 4 a month.[68] Similar precautions may have been necessary in our period as well, and the maintenance of a militia would have reduced the expense of keeping the mercenary force, besides adding to the dignity and prestige of the corporation. In this connection we should not forget that even village communities in our period used to maintain their own militias.[69]

The guild banks were among the most stable banks of our period, inspiring the highest amount of public confidence. The village communities also had their own banks as shown already,[70] and these must have been equally stable institutions. Private individuals also must be then, as now, carrying on banking business.

Let us now proceed to ascertain the rate of interest. There is sufficient epigraphical evidence to help us in this matter. A Kanheri inscription of the time of Amoghavarsha I[71] mentions a certain investment in a local bank, which had agreed to pay an interest in perpetuity upon it. This record states that the rate of interest was to be determined by experts from time to time. This provision was a reasonble one; the guild had to pay the interest in perpetuity, and no definite rate could be guaranteed for all time to come. The rate must vary with the conditions of the money market. It is, however, worth noting that a similar saving clause does

67. C. I. I., III, No. 18. 68. p. 334. 69. *Ante*, pp. 190-91.
70. *Ante*, pp. 208-9. 71. I, A., XIII, p. 133.

not occur in the numerous other inscriptions of our period. which state the agreed rate of interest on deposits given in perpetuity. It is, however, not unlikely that in practice the banks of the guilds and the village communities, which had bound themselves to supply interest at a certain rate, may have been allowed some latitude, if the condition of the money market was severely adverse to them.

Another Kanheri inscription of the same period [72] supplies some data to determine the rate of interest of the locality. We find that the premier of the local S'ilāhāra dynasty had to invest 160 Drammas in order to provide annually 20 Drammas for the Buddha worship, 3 Drammas for the building's repairs, 5 Drammas for the robes of the monks and 1 Dramma for the purchase of the books; 160 Drammas could thus fetch, by way of interest, 29 Drammas annually. The rate of interest, which prevailed at Kanheri towards the end of the 9th century is thus found to be about 17 percent per annum.

We get copious data to determine the current rate of interest during the latter half of the 10th century A.D. An inscription from Tiruvurrur in Chingleput district, dated in the 22nd year of Kṛshṇa III, [73] mentions an investment on which the village assembly of Kuattur had agreed to pay in perpetuity an interest of 15%. This rate of interest seems to have been not far removed from the normal rate on perpetual deposits; a number of inscriptions from Tanjore belonging to the first half of the 11th century disclose $12\frac{1}{2}$% as the current rate on such deposits.[74] Sometimes the interest on capital in cash *i.e.*, Kaḷanjus, is stated in kind *i. e.*, in Kalams of paddy. But here again, if we convert the Kalams into their cash equivalent, the rate of interest is found to be varying between

72. *Ibid*, p. 136.
73. *Inscriptions from Madras Presidency*, Chingleput, No. 1048.
74. S. I. I., II, pp. 95, 97, 98, 99, 101-3.

10 to 15%. Thus an inscription of the time of Kṛshṇa III [75] records a gift of 20 Kaḷanjus by a queen of Vaidumba Mahārāja, a feudatory of that emperor. The interest on these 20 Kaḷanjus is stated to be 20 Kalams of paddy. Another inscription from south Arcot district, belonging to the reign of the same emperor, shows that the rate of interest in that locality also was 1 Kalam per Kaḷanju.[76] This Kalam is, however, by the Perilmai measure which was 25% bigger than the normal Kalam, as will be soon shown. The rate of interest will thus work out to be 1¼ Kalam per Kaḷanju, if we take the Kalam to consist of 12 Marakkals of 8 and not of 10 Nāris. The price of paddy at this period varied between 8 to 12 Kalams per Kaḷanju, as will be soon shown; an interest of 1 Kalam per Kaḷanju would thus be somewhere between 8 to 12½%, and an interest of 1¼ Kalam would be between 10 to 15%.

In some localities, however, much higher rates prevailed. A Bāṇa inscription, dated 915 A.D.,[77] states that the interest on 20 Kaḷanjus was to be 5 Kaḷanjus. The rate of interest in this case is, therefore, 25%. A still higher rate of interest is seen to prevail in a record,[78] belonging to the time of Parāntaka I, *i. e.*, the first half of the 10th century. A local temple at Annamalai, which had to pay to the assembly a tax of 18 *īlakkāsu* on the lands belonging to it, is seen arranging for the annual payment of 6 *īlakkāsu* by depositing a capital of 15 *īlakkāsu* with the members of the village assembly. The rate of interest here works out to be as high as 40%. This rate is much above the normal one; it may be due to the village assembly being in urgent need of funds for meeting some pressing need of the hour; it is also possible that the assembly may have decided to show a special favour to the

75. *Inscriptions from Madras Presidency*, N. Arcott., No. 636.
76. E. I., VII, pp. 188 ff.
77. E. I., XI, p. 224.
78. S. I. I., III, p. 241.

deity of the village by giving an indirect concession in the land ax by allowing an abnormal rate of interest on the capital deposited by the temple authorities for that purpose.

Interest at high rate like 30 or 40% is only exceptional; in the vast majority of the records of our period, the rate of interest, when the capital was in cash, is found to be varying between 12 to 15%. It is interesting to note that the rate permitted by Manu,[79] Yājñavalkya,[80] and Kauṭalya[81] on the capital in cash is also 15%.

If the capital advanced was in kind we find that the rate of interest was much higher. Ukkal inscription No. 5, belonging to the time of Kampanavarman,[82] records an agreement of the villagers to pay an interest of 100 *kādis* on a capital of 400 *kādis* of rice, while another from the same locality mentions an interest of 500 *kādis* on a capital of 1000. The rate of interest in these cases works out to be 25% and 50% respectively. Here again epigraphy is seen confirming the testimony of the Smritis. Kauṭalya [83] permits an interest of 50% in the case of the capital in grain, and Manu,[84] Yājñavalkya,[85] and Vasishṭha,[86] who do not permit the capital in cash to be exceeded by the interest, declare that in the case of the capital in corn the interest may amount to two times the capital, showing thereby that the normal rate of interest permitted on the corn was about twice as high as that allowed on the capital in cash.

It must be remembered that the normal rate of interest of 12 to 15% on the cash capital was the one which the banks of the guilds and the village communities, whose security was unquestionable, were allowing on permanent deposits which were never to be withdrawn. Ordinary debtors could have obtained loans from these banks obviously at a much

79. VIII, 41. 80. II, 37. 81. III, 15. 82. S. I. I., III, p. 13.
83. III, 11. 84. II, 39. 85. VIII, 151. 86. II, 48.

higher rate of interest. It is, therefore, very probable that these banks may have charged an interest of about 20% to the debtors, who could offer good security for the loan, and that private money lenders may have charged about 25%. This inference is supported by the statement of Manu that a person charging interest at 24% is not guilty of sin.[87] If the security were of doubtful value, the rate of interest must have been still higher, say 30 to 35%. The statements in Manu and Yājñavalkya[88] that Brahmanas, Kshatriyas, Vaishyas, and Sudras should be charged interest at 24%, 36%, 48%, and 60%, respectively would seem to show that the poorer classes like the tillers of the soil, who could not probably have given quite a good security, were charged interest varying between 30% to 50%. This conclusion is fully supported by the above epigraphical evidence, which shows that the depositers could get from the banks of the best security an interest of about 15%. One can now well understand why the Smritis hold the usurer in low estimation and declare him to be a person unfit for being invited for a S'rāddha. The rates of interest figuring in the examples given in the *Līlāvatī* by Bhāskarāchārya vary from 36 of to 50%.[89]

Inscriptions of Kṛshṇa III and his Chola contemporaries supply interesting data to determine the prices and the standard of living towards the close of the 10th century. The prices given are usually the barter prices in paddy, but they can be converted into their cash equivalents. A knowledge of the various measures mentioned therein is necessary to work out these prices and the following table, the first two columns of which are borrowed from a table prepared by Hultzsch,[90] will supply the necessary information.

87. VIII, 141. 88. II, 37. 89. Vv. 92 and 94.

90. S. I. I., II, p. 48 n. 5 and p. 77 n. I.

	Old names		Old names	Equivalents in lbs. or tolas	Probable equivalents in our time
5	Śevudu.	1	Āṛakku.	$3\frac{3}{4}$ tolas	These measures in our time were either of the same capacity or perhaps 16% bigger in each case in the district of Tanjore.
2	Āṛakku.	1	Uṛakku.	$7\frac{1}{2}$ tolas.	
2	Uṛakku.	1	Uṛi.	15 tolas.	
2	Uṛi.	1	Nāri or Padi	$\frac{3}{4}$ lb.	
8	Nāri	1	Kuruṇi or Marakkal.	6 lbs.	
2	Kuruṇi	1	Padakku.	12 lbs.	
2	Padakku	1	Tūṇi.	24 lbs.	
3	Tūṇi.	1	Kalam	72 lbs.	

The above table gives the contents of the Marakkal, as determined by the Āḍavallāṉ or Rājakesari measure, which was current in the district of Tanjore in c. 1000 A.D. The value of a Marakkal differed in the past as it differs now in different districts. In the South Arcot district in the time of Kṛshṇa III, the Marakkal prevailing was the one determined by the Perilmai measure which was 25% larger than the ordinary Marakkal, since it was equivalent to 10 and not 8 Nāris.[91] It may be pointed out that even today, the Marakkal of the South Arcot district is larger than that of Tanjore, but the excess today is 50% and not 25%. The Mādevi measure of Marakkal, that is mentioned in another record of Kṛshṇa III[92] hailing from the same district seems to be identical with the Perilmai measure. At Annamalai the Marakkal was determined by the Annamaa measure,[93] at Takkolam it was fixed by the Kavaramoli measure.[94] Since these places are near the district of Arcot, it is permissible to infer that these last two measures like the Perilmai one were larger than the Āḍavallāṉ one. It may be pointed out that even today there is a great diversity of measures prevailing

91. E. I., VIII, p. 188.
92. E. I., VII, p. 36.
93. S. I. I., III, p. 241.
94. *Ibid*, p. 367.

in Tamil country; the Kalam of Trichy, South Arcot, and Tanjore is equal to 48, 36, and 24 Madras measures respectively. While trying to find out the prices, we shall have to take great precautions in determining the precise contents of the Marakkal in use.

The Kalam that is prevalent today in the district of Tanjore is equal to 24 Madras measures, the contents of each of which when filled with rice are about 3 lbs. in weight. The present day Kalam of Tanjore is thus equal to about 72 lbs.; the results in the column 3 of the above table can be easily deduced from this datum by making the necessary calculations.

It is, however, by no means certain that the Kalam by the Āḍavallāṉ measure, which was in use in Tanjore in our period, was exactly equal to the modern Kalam there in vogue. It may have been bigger or smaller or equal. In South Arcot district, we have seen above that the Kalam today is 50% and not 25% bigger than the Tanjore Kalam; so these measures have been by no means unchanged in the last 1000 years. Our records, however, supply us evidence to conclude that the modern Kalam at Tanjore is approximately equal to the one in vogue towards the end of the 10th century. A number of inscriptions state that one *uri* of ghee was required to burn one lamp, day and night. The *uri* in the above table is equal to 15 tolas, and it will be found that if a ghee lamp of one flame of moderate dimensions fed by two wicks is kept burning day and night, it will require 15 to 17 tolas of ghee. 15 tolas are just sufficient for the purpose, but it is possible that the endowments may have provided for some margin, or that the wicks may have been bigger than those used now-a-days, requiring a somewhat greater supply of ghee. If we assume that the latter was the case, then the *uri* referred to in our records would be 17 to 18 tolas, or say 17½ tolas, *i. e.*, ⅙ bigger than the present one. Under that assumption the Kalam would be also about 16% bigger than the present Tanjore Kalam, *i. e.*, about 84 lbs.; otherwise it would be approximately equal to the modern one, *i. e.*, 72 lbs.

Having determined the modern equivalents of the various measures that we shall have to deal with while determining the prices, we can now undertake that task with fair confidence. It must be remembered at the outset that even in modern times the prices are not fixed but fluctuate with scarcity, wars, famines and bumper crops. We must be, therefore, prepared to find a certain fluctuation in prices, as they may be disclosed by our inscriptions.

Let us first find out the price of paddy which was the staple corn in the south. Two inscriptions[95] on the central shrine of the Rājarājeśvara temple at Tanjore, one on the southern and the other on the northern wall, enumerate a number of villages, that were assigned by king Rājarāja before the 29th year of his regin, *i. e.*, before 1014 A.D. In the case of each village the precise acreage under cultivation and the land tax due therefrom have been stated with meticulous accuracy. The taxation of about 29 villages is given in paddy and is found to be 100 Kalams of paddy by the Āḍavallāṉ measure per *veli*. In the case of 5 villages, however, the amount of tax is given in cash, and is seen to be 10 Kaḷanjus per *veli*. Since the villages belonged to the same division, it is fair to conclude that 10 Kaḷanjus of gold were equal to 100 Kalams of paddy by the Āḍavallāṉ measure. The price of paddy would thus be 10 Kalams per Kaḷanju towards the end of the 10th century A.D.

Two inscriptions from North Arcot district, belonging to the reign of Kṛshṇa III,[96] inform us that the interest on a Kaḷanju of gold was a Kalam of paddy. In this district, the

95. S. I. I., II, Nos. 4 & 5.

96. *Inscriptions from Madras Presidency*, North Arcot, No. 636; E. I., VII, pp. 188 ff.

Marakkal was measured by the Madevi's measure, which was 25% bigger than the Āḍavallāṉ measure. The interest of 20 Kalams would thus be equal to 25 Kalams by the Tanjore measure. The rate of interest allowed on permanent deposits by the banks in this part of the country at this time was about 15%.[97] The interest on 20 Kaḷanjus would thus be 3 Kaḷanjus which would be the price of 25 Kalams by the Āḍavallāṉ measure. A Kaḷanju could thus procure 8⅓ Kalams of paddy in c. 960 A.D. in the Tamil districts annexed to the Rāshṭrakūṭa empire. This price is about 20% dearer than the price prevailing under Rājarāja, which, as we have seen above, was 10 Kalams per Kaḷanju. It is very likely that the prolonged and bloody wars that were waged in this province between the Cholas and the Rāshṭrakūṭas by this time, may have made articles dearer; we may, therefore, assume that the normal prices towards the middle of the 10th century A.D. in the districts annexed to the Rāshṭrakūṭa empire were 10 Kalams a Kaḷanju.[98] A gold Kaḷanju was about a quarter of a tola in weight and thus was equal to about Rs. 5 of today. Since the ratio of paddy to rice is 5: 2, 10 Kalams of paddy would be equal to 4 Kalams of rice. Four Kalams by the Āḍavallāṉ measure would be equal to either 144 or 168 seers according to the table giveṉ on p. 376. Rs. 5 could thus procure about 150 seers of rice. *Rice was thus sold at about 30 seers a rupee.* Before the recent fall in prices ordinary rice was sold at about four to five seers a rupee; so the prices have gone up by about 700%.

Several records enable us to ascertain the price of ghee.

(1) A Bāṇa record, dated 915 A.D.,[99] leads to the conclusion that four Kaḷanjus could fetch 190 *nāris* of ghee that

97. *Inscriptions from the Madras Presidency*, Chingleput, No. 10; *ante* p. 360

98. E. I., XI, p. 224.

99. If the interest is assumed to be 12½% and not 15% the price in this case also will work out to be 10 Kalams a Kalanju.

were necessary to keep a lamp burning throughout the year. The table on p. 376 would show that 180 *nāris* are equal to 135 lbs.; 4 Kaḷanjus, *i. e.*, Rs. 20 could thus bring 67½ seers of ghee. Ghee was thus sold at 3 to 3½ seers a rupee at the beginning of the 10 century. The ratio of the prices of ghee and rice would thus be about 9 : 1.

(2) Another record belonging to the end of the 10th century A.D.[100] states that the interest on 12 Kaḷanjus could purchase 90 *nāris* of ghee required to burn one perpetual lamp throughout the year. If we assume that the rate of interest was the normal one, *i. e.* 12½%, the price of ghee, as given by this record, is found to be 4½ seers a rupee. This price is cheaper than the one ascertained in the previous paragraph, but it may be pointed out that the inscriptions are separated by about 75 years and that the rate of interest assumed is hypothetical. The relative prices of rice and ghee, as deducible from this record, would be 7½ : 1.

(3) An inscription of the time of Parakesarivarman Uttamachola (c. 975 A.D.) informs us that one Padakku of paddy could fetch one *uri* of sweet ghee;[101] another of the time of Rājarāja (c. 1000 A.D.) states that four *nāris* of paddy was the price of one Ārakku of sweet ghee;[102] a third one,[103] about 50 years later, observes that one Urakku of ghee was equal in value to one Kuruṇi of paddy. If we work up these figures from the table supplied on p. 376 we shall find that in each of these three cases the ratio of the prices of sweet ghee and paddy is the same, *viz.*, 1 : 32. Rice is about two-fifths of paddy, and therefore, the ratio of the prices of rice and sweet ghee would be about 1 : 12. Since rice was sold at about 30 seers a rupee, the price of sweet ghee would be about 2½ seers a rupee.

100. S. I. I., III, p. 357.
101. S. I. I., III, p. 282.
102. *Ibid*, II, p. 94.
103. S. I. I., II, p. 149.

This price is much dearer than that deduced from records Nos. 1 and 2 above, where we found it to be $3\frac{1}{2}$ to $4\frac{1}{2}$ seers per rupee. But the difference is due to the fact that the ghee required in these two cases was for burning a lamp, and must have, therefore, been of quite an ordinary quality. The ghee in all the cases in paragraph 3 above is described as sweet and was, therefore, naturally dearer. We may, therefore, conclude that good ghee was sold at about $2\frac{1}{2}$ seers a rupee and ordinary one, at about $3\frac{1}{2}$ to 4 seers a rupee. The present day variations between the prices of good and bad ghee are equally great. It will also be seen that the relative prices of good ghee and rice today are also the same; rice is sold, (to quote 1930 rates) at about $4\frac{1}{2}$ seers a rupee and good ghee at about Rs. $2\frac{1}{2}$ a seer. The price ratio in thus about 1 : 11.

Let us now consider oil prices. Two records belonging to the third quarter of the 10 century A.D. supply the necessary data. In one of these[104] we are informed that one *nāri* of oil costs one Tūṇi *i. e.*, 32 *nāris* of paddy, *i. e.*, $12\frac{1}{2}$ *nāris* of rice.

Oil is thus seen to be as costly as sweet ghee. The same conclusion is driven home to us by another record,[105] which records an investment of 30 Kaḷanjus for purchasing 90 *nāris* of oil. The rate of interest is not stated, but the investment is sufficiently high to indicate that oil was dearer than ghee of indifferent quality. At present oil is relatively very much cheaper than ghee. The dearness in our period may suggest that oilseeds were not then so common as they are now. The price of oil in our period would be about $2\frac{1}{2}$ seers a rupee.

The prices of curds are supplied by two records of the time of Rājarāja.[106] We are told in these records that one *nāri* of curds used to cost 3 *nāris* of paddy, *i. e.*, $\frac{6}{5}$ *nāris* of rice. Curds was thus about 20% dearer than rice and, therefore, must have been sold at about 24 seers a rupee.

104. S. I. I., II, p. 105. S. I. I., III, p. 262.

106. S. I. I., II, p. 74; p. 129.

The price of pulse at the end of the 10th century can be worked out from two inscriptions of Rājarāja.[107] The ratio of prices between the pulse and rice, as given in both these records is the same, *viz*., 6 : 5 ; 5 *nāris* of pulse used to cost 6 *nāris* of rice. In northern India the pulses are usually cheaper than rice, but the thing seems to have been the reverse in the south during our period. From the above price ratio we can conclude that about 25 seers of pulse could be purchased for a rupee in our period.

The prices of a number of miscellaneous articles, used for the soup and vegetables, can be ascertained from inscription No. 26 in the Rājarājeśvara temple. The prices of these articles in the Rāshṭrakūṭa dominions could not have been much different.

SALT. The record states that $1\frac{1}{3}$ *urakku* of paddy could procure the same quantity of salt. The ratio of paddy to rice being 5 : 2, and the latter being procurable at 30 seers a rupee, salt must have been sold at about 75 seers per rupee. The relative ratio of the prices of these two commodities is the same today. In Akbar's time, however, a pound of salt was, when measured in terms of food grains, $2\frac{1}{4}$ times dearer.[108]

PEPPER. Five Nāris and 1 Urakku of paddy was required to purchase one Ārakku and $1\frac{3}{4}$ S'evidu of pepper. 210 S'evidus of paddy were thus required for purchasing six S'evidus of pepper. Pepper was thus 31 times costlier than paddy, or about 12 times costlier than rice. The present ratio of the prices of these articles is the same.

MUSTARD. 2 Nāris, 1 Ārakku, and 1 S'evidu *i. e.*, 96 S'evidus of paddy or 38 S'evidus of rice were required for 1 Ārakku and 1 S'evidu *i. e.*, 6 S'evidus of mustard. The latter commodity was thus $6\frac{1}{3}$ times costlier than rice. To use the present terminology its rate was five seers a rupee.

107. S. I. I., II, pp. 74 and 149.
108. Moreland: *India at the Death of Akbar*, p. 153.

JĪRAKA or CUMIN. One Nāri of paddy fetched $\frac{15}{16}$ S'evidu of Cumin. The ratio of prices between these two articles works as out 40 : $\frac{15}{16}$ *i. e.*, 43 : 1. Cumin was thus about 17 times costlier than rice. It must, therefore, have been sold at about two seers a rupee. At present it is only 12 times costlier than rice.

CARDAMOM SEEDS. A Kāsu *i. e.*, 15 grains of gold or about Re. 1 and 10 as., could fetch one Kuruṇi and four Naris *i. e.*, 9 lbs., of cardamom seeds. The rate was thus about 5$\frac{1}{2}$ lbs. a rupee. The present rate in northen India *e. g.*, at Benares is 12 as. a lb. The commodity was thus only about four times cheaper than today; it was thus relatively dearer.

CAMPHOR. This article was in our period very much costlier than it is today. From one record[109] we learn that one golden Kāsu *i. e.*, about Re. 1 and 10 as. were required to purchase 2$\frac{1}{2}$ Kaḷanjus *i. e.*, $\frac{5}{8}$ tola of camphor. In another record [110] the price is stated to be 3 Kaḷanjus *i. e.*, $\frac{3}{4}$ tola a Kāsu. A tola of camphor was thus costing in our period about 2$\frac{1}{4}$ rupees. *Līlāvatī vv.* 76,100 gives 1$\frac{2}{3}$ and 2 Nishkas as the price of one Pala of camphor. A Nishka of Bhāskara weighed about $\frac{1}{3}$ tola, and Pala 3 tolas. A tola of camphor thus required $\frac{1}{6}$ tola of gold *i. e.*, roughly Re. 1–12 as. At present the same quantity of that commodity costs about 1 anna, so the price is about 36 times cheaper. Camphor had to be imported from abroad, and its price shows that the danger and cost of the sea transport were very great. There was the danger of piracy, and the import merchants had to borrow money for their trade at 120% per annum.[111]

FRUITS. Plantains were sold at 1200 per Kāsu, [112] *i. e.*, for 26 as. A pice could thus fetch 10. They were thus about 6 times cheaper than now. *Līlāvatī v.* 89 gives one silver Dramma (=60 gr.) as the price of 300 mangoes; this shows that mangoes were sold at the rate of 60 an anna.

109. S. I. I., II, p. 75.
110. *Ibid.* p. 132.
111. Yājnavalkya, II, 37.
112. S. I. I., II, p. 151.

SUGAR. The price of this article is mentioned in several records; one [113] states that three Palams and 1 Kaśu of sugar cost 2 Nāris, 1 Uri, 1 Arakku, and 4 S'evidus of paddy; another observes [114] that one Palam of sugar could be had for 2 Nāris of paddy, while a third [115] one informs us that half a Palam of sugar required $1\frac{1}{2}$ Nari of paddy. These prices are very divergent, and it is not possible to work them out, because Palam is an indefinite and variable measure. Amara says that it is equivalent to 4 Karshas or 3 tolas; in medical works it was and is taken to be 8 tolas; some other Koshas equate it to 5 Karshas or 4 tolas. Since we do not know the value of the Palam in vogue at Tanjore during our period, it would be hazardous to offer any conjecture about the price. If we take the Palam to be 5 tolas and the average price of sugar to be about $1\frac{1}{2}$ Nāri of paddy, *i. e.*, about 12 tolas of rice, we find that sugar was about $2\frac{1}{2}$ times costlier than rice. So it was much dearer than it is now. The conclusion is of course hypothetical.

CATTLE. A record [116] of Rājarāja throws some light on the prices of ewes and cows. A ewe cost about $\frac{1}{4}$ of a Kāsu *i.e.*, about 6 to 7 as. and a cow $\frac{3}{8}$ of a Kāsu, *i. e.*, about Re. 1 and 2 as. The cost of the cow was about three times the cost of an ewe, a conclusion which is further supported by the fact that a perpetual lamp required 32 cows or 96 ewes or 16 she-buffalos. The price of a she-buffalo would thus be about Rs. $2\frac{1}{4}$.

LAND PRICES. One record [117] from Melpadi, where Kṛshṇa III was encamped when he had issued the Karhad plates in 959 A.D., states that the assembly of the village received 15 Kaḷanjus and assigned 1000 Kulis *i. e.*, $\frac{1}{2}$ Veli or about $3\frac{1}{4}$ acres of land, rendered tax free, for burning

113. *Ibid*, p. 129. 114. S. I. I., III, p. 282. 115. S. I. I., III, p. 77.
116. S. I. I., II, p. 479. 117. S. I. I., III, No. 19.

a perpetual lamp. An acre of tax-free land would thus be costing about Rs. 25.

(2) Another record[118] from the same place states that $\frac{1}{40}$ Veli of tax-free land was purchased for three Kaḷanjus and assigned to the temple for burning a perpetual lamp. Here a Veli of tax-free land is seen costing 120 Kalanjus; so the price is about Rs. 100 an acre.

(3) Similar data from other records[119] show that the prices of land were 34, 19, 17 and 11 Kaḷanjus per *veli*. in different localities. These are wide variations in prices; but even today the prices of land vary considerably according to the quality. The land, referred to in paragraph two above, seems to have been of good quality, while the pieces, the prices of which are given here, seem to be very inferior. To sum up, wet fertile land appears to have been sold at 125 Kaḷanjus a Veli when they were tax-free; ordinary lands were about four times cheaper.

We can state the prices of land in the terms of their annual produce. The Melpadi inscription[120] shows that land purchased for 15 Kaḷanjus was sufficient for feeding one perpetual ghee lamp, which used to consume 180 Nāris, *i.e.*, about 67 seers of ghee. 180 Nāris of ghee used to cost about four Kaḷanjus.[121] The price of this piece was thus about four times the annual net produce. We have seen already how the banks of our period were allowing an interest of about 15% to their depositors, how Manu states that the person who charges an interest of 24% is not guilty of sin, and how ordinary persons in our period had to pay an interest of about 30 to 40 per cent on their debts. If the rate of interest was thus so high, it is but natural that the land should cost only about four times its net produce, and yield an interest of about 25% on the capital invested.

118. *Ibid*, No. 24. 119. *Ibid*, Nos. 28, 48, 54, 64, 68.
120. S. I. I., III, No. 19. 121. *Ante*, p. 380.

Below is given a list of the prices as determined above in a tabulated form. These prices prevailed in the Tamil districts of the Rāshṭrakūṭa empire; and those in the empire proper could not have been much different.

Articles	Ancient Prices		Modern equivalents	
Rice	1 Kaḷanju	10 Kalams	1 Rupee about	32 seers
Ghee good	1 ,,	33 Nāris	1 ,, ,,	$2\frac{1}{2}$ seers
,, bad	1 ,,	50 Nāris	1 ,, ,,	$3\frac{1}{2}$-4 seers
Oil	$12\frac{1}{2}$ Nāris of rice	1 Nāri oil	1 ,, ,,	$2\frac{1}{2}$ seers
Pulses	6 Nāris ,,	5 Nāris pluses	1 ,, ,,	25 seers
Salt	2 Nāris ,,	5 Nāris salt	1 ,, ,,	75 seers
Curds	6 Nāris ,,	5 Nāris curds	1 ,, ,,	24 seers
Pepper	12 Nāris ,,	1 Nāri pepper	1 ,, ,,	$2\frac{1}{2}$ seers
Mustard	$6\frac{1}{2}$ Nāris ,,	1 Nāri mustard	1 ,, ,,	5 seer
Cumin	17 Nāris ,,	1 Nāri cumin	1 ,, ,,	2 seers
Camphor	3 Kaḷanjus	1 golden Kasu	$2\frac{1}{4}$ rupees ,,	1 tola
Plantains	1200	1 ,, ,,	1 pice	10 plantains.
Cardamom seeds	1 Kasu for 12 Nāris		1 rupees for	3 seers
Ewe	$\frac{1}{4}$,, ,,	1 ewe	6 as. ,,	1 ewe
Cow	$\frac{3}{8}$,, ,,	1 cow	Re. 1–2 as. ,,	1 cow
She-Buffalo	$\frac{4}{8}$,, ,,	1 she buf.	Rs. 2–4 as.	1 she-buf.

Table of the Current Rates of Interest

Interest on permanent deposits ...	12–15 per cent
,, to debtors of good credit ...	20–24 per cent
,, ,, debtors of ordinary credit ...	30 ,, ,,
,, ,, ,, ,, bad credit ...	40–50 per cent
Interest on capital invested in landed property	20–25 per cent
Interest on corn given by village communities	25–50 per cent

In a recent monograph of the Royal Asiatic Society,[122] it has been asserted that the prices of the food-stuffs towards the beginning of the 11th century A.D., which have been tabulated above, were about 725% higher than the prices

122. Dr. Pran Nath, *A Study in Ancient Indian Economics*, p. 102.

current in the Gupta period. The theory of this tremendous rise in prices is indeed arresting, and let us see whether the prices under the Cholas and the Rāshṭrakūṭas were really so much higher than those under the Imperial Guptas.

The first argument to support this tremendous rise in prices is based upon a comparison of the meal-charges per head in the two periods. It is argued that the Sanchi inscription of Chandragupta II[123] shows that a capital of 23 Dīnāras was sufficient to feed 10 monks in the 5th century A.D., whereas the Ukkal inscription No. 1[124] shows that an investment of 200 Kalanjus was necessary to feed 12 Brahmanas in c. 1000 A.D. The capital charge per head was thus $2\frac{3}{10}$ Dīnāras in the Gupta period, whereas it was $16\frac{2}{3}$ Kalanjus at c. 1000 A.D. 'If we divide $16\frac{2}{3}$ by $2\frac{3}{10}$,' argues the author, 'we get the purchasing power of a Dīnāra as equal to that of $7\frac{1}{4}$ Kalanjus, or in other words, we find the prices of food stuffs rose seven and a quarter times from the 5th to the 11th century A.D.'[125]

There are a number of fallacies in the above argument. The division of $16\frac{2}{3}$ by $2\frac{3}{10}$ to find out the rise of prices between the two periods is unmathematical; for, the one figure is that of Kalanjus, while the other is that of Dīnāras. A Dīnāra of the time of Chandragupta II, during whose time the Sanchi inscription was engraved, was a golden coin, about 125 grains in weight, whereas a Kalanju of our period was only about 50 grains in weight. Dr. Pran Nath has himself stated in his book that the weight of a Kalanju was only about 57·6 grains.[126] $16\frac{2}{3}$ Kalanjus were thus equal to about $6\frac{2}{3}$ Dīnāras. To ascertain the comparative rise in prices, we shall have to divide $6\frac{2}{3}$ by $2\frac{3}{10}$. If all the other assumptions were correct, the rise in prices would be about 300% only.

123. C. I. I., III, No. 5.
124. S. I. I., III, No. 1.
125. Pran Nath, p. 102.
126. *Ibid*, p. 91.

The assumption, however, that the capital outlay in the two periods in question was $2\frac{3}{10}$ Dīnāras and $16\frac{2}{3}$ Kalanjus respectively is based on shaky grounds. The capital outlay in the Gupta period was much higher than $2\frac{3}{10}$ Dīnāras. The Sanchi inscription of Chandragupta II, upon which Dr. Pran Nath relies for fixing this figure, is unfortunately fragmentary, but the extant portion makes it quite clear, that something in addition to the capital of 25 Dīnāras was given for the feeding of 10 Brahmanas and the burning of two lamps. The relevant portion reads as follows :—

आम्रकार्दवः मञ्ज-शरभङ्ग-आमरातराजकुलमूल्यक्रीतं ईश्वरवासकं पञ्चमण्डल्यां प्रणिपत्य ददाति पञ्चविंशतिश्च दीनारान्। तद्दत्यार्धेन यावच्चन्द्रदिवाकरौ पञ्च भिक्षवो भुञ्जन्तां रत्नगृहे च दीपको ज्वलतु।

Fleet translates this passage as follows:—

'Having prostrated himself in the assembly of five persons Āmrakārdava gives (the village or allotment of) Is'varavāsaka... purchased with the endowment of Mania, S'arabhanga, and Āmarāta of the royal household and (also gives) 25 Dīnāras. With the half of that donation, as long as the Sun and the Moon endure, let five Bhikshus be fed and a lamp burnt in the Jewel house.'

The particle *cha*, occurring in the first sentence quoted above, makes it clear that the donation consisted of something in addition to 25 Dīnāras. That additional donation is also explicitly described as (a field or allotment called) Is'varavāsaka, which was purchased with the capital supplied by the royal officers mentioned in the record. That the capital outlay for feeding 10 Bhikshus was not 23 Dīnāras is further proved beyond all doubt by another inscription from Sanchi itself, where[127] it is expressly stated that a capital

127. C. I. I., III, No. 62.

outlay of as many as 12 Dīnāras was necessary to feed one monk in the middle of the 5th century. Cf.:—

चातुर्दिशआर्यसंघायाक्षयनीवि दत्ता दीनारा द्वादश। एतेषां दीनाराणां या वृद्धिरुपजायते तया दिवसे दिवसे संघमध्यप्रविष्टभिक्षुरेको भोजयितव्यः।

Fleet translates the passage as follows:—

'12 Dīnāras are given, (as) a permanent endowment to the community of the faithful, collected from the four quarters of the world... With the interest that accrues of these Dīnāras, day by day, one Bhikshu, who has been introduced into the community, should be fed.'

This Sanchi inscription is no doubt later by about 40 years than the Sanchi inscription of Chandragupta II, but it cannot be argued that the prices had soared higher in the interval. At the time of the earlier inscription, Sanchi was the centre of a big military campaign, at the time of the later one there was peace in the locality, though there were wars going on elsewhere in the empire. So there is nothing to support the view, that the capital outlay disclosed by the later record at Sanchi, represents an abnormal figure. The capital outlay for feeding a monk guest in the 5th century was thus 12 Dīnāras and not $2\frac{3}{10}$ Dīnāras as argued in the book under discussion.

The dinner provided for by the Ukkal inscription No. 1, which required a capital outlay of $16\frac{2}{3}$ Kaḷanjus, was a sumptuous one; the record states that each of the 12 Brahmanas was to be supplied with 1 Ārakku of ghee, 5 dishes of curry, 5 Urakkus of curds, 2 areca nuts and betel leaves, till they were satisfied. The meal supplied to the guest Bhikshu at Sanchi was also, very probably, equally rich. In the 7th century A.D. Bhikshus, when they were guests, were fed in a right royal fashion.(128) I-tsing says(129) that if the food supplied was just enough to satisfy the hunger,

128. I-tsing, p. 50. 129. *Ibid*, p. 40, p. 47.

the host was ridiculed. Usually the leavings at the table of one man could satisfy three persons, but in the case of a meal supplied by a rich host, they could not be eaten even by 10 men. These observations will explain why the cost of feeding one Bhikshu was as high as the interest of 12 Dīnāras or 30 Kaḷanjus. Like I-tsing, the donor at Sanchi might have been warned that if the food supplied was just enough for the appetite, he would be ridiculed. The capital provision of 12 Dīnāras or 30 Kaḷanjus, that has been made in the Gupta inscription No. 62, may thus have been, to some extent, in excess of the actual needs of the situation. We may perhaps presume that for the real cost of a rich dinner where there was no waste, a capital outlay of about 8 Dīnāras or 20 Kaḷanjus was sufficient. The capital outlay for a similar meal in the south in our period was 16 or 17 Kaḷanjus as shown already. The capital outlay for an ordinary meal in the 10th century was only about 8 Kaḷanjus as will be shown later. It will be thus seen that the prices of our age, far from being 725% higher than those of the Gupta period, were actually somewhat lower. Precise comparison is unfortunately not possible, as we have not any information about the cost of an ordinary meal and the actual rate of interest in the Gupta period.

The arguments from the Dharmaśātra, adduced to support the theory that the price of the cow in the 11th century *viz.*, 56 Paṇas, was about 500 per cent. higher than that in the 5th century, *viz.*, 12 Paṇas, are equally weak. In the first place, the assumption underlying the whole line of argument here, *viz.*, Manusmṛti, Mūlyādhyayanapariśishṭa of Kātyāyana, Dānamayūkha of Nīlakaṇṭha, Vasishṭha Dharma-Sūtra, Yājnavalkyasmṛti, and the Arthaśāstra of Kauṭalya are contemporary works written in the 5th century A.D., cannot be accepted by any student of the Dharmaśāstra literature. To maintain that the price of a cow in the time of Manu,

Yājnavalkya, and Kauṭalya was 12 Paṇas, because the ransom for a lost cow was two Paṇas according to these authorities, is hardly correct, for there is nothing to prove that the ransom was to be exactly $\frac{1}{6}$th the price of the lost article. The line in the Manusmṛti cited to support this contention, *viz*.

आददीताथ षड्भागं प्रणष्टाधिगमान्नृपः ।

is immediately followed by

दशमं द्वादशं वापि सतां धर्ममनुस्मरन् ॥ (130)

Two Paṇas can, therefore, just as well represent the $\frac{1}{6}$th as the $\frac{1}{10}$th or the $\frac{1}{12}$th price of the cow. The price of a cow, even if we accept this line of argument as valid, can be 12, or 20 or 24 Paṇas. The fact, however, is that the ransom prescribed for the recovery of a lost article had no mathematical ratio with its price. If we accept the theory that it was everywhere one sixth the price of the article, we shall have to assume that the price of a slave was only 30 copper Paṇas, since Kauṭalya prescribes a ransom of 5 Paṇas for the recovery of a biped. A slave would thus be only $2\frac{1}{2}$ times costlier than a cow. Another corollary of this proposition would be the necessity to assume that the price of a cow was the same as the price of a she-buffalo, since the ransom for both is the same, *viz.*, two Paṇas. We have shown above that a she-buffalo was three times costlier than a cow and Dr. Pran Nath's view is also the same.(131) It may be further pointed out that immediately after stating the ransom for horses, cows, etc., the Arthaśāstra adds that in the case of jewels and metals, the ransom was to be only 5%.(132) The ransom figures in the case of animals were higher because the custodian had to spend for their maintenance during the time they were with him. The ransom thus seems to have varied, not with the price of the article, but with the cost of its custody. Nibandha

130. VIII, 33. 131. P. 104. 132. Book III, chap. 16.

writers expressly say so. Nilakaṇṭha, while beginning the section on *Praṇashṭādhigama*, expressly observes :—

परस्वामिकनष्टलब्धपशूनामेकदिनरक्षणे भृतिमाह ।[133]

'Now is discussed the cost of maintenance for protecting one day animals belonging to others.' Vijñāneśvara also says that the sums of four Paṇas and the like that have to be paid to the king were for the cost of protection.[134]

The argument that the price of an ox was 12 Paṇas in the 5th century, since the penalty for an unnatural offence is a white ox according to Vasishṭha-Dharma-Sūtra and 12 Paṇas according to Kauṭalya, is also untenable. It presupposes that the two authors held similar views about punishments. A glance, however, at the treatment of this topic by these two authors shows that their views were widely different. Kauṭalya imposes only a fine upon a Kshatriya for having intercourse with a Brahmana lady.[135] Vasishṭha, on the other hand, condemns the Kshatriya culprit to death by burning.[136] Dr. Pran Nath's view that the Arthaśāstra and the Vasishṭha-Dharma-Sūtra prove, between themselves, that the price of a cow in the 5th century A.D. was about 12 or 13 Paṇas is thus untenable.

All the arguments advanced from the Dharmaśāstra literature to prove that the price of the cow in the 5th century A.D. was about 12 or 13 Paṇas thus fall to the ground. It cannot be, therefore, argued that the 11th century price, *viz.* 56 Paṇas was about 500% higher than the 5th century one. There must have been variations of prices in the Hindu period, but they do not seem to have been so great.

We have shown above that the price level of 1930 A.D. was about 700% higher than that in the 10th century; rice was sold at about 30 to 32 seers a rupee in our period and it was sold at about 4 to 5 seers a rupee three years ago.

133. *Vyavaharamayukha*, p. 123. 134. On Yājnavalkya, II, 174.
135. Book IV, Chap. 13. 136. XXI, 5.

It seems that the prices continued to be more or less on the same level during the next seven centuries. At the beginning of the 17th century A.D., rice was sold at Surat at about 32 seers a rupee.[137] We know the prices of a number of other articles in the 17th century *e. g.*, wheat, gram, etc., but unfortunately the corresponding prices in our period are unknown. The only price that can be compared is that of rice and this is fortunately an article that can be well utilised in this connection. By the middle of the last century rice was sold in the Deccan at about 21 seers a rupee; my grand uncle, who recently died at the age of 90, had purchased this commodity at this rate in the sixties of the last century. It would, therefore, appear that the rise in prices from the 10th to the middle of the 19th century was only about 50%.

Whether the Deccan administrations of our period used to control the prices or not is not known. Kauṭalya favours such a procedure, for according to him it was one of the duties of the Superintendent of Market, Paṇyādhyaksha, to regulate prices; any excess price that was realised by the vendor was confiscated to the state.[138] Somadeva, a Deccanese writer of our period, favours the same proposal.[139] It cannot be, however, confidently argued that Somadeva's rule was based upon contemporary practice in the Deccan, for in many places he merely summarises the Arthaśāstra of Kauṭalya. Whether prices were regulated by the state or not, must therefore be left an open question.

Let us now ascertain the cost of living in our period. We have seen already that a capital outlay of 16 or 17 Kaḷañjus was sufficient to supply a rich meal throughout the year. Unfortunately the rate of interest is not stated, so no very accurate conclusions are possible from this inscription. An inscription of the time of Uttamachola gives the exact

137. Moreland, *From Akbar to Aurangzeb*, p. 171.
138. IV, 2; II, 16. 139. *Nitivākyāmṛta*, VIII, 16.

expenses of a rich meal of the period.[140] 'For feeding 25 Brahmanas in the feeding house...is required, for 1 year, 937½ Kalam of paddy for vegetables, firewood, ghee, curds, different spices, betel leaves and nuts, including the pay of the cooks, at the rate of 1 Kuruṇi and 2 Nāri of paddy per day for each person.' Another record,[141] about 25 years later, makes provision for the purchase of 25 Kalams of paddy in order to supply one meal to 240 S'iva-yogins. Both these records lead to the same conclusion, *viz.*, 37½ Kalams of paddy were required to supply a good meal to one individual throughout the year. 37½ Kalams of paddy are equal to 15 Kalams or about 540 seers of rice; 1½ seer are thus seen provided for each individual per diem. The cost in cash per individual per annum would be 3¾ Kaḷanjus (since paddy was sold at about 10 Kalams per Kaḷanju), *i. e.* about Rs. 19, since one golden Kaḷanju weighed about a quarter of a tola.

The cost of a poor meal seems to have been half of this amount. An inscription[142] of the time of Parāntaka I (*i. e.* of the first half of the 10th century A.D.) records an investment of only four Kaḷanjus for feeding one Jain devotee at the local Jain temple. The rate of interest is unfortunately not stated, but it is worth noting that the capital invested is about one fourth of that invested for supplying a rich meal to a Brahmana at Ukkal. The Jain devotee is allowed only one meal in the day and that too is to be very simple. For two ordinary meals a day, we may, therefore, assume that a capital outlay of about 6 or 7 Kaḷanjus would have been necessary. We may, therefore, conclude that the cost of a simple meal was less than half of that of the rich meal. The latter required 37½ Kalams of paddy per annum per individual; the annual expenses of an ordinary meal could under no circumstances have exceeded 20 Kalams of paddy *i. e.* 288 seers of rice. Allowance of rice

140. S. I. I., III, No. 151. 141. S. I. I., II, No. 28.
142. S. I. I., III, No. 97.

per day per individual will be found to be ⅝ of a seer under this arrangement and that is quite sufficient to meet all the expenses connected with two ordinary meals consisting of the usual soups and vegetables.

Let us now ascertain the wages of our period and see how far they were above the subsistence allowance.

Some of the records from Karnatak supply us information about the wages of the various classes, but there arises considerable difficulty in interpreting them. The inscriptions inform us that so many Mattars of land were assigned to certain persons as their annual wages of work. The net produce of the land given is not stated, and we do not also know the precise dimensions of a Mattar. The grant of a S'ilāhāra prince records an assignment of 2000 Mattars, measured by the Tambola rod of the village, of two Mattars measured by the Magun rod, and of the three Mattars measured by the small rod of the paddy fields.(143) Since one and the same record mentions three different measures of the Mattar, it is clear that the unit differed considerably with the different localities. An inscription from Tilgund(144) states that the yield of a Mattar was two Khaṇḍugas *i. e.*, Khandis which are equal to 40 maunds by measure (and not by weight). The net produce per acre varies from 6 to 12 maunds in the Deccan according to the quality of the soil, and since the net yield per Mattar is given as 40 maunds, we may assume that this measure was equal to about five acres. An inscription from Managoli(145) states that five Mattars were assigned to the teacher of the Kaumāra grammar and two Mattars to each of the 4 Brahmana families constituting the settlement of the god. The salary of the village Sanskrit teacher of our period was thus 2½ the amount necessary for an ordinary Brahmana family to live in ease. We do not know the net produce of

143. E. I., IV, p. 66. 144. I, A., XIX, p. 274, n. 29.
145. E. I., V, p. 22.

the lands given in endowment, and so the salary cannot be stated either in terms of corn or of cash. If we assume that a Mattar is equal to 5 acres, and each acre yielded 8 maunds of Jwari, the income of the Sanskrit teacher would be 200 maunds of Jwari and of the temple Brahmana 80 maunds of Jwari (by measure). An ordinary family of 5 in the Deccan would require about 40 maunds of Jwari for its entire meal expenses, including ghee, oil, fuel &c. The temple Brahmana family was getting a fairly decent income, and the Sanskrit teacher was getting 5 times the amount necessary for the maintenance of his family.

The Hebbal inscription, dated 975 A.D.,[146] records an assignment of five Mattars to each of the temple dancing girls. This apparently seems to show that the Sanskrit Pandit was getting the same salary as the dancing girl, but we must remember that the respective lands were situated in different localities and their quality and produce may have been different.

The salary of the principal of a big Sanskrit College was 50 Nivartanas.[147] A Nivartana was a little less than 5 acres, and therefore, this salary would be equal to the net produce of 250 acres of land. We do not know the quality of this piece of land, but if we suppose that it was neither too bad nor too good, the conclusion would be that the principals of famous colleges were getting about 20 times the income of the ordinary Brahmana, and 10 times the income of the village Sanskrit teacher. This conclusion is, however, a tentative one as it is not based on sure premises, since neither the dimensions of a Mattar nor its precise produce is definitely known.

Definite information about wages is, however, available from contemporary records hailing from Tamil country. An inscription of Rājarāja at Tanjore[148] gives the scales of the

146. E. I., IV, p. 351. 147. E. I., IV, p. 60. 148. S. I. I., II, p. 320.

salaries of several temple officials. Some other records also supply information on this point. It is given in a tabulated form below.

Table of Wages

Name	Wage per annum
Accountant	200 Kalams of paddy *i. e.* about 80 maunds of rice.
Sub-accountant	75 ,, ,, ,, ,, ,, 30 ,, ,, ,,
Carpenter-master	150 ,, ,, ,, ,, ,, 60 ,, ,, ,,
Temple-watchman	100 ,, ,, ,, ,, ,, 40 ,, ,, ,,
Drawer of water[149]	60 ,, ,, ,, ,, ,, 24 ,, ,, ,,
Temple-brahmachārin	61 ,, ,, ,, and four or five Kāsus.[150] *i. e.*, about 30 maunds of rice.

These wages are fairly liberal and much above the subsistence allowance. Since the food expenses per head for an ordinary meal were 20 Kalams, and for a good meal, 37 Kalams per annum, the accountant and the carpenter-master were getting much more than was necessary for maintaining a family of five, consisting of the husband and the wife, two children, and an old man. In the case of the carpenter the income was probably further increased to some extent by the earnings of his children, who must have acted as his assistants. In the case of the temple watchman and the drawer of water the family income must have been something above 100 and 60 Kalams respectively, as the women and children of the family must also be earning members to some extent. So they too were able to get much more than their subsistence necessities. The temple Brahmachārin had no family to maintain and he must have been quite well off with

149. S. I. I., III, Ukkal, No. 4. 150. S. I. I., II, No. 66.

his 75 Kalams. The sub-accountant alone seems to be in a comparatively unsatisfactory position; his family members were probably unearning ones, and hence his 75 Kalams could just have maintained 3 adults and 2 children. But he was probably at the beginning of his career, and may have expected to be promoted to the position of the accountant in due course. While considering the family budgets of our period, we must further remember that each family was largely self-reliant as far as its clothing requirements were concerned. People, therefore, were comparatively better off than they are at present; for the grain equivalents of the present-day wages do not come up to the same figures. The same conclusion is supported if we consider the salaries after converting them into cash. The drawer of water was getting in our period 60 Kalams in rural areas; 60 Kalams are equal to 6 Kaḷanjus or 30 rupees. The prices in the present times are 7 times higher than they were in the 10th century, and, therefore, in order to be equally well off, the unskilled labourer in the village ought to get Rs. 210. He, however, hardly gets more than Rs. 150–180 at present.

CHAPTER XVI

Education and Literature

Section A: Education

The theory that the compulsory education of the masses is a duty of the state is a very modern one, and we must banish it from our minds while examining the educational arrangements in the medieval or ancient times, whether in the west or in the east. The knowledge of the 3 R's was not regarded as a necessary part of the equipment of every citizen; members of the industrial classes paid more attention to the initiation of their boys in the mysteries of their professions than in those of the 3 R's. The village communities of the Deccan had arranged for the services of a permanent residential staff to meet their normal public needs by the grain-share system; the carpenter, the smith etc., whose services were required by every villager were assigned a grain share which was paid to them annually at the time of the harvest by all the villagers. The teacher does not figure among the grain sharing servants of the community, a fact which shows that the community at large did not regard the primary teacher as essentially necessary for the ordinary villager. It is very probable that only the children of the Brahmanas and the trading classes cared to be literate, and the arrangements for educating them could not be obviously made at the cost of the whole community, by assigning the village teacher a grain share from every villager.

Our epigraphical materials do not throw any light on the arrangements made in the ordinary village for the primary education. Nor do the Smritis or the foreign travellers help us in the matter. It would seem that the village priest, or accountant, or some members of their families were undertaking the task of giving primary education to such village boys as cared to have it. The guardians were very probably paying the fees annually at the time of the harvest, according to their means, rather than according to a fixed scale. The teacher could supplement his income by the customary gifts in kind or cash that he used to receive on festivals like Dasara, or at the times of the thread or marriage ceremonies in the houses of his pupils. In many cases the teacher probably possessed some elementary knowledge of medicine and was also employed for writing letters, bonds and leases. Some such system prevailed in the Deccan at the advent of the British rule as I have learnt from many an octogenarian, and it is very likely that the state of affairs may have been similar in our period.

We have ample evidence to enlighten us as to the arrangements for higher education that were made during our period. Higher education in our age meant Sanskrit education, and Veda, Vyākaraṇa (grammar), Jyotisha (astronomy and astrology), Sāhitya (literature), Mīmāṇsā, Dharmas'āstra, Purāṇas and Nyāya (logic) were the main branches thereof. The donee of the Dhulia plates of Dhruva, dated 779 A.D., [1] is described as well versed in Vedas, Vedangas, history, Puranas, grammar, Mīmāṇsā, logic, Nirukta, and liturgy. Of these grammar is still the most extensively studied branch; Alberuni informs us that it was held in the highest estimation in his days, and curiously enough, the only place where epigraphs of our period specify the subject of a teacher is one where he happens to be the expounder of Kaumāra grammar.[2] Grammar was the key subject to the knowledge of the rest of the sciences and, therefore, we may well presume that it was held in high estimation and extensively studied in the Deccan as in the north.

The Dharmas'āstra literature no doubt lays down that the whole of the Veda was to be studied for 12 years by the first three castes, but it is fairly clear that the society of our period did not pay much attention to this injunction. The Vaishyas of our period had already lost their privilege of the Vedic studies as has been already shown in the last chapter,[3] and the Kshatriyas too, though permitted to study the Vedas, were largely following the Pauranic ritual.[4] The normal Kshatriya youth, who intended to follow the hereditary profession of his caste, must have devoted the largest part of his time to the military training. Even in the epic period he had only a smattering of the Vedic knowledge, and we may, therefore, well conclude that in our period the cases of the

1. E. I. VIII p. 182.
2. E. I. V. p. 22.
3. *Ante*, page 332.
4. *Ante*, p. 332.

Kshatriyas taking seriously to Vedic education may have been very rare. Among the Brahmanas themselves, only the professional priests must have concentrated on the study of the sacred lore; the average Brahmana who intended to take up to government service, trade or agriculture would hardly have troubled himself much about remembering the exact accent of the Vedic Mantras. Vedic sacrifices too had gone out of vogue and epigraphical evidence shows that the Puranas and the later Smritis were exercising a remarkable hold on the society as shown already in Chapter XIII. Proficiency in the Dharmaśāstra must have been regarded as a passport to government service in the judicial branch, and we may, therefore, presume that the study of this subject was more popular in our period than the study of the Vedas. It may be pointed out that the term Vedic study in our period did not mean only the cramming of the Vedic Mantras; in some centres the meaning was also studied as the title *Vedārthada* occurring in one of our records would show.[5] Astrology was wielding great influence on the popular mind as shown in the last chapter; royal courts used to maintain astrologers[6] and a number of works on astronomy and astrology were composed in our period. We may, therefore, well presume that this subject was fairly popular in the Sanskrit schools and colleges of our time as is still the case to some extent. One record slightly falling outside our period records an endowment to found a College where the work of the famous Bhāskara alone were to be studied.[7]

Arrangement for the higher education was made in three places, (i) Mathas associated with temples endowed by the state or private charity, (ii) *agrahāra* villages granted to Brahmana settlements, and (iii) special educational institutions conducted by private individuals or village communities with the help of the public and the state. At Hebbal in

5. I. A., XIV, p. 69. 6. Kavi plates, I. A., V., p. 145. 7. E. I., I. p. 30.

Dharwar district there existed a Matha in the Bhujjabes'vara temple; an inscription, dated 975 A.D., records the grant of 50 *mattars* (probably equal to 200 acres) of land for the Maṭha, where students were fed and taught.[8] Two 12th century inscriptions, one from Managoli dated 1161 A.D.,[9] and the other from Belgamve dated 1183 A.D.,[10] show that there existed Sanskrit schools in these villages associated with the local temples; at the latter place the temple authorities of the Dakshiṇes'vara temple, where the school was located, were enabled by private charity to provide for the boarding of the scholars free of charge. An inscription at Jatiga Rāmes'vara hill in Chitaldurg district, dated 1064 A.D., records a grant of 50 *mattars* of land to the Rāmes'varam temple for defraying the expenses of the temple worship, and for imparting education.[11] Part of the donation of Bhadravishṇu, given to the Buddhist Vihāra at Kanheri, in the reign of Amoghavarsha I, was for purchasing books. The Buddhist monastery at Kanheri like the one at Valabhi[12] was obviously maintaining a library which was very probably required for the school connected with it. We learn from the Chinese travellers that the Buddhist monasteries used to attend to the training not only of the monks but also of the children of the laity.[13] Indirect help to the cause of education was given by some of the temples, which used to give free food to the students in the feeding houses attached to them.[14] Some of the records mentioned above fall just outside our period, but they may be well utilised to illustrate further the state of affairs in our age.

The Kalas inscription[15] from Dharwar district shows that Kalas, which was an *agrahāra* in our period, was

8. E. I., IV, p. 358.
9 E. I., V, p. 22.
10. *Mysore Inscriptions*, No. 45.
11. E. I., IV, p. 214.
12. I. A., VII, p. 67.
13. I-tsing, p. 155.
14. Kharepatan grant, E. I., III, p. 360.
15. E. I., XIII, p. 317.

maintaining a Sanskrit College. All its 200 Brahmana householders are described in v. 30 of the record as well versed in grammar, works on polity, the science of literary composition, the legendary lore and the great logic of *Ekākshara* sage and writing of interpretations *i. e.* commentaries. V. 25 observes that Kalas can pride itself, inter alia, on its brilliant dispensation of lore. The main purpose of the grant is to record an endowment, part of which was reserved for the salaries of professors. It is, therefore, quite clear that this *agrahāra* village was maintaining a college where grammar, Puranas, Nyāya, literature and works on polity were taught. The students must have flocked to the place from distant places. The inscription, which gives information about this college is dated in the reign of Govinda IV, but it is likely that this institution may have been flourishing throughout the 10th century.

The small village of Salotgi in Bijapur district was another *agrahāra* village, that is known to have been maintaining a big college in the reign of Kṛshṇa III. The college must have been flourishing for a fairly long time, for it has transformed the original name of the village Pāviṭṭage into Saloṭgi, which is a combination of the words S'ālā and Pāviṭṭage. From one of the inscriptions from this locality[16] we learn that the college was located in a big hall attached to the temple of Trayī-purusha, which was built by Nārāyaṇa, a minister of Kṛshṇa III, in 945 A.D. The record expressly states that the college attracted students from far and near, and 27 boarding houses were necessary to accommodate them. An endowment of 12 Nivartanas (probably equal to 60 acres) was necessary to defray merely the lighting charges of the institution. The pay of the principal of the college was the income of 50 Nivartanas of land *i. e.* about 250 acres. The institute had received a magnificent endowment from a local magnate, and the inhabitants of

15. E. I., IV, p. 60.

the village had agreed to pay 5, 2½, and 1¼ coins on the occasion of marriages, thread ceremonies, and tonsures respectively, besides agreeing to feed as many students and teachers as possible, at the dinners that may be given on these and similar occasions. A later inscription from the same place informs[17] us that when the college hall built in 945 A.D. crumbled down, it was built again by a local feudatory in the next century.

There existed scores of *agrahāra* villages in our period given to Brahmana donees, who in many cases are expressly described as engaged in the six scriptural duties consisting of learning, teaching etc.[18] It is, therefore, fairly likely that many of these villages must have been maintaining educational institutions, more or less similar to those at Kalas and Salotgi.

Ordinary villages also had sometimes their own schools and colleges. One institution for Sanskrit education existed at Belur in Bijapur district in 1022 A.D.,[19] another at Soratur in Dharwar district in c. 950 A.D.,[20] a third one at Bijapur during c. 975–1075 A.D.,[21] a fourth one at Yewoor in 1077 A.D.[22] and so on. These are the institutions the memory of which has been accidentally preserved in records, that have withstood the ravages of time; there may have probably existed many more. We may, therefore, fairly conclude that the facilities for higher education during our period can compare fairly well with those afforded in the present age.

These institutions were financed partly by state aid and partly by private charity. The *agrahāra* village institutions can well be regarded as being indirectly financed by the

17. E. I., IV, p. 64.
18. E. g., Chittarājadeva's grant, 1024 A.D., I. A., V, p. 278.
19. I. A., XVIII, p. 273.
20. I. A., XII, p. 253.
21. I. A., X, p. 229.
22. I. A., VIII, p. 21.

state, since it was the state that used to alienate the village revenues to Brahmanas, who, being freed from the anxiety of their maintenance, could devote their energies to the cause of education. The *ishṭāpūrta* theory was inducing a number of private individuals to endow educational institutions. We have seen already how a minister of Kṛshṇa III had built the college hall at Salotgi; when it crumbled down it was re-erected by a local chief. A record from Soratur,[23] dated 951 A.D., records the gift of 12 *mattars* of land made by the officer of the division for the Maṭha and education. The Mahājans of Belur had granted in 1022 A.D., 12 *mattars* for the purpose of feeding and clothing the local students.[24] At Salotgi, as shown already, a local magnate had endowed the college and the inhabitants had levied a voluntary cess as their contribution. At Habale in Dharwar district a private individual had given five *mattars* of land for education in 1084 A.D.

The guild at Dambal, which owned 18 cities, is described in a record from the place as maintaining a college.[25] It is, therefore, not unlikely that some of the big guilds of our period may have been either maintaining or supporting educational institutions. The state also used to sanction grants specially and directly for education, in addition to its indirect help given by the creation of the *agrahāras*. The Bahur plates of Nripatungavarman record a grant of three villages for the maintenance of a college, made by the king at the request of his minister.[26]

Section B : Literature

A detailed discussion about the dates of the various authors of our period, or an enquiry into the problem connected with the authorship of some of the works composed in it, is

23. I. A., XII, p. 253.
24. *Ibid*, X, p. 129.
25. I. A., VIII, p. 185.
26. E. I., IV, p. 180.

obviously not within the scope of the present work. The reader will have to consult the standard works on literary history for that purpose. The general condition of the literature of our period, its main features, the principal writers of the age and their contributions, and how far they were influenced by the spirit of the age would be the main points that will engage the attention of a general historian, and these only will be discussed in the present section.

The main energy of the schools and colleges described in the last section was devoted to the study and cultivation of Sankrit; the Canarese literature had begun to flourish in Karnatak, but it is doubtful whether it had reached the stage when it could be recognised as a subject of study in secondary schools and colleges. As to Maharashtra, the Marathi language itself does not make its appearance in epigraphical records till the end of our period:[27] there could hardly have existed much literature in it. Even the late Mr. V. K. Rajwade has admitted that there was hardly any cultured literature in it till the end of the 10th century A.D.[28]

A glance at the inscriptions of our period is sufficient to indicate the firm hold of the *kāvya* or classical style of writing upon the Deccan of our period. All the merits and defects of that style are reflected in our epigraphs. The composers of our grants were no doubt poets of mediocre ability, but they had carefully studied standard works of the classical Sanskrit literature. Kielhorn has shown how the poets, who have composed the *s'āsanas* of the Rāshṭrakūṭas were greatly indebted for their expressions to works like the *Vāsavadattā* of Subandhu and *Kādambarī* and *Harshacharit* of Bāṇa.[29]

27. Rajvade's contention that the language existed in the 5th century A.D., is untenable; the inscriptions he refers to are either forged or do not contain any Marathi passages.

28. Rajvade, *Jnyanes'vari'*, Introduction, p. 62.

29. E. I., VI, p. 242.

The author of the Kadba plates of Govinda III[30] imitates in the prose portion of the record the style of Bāṇa. The general impression left on our mind after a perusal of the epigraphical poetry is that if it is not of the first order, the reason is rather the lack of *Pratibhā* or poetic genius than that of *abhyāsa* or practice according to approved model. It is further interesting to note that most of our epigraphical poetry is in the *Vaidarbhī* style, the *Gauḍī* hardly makes its appearance. The significant fact would show that the names like *Vaidarbhī, Gauḍī* and *Pāñchālī*, that were given to various poetic styles owed their origin to actual literary fashions of the provinces concerned.

Modern research has succeeded in determining the dates of several writers in Sanskrit literature, but it has not been equally successful in discovering their home provinces. Kumārila, Śankara, Sarvajnātman and Vāchaspati in the realm of philosophy, Lalla and his pupil Āryabhaṭṭa II in the sphere of astronomy, and Kāmandaka, and probably Śukra[31] in the domain of the political science flourished in our period. But some of these certainly did not belong to our province, and the home of others is not known; so a discussion about them is hardly relevant in the present work. The same is the case with most of the later Smritis and Puranas. It has been already shown in several places in chapter XIII how the theories and practices recommended in these works had a remarkable hold on the Deccan of our period. It is clear that the Smritis and Puranas of our age were in close sympathy with it, and that the two were mutually influencing each other.

30. E. I., IV, p. 340.

31. The reference to guns and gun-powder in this book may only show that some portions in it are interpolations. The book as a whole seems to be not much later than our age.

It was during our period that the literature on poetics flourished luxuriantly in the beautiful valley of Kashmir. The rugged Deccan had, however, hardly any contribution to make to that department. The *Sarasvatīkaṇṭhābharaṇa* of Bhoja and the *Kāvyānuś'āsana* of Hemachandra belong to a later period and are besides mere compilations. The *Kavirājamārga* of Amoghavarsha shows that works of poetics were studied in the Deccan during our period, for the work is mainly based on the *Kāvyādarś'a* of Daṇḍin;[32] but no Deccanese writer came forward with any distinctive contribution of his own to that science.

Hindu Sanskrit writers, having any compositions of permanent value to their credit, are indeed few in our period. The colophon of the Benares edition of the *Karpūramañjarī* of Rājaśekhara describes the author as the crest jewel of Mahārāshṭra, but this province can hardly claim that poet since he spent most of his life at Kanauj or Tripuri. Dr. D. R. Bhandarkar has shown that Trivikrama, the author of the *Nalachampū*, is identical with the Trivikrama, who has composed the Begumra plate of Indra III, dated 915 A.D.[33] The *Nalachampū* is the earliest of the extant *champūs*, and therefore, the Deccan may perhaps claim to be the first in that field. The *Kavirahasya* of Halāyudha was composed in the reign of Kṛshṇa III. The poem is really a *dhātupāṭha* explaining the conjugational peculiarities of roots having the same form, but the verses also contain a eulogy of the Rāshṭrakūṭa emperor Kṛshṇa III.[33] The work, therefore, belongs to the class of *Bhaṭṭikāvya* and *Rāvaṇārjunīya*. The *Udayasundarīkathā* of Soḍhala, a Kāyastha from Valabhi, was composed towards the close of our period under the patronage of Mummunirāja, a king of Konkan.[34] These

32. E. I., IX, p. 28.
33. Winternitz, *Geschichte*, III, p. 72; B. G. I., ii, p. 208.
34. Keith, *History of Sanskrit Literature*, p. 136.

are the only Hindu Sanskrit works that can be undisputedly ascribed to the Deccan of our period. The output is indeed poor both in quantity and quality.

Many Rāshṭrakūṭa emperors like Amoghavarsha I, Kṛshṇa and Indra III were either themselves Jains or patrons of that religion; the same was the case with many of their feudatories and officers as shown in chapter XIII.[35] It is, therefore, no wonder that the contribution of Jainism to literature should have been considerable. Haribhadra flourished by the middle of the 8th century A.D., but his works cannot be considered here as his province is not known. Samantabhadra, the author of the *Āptamīmansā*, which contains a most interesting exposition of the *Syādvāda*, flourished before our period, but several commentaries were written on his work in the Deccan from the middle of the 8th century A.D. onwards. Akalankadeva's commentary *Ashṭas'ati* was written early in the Rāshṭrakūṭa period. S'ravana-Belgola inscription No. 67 refers to Akalankadeva as describing his own greatness to Sāhasatunga who, it is conjectured, may have been Dantidurga. There is a tradition to the effect that Akalankadeva himself was a son of Kṛshṇa I,[36] but more evidence would be required to accept it as historical. Vidyānanda, the author of *Ashṭasahasrī*, which is a more exhaustive commentary on the *Āptamīmānsa*, flourished a little later. He is mentioned in S'ravana Belgola inscriptions.[37]

The Jain contribution to logic in our period is not inconsiderable. Māṇikyanandin, who flourished in the latter half of the 8th century is the author of a work on logic called *Parīkshāmukhasūtra*,[38] which was commented upon by Prabhāchandra in the first half of the 9th century. Besides writing this commentary which is named as *Prameyakāmala-*

35. *Ante*, pp. 310–4.
36. Peterson's Report, No. 2, p. 79.
37. E. C., II, No. 254.
38. Vidyabhushna, *A History of Indian Logic*, p. 179.

mārtanda this writer has also written *Nyāyakumudachandrodaya.* Another Jain writer on logic of this period is Mallavādin, who was probably the founder of a Jain Digambara monastery at Naosari which is no longer in existence. The Surat plates of Karkka Suvarṇavarsha which I am editing, (E. I., XXI), record a grant to his desciple's desciple given in 821 A.D. This author wrote a commentary called *Dharmottaratippaṇaka* on the *Nyāyabinduṭīkā* of Dharmottarāchārya.[39] That a book on logic written by a Buddhist should have been commented upon by a Jain is quite in consonance with the spirit of harmony that prevailed in our period.

Quite a galaxy of Jain writers flourished in the court of the Jain emperor Amoghavarsha I, who was well known for several centuries as a great patron of literature.[40] Jinasena, his spiritual preceptor, is the author of *Harivans'a*, which was finished in 783 A.D. He has placed the workers in the field of Ancient Indian history under great obligation by mentioning the contemporary kings that flourished in that year in the colophon of this work. He did not live to finish his *Ādipurāṇa,* which had to be completed by his desciple Guṇachandra, who was the spiritual preceptor of Lokāditya, the governor of Banavasi 12000.[41] The *Ādipurāṇa* is a Jain work dealing with the lives of Jain Tīrthankaras and saints. In his *Pārs'vābhyudaya* Jinasena has performed the wonderful feat of utilising each line of the love-poem *Meghadūta* for narrating the life of the Jain saint Pārśva. The concluding line of each verse in Jinasena's poem has been borrowed from the successive stanzas of the *Meghadūta.* The *Amoghavṛtti* of S'ākaṭayāna,[42] a work on grammar, and the *Gaṇitasārasangraha* of Vīrāchārya,[43] a work on mathematics, were also composed in the reign of Amoghavarsha I. The

39. *Ibid*, pp. 194–5.
40. I. A., 1904, p. 197.
41. I. A., XII, p. 216.
42. I. A., 1914, pp. 205 ff.
43. Winternitz, Geschichte, III, p. 57?.

Kavirājamārga, the first work in the Canarese on poetics, has been attributed to this emperor, but whether he was himself its author or merely its inspirer, is still a matter of controversy.[44] The authorship of the *Pras'nottaramālā* is also in dispute, as it has been variously attributed to S'ankarāchārya, Vimala, and Amoghavarsha I. The colophon of the Tibetan translation of this booklet shows, as Dr. F. W. Thomas has pointed out, that Amoghavarsha was believed to be its author at the time it was rendered into the Tibetan.[45] It is, therefore, very likely that he was its real author.

Gangadhārā, the capital of a feudatory Chālukya house in southern Karnatak, was a centre of considerable literary activity by the middle of the 10th century. It was there that Somadeva flourished and wrote his works *Yasastilaka* and *Nītivākyāmṛta*[46]. The first of these works, though sectarian in purpose is of no inconsiderable literary merit; it belongs to the variety of the *Champu* and its author shows considerable skill in the treatment of his theme. The second work is on the science of politics; it has, however, hardly much independent value as it is largely based on the *Artha-s'āstra* of Kauṭalya. The work is, however, almost entirely free from any sectarian tinge and is written from a much higher moral point than the *Arthas'astra* of Kauṭalya.

Karnatak was a great stronghold of Jainism in our period and the Jain authors had not forgotten that the founder of their religion had preached in the vernacular. We, therefore, find a number of Canarese authors in the 10th century, most of whom were Jains. The earliest and foremost among these is Pampa, who was born in 902 A.D. Though a native of Āndhrades'a he became the *ādikavi* of the Canarese literature. His *Ādipurāṇa*, which was finished in 941 A.D., is a Jain work, but his *Vikramārjunavijaya* is a more or less

44. I. A., 1904, pp. 199. 45. J. B. B. R. A. S., XXII, pp. 80 ff.
46. *Yas'astilakachampu*, p. 419.

historical work, where he glorifies his patron Arikesarin II as Arjuna.[47] It is from this work that we get valuable information about the northern campaigns of Indra III in which his feudatory, Arikesarin II, had participated. Asanga and Jinachandra are other Canarese writers of this period, who are referred to by Ponna, but whose works are not yet forthcoming. Ponna himself flourished in the third quarter of the 10th century and is said to have been given the title of '*Ubhayakavichakravartin*' 'Supreme among the poets of both (*i. e.* Sanskrit and Canarese) the languages' by Kṛshṇa III, on account of his proficiency as a poet both in Sanskrit and Canarese. *S'antipurāṇa* is his principal work.[48] Chāmuṇḍarāya, a Jain general and minister of the Jain ruler Mārasiṃha II, was the author of the *Chāmuṇḍapurāna* which was composed in the 3rd quarter of the 10th century.[49] Raṇṇa, another Canarese writer of the 10th century, was born in 949 A.D. His *Ajitatīrthankarapurāṇa* was finished in 993 A.D.[50] That Jain religious works of our period should have been mostly composed in the form of Puranas shows the immense influence and popularity of these works in the Deccan of our period.

It is interesting to note that there is hardly any output of Prakrit or Marathi literature during our period. Dhanapāla's Prakrit dictionary, *Pāïyalachchhī*, was composed in our period but the author lived in Dhārā, and not in the Deccan, and his work being a dictionary, can hardly come within the category of literature. The Marathi language existed in our period, for the earliest composition in it seems to go back to the 3rd quarter of the 10th century A.D..[51] There is, however, no

47. *Karnātakabhāshābhūshana*, Introduction, pp. XIII-XIV.

48. *Ibid*, p. XV. 49. E. I., V, P. 175. 50. E. I., VI p., 72.

51. See Bhave: *Mahārāshtra-sāhitya*, Chap. I. It may be, however, pointed out that the inscription '*Sri-chāmuṇḍarāye karaviyale*' on the Gommatesvara statue may not be contemporary with Chāmundarāya.

Marathi literature belonging to our age.[52] Marathi was not the mother tongue of the Rāshṭrakūṭas and Jainism, which had given an impetus to Canarese literature, was not very strong in Maharashtra. It is, therefore, no surprise that there should have been no output of the Marathi literature during our period.

CHAPTER XVII

Conclusion

Our task of giving a comprehensive picture of the Deccan under the Rāshṭrakūṭas has now come to an end, and only a few words are necessary by way of epilogue.

The Rāshṭrakūṭas were, on the whole, an able set of rulers. Their empire was certainly more extensive than that of any of their Hindu successors in the Deccan. It is possible that the Āndhras and the early Chālukyas, who preceded them, were perhaps ruling, for some time, over more extensive areas; but neither of them could claim an equally brilliant career. The Chālukyas could boast of having only repelled successfully the attempted invasion of Harsha. The Āndhras could no doubt launch an expedition into the Madhyadeśa and overthrow the Kaṇvas, but the latter, at the time of the Āndhra victory, were mere petty rulers. In no other period of Ancient Indian History did the Deccan enjoy the same high political prestige, which it did under the Rāshṭrakūṭas. The observation of Sulaiman, that the Rāshṭrakūṭas were the most feared and powerful rulers of India, is no flattery, but a mere statement of facts. A glance at the Indian History shows that it is usually the northern

52. The Marathi translation of the *Panchatantra* seems to be slightld more archaic than the *Dnanes'vari*, but it cannot go back to our perioy See Joshi, *Marāthi Bhāshechi Ghaṭanā*, p. 58.

Indian powers which try to expand at the cost of their southern neighbours. During the Rāshṭrakūṭa regime, neither the Pālas nor the Gurjara-Pratihāras could entertain such ambitions. Nay, we find that the latter were several times signally defeated in their own provinces by the Rāsṭrakūṭas. Three times the armies of the Râshṭrakūṭas crossed the Vindhyas and defeated their northern opponents, who were, unlike the Kaṇvas, strong and ambitious rulers, attempting to establish their own hegemony in the north. The Rāshṭrakūṭas could capture the Gurjara-Pratihāra capital; the latter could not even cross the Rāshṭrakūṭa border in retaliation. The Pallavas were a perpetual source of anxiety to the early Chālukyas; no southern neighbour of the Rāshṭrakūṭas, though given repeated provocation, ever dared to invade the empire from the south.

The Rāshṭrakūṭa empire lasted for about 225 years. It is interesting to note that very few Hindu dynasties have ruled in their full glory for so long a period. The Mauryas, the Imperial Guptas, the early Chālukyas all collapsed in less than two centuries. The Āndhras no doubt ruled for about four centuries and a half, but it is not certain that the Pauranic list of the Āndhra kings belongs really to one dynasty. The Gurjara-Pratihāra dynasty can certainly claim a longer career, but it had attained no imperial position before the time of Vatsarāja (c. 775 A.D.), and its empire was shorn of much of its glory after the severe blow given by Indra III in c. 916 A.D. Most of the Rāshṭrakūṭa rulers were able ones; in a list of about 14 kings, only three are found to be vicious or inefficient. Dantidurga, Kṛshṇa I, Dhruva, Govinda III, Indra III and Kṛshṇa III form a galaxy of able and ambitious rulers, the like of which can hardly be claimed by any other dynasty.

The most glaring defect of the Rāshṭrakūṭa polity was its inability to secure a peaceful succession to the throne at the death of its previous occupant. There was a war of succession almost at every alternate accession. The dynastic history of no other Hindu dynasty is probably disfigured by so many wars of succession. It is, therefore, the more remarkable that the empire should have had so long and glorious a career.

A superficial reader of the Muslim chroniclers is likely to get the impresion that the Rāshṭrakūṭas were following an anti-national policy by siding with the Muslims and fighting against the Gurjara-Pratihāras. It has been, however, shown already[1] that the statements of these writers, that the Rāshṭrakūṭas were partial to the Muslims, and that none but the Muslims ruled over the Muslims in their dominions, only show that the Muslim Kazis were allowed to look after the religious and judicial affairs of the foreign colony. The friendly policy followed towards the Muslim traders was, in a great measure, necessitated by the dependence on Arabia for the supply of horses to the army. Merchant Sulaiman, who was acquainted with the state of affairs only in the Deccan, observes that none among the natives of India or China had embraced the Muslim faith or could speak the Arabic language.[2] It is, therefore, clear that the Muslim traders, settled in the Rāshṭrakūṭa ports, had initiated no activities injurious to the interest of the Rāshṭrakūtas or their subjects. There is no evidence whatsoever to show that the Rāshṭrakūṭas had made any political alliance with the Muslim rulers of Sindh in their wars with the Gurjara-Pratihāras.

It is, however, a pity that the Rāshṭrakūṭas should have neglected altogether the branch of naval defence. The reasons for this have been already discussed.[3] This weakness of the administration was, however, not peculiar to the

1. *Ante*, p. 187. 2. Sulaiman Saudagar, Hindi translation, p. 84.
3. See *ante*, p. 247.

Rāshṭrakūṭas, for most of the Deccan empires had neglected the naval arm. It must, however, be remembered that no naval invasion of the Deccan had occurred in historic times; it is, therefore, in a way natural that it may have been thought that it was unnecessary to waste any money over the navy. Safety of the oversea trade, however, aught to have opened the eyes of the Hindu governments to the necessity of the navy.

The careful student of the Hindu history cannot help regretting that the political thinkers in India should ever have adumbrated the principle that a conqueror should not supplant, but merely reduce, the conquered king, and that it should have been so widely respected. The resources of the empires, like those of the Rāshṭrakūṭas, were unnecessarily frittered away in suppressing the rebellions of feudatories, who should never have been allowed to exist. The present writer believes that if the policy of ruthless annexation had been followed consistently since the days of Chandragupta Maurya, there would have been evolved in India stronger and stabler states, and it would not have been possible for foreigners like the Scythians, Hunas, and Muslims to get so easy a footing in India.

The Rāshṭrakūṭa administration was certainly efficient. The 20th century would naturally disapprove of a system of administration under which a large number of civil officers were recruited from the army. But it may be pointed out that the bifurcation between the civil and military, and executive and judicial functions is more recent than our period, and the recent history of Italy, Poland, Spain, Portugal and Germany shows that it is by no means certain that some states in future may not revert back to the old system where the military commanders, being persons of proved vigour and efficiency were entrusted with important administrative posts. Probably the exigencies of a forward policy were responsible for the appointment of so many military commanders to civil posts. The evils of the system were probably to a great extent mitigated by the fact that the military officers were after all sons of the soil and were assisted by hereditary district, Taluka, and village officers. Democratic institutions like elected parliaments, responsible cabinets etc., were absent, but it may be pointed out that they existed nowhere else in contemporary times. The Rāshṭrakūṭa subjects, however, enjoyed a substantial amount of self-government by the circumstance that large powers were delegated to local bodies where they had an effective voice. How far the administration secured the material, moral and cultural progress of the people is the next question to be considered. Sufficient evidence has been adduced in chapter XV to show that the Deccan was economically strong and prosperous under the Rāshṭrakūṭas. Otherwise their aggressive wars would have been impossible. Commerce was brisk, and several industries flourished. The mines were also yielding rich income. The high compliments paid to the Deccanese character by the Chinese and the Muslims would show that the moral welfare was also looked after. It is, however, difficult to determine how much of the credit in this respect has to be given to the state and how much to religion. In religious matters the state maintained a catholic and tolerant attitude. Jainism, Buddhism and Hinduism lived side by side in peace and harmony. It may be pointed out that during our period, there was no such harmony in Tamil country, where the Jains were ruthlessly persecuted by the Saivaits.

The effort of the state to promote the cultural wellbeing of the subjects can, to some extent, be judged from the chapter dealing with Education and Literature. Both these received the royal patronage in a liberal measure; if the literature did not flourish more luxuriantly than it actually did, the fault seems to be not of the state. It must be, however, admitted that fine arts do not seem to have received any impetus in the age of the Rāshṭrakūṭas. The Mauryan, Gupta, Chālukya and Pallava ages had their own distinctive and creditable contributions in the sphere of fine arts; no such claim can be made for the Rāshṭrakūṭa age. Fine arts seem to have been practically neglected by the Malkhed Court. The rock-cut temple at Elora is no doubt an architectural wonder; but it is the only imposing monument of the age, handed down to the posterity, and there is no evidence to show that any other monuments of equal magnificence have been subsequently destroyed. The Elora temple, again, may, not unlikely, have been the work of artists imported from Kanchi.

In the religious and social spheres, our age was an age of transition. It was towards the end of our period that Buddhism, reconversions into Hinduism, intercaste dinners and marriages, and religious *parishads* having powers to settle socio-religious matters, disappeared from the Hindu society. *Vratas*, tonsure of widows, provincial sub-castes, the association of dancing girls with temples, the resuscitation of the Satī custom in the Deccan, and the more intricate Smārta ritual are innovations that can be traced either to our, or to the immediately succeeding age. It is probable that our age believed that most of these changes were changes for the better, but the subsequent history of the Hindu society has shown that they have weakened its unity and cohesion. One cannot help thinking that the thinkers of the age should have taken a longer view of the situation, and realised the full consequences of the new changes that were being either forced upon or recommended by them.

ERRATA

Page	*Line*	*Read*	*For*
5	19	Hoshangabad	Houshangabad
7	8	Nannarāja	Nannāraja
10	11	Indra II	Indra I
34	2	the last	last
35	10	the last	last
49	13	the last	last
51	8	तस्यानुजो	तस्यानुजा
62	20	Śivamāra	Muttarasa
62	last	कृतघ्न	क्रितघ्न
64	34	चक्रायुधाय	चक्रायुघाय
71	11	the last	last
85	7	in	is
88	22	Karṇāṭakaśabdā-nuśāsanam	Karṇāṭakaśaabdā-nuśāsanam
92	top	92	20
92	10	staying	statying
95	12	Kirnapur	Kiranyur
95	13	250	150
106	31	°वर्षो	°वर्षों
108	14	Amoghavarsha III	Amoghavarsha II
123	6	was	wa
127	16–17	Bhīmaparākrama	Bhīmapapākrama
129	22	Govinda IV	Govinda II
151	9	Raṭṭarājya—	Raṭṭārajya—
160	4	in	is
156	29	XVI	XV

165	13	Rāshṭrakūṭa	Rāshṭragkūṭa
166	28	समादिष्टः	समादिष्टः
195	16	to interfere	interfere
199	26	still	till
218	18	tola	atol
257	19	Rāshṭrakūṭas	Rāshṭrākūṭas
259	8	in contradiction to	in contradiction of
259	9	burnt	burn
264	12	and control,	, and control
265		Karṇāṭabhāshā-bhūshaṇa	Karṇāṭabhasahā-bhūshāṇa
267	21	indignities	indignitiest
278	29	Amoghavarsha I	Amoghavarshal
281	26	founded	funded
294	9	buffaloes	buffalos
308	20	Kāmpilya	Kāmpailya
337	8	Pāraśava	Pārāśava
345	21	but	bu
364	10	Paramamāheśvara	Paramamaheśvara
374	2	tax	ax
375	2	from	to

ADDENDA

Pp. 52–3. The conjecture hazarded here that Śrīvallabha mentioned by Hariṣeṇa in the colophon of the *Harivanś'a* as ruling the Deccan in the year 783 A.D. would be Dhruva rather than Govinda II, is now confirmed by an unpublished grant of Dhruva lying in the treasury of the State of Bhor, which is dated in S'aka 702 *i. e.* 780 A.D., and is issued by Dhruva Dhārāvarṣa. The plates will be shortly published.

P. 85. The statement in the book that Dantivarman had succeeded his elder brother Dhruva II was based on the fact that there was a long interval of 21 years between the last known date of Dhruva II and the first known date of his successor Kṛṣṇa. Recently, however, a new grant of Dhruva II has come to light, which I am editing for the *Epigraphia Indica*, and which reduces this interval to a period of less than four years. The passage giving the date is in words, but is defective; it reads शकनृपकालातीतसंवत्सरशतेषु षडुत्तरेषु. The word for the number of centuries is omitted by inadvertence, but there can be no doubt that the expression was intended to be संवत्सराष्टशतेषु. This record thus supplies 884 A.D. as the latest date for Dhruva II. It, therefore, now looks extremely improbable that Dantivarman could have reigned between Dhruva II and Kṛṣṇa Akālavarṣa II. In my paper on this plate I have adduced reasons to show that Kṛṣṇa Akālavarṣa II was very probably a son of his predecessor Dhruva II and not of his brother Dantivarman.

Pp. 124–5. The sack of Malkhed. In Śāradāśrama Vārṣika, p. 6, Prof. Hiralal Jain has suggested that the sack of Malkhed by the Paramāra ruler Sīyaka may have taken place in 962 A.D. and not 972 A.D. He relies on the colophon of the *Mahāpurāṇa* of Puṣpadanta, which according to its colophon was completed on the 11th of June 965 A.D., and which refers to the sack of Malkhed in a verse of its 87th chapter. Until the Purāṇa is published, it will be difficult to assess the value of these passages. It, however, seems extremely improbable that the Rāshṭrakūṭa capital could have been captured during the reign of the mighty emperor Kṛṣṇa III. He was holding even Tamil districts down to the last year of his reign; this would have been impossible if the Rāshṭrakūṭa prestige had been shattered by the capture and plunder of the imperial capital in 962 A.D. We must further note that the Malva Praśasti distinctly states that the opponent of Sīyaka was Khoṭṭiga:— श्रीहर्षदेव इति खोट्टिगराज्य-लक्ष्मीं जयाह यो युधि। This statement in the Paramāra official document would show that the sack of Malkhed took place during the reign of Khoṭṭiga, rather than that of Kṛṣṇa. We must, therefore, accept 972 A.D., as the date of the event as supplied by Dhanapāla in the colophon of his *Pāiyalachchhī*.

P. 309. The identification of Kāmpilya suggested here is wrong. The new copper plate of Dhruva II, dated 884 A.D., makes it clear that this Kāmpilya is to be identified with the village Kāpliā in Bardoli Taluka, Surat district.

BIBLIOGRAPHY*

Original Sources

Inscriptions of the Rāshṭrakūṭas, their predecessors, contemporaries, and successors, as published in Epigraphia Indica, Epigraphia Carnatica, Inscriptions from Madras Presidency, Indian Antiquary, Journals of the Bombay Branch of the Royal Asiatic Society, Asiatic Society of Bengal, Royal Asiatic Society, etc. References to these inscriptions can be found in the foot-notes in the text.

Almost all the books in Sanskrit, bearing upon the Dharmas'āstra, Nītis'āstra and Arthas'āstra. The reader will find specific names in the foot-notes.

Fleet, Corpus Inscriptionum Indicarum, Vol. III. Calcutta, 1888.

Hiralal, List of Inscriptions from the Central Province and Berar. Nagpur, 1916.

Rapson, British Museum Catalogue of Coins of the Āndhras, Kshatrapas, etc. London, 1908.

Pathak, Kavirājamārga of Nṛpatuṅga.

Somadeva, Yas'astilaka. Kāvyamālā series.

Rice, Karṇāṭakabhāshābhūṣaṇa of Nāgavarma. Banglore, 1884.

Abhidhānarājendra. Rutlam, 1913.

Stein, Rājataraṅgiṇī. Bombay, 1892.

Yas'ahpāla, Mohaparājaya. Baroda, 1918.

Accounts by foreigners

Watters, On Yuan Chwang, Vols. I and II. London, 1904.

Takakusu, Itsing's Travels. Oxford, 1896.

**All these Books are available at the Oriental Book Agency, Poona.*

Elliot, History of India. Vols. I and II. London, 1870.

Sachau, Alberuni's India. London, 1888.

Gibb, Ibn Batuta. London, 1929.

Cordier, Yule's Travels of Marco Polo. London, 1926.

Schoff, The Periplus of the Erythræon Sea. London, 1912.

M'crindle, Ancient India, as described by Megasthenes and Arrian. Calcutta, 1926.

Maulvi Maheshprasad Sadhu, Sulaiman Saudagar, Hindi translation, published by the Nāgarī Prachāriṇī Sabhā, Benares. 1922.

Tavernier, Travels in India. Calcutta, 1905.

Bernier, Travels in the Mogul Empire (2nd Edition), Oxford. 1914.

Modern Works

Fleet, The Dynasties of the Canarese Districts of the Bombay Presidency. Bombay, 1899.

R. G. Bhandarkar, Early History of the Deccan, Bombay Gazetteer, Vol. I, part I. Bombay, 1896.

Bhagwanlal Indraji, Early History of Gujrat, Bombay Gazetteer, Vol. I, part II. Bombay, 1896.

C. V. Vaidya, History of Hindu Mediæval India. 3 Vols Poona, 1921–26.

Rapson, Indian Coins.

J. Dubreuil, Pallavas. Pondichery, 1917.

Pran Nath, A Study into the Economic Conditions of Ancient India. London, 1929.

Bhandarkar Commemoration Volume. Poona, 1917.

Altekar, A History of the Village Communities in Western India; 1927, Bombay.

Altekar, A History of the Important Ancient Towns and Cities in Gujrat; Bombay, 1925.

Majumdar, Corporate Life in Ancient India. Calcutta, 1918.

Jayaswal, Hindu Polity. Calcutta, 1924.

D. R. Bhandarkar, The Carmichæl Lectures, Calcutta, 1921.

Ghosal, Hindu Revenue System. Calcutta, 1929.

Sen, Hindu Jurisprudence. (Tagore Law Lectures).

R. D. Banerji, The Palas of Bengal. Calcutta, 1915.

Oldenberg, The Buddha, English Translation. London, 1882.

Winternitz, Geschichte der Indischen Litteratur. Lepzig, 1920.

Keith, History of Sanskrit Literature. Oxford, 1928.

Nahar and Ghosh, Epitome of Jainism. Calcutta, 1917.

Codrington, Ancient India. London, 1926.

Peterson. Report on the Search of Sanskrit Manuscripts. Bombay, 1877.

Vidyabhusan, A History of Indian Logic. Calcutta, 1921.

Moreland, India at the Death of Akabar. London, 1920.

,, From Akabar to Aurangzeb. London, 1923.

,, Agrarian System in Muslim India. Cambridge, 1929.

Ball, A Manual of Geology in India. Calcutta, 1881.

La Touche, A Bibliography of Indian Geology and Physical Geography. Calcutta, 1917.

INDEX

A

B

C

P

R

S

W

Y

Z